EUROPEAN EMPIRES
IN THE
AMERICAN SOUTH

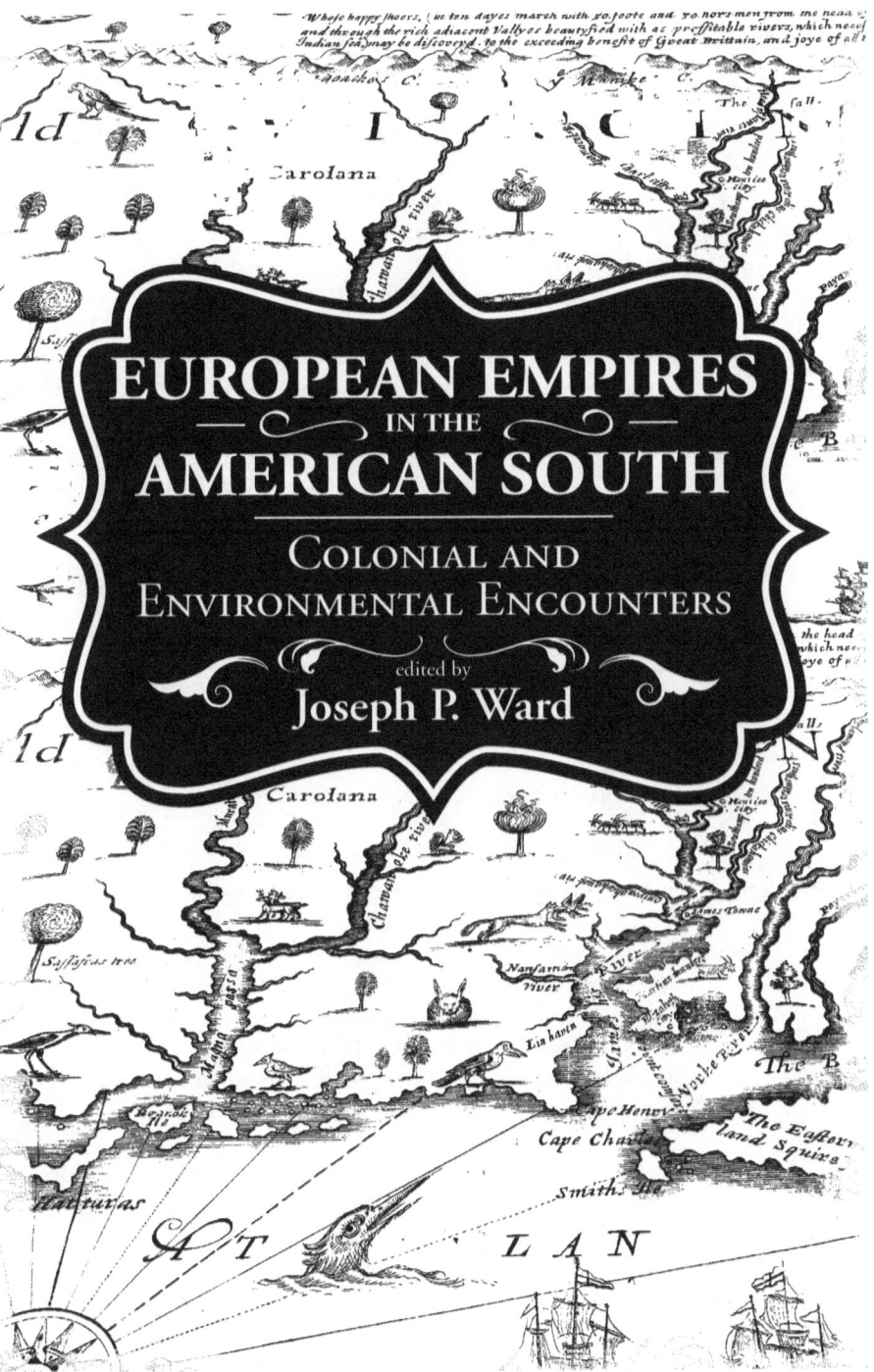

EUROPEAN EMPIRES IN THE AMERICAN SOUTH

COLONIAL AND ENVIRONMENTAL ENCOUNTERS

edited by
Joseph P. Ward

University Press of Mississippi | Jackson

Chancellor Porter L. Fortune Symposium
in Southern History Series

www.upress.state.ms.us

The University Press of Mississippi is a member of
the Association of American University Presses.

A somewhat different version of Chapter One appeared as "Gendered
Language and the Science of Colonial Silk" in *Early American Literature* 49,
no. 2 (Summer 2014): 271–325. doi: 10.1353/eal.2014.0024.

Copyright © 2017 by University Press of Mississippi
All rights reserved

First printing 2017
∞

Library of Congress Cataloging-in-Publication Data

Names: Ward, Joseph P., 1965– editor.
Title: European empires in the American South: colonial and environmental
encounters / edited by Joseph P. Ward.
Description: Jackson: University Press of Mississippi, [2017] | Series:
Chancellor Porter L. Fortune Symposium in Southern History Series |
Includes bibliographical references and index. |
Identifiers: LCCN 2017020581 (print) | LCCN 2017021629 (ebook) | ISBN
9781496812209 (epub single) | ISBN 9781496812216 (epub institutional) |
ISBN 9781496812223 (pdf single) | ISBN 9781496812230 (pdf institutional)
| ISBN 9781496812193 (cloth: alk. paper)
Subjects: LCSH: Southern States—History—Colonial period, ca. 1600–1775. |
Southern States—Colonization—History. | Southern States—Economic
conditions. | Southern States—Social conditions. | Southern
States—Politics and government.
Classification: LCC F212 (ebook) | LCC F212 .E94 2017 (print) | DDC
975/.02—dc23
LC record available at https://lccn.loc.gov/2017020581

British Library Cataloging-in-Publication Data available

CONTENTS

Acknowledgments   vii

Introduction   3
JOSEPH P. WARD

1   Colonial Industry and the Language of Empire   8
    Silkworks in the Virginia Colony, 1607–1655
    ALLISON MARGARET BIGELOW

2   "The Confines and Boundaries of the Land"   37
    The Struggle for Fort King George and the Southern Frontiers, 1721–1725
    ALEJANDRA DUBCOVSKY

3   Negotiating Slavery and Empire   57
    Yamasee Indians in the Early Southeast
    DENISE I. BOSSY

4   The Seller King   87
    Revisiting Control and Authority in French Louisiana
    ALEXANDRE DUBÉ

5   "A Well Grounded Christian Commonwealth"   122
    Nicholas Trott of South Carolina and Britain's Atlantic Empire
    TRAVIS GLASSON

6   The Empire, the Emperor, and the Empress   149
    The Interesting Case of Mrs. Mary Bosomworth
    JOSHUA PIKER

7   **The American South in the French Empire**   169
    Les Étés Longs et Chauds
    CHRISTOPHER MORRIS

8   **Incidental Imperialist**   188
    John Bartram's Florida Travels, 1765–1766
    ROBERT OLWELL

9   **Urbanity and the Endurance of Global Empire**   218
    Charleston and Calcutta before and after the American Revolution
    JONATHAN EACOTT

    Afterword   240
    KATHLEEN DUVAL

    About the Contributors   245

    Index   247

ACKNOWLEDGMENTS

This project began with the 2013 Porter Fortune Jr. History Symposium at the University of Mississippi. The editor thanks the symposium participants as well as all those who contributed to making the event successful, especially History staff members Kelly Brown Houston and Betty Harness. The editor also thanks the external readers of the manuscript for the University of Mississippi Press, whose comments and suggestions greatly strengthened the present volume, as well as the press's outstanding editorial and production staff members, especially Craig Gill and Emily Bandy. Kristi Ezernack, Michael Levine, Sabine Barcatta, Paige Smitten, and Jessica Nelson contributed significantly to the final stages of the volume's production.

EUROPEAN EMPIRES
IN THE
AMERICAN SOUTH

INTRODUCTION

Joseph P. Ward

The seeds of early modern European empire in the Atlantic World first germinated in the imaginations of those who dreamt of a world in which their ambition to shape events would be given free rein. The would-be imperialists convinced themselves to subscribe to at least two clearly false assumptions: that they had the skill and ability to remake the distant lands in their own image, and that the enterprise would quickly prove to be immensely profitable. The unfolding of events would prove that Europeans were no better able to create order and unity in the New World than they had been in the Old, but over time they came to realize that more modest ambitions had the advantage not only of being achievable but also of creating durable—albeit limited—relationships of some advantage to themselves, especially if such relationships ignored the political borders that imperialists tried to impose upon them.[1]

The present volume examines the process of European expansion into the Atlantic by focusing on a region that came to be known as the American South. During the three centuries after Europeans began to cross the Atlantic with confidence, they interacted with one another, with Native people, and with enslaved Africans in ways that made the South a significant arena of imperial ambition. As such, it was one of several similarly contested regions around the Atlantic basin, but without claiming that the South was unique during the colonial era, the essays that follow here suggest that it is a fruitful subject for research seeking to shed new light on the long-term process of global social, cultural, and economic integration.

In this way, the essays offer examples of colonial encounter for those who are curious about how the broad processes of historical change influenced particular people and places. In recent years, several important essay collections have addressed the Atlantic World generally and/or the specific experiences of Spanish, British, and French imperial projects in the South.[2] A key aspect of each of these colonial schemes was finding ways to engage profitably—from the European perspective—with Native Americans. The consequences of Indian encounters with European invaders has long been a principal feature of ethnohistorical research, but during the last long generation, scholars of Native Americans in the South have increasingly viewed their subject in an Atlantic World context.[3] With such scholarship as its foundation, the goal of the present volume is to bring together specialists in each of the three major European colonial powers that competed over the South in the hope that, taken together, they will advance the state of knowledge in the field.

Reflecting the nature of the subject at hand, the essays are arranged in a loose chronological order that allows for themes to emerge and overlap from chapter to chapter. Among the most common topics covered in what follows are the efforts by Europeans to integrate southern people—Indian, African, and European alike—into their aspiring empires. Apparent throughout the volume is evidence of the power of the concept of "empire" to hold the imagination of all concerned, despite the many obvious challenges that would-be imperialists faced when striving to bring their ambition to fruition. If Europeans found it difficult to control people in the American South, in many ways their challenge was even greater when managing—or, more importantly, even understanding—the southern environment, the other prominent theme of the volume. The colonists persisted in endeavoring to recreate familiar surroundings, both rural and urban, in unfamiliar settings long after experience should have convinced them of the project's futility.

The analysis begins with Allison Margaret Bigelow's examination of silkworks in seventeenth-century Virginia. British projectors hoped that Virginia silk could rival Spain's American silver as a source of imperial wealth. Silk failed as an industry, but it remained the focus of reformers seeking a commercially viable alternative to tobacco and sugar as the foundation for colonial agriculture. The rivalry between Britain and Spain serves as the backdrop to Alejandra Dubcovsky's essay about the limitations of communication between European capitals and the colonial frontier as the aspiring global powers sparred over the construction of a modest British fort. Neither formal diplomatic negotiations in London nor the more informal, spontaneous efforts of local commanders could produce a common framework for the resolution of the dispute. Too often the parties spoke past, rather than with, each other as they each tried to assert their control over a patch of ground on the other side of the sea. Denise I. Bossy's essay on Indian and African slaveries in the Southeast then shows how the Spanish first learned about, and then adapted to, the lack of commercial slave trading among Indians. Although the Spanish imported African slaves in the early seventeen century, their numbers would remain relatively small until the mid-eighteenth century as they continued to rely on Indian labor. By the early eighteenth century, however, Indians—and especially the Yamasees—found themselves similarly threatened by the British, which led them to see Spanish territory as a potential staging ground from which to push back against the plantation economy.

The tenuous nature of the French claim on Louisiana during the reign of Louis XV (r. 1715–1774) is the focus of Alexandre Dubé's essay. In the early eighteenth century, French ambition for its American empire was evident through the wide array of goods—not just food, but manufactured consumer goods such as blankets and paper—that the royal government undertook to supply to colonists. During the second quarter of the eighteenth century, the French king was the greatest single source of imported goods in the Mississippi Valley. These goods became an essential element in the trade between colonists and Native peoples, a trade that, it was hoped, would cement ties between the two groups. In this way, the king-as-merchant was a central actor in an elaborate effort to integrate Indian societies into the French mercantilist system. The imperial effort to assert metropolitan control more firmly over the colonies is readily visible in Travis Glasson's study of Nicholas Trott. He was an influential—though somewhat controversial—figure in South Carolina in the early eighteenth century who aggressively supported efforts to give the Church of England great influence in colonial society. In both his political and scholarly work, Trott embodied both the strengths and the limitations of the emerging British Empire. Joshua Piker's essay on Mary Bosomworth analyzes her imperial ambition in the context of British expansion into Georgia. When in August 1749 a large group of Creeks visited Savannah, the capital of colonial Georgia, it provided a space for the intersection of three imperial dreams: Britain's; that of Malatchi, the Creek leader who was asserting a claim that the loose assortment of towns that he led was an empire; and Mary Bosomworth's, as she tried to assert privileges based on her complex ancestry. The coexistence of these overlapping—and therefore incompatible assertions—reflected a central feature of the lived experience of empire in the eighteenth-century Atlantic, namely that the distance between imperial theory and practice grew by the year.

Christopher Morris's essay on French struggles to adapt themselves to Louisiana's climate shows how mightily they struggled to fit their colonial enterprise in the American South into their larger imperial project. Compared to French Canada, the climate in Louisiana seemed hot, but it was also cooler than French possessions in India, Africa, and the West Indies. In their effort to place Louisiana in its proper context, the French engaged in an early modern scientific conversation about climate and history, clinging to the deeply rooted theory of geosymmetry, which maintained that regions of similar latitude would have similar climates no matter which continent they occupied. Robert Olwell's "Incidental Imperialist: John Bartram's Florida Travels, 1765–1766" describes how Bartram avidly explored the frontier as it was altered by the Treaty of Paris, suggesting that Britain's brief control of Florida (1763–1783) was an example of the relationship between the acquisition of knowledge and the acquisition of power. Jonathan Eacott's chapter uses the concept of "imperial urbanity" to explore the cultural similarities between Charleston and Calcutta during the eighteenth century, with an emphasis on their shared genteel culture. By comparing Charleston and Calcutta, Eacott encourages historians to place the British colonial enterprise in the American South in a broader frame, one that encompasses an emerging tropical empire that survived the American Revolution. His research highlights the remarkably similar material cultures of these two nodes in the imperial network located half way around the world from one another. In the final essay of the volume, Kathleen DuVal notes that despite the many failings of imperial enterprises in the South, over time the Europeans were able to extract valuable knowledge and resources, assets that facilitated their rise to global dominance in the age of industry.

Taken together, then, the essays in this volume bring to light new evidence of the ways in which the modern South—like so many other parts of the postcolonial world—is built upon the wreckage of imperial collapse. Many of the social, economic, political, and environmental pathologies of today's South took root in failed efforts of Europeans centuries ago to reshape the New World in their own image.[4] That said, this volume also provides material to support those who see the folly in efforts to limit the diversity of southern culture in order to preserve its mythical homogeneity.[5] The notion that only certain people, certain attitudes, and certain behaviors are properly southern is as quaint, and unfounded, as the notion that the weather in Williamsburg really ought to be the same as that in Seville.

Notes

1. An overview of European imperial projections is offered in Paul W. Mapp, *The Elusive West and the Contest for Empire, 1713–1763* (Chapel Hill: University of North Carolina Press, 2011). On the early modern European state system and its engagement in expansion into the Atlantic basin, see Alison Games, "Atlantic History: Definitions, Challenges and Opportunities," *American Historical Review* 111, no. 3 (June 2006): 741–57, and J. H. Elliott, *Empires of the Atlantic World: Britain and Spain in America 1492–1830* (New Haven, CT: Yale University Press, 2006).

2. On the European engagements with the Atlantic World generally, see Bernard Bailyn and Patricia L. Denault, eds., *Soundings in Atlantic History: Latent Structures and Intellectual Currents, 1500–1830* (Cambridge, MA: Harvard University Press, 2009); Jack P. Greene and Philip D. Morgan, eds., *Atlantic History: A Critical Appraisal* (Oxford: Oxford University Press, 2009); and Louise A. Breen, ed., *Converging Worlds: Communities and Cultures in Colonial America* (New York: Routledge, 2012). For an emphasis on the South during the period of European colonization in the Atlantic, see Bradley G. Bond, ed., *French Colonial Louisiana and the Atlantic World* (Baton Rouge: Louisiana State University Press, 2005); Peter C. Mancall, ed., *The Atlantic World and Virginia, 1550–1624* (Chapel Hill: University of North Carolina Press, 2007); and Kenneth G. Kelly and Meredith D. Hardy, eds., *French Colonial Archaeology in the Southeast and Caribbean* (Gainesville: University Press of Florida, 2011).

3. Charles Hudson and Carmen Chaves Tesser, eds., *The Forgotten Centuries: Indians and Europeans in the American South, 1521–1704* (Athens: University of Georgia Press, 1994); Charles Hudson and Robbie Ethridge, eds., *The Transformation of the Southeastern Indians, 1540–1760* (Jackson: University Press of Mississippi, 2002); Steven C. Hahn, *The Invention of the Creek Nation, 1670–1763* (Lincoln: University of Nebraska Press, 2004); Julie Anne Sweet, *Negotiating for Georgia: British-Creek Relations in the Trustee Era, 1733–1752* (Athens: University of Georgia Press, 2005); Robbie Ethridge and Sheri M. Shuck-Hall, *Mapping the Mississippian Shatter Zone: The Colonial Indian Slave Trade and Regional Instability in the American South* (Lincoln: University of Nebraska Press, 2009); and Robbie Ethridge, *From Chicaza to Chickasaw: The European Invasion and the Transformation of the Mississippian World, 1540–1715* (Chapel Hill: University of North Carolina Press, 2010).

4. Indeed, a sense of abiding grievance against the early modern colonial empires can be seen in B. B. Kendrick's presidential address to the Southern Historical Association, "The Colonial Status of the South," delivered one month before the Japanese attack on Pearl Harbor, in *The Pursuit of Southern History: Presidential Addresses of the Southern Historical Association, 1935–1963*, ed. George Brown Tindall, 90–105 (Baton Rouge: Louisiana State University Press, 1964). On the longer-term relationship between the South and Europe, see Cornelis A. van Minnen and Manfred Berg, eds., *The U.S. South and Europe: Transatlantic Relations in the Nineteenth and Twentieth Centuries* (Lexington: University Press of Kentucky, 2013).

5. Trent Watts, *One Homogenous People: Narratives of White Southern Identity, 1890–1930* (Knoxville: University of Tennessee Press, 2010).

COLONIAL INDUSTRY AND THE LANGUAGE OF EMPIRE

Silkworks in the Virginia Colony, 1607–1655

Allison Margaret Bigelow

On November 28, 1653, three years after his failed attempt to sell some two hundred copies of the *Eikon basilike* to Virginia planters, a beautifully bound but politically precarious celebration of the recently beheaded King Charles I, John Ferrar (c. 1588–1657), former deputy of the Virginia Company, sent to Samuel Hartlib (c. 1600–1662) an account of his daughter Virginia's silkworm experiments, bookended with three travelers' reports on Turkish sericulture. If colonial readers were unresponsive to his home-bound book, Ferrar figured that an international community of New World projectors might give greater purchase to a new model of silkwork. Hartlib circle correspondents like the Ferrars sought to rehabilitate the silk colonies in Virginia to establish continuity with the past and open a space for their own midcentury reformations, and they phrased their proposed improvements in explicitly gendered terms that were designed to enable the economic, cultural, and religious remaking of a young virgin colony rich in mulberry trees and already burdened with what Ferrar alliteratively called the "toyl you take about your Tobacco."*

---

* Samuel Hartlib and John Ferrar, *The Reformed Virginian Silk-worm, or A Rare and New Discovery of a Speedy Way, and Easy Means, Found Out by a Young Lady in England, She Having Made Full Proof Thereof in May, Anno 1652. For the Feeding of Silk-worms in the Woods, on the Mulberry-trees in Virginia and Also to the Good Hopes That the Indians, Seeing and Finding That There Is Neither Art, Skill, nor Pains in the Thing, They Will Readily*

These midcentury reformers were not the first promoters of colonial silkworks, nor were New World projectors the first to argue that a reformed colonial industry was central to the English pursuits of right Christianity, straight commerce, and true natural knowledge. Richard Hakluyt (1551?–1616), who framed his *Principal Navigations* (London, 1589–1600) with that tripartite focus, was perhaps one of the earliest English writers to speculate that colonial silkworks could counter the hegemony of Spanish silver in the global economy. In his *Discourse Concerning Western Planting* (1584), Hakluyt proposed that with the right cultivation of American wealth, "wee may abate and pull down their hygh myndes," replacing mining and metallurgical models of colonization with agricultural regimes of cultivation, like "plantinge of sugar canes as the Portingales have done in Madeira in maynetenance and increasing of silke wormes for silke, and in dressing the same."[1] Silkworks were eagerly endorsed by the Stuart monarchy, as James VI of Scotland, also known as James I of England, required in 1607 that English landholders plant ten thousand mulberry trees on their estates. The trees, like the order, came from the Crown, which sold them at a rate of "three farthings the plant, or 6 s. the hundred, containing five-score plants." In the early 1620s royal sericulturalist John Bonoeil recommended that colonial landowners plant no fewer than two or three thousand trees, anything less being "onely for women wantonly to keepe a few Silk-wormes, with a few Mulbery trees, more for pleasure than for profit." The Virginia assembly never managed to enforce the large-scale program, however, only requiring by midcentury that landowners plant ten mulberry trees for every one hundred acres of their estates.[2]

Although the trees took root, colonial silkworks failed repeatedly, returning neither pleasure nor profit to the planters. Some writers, like Captain John Smith (c. 1580–1631), blamed these failures not on the effeminate husbandmen that Bonoeil observed, but rather on a shortage of experts. Smith noted that the worms prospered "till the master workeman fell sicke: during which time, they were eaten with rats," while other projectors, like Dr. Robert Child (1613–1654), pointed to a more general "want of hands" in the labor-poor colony. Although colonial observers like Smith and Hartlib circle correspondents like Child had different ideas about the place of experts and the role of labor in the cultivation of colonial silk, both groups agreed that because humans were partly responsible for the failure of the Virginia

---

Set Upon It, Being by the Benefits Thereof Inabled to Buy of the English All These Things That They Most Desire, Early English Books Online (subsequently EEBO) (London: John Streater for Giles Calvert, 1655). Subsequent citations will be noted parenthetically.

silkworks, then they might also play a hand in the solution to the problem and the reformation of this key colonial industry.[3]

With this idea Virginia Ferrar (1627?–1688), anagrammed by her cousin "F[errar] C[ollett]"as "Rare Fair Virgin" and named by her father after the colony "so that speaking unto her, looking upon her, or hearing others call her by her name he might think upon both at once," set out to test different feeding methods and silkworm habitats.[4] For however rich the Virginia colony was in mulberry trees, the early-seventeenth-century silkworks had failed to thrive without proper food sources and growing spaces for the worms. From her earlier trials, Virginia Ferrar had concluded that mulberry tree leaves were more advantageous than other food sources, namely lettuce; as a follow up to those first experiments, Virginia Ferrar designed a second round of tests to determine the ideal habitat for silkworm cultivation. Controlling for food sources, she fed the same amount of leaves to groups of worms housed in two different locations: indoor worms that she grew in cabinets in her bedroom chamber, and outdoor worms that she cultivated in the family garden. After comparing the sizes and survival rates of the two groups at the end of their forty-five-day cycle, she concluded "in triall and experiment" that outdoor worms produced the best silk outcomes.

The tale of these trials, a story spun as artfully as the homebound books but with wider circulation, formed part of a transatlantic exchange of natural knowledge that belied the more restricted geography of the garden plot and the intimate corners of Virginia Ferrar's bedroom. It also threw into sharp relief the explicitly feminized program of silk work and colonial labor promoted by mid-seventeenth-century reformers in the hopes of refashioning the English experiment in colonial Virginia. Two years after Hartlib received the report, the Polish émigré appended it to related silkworm letters from Germany, Ireland, and England and published the transcultural assemblage as *The Reformed Virginian Silkworm; or, A rare and new discovery of a speedy way, and easy means, found out by a young Lady in England, she having made full proof thereof in May, anno 1652* (London, 1655).

The curious circumstances of English projections for Virginian silk, and their supporting publications, leave us with a few questions about the nature of colonial planting and English imperial designs. Why, at the height of the Protectorate, might an international body of Puritan readers and reformers have endorsed the Stuart monarchy's silkworks? And why might this colonial scientific community have framed its proposals around the labor of a female sericulturalist and feminized silkworms? What can this history tell us about the gendered nature of English planting in an era of early modern European imperial competition for the Americas? This essay addresses these questions by tracing the linguistic gender of silkworms and scientists in seventeenth-century sericultural treatises, a subset of a rich body of English agricultural literatures that transmitted some of the most important technologies and methods to grow crops known and unknown in the New World, and a textual corpus that provided some of the most formative terms of colonial policy—planting English bodies in America and harvesting new souls.[5] I map the shifting male, female, and neuter pronouns of silkworm treatises onto proposed shifts in agroeconomic colonial industries and cultural models of colonization. Reformers hoped that by replacing tobacco with silk they might diversify the colonial economy, and then, that this economic stability would improve relations between and among indigenous practitioners, colonial planters, and the international brotherhood of Protestant projectors committed to the restoration of Adamic empire. As a source of colonial wealth, silk was an undisputed failure—and repeatedly so. But as part of a broader design to reform the political, cultural, and economic relationship between England and its foreign plantations, colonial silkworks contributed an important register to the organizing grammar of settlement. Facts and experiences on the ground could be sanitized by a religioscientific discourse that refashioned spaces of violence into sites of cultivation; the reformed virgin colony would not be an embarrassing exporter of what John Ferrar had called "that contemptible, beggarly *Indian* weed," but rather a pure producer of fine, first-rate silk (27).

This model of colonial design emerged during a formative moment in the development of English imperial identity; as such, silk became one of the key industries that Hartlib Circle reformers identified as a source of natural knowledge that could underwrite their imperial projections. By the end of 1655, English soldiers had invaded Jamaica and supplanted Spanish colonists from the island that became the Crown jewel in the imperial economy and the colonial scientific knowledge economy.[6] But New World projectors did not know how the story would end when they traded ideas and improvement schemes advancing the small-scale, decentralized production of wines, silks, and honey, explicitly feminized emblems of sensuality and sweetness that signified far different cultural values and imperial images than the industrial-scale regimes of rum, tobacco, and sugar that dominated Atlantic trade. The political, economic, and cultural shifts required to translate imperial aspirations from wine to rum, honey to sugar, and silk to tobacco were registered in agricultural treatises, proposals, and instruction manuals that called for the reformation of these colonial industries. With a better command of the science of sericulture and apiculture, reformers like Virginia and John Ferrar and Hartlib circle projectors argued in texts like the *Reformed Virginian Silkworm* (London, 1655) and *The Reformed Commonwealth of Bees* (London, 1655) that feminized modes of colonial labor—human and nonhuman alike—could become commercially viable ways to wealth and the fulfillment of millenarian ends.[7]

Although literary scholars have focused their studies of gender and seventeenth-century science on single-author texts that fall largely within the purview of natural philosophy, agricultural scientific literatures, and especially sericultural works like the Ferrar epistle, which were equal parts instructional and promotional, represent an important genre whose gender-inclusive, transnational, and commercialized modes of practice and knowledge production puts pressure on some of the longest-held theories of gender and early modern science. This body of literature is not often praised for its literary merit or felicity of expression, and yet literary methods can productively help us to root out the gendered languages of silkworm treatises such that we understand both the complex marking role of linguistic gender within the treatises and the "natural" place of gender within English imperial designs more broadly.[8]

Agricultural historians, meanwhile, have tended to concentrate more on technical innovations in farming instruments, methods of planting, and species selection, or else on large-scale reengineering projects like enclosure or fenlands drainage.[9] While these new crops and technologies are essential parts of English agrarian history—with important biopolitical implications for the movement and management of a population whose scientific advances were shaped by religious institutions, commercial networks, and cultural norms as much as by early modern natural knowledges[10]—this focus on measurable outcomes has overshadowed a more careful attention to the language in which agricultural writers explained and justified their novel designs. Because most of the ideas proposed by writers like Sir Hugh Platt (1552–c.1611), Gervas Markham (1568–1637), and Walter Blith (c. 1605–1654) were not practiceable, their language is an important vehicle for understanding seventeenth-century ideas about technologies and improvements rather than actual technologies or improvements.

When the conditions of agricultural labor changed, so too did these writers modify the pronouns that they used to describe soils, seeds, and silkworms in practical manuals and philosophical discourses alike. For example, Sir Hugh Platt famously complained that unschooled English husbandmen ("al these simple sots") spoiled the fertility of their lands by too zealously plowing into unprepared soil, such that "the hungry seede intime will drinke vp all of the salt of the earth, whereby the earth being robd of her salt, can bring forth no more fruit, vntill it bee dunged againe, or suffered to lie fallow a certaine time." Thus, when Platt described fecund land that needed little labor, it was a she ("robd of her salt"), but when he referred to barren soil that required heavy husbanding, it was an it ("vntill it bee dunged again").

The marking pronouns of Platt's late sixteenth-century book were echoed by mid-seventeenth century writers like Gervas Markham, for whom a "barren, dry, and dejected earth" required that the greatest labor "be bestowed upon it, both in manuring digging, and in trenching," while "the more rich it is, lesse cost of such labour, and more curiosity in weeding, proyning, and trimming the earth, for, as the first is too slow, so the later [sic] is too swift, both in her increase and multiplication." This second group of rich earths were marked as feminine spaces ("her increase and multiplication") because of the interaction of art and nature that they demanded; like Platt's explanation, Markham's neuter pronouns mark the spaces that require the greatest degrees of human care, while feminine pronouns index more "curious" husbanding of naturally fertile soils.[11]

Some scholars see the shifting gender pronouns of seventeenth-century agricultural scientific discourse as signs of an animistic view of nature that would ultimately be replaced with the mechanical philosophies of institutional bodies like the Royal Society of London.[12] But even late century natural philosophers like John Evelyn (1620–1706), whose presentation to the Royal Society in 1675 was published the following year as *A Philosophical Discourse of Earth*, shifted between neuter and feminine pronouns to signal important changes in the nature of soils and human responses to them. In a passage that extolled the universally fertile properties of nitrous salt, "which renders *AEgypt* so luxuriously fruitful after the inundations of *Nile;* and the *Nitrous* grounds of *Jamaica,* and other places," Evelyn intermixed neuter and feminine pronouns to describe the interactions of plant and planter vis-à-vis the salt that "resuscitates the dead and mortifi'd Earth, when languishing and spent by our indulgence to her verdant Offspring, her vigour seems to be quite exhausted, as appears by the rains and showers which gently melt into her bosome what we apply to it, and for which cause all our Composts are so studiously made of substances which most ingender or attract it." When the husbandman intervened too eagerly into the earth, he spoiled the virtue of explicitly feminized soil ("her verdant Offspring," "her vigor,"), but when he remedied her worn-out "bosome" with "studiously made" salts, he restored both the earth and the broader concept of agricultural fertility to a gender-neutral "it" ("what we apply to it," "which most ingender or attract it").[13] For Platt and Markham, as with many colonial promoters, nature's unspoiled fertility was feminine, while human intervention shifted the soil into a gender-neutral position. For Evelyn, however, feminine earths were those that had been excessively fertilized by humans, whether in Egypt or the New World, and neuter lands were those properly balanced by well-informed practices and principles of husbandry. Although they defined feminine and neuter lands in different terms, and thus with opposite relationships to human agency, all three writers used shifting gender pronouns to signal the intervention of planters who plotted their work with good and bad practices and right and wrong knowledges. The point here is not that cosmological bodies like soils were consistently gendered as male, female, or neuter, but rather that these gendered ascriptions shifted in accordance with changes in, on, and under the ground, and that these pronominal changes indexed different forms of labor, embodied practices, and stewardship.

We might expect to find similarly shifting gender pronouns in silkworm treatises, a literary corpus dedicated to an insect (*Bombyx mori*) whose "shifts," "sicknesses," and "strange and mystical transmigrations," as early modern writers called them, index their movement through a four-part life cycle of infancy, adulthood, and emergence as caterpillars that spin cocoons of silk thread for humans to unwind.[14] But instead of registering silkworm shifts through shifting gender pronouns, a different gendered pattern emerges in the circum-Atlantic archive. The silkworms tended by male growers begin with masculine pronouns that shift into feminine referents when the worms reach their reproductive maturity, while silkworms grown by women are glossed with feminine pronouns throughout the entirety of the life cycle. The gendered pronouns in the treatises thus serve as linguistic markers of the women and men whose different ideas and methods influenced the "natural" models of what Karen Kupperman has called "colonial design."[15] By tracing those pronouns through multiple editions of collaboratively authored texts, we can appreciate the ways in which gendered models of colonial scientific industries shaped emerging ideas about the reformation of English empire and colonial subjects, English and non-English alike, in the seventeenth century.

The story of English silkworks in colonial Virginia, as they were practiced on the ground, is quite short. (For an analysis of how English natural scientific programs were put into practice in the organization of American space in the eighteenth century, see Robert Olwell's essay in this volume.) Large mulberry trees grew abundantly in the colony, but these red-berried varieties (*Morus rubra*) were not the right sort for silkworms. Early modern sericulturalists considered that the white mulberry tree bore three different kinds of berries, white, black, and red, "all which three sorts," John Bonoeil explained, "notwithstanding the difference of the colour of the fruit, beare but one name of the white Mulbery tree." Although Bonoeil recommended the black berry (*Morus nigra*) variety of the white mulberry tree, white mulberries (*Morus alba*) had long been agreed upon as the best source of silkworm food, and even late nineteenth-century promoters like the Women's Silk Culture Association declared that "the silk which it produces is of the finest quality."[16] Red mulberries are consumed by humans and livestock, but *Bombyx mori*, the flightless silkworm that had been domesticated by Chinese sericulturalists four thousand years earlier and the variety best suited for industrial-scale silk production, do not take to the leaves as well.[17] (Although reformers had contemplated the use of native silkworms in their colonial designs, the English ultimately followed Spanish precedent by introducing domesticated worms from the Old World into their American colonies.)[18] From the reports of John Smith, it is clear that indigenous Virginian growers, who planted "great Mulbery trees" by their houses, knew the difference between the mulberry species, as did European sericulturalists like the French grower in Bermuda who sought "to make triall of the Mulberries for Silke, but he did not bring any thing to perfection; excusing himselfe, they were not the right Mulberies he expected." Early colonial recorders like Smith and expert silkmasters alike gave accurate reports about the true nature of native mulberry trees in Virginia and the ways in which they were managed by indigenous growers, and there was some evidence that government committees took these accounts to heart. For example, fifteen years after Smith's *General History* was published in London, Sir Francis Wyatt (1588–1644) returned to govern Virginia for another term, and he came charged with explicit instructions from the Stuarts to survey the state of white mulberry cultivation.[19]

Nevertheless, well-educated, empirically oriented English reformers chose instead to give credence only to some interpretations of the landscape, to invest meaning in different kinds of facts, and to draw conclusions about the possibilities of colonial silk based on their own senses of the matter. As a technical practice, economic sector, and colonial scientific industry, large-scale silkworks failed in short order in seventeenth-century Virginia. But they left a rich legacy of projecting colonial possibilities—indeed, silkworks were proposed as economic and social remedies for places as different as eighteenth-century Georgia, nineteenth-century New England, and twentieth-century California[20]—and the discursive archive of colonial silkworks thus opens up new questions about gendered language, vernacular science, and coloniality. I take up these questions in the remaining two parts of this essay. The first part examines the gendered language of silkworm treatises, while the second part explains the implications of that language on reformist visions of inter-imperial rivalry, the nature of English empire, and the place of indigenous American communities in that empire.

Natural Shifts and Pronominal Resiliency: The Gendered Languages of Colonial Silkworks

In 1650, Edward Williams published three texts on colonial Virginia, all of which were printed in London by Thomas Harper for John Stephenson.[21] Two of the volumes, *Virgo Triumphan, or Virginia in Generall,* and *Virginia, More Especially the South Part Thereof, Richly and Truly Valued . . . The Second Edition,* included substantial sections on silkwork and silkworm rearing, though they were primarily designed as promotional pitches to public patrons (Parliament and the Council of State) and private investors on both sides of the Atlantic ("to the worthy Gentlemen Adventurers and Planters in VIRGINIA"), respectively. The third text, *Virginia's Discovery of Silkworms . . . and Implanting of Mulberry Trees,* was advertised as an instruction manual to be put into practice by "all the Virginia Merchants, Adventurers, and Planters," and it contains Williams's most extensive account of silkworm cultivation and silk spinning. There is a good deal of borrowing among the three volumes, as the first edition's address to Parliament (but not the council) was reprinted in the second edition, and the *Discovery of Silkworms* was also appended to this edition. In this essay, I quote primarily from the stand-alone edition of the *Discovery of Silkworms,* though the overlap in the three texts, and the collaborative nature of their authorship, should suggest that the gendered language of the treatise is not an isolated example.[22]

Williams grounded his faith in the sure success of silkworm rearing by establishing the natural accord of a colonial silkman and the Virginia silkworm. The former, a "governour," had been removed from England, while the latter was "aboriginally native" to "the South of Virginia" and had been "transplanted" to the colony. The two non-native bodies shared a particular kind of correspondence in their gendered positions and labor relationship: "Whatever we naturally desire and abhore, does this Creature by the prosperity or infelicity of his labour show a most experimentall refinement" (10). The silkworm's outward revelation of the "natural desire" of the planter was revealed by its "mak[ing] his affection of habitation" match that of the "master" (10) and would thus fail to thrive "if wee sort him not with a lodging proper and agreeable to his nature" (10). In a labor-intensive attention to the silkworm home, Williams recommended that silkmen monitor the worm carefully, ensuring "his disposition and safety" as an infant ("the beginning of his apprentissage") and later tending to "his station" to maximize "the benefit of his labours" in the days leading to the worm's emergence into adulthood (10, 12, 19, 26).

But once the worms were ready to be mated, the governor was instructed to perform a purification ritual that reconciled what had been a masculine "affinity" between master and mastered into a generative complementarity that accommodated the changing states of the newly feminized worms. As Williams told it, the silkman's body was so thoroughly infused with tobacco that he had to "purifie the ranknesse of his own breath" before he could enter the silkworm houses at this crucial reproductive stage. He was instructed "when fasting" to draw near them only upon taking "good Wine . . . with the odour whereof the worme is highly cherished" (21). After purifying the inner temple of his physical body with this prepatory work, the governor attended to the outer temple with fully sensory rites, sweeping the floor of the silkworm house, coating it in vinegar, and "strawing" it with lavender, spike, rosemary, thyme, and other such "quickening armoatics" like frankincense, benzoin, and storax (21).

As he became "master of an exact purity," Williams's silkman protected "the chast and magnificent Creatures" from the "ill breathings" that "make this innocently noble Creature express her resentment by her own death, or sicknesse" (21). Here is the crucial gender shift in the treatise as the worms shift from male to female pronouns, reflecting their changing states of fertility and their changing relationship to a tobacco-stained planter who emerged as a pure cultivator of the sources of silk. It is worth nothing that these pronouns have nothing to do with the biological sex of the worms, for Williams also explains in great detail how to distinguish the male from the female before and after they hatch from their cocoons:

> The Male of the worme, when grown great, is knowne from the Female, by a wrinkled head, and a great appearance of eyes; the Female hath the head round without any such appearance. In the Bottomes of Balls the Male is knowne, as having workd himselfe into a Bottome, long, slender, and by much sharper at one end then the other: the Bottomes of the Female are bigger, softer, round at one end, halfe pointed at the other. The Sex in those

Butterflyes is thus distinguished: the Male is lesser of body then the Female, stirring the wings more often and more strongly. (26)

Before and after the worms reached their full reproductive maturity, then, there were physical and behavioral properties that distinguished biologically female and male silkworms; the gender pronouns that marked young worms as linguistically male and adult worms as grammatically female were not about biological sex. Rather, this transformation of the sexual economy of purity in colonial industries like silk was realized through ceremonial performance and linguistic resexing of silkworms, an embodied act of labor and a discursive move that allows the "governor" to change colonial silk from a source of natural possibility to an industry with real commercial viability. Improved planters like Williams's could harvest the reproductive labor of silkworms whose molting masculinity and grammatical shift from male to female registered a shifting model of colonial labor, signaled a new understanding of the gendered relationship between grower and grown, and suggested that an alternative model of colonial industry was both possible and practiceable.

For John Ferrar, it was clear that colonial silkworks could serve as England's American answer to Spain's American silver, such that a reformed Virginian colony could ultimately "rival *Peru* for wealth" (26). Channeling the Iberian command to *seguid vuestro jefe* (follow your leader), John Ferrar instructed seventeenth-century planters to replace the economic weight and social nothingness of tobacco smoke with a program of silkworm cultivation that had been empirically tested by his daughter Virginia. "Do but as she hath done; follow but with good courage your cheerfull leader, and doubtless you shall finde (what she desires you may,) namely, *Great profit and pleasure* in an honest imployment. This Silken-Mine will be to you of more benefit then a Mine of silver" (9).[23] Less clear than John Ferrar's invocation of Spanish American precedent and his shifting colonial economic model was the gendered language that Ferrar used to describe his daughter's trials. In a series of confused feminine pronouns, John Ferrar established the full interchangeability of the feminized silkworm and the female experimenter, for "when her young Mulberry-tree in her Garden began to put out its buds, then her Silkworm-eggs began to hatch, as the nature of this wise creature is, when her food begins once to appear, she comes forth of her shell: she presently laying a Mulberry-leafe upon these little crawling creatures they came all upon it instantly: then she carried the leafe and them upon it to the tree, upon whose leaves they made hast to be" (10). In contrast to the worms grown in cabinets, the garden silkworms "day and night fed themselves, creeping from leafe to leafe, and branch to branch at their own liberties most pleasing to themselves" until, when the time came, "the wormes, as their nature is, cast off or slipped out of their skins four severall times, still growing greater and greater to the singular delight and content of their Mistris" (10). Despite the clear report of agricultural change—those four-part productive sheddings of skins to molt into reproductive adulthood—and the generic conventions within agricultural scientific literatures against this sort of pronominal fixity in explanations of botanical changes, John Ferrar's pronouns consistently marked the femininity of the silkworm and silkwoman.

After measuring their growth, Virginia Ferrar made two key determinations that, if followed, would change the spatial organization of colonial silkworks and reduce the labor of sericulturalists. First, she found that worms did not need manmade houses, for "they grew and thrived wonderfully, and surpassed in largeness of body those other worms she kept in her chamber" (10). Second, she concluded that growers did not need to perform elaborate ceremonies to mate the worms, disagreeing very much with Edward Williams's model of embodied intervention into silkworm reproduction (10). With both of these results, "not heretofore thought of, nay, as it were, held impossible by such Authours as have written of the ordering and feeding of Silk-worms," Virginia Ferrar offered an international body of Protestant reformers an empirically proven model and new methodological program for the production of their much sought after "plain Silk" (9, 40). Now "Crowned" with an excess of happiness," she sought to apply her findings to the nascent silkworks of "her dearly beloved *Virginia* (for so you must give her leave to call it"). If what was most natural worked best in England, as her results suggested, then perhaps a less elaborate method would improve the cultivation of worms in the virgin colony, or, John Ferrar wrote, "so she concluded, and so must all you" (9). To that end, Ferrars reported that "very poor and slight houses in Virginia will do the deed," and the hearty labor of the "stout and robustous" worm "pays you ten thousand fold what you bestow onto her" (23), suggesting that naturally fertile feminized worms required less husbanding than what Williams's master-governor had bestowed upon "this delicate nice Creature" (7). The gendering of silkworms and scientists in the Ferrar and Williams treatises reveals important differences in the practices, experiences, and expressions of male and female sericulturalists, even—and especially—when the linguistic gender of the worm did not match the culturally dominant ideas about that gender. By translating the study of gender and science from theoretically oriented single-author texts to multivocal treatises circulated throughout the Anglophone Atlantic, we can more fully appreciate the complex marking role of gendered language in seventeenth-century scientific discourse and gendered agricultural practices in English designs for a silk industry in colonial Virginia.

Gendered Language and the Making of Empire: Inter-Imperial Discourse, Indigenous American Communities, and the Nature of Colonial Planting

The silkworm treatises that circulated throughout the information and material networks like the Hartlib circle recorded men's and women's work in different ways. When we treat the language of these texts as what philosopher Ralph Waldo Emerson (1802–1883) calls "fossil poetry," we can map their alternately shifting pronouns and pronominal resiliencies onto the technical practices, cultivation methods, and theories of sericulture advanced by women and men in this key moment in the formation and reformation of English imperial systems.[24] While a close reading of different accounts of silkworm growing reveals the contributions of both women and men to the silkworks proposed for colonial Virginia, the treatises do much more than simply instruct planters how to replace their curing of tobacco with the spinning of silk. The move from tobacco to silk, as with similar proposals to harvest honey from the colonies, was designed as a way to instantiate reformed commonwealths of silkworms and bees, *The Reformed Virginian Silkworm* (London, 1655) and *The Reformed Commonwealth of Bees* (London, 1655), two naturalized models of feminized labor and industry in which raw fruits were carefully cultivated by human hands.[25] In displacing tobacco plantations from their visions of English planting and their definitions of English planters, Hartlib circle projectors offered an alternative metaphor of colonial cultivation, one produced from equal parts linguistic resexing, religioscientific reformation, and empirically measured improvement. In the remainder of this essay, I will explore three specific implications of the gendered language of the treatises as it bore upon the development of English imperial identities in comparison with competing imperial traditions, indigenous American communities, and refashioned English subjects.

First, as it was conceived by seventeenth-century reformers, colonial silk was an inherently transcultural industry that blended European, Middle Eastern, and Asian traditions into a rich projection of New World wealth. In early modern England, silk culture was transmitted by French experts that the Stuart monarchy had solicited[26] to take advantage of the labor of displaced French and Dutch Protestants whose weaving competencies[27] offered England a way to counter the hegemony of Iberian American silver in global markets.[28] Virginia's supposed geographic parallels with China and the Middle East allowed colonial projectors to imagine that its native mulberry trees were evidence of providential design and to fashion colonial silkworks into the stuff of mercantile exchange. By shifting Virginia's economic center from tobacco to silk, reformers hoped to diversify the imperial economy in monetary and cultural terms, converting land- and labor-intensive colonial modes of tobacco production into land-poor but labor-rich industries like sericulture and apiculture. The proposed economic and social shift from the nothingness of tobacco, all "smoak and vapour," into the feminized goods proper to English colonies in "*Ireland, and other new Plantations throughout the whole Globe*" revealed the ways in which seventeenth-century projectors were beginning to redefine an English imperial project in global terms.[29]

These seventeenth-century reformers were fully and deeply convinced of the urgency of their task, both for the earthly ends of the English Empire and the spiritual restoration of Adamic empire. It should not be surprising, then, that they looked south and east, near and far, for models upon which to fashion their designs. When midcentury reformers like the Ferrars proposed their silkworks in colonial Virginia, they did so with good knowledge of Iberian American silk production in western Mexico, where Spanish colonists had successfully collaborated with Mixte-Zapotec sericulturalists in the earliest colonial American silkworks. As recently recovered manuscript evidence reveals, the Ferrars repurposed several pages of the Gerhard Mercator's (1512–1594) *Atlas; or, a Geographicke Description of the World* (1569; London, 1635), beginning in the pages of "New Virginia" (904), flowing backward into the body of the chapter (903), and ultimately concluding in New Spain (905), to debate the merits of American silk industries. Over the course of several years, Virginia, who signed her entries with a decorative "V," and John, who marked his contributions with the initials "J.F.," exchanged ideas in prose and picture about the methods of cultivating native silkworms, probably *Antherae polyphemus, Anisota senatoria*, and *Hyalophora cecropia*, relative to the transplantation of worms from Europe.[30]

The extensive, detailed, intralineal conversation that figures Iberian America as a palimpsest for British America in some ways reflects the practices of English silk promoters in Virginia and Carolina, where Spanish colonists had unsuccessfully sought to introduce silk culture between 1521 and 1525. Although there were no Spanish silk colonies in the Chesapeake when Protestant reformers advocated for colonial silkworks, New Spain nevertheless offered an important precedent for imperial modeling. In 1542 silk weavers were the first artisans to establish themselves as a guild in the imperial viceroyalty of New Spain, where their professional network collectively spun the raw fruits of western Mexican silk colonies into textiles that were easily trafficked throughout the far reaches of the Hapsburg Empire. Spanish American silkworks ran successfully in Michoacán, Nueva Galicia, and Oaxaca, expanding throughout the sixteenth century eastward into Yucatán and northward into Pánuco. The planting of new silk colonies stopped shortly after 1572, when merchants found ways to route cheaper silks from China to Acapulco through the port of Manila, claimed by Spain in that year. In the earliest years of colonial development in New Spain, then, before the development of amalgamation technologies that would dramatically restructure the viceroyalty around the mining and minting of silver, silk proved to be the type of natural resource that could connect indigenous communities whose skilled cultivation of raw goods in the provinces could be profitably manufactured in the colonial center. This model of intracolonial networking offered subsequent generations of imperial theorists, like mid-seventeenth-century Hartlib circle correspondents, a model of a small-scale industry that harvested colonial wealth and wove together different body politics in the name of a common empire.[31]

For as much as the history of Iberian American silkworks may have prefigured English designs in Virginia, the Ferrars and reformers like them had a distorted sense of the colony's potential to support a silk industry. Some of these distortions may have come from the same Mercator *Atlas,* whose neatly aligning right angles along the equator lead to increasingly incorrect representations of northern and southern spaces; Greenland is roughly ten times the size of Africa, whose "opposite Regions" reformers associated with China, Japan, Persia, the Mediterranean, and Virginia along a common parallel of silk culture.[32] Whatever they knew about Hapsburg imperial models in western Mexican silkworks, midcentury reformers knew very little about the geography of the colony whose western limits ("the Backe of the Mountayns beyond Jeames River Falls") might reveal a passage to China and "the East Indies" "as benefisiall as the West Indies were to the king of Spayne." In a heavily annotated edition of William Bullock's (b. 1617?) *Virginia Impartially Examined, And Left to Public View* (London, 1649), John Ferrar argued that such an opening "to a West Sea / or South Sea over the / hills: an 8 or 10 days / March naye it maybe / not a 4 days Journy with 40: or 50. Men."[33] As English reformers invoked these very different Hapsburg and Chinese

Empires to make their own case for colonial silkworks in Virginia, their arguments threw into sharp relief the ways in which eastern and western models of empire in the Old and New Worlds both shaped and marked the limits of seventeenth-century projections of geography, vernacular science, and natural knowledge.

In his second edition of *Virginia Richly and Truly Valued* (London, 1650), Edward Williams argued for a new plantation between Spanish Florida and English Virginia because the region's latitudinal similarity ("parallel") to China produced the very commodities—"visible silver" and "China root, of which some wee have already discovered"—required to excel the jewelhouses of the East (17). "Whatever singularity of Nature that Nation may imagine her selfe Victorious over others will be found equall in this Garden of the World," he wrote, "this emulous Rivall of China, Virginia: And the Chineses may with as great justice deny the Europeans the benefit of both eyes, as boast that they precede in any thing except Antiquity of habitation, and a long experienced industry, this great Luminary of the new World Virginia" (19). John Ferrar literally mapped these beliefs onto colonial Virginia by plotting the Chesapeake between Carolina and Maryland on the "Sea of China and the Indies," a distance of "ten dayes march with 50 foote and 30 horsmen from the head of the Ieames River," whose currents "necessarily must run into ye peacefull Indian sea" (see Figure 1.1).

Outdated even in its original edition, the map was nevertheless widely reprinted in midcentury texts like Williams's *Virginia's Discovery of Silkworms* (1650), the second edition of *Virginia Richly and Truly Valued* (1650), and Hartlib's *Rare and New Discovery of Silkworms* (1652), and it continued to circulate through the 1680s by way of William Blathwayt (c. 1650–1717), then serving as secretary of the Privy Council committee on Trade and Plantations. (For a study of geosymmetrical readings of the American South in the eighteenth century, see Christopher Morris's essay in this volume.) New World projectors like Edward Williams acknowledged the foolishness of planting commodities in ill-suited climates, insisting "wee must not therefore conforme the nature of the Climate to our Rules, but our Rules to it," and thus he likened the local conditions of Virginia to those of China to make his case for geosympathy (35 [actual page 27]). In the same year that Russian officials would arrange to deal directly with sericulturalists in China, thus making Russia an important silk market, Williams charted the advantages of Virginia and Carolina relative to Persia (10–11) and China (11–21), asking his readers "Why may not Virginia in her future felicity of silke be a new China and Persia to Europe? . . . why may not the Cloves perfum Virginia with as

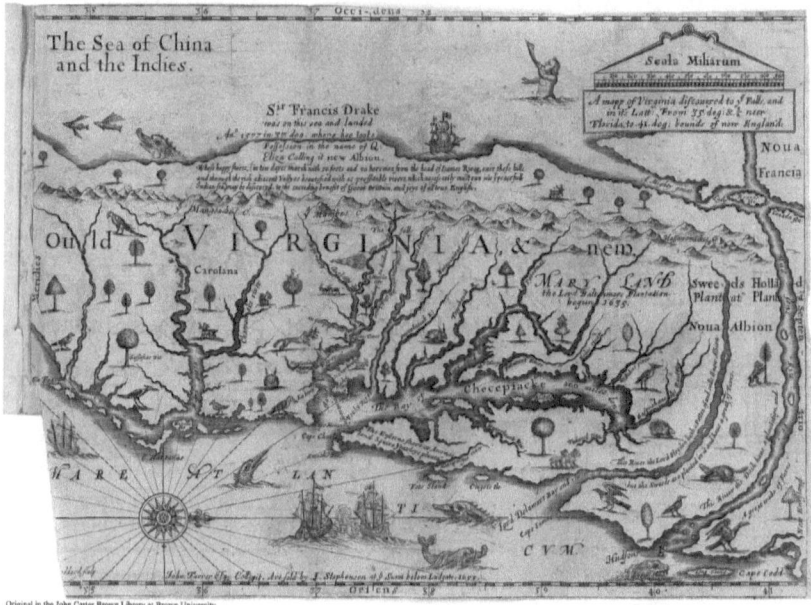

Figure 1.1. John Ferrar, "A mapp of Virginia discouered to ye Falls, and in it's Latt: From 35 deg;," c. 1651. Courtesy of the John Carter Brown Library at Brown University.

aromatic redolency as the Philipine Gardens" (39). If the reformed Virginia colony could be a new Persia or an English Philippines, so too could silk enable a universal cosmology of Englishness. Richard Ferrar, for one, styled himself "a *Virginia*-Planter in England" who sung the accomplishments of his cousin, "the Virgin-Lady *Virginia*," for having adopting silk "Work / Ador'd by th' *Persian*, and their neighbouring Turks" to the colony that "boasts thy name in happy houre."[34] In both cases, the real geographies of non-European silk producing regions like China and the Middle East informed imaginary geographies of colonial Virginia, making a pre-Christian space in the New World suitable for conversion into a Protestant monetary and spiritual economy, as reformed planters recuperated silk from its non-Christian origins in the empires of the East. Williams insisted that this religioscientific refashioning of the colonial silk industry, performed "by an innocent Magick" that was, at the same time, "made our owne by the Midwifry," would "convert that Countrey" and its heathen wealth into a luxury good spun in the heart of reformed Christendom, "our Maid of admiration and envy Virginia" (35).

While its supposed similarity with China convinced midcentury projectors like Williams not only that the mulberry tree rich virgin colony would be "no lesse proper for all European commodities, then all those staples which entitle *China, Persia,* and the other more opulent Provinces of the East to their wealth, reputation, and greatnes," there was one area in which Virginian silkworks would require a departure from the Chinese imperial model of cultivation, "the most Christian of all improvements, the converting many thousands of the Natives" (B3v). Some reformers argued in favor of collaborative colonial and indigenous silkworks that followed the Iberian model from western Mexico, while others were adamantly opposed to the incorporation of Native knowledge in the imperial silk economy, insisting that Native growers' labor was more valuable than their natural knowledge. Proponents on both sides agreed that unifying indigenous American communities in the production of silk—in some form—would benefit Native people and, especially, the transatlantic body politic of *"England,* as all men that have their eyes in their heads, and English hearts in their bodies, see and apparently know," as John Ferrar affirmed as "nothing more sure and certain" (13).

In the first group, Virginia Ferrar requested a report of silkworm lifecycles, habitation, and reproduction, "what by any *English* or *Savage* hath bin any way observed in her," and she was especially eager to compare the feeding habits of mother worms after they laid their eggs, noting that "these in the old World never eat after they once begin to spin" (22). In case the planters had missed the point, she concluded her request with a specific solicitation of Native knowledge of silkworms: "what do the *Savages* call them, or know any use of them?" (23) Her father, however, was less optimistic about the "Manner of the Indian frindshipp," and he instead proposed that English planters pay indigenous people to grow, harvest, and collect silkworms (16). By giving Native growers five pounds' worth of "any Commodity they desire" in exchange for one pound of silkworm bottoms, "by the blessing of Almighty God, there may be good hope of their civilizing and conversion; so that they may be likewise great gainers, in body and soul" (11). These fixed terms of material redemption, as they were proposed by John Ferrar, were complicated by redemptive religioscientific practice, for indigenous people were at once understood to be valuable contributors to the silkworm colonies and as unredeemed souls whose incorporation into the English spiritual economy would enable the full realization of the reformist ends of *The Reformed Virginian Silkworm.*

In this sense, reformers like John Ferrar hoped that Virginia would offer them a chance to rewrite the imperial monetary history of silk, which for some three thousand years had served as currency in China before it was replaced with paper money in the late thirteenth century. Under the emperors of the Song Dynasty (960–1279), paper money and copper cash (*weng*) were intermittently substituted for silk in long-range transactions, and with the imperial imposition of the Yuan Dynasty (1260–1368), silk was replaced with silver. Although Kublai Khan's empire lasted only one hundred years, a brief moment in Chinese imperial history, it influenced the succeeding Ming emperors (1368–1644) in ways that deeply shaped that dynasty's cultural institutions, economic practices, and administrative policies, including its standardization of monetary systems for local and long-distance transactions.[35] As Dennis O. Flynn and Arturo Giráldez have shown, the collapse of the paper system led China to adopt a silver bullion standard that ultimately allowed early modern Hapsburg traders to command extremely favorable rates for American silver relative to the exchange value of precious metals in Europe. The place of China in terms of geographic similarities, monetary systems, and modes of exchange thus figured formatively into seventeenth-century English attitudes and orientations on silk in Virginia.[36]

Given the shortage of currency in Virginia and the English colonies in America more broadly, Ferrar's idea to exchange English goods measured in hard currency for natural resources measured in weight might seem especially far-fetched. How would English colonists obtain the currency to pay indigenous sericulturalists? Was not the absence of credible currency the very reason why reformers were seeking alternative sources of colonial wealth and proposing new models of colonial development? Colonial Iberian amalgamation technologies developed in the mid-sixteenth century made it possible to mine, refine, and mint every variety of American silver in mineral-rich New Spain and Alto Perú; by comparison, British America's reliance upon tobacco as an exchange medium forced the colonies to compete with each other for access to currency, while England used what little specie it had to subsidize its own imports. The use of a cured crop put English subjects on both sides of the Atlantic at what John Huxtable Elliott calls, with great understatement, "an obvious disadvantage" in both local and global markets. Such was the colonists' near complete dependence upon tobacco that the Virginia Assembly used it to compensate landholders for their planting of mulberry trees.[37]

John Ferrar invoked this point of weakness in the Virginian monetary economy and married its remedy to another imperial aim, the conversion of indigenous people to Christianity. To accomplish this most Christian of tasks, he argued, it was necessary to join Native and non-Native communities in a common economic project. Such a refashioning of the early English Empire in the New World would require an equal reformation of Native communities and English subjects. To that end, Hartlib circle correspondents defined reformed planters as women or men whose study of nature, transatlantic exchanges, and application of experientially tried practices allowed for the improved husbanding of colonial commodities and the development of a more competitive global marketplace centered in England. As correspondents like William Potter (fl. 1650) suggested, these goods would help to make England the center of the economic world: "by meeting here (as in a center) might furnish each other with returns, so as *England* would become as it were a general Market or Faire to other Nations, to the great enriching thereof."[38] The *Reformed Virginian Silkworm* was thus part of a tripartite plan to reshape colonial industry, indigenous communities, and English planters with a gender-inclusive, commercially viable science of vendible commodities like "plain Silk."

Virginia Ferrar's "plain" model of silkwork should not be taken to imply that the knowledge she contributed to the circum-Atlantic community of reformers was considered simple, or that her methods were not intimately connected to the proposed production of wealth in the colonies. John Ferrar enthusiastically suggested to Hartlib circle correspondents that his daughter's intellectual labor and empirical trials could reform the source of colonial wealth into a serviceable instrument of empire: "that this her invention being thus made known unto you, her beloved friends in *Virginia*, she is most confident, and assures herself you will all there instantly without further delay (which will be the joy of her heart) become great and rich Masters of this noble Silk-work to all your unspeakable wealth" (9). Upon seeing the planters earnestly applied in the harvesting of silk, "the Indians shall behold and see you begin the business, they will with all alacrity set upon it likewise, and imitate you," fulfilling with their labor the prophecy of peaceful colonization and profitable conversion in Virginia. As Ferrar contemplated the productive incorporation of indigenous labor into reformed colonial silkworks—"how much then indeed will *Virginia's* happiness be every way raised to the height of Blisse"—he invoked the apocalyptic passage from the Old Testament in which Michael, the archangel and "great prince which standeth for the children of thy people," delivered the chosen people of Israel whose names are inscribed "in the book" (Daniel 12:1–2). Ferrar writes, "The promise being made, *That they that be wise shall shine as the brightness of the Firmament, and they that turn many to righteousnesse, as the stars for ever and ever;* which the God of wisdom and power grant to you all in *Virginia*, and so, Lord, prosper this work in their hands, Lord, prosper their handy-work; good luck I wish you all in the name of the Lord, *Amen, Amen, Amen*" (11). Just as the Book of Daniel is marked by a shift from its initial third-person narration (books 1–6) to its conclusion in the first-person (books 7–12), so too does Ferrar's use of scripture move him from his third-person description of the trials of "the Lady" and the labor of indigenous people into a direct address to colonial planters delivered with heavily sermonic intonation. The "unspeakable wealth" promised by silk, a luxury good spun from colonial fruits, was not an end in and of itself; rather, a better science of silk was necessary to support the earthly and otherworldly aims of this international community of pansophic Protestant projectors.

Although Virginia Ferrar's methods of silkworm growing were never put into practice on an industrial scale in colonial Virginia, exchanges of information and material samples helped to strengthen communication and economic networks among an international community of reformers. In many ways, the creation or reinforcement of these networks of knowledge, at once grounded in the local and part of a universal pursuit of human and heavenly empire, was perhaps the most tangible outcome of Virginia Ferrar's silkworm trials. For instance, growers in Dublin used the London-centered epistolary networks of the Hartlib circle to speak with each other about silkworm cultivation methods and food sources, including lettuce leaves and "the hearb called *Dantedelyon*" (31). While one correspondent found that Virginia Ferrar's "Experiment is most Natural to my apprehensions that the Worms should feed and thrive best upon the leaves growing on the Trees, rather then in the Houses, and that they, like other Caterpillers (of whom these are a sort) did at first breed so, and that Houses were rather an Invention for expediency," another disagreed with the "Gentlemans Reason why he likes the Proposition concerning feeding of Silk-worms upon the Trees," rejecting the analogical thinking of the first respondent and instead insisting that human interventions like "industry," "home-helps," and "contrivances" never fail to improve "almost all Plants . . . to such a degree of excellency to the eyes, nose or palat." As they circulated within readership communities like the Hartlib circle, Virginia Ferrar's studies of silkworm lodgings and food sources became part of a larger debate among seventeenth-century Protestant reformers throughout the circum-Atlantic world about the limits of human agency in making, testing, and applying of natural knowledge in an era of colonial planting.[39]

On a more local level, too, silk culture offered English reformers the opportunity to remap relationships with their neighbors during a tumultuous time of civil war. In his letter to Hartlib, John Ferrar reported that he had received two recirculated documents, a letter that Hartlib had sent to "My good Cosen Mr. W" [William Ferrar? (1626–1678)] and a copy of a letter that Hartlib had received from a correspondent in Ireland. This second letter glossed a local woman's "happy success" with mulberry trees and lettuce leaves, and the writer explained his own trials with lettuce, ultimately urging Virginia Ferrar to conduct her own experiments with the alternative food source (31). John Ferrar thanked the man for sharing his news with the community of Little Gidding, "though Strangers to you," and reported that Virginia Ferrar had indeed conducted two separate experiments with lettuce. In 1651 she had "tried her-self to have kept some with Lettice leavs," but despite initially promising results, "when the time of spinning came they would not spin, but then dyed" (31). In her second experiment, she partnered with "a Gentleman near her" to try a hybrid program of lettuce leaves and mulberry tree leaves. They fed lettuce to the worms for the first three stages of the lifecycle ("25 daies") and finished the regimen with mulberry leaves in the twenty-odd days leading up to the spinning of silk, producing worms that "did very well and spun as good Bottoms as those wholly kept with Mulbery leaves" (31). Newly encouraged by the report from Ireland, Virginia Ferrar determined to make a third trial "and to give you an accompt of her success in *June* next, if God permit" (32). The epistolary networks of the Hartlib circle thus connected female and male growers in Ireland, England, and Virginia, and they created opportunities for sericulturalists like Virginia Ferrar to collaborate with her local neighbors and lettered correspondents in the making of new silkworm knowledge. At once transatlantic and international, these exchanges of ideas, reports of failures, and suggestions for improvement also led to local applications of new growing methods and collaborative practices in England and its Atlantic colonies alike.

The same Hartlib circle and extended kinship networks that supported these flows of natural knowledge also allowed reformers to exchange material samples required for experimentation. According to their own report, John and Virginia Ferrar received specimens like "a sample of *Virginia* Silk-grass" that they resent to Hartlib, "as she [Virginia Ferrar] hath great hopes this will prove a commodity next to the Silk there, as skilfull men and Artists do assure her of it, and thousands of poor people will be set a work with it, if it prove there to be in quantity" (33). In verse as well as in prose, they name other collaborators dedicated to "The infinite, speedy, great wealth she [the worm] will produce to her protector" in the virgin colony whose "rare Superlative Climate, Breeding them on so many several kinds of Trees in her Woods where they live, Feed and Spin, their large, strange, double-bottoms of Silk" (33). The Ferrars, in turn, shipped silkworm eggs to sericulturalists like Virginia's cousin Mary Ward (née Mapletoft, 1629–1665),

Mr. Lawrence Ward (d. 1660), and Dr. Richard Russell in Norfolk, as well as a Mr. Wright in Nansemond County and "her kinsman Esquire Ferrar," (32, 26).[40] The Ferrar treatise ends with a poem whose rhyming couplets run some five and a half pages in celebration of loyal planter Edward Diggs (1620–1674), whose "two *Armenians* from Turkey sent / Are now most busy on his brave attempt"; William Bernard (c. 1598–1662), "worthy *Bernard* that stout Colonel"; George Lobs, "that prudent old Planter / Tels her that Worms ne're spun Silk daintier"; Mrs. Thomas Burbage and one "Mistress Garret," keepers of a "pleasant Mulberry Grove" whose contributions to the colonial silk industry invite the direct address, "Lets give those Gentlewomen their full dues" (37–38).[41] These "Rhyming lines (for verses they deserve not the name)" were assembled "out of Letters, that were sent her from *Virginia*." In versifying verbatim passages from the treatise, the concluding panegyric inscribes a kind of gender complementarity among the female growers, feminized silkworm, and the "Gallant Silken Trade" of natural knowledge, material samples, and expert growers from the Middle East whose arrival in the Virginia colony prompted Ferrar to wish Diggs "Courage, brave Sir: sith Ayde from God is sent / Proceed, go on, drive forth thy great intent" (32, 33, 38). In a determinative moment in the formation of English imperial identities, communication channels, and economic networks, these gender-inclusive local and circum-Atlantic exchanges of materials and debates about sericultural labor helped to shape broader ideas about vernacular science, colonial commodities, Native communities, and the nature of English Empire in the New World.

Even though the silk industry never came to economic fruition in colonial Virginia, this broad movement in botanical goods, natural scientific knowledge, and skilled artisans who put those ideas to work led to two important developments in English colonial planting. First, silk put English reformers in dialogue with other imperial systems, namely the Hapsburgs and Chinese, at a time when England had no empire to speak of. Second, silkwork offered a way to incorporate people from very different language communities and social worlds into a unified economic project. Despite its failures as an economic sector, the discursive process, technical skills, and material practices required to project a new model of industry laid important groundwork for early modern English knowledge about empires and the limits of religioscientific improvement.[42]

In signaling what English agricultural practitioners and colonial planters knew and did not know about fertility, growth, and increase in the virgin colony, the gendered language of sericultural treatises marked the epistemological boundaries of English natural knowledge and the limits of its spiritual aims. Colonial silk may have failed to reform the 'all liberal Virginia' bemoaned by New World projectors. But the ways in which imperial apologists dedicated themselves to empirical testing of the science of silkworms, collaborative exchanges of information throughout increasingly robust channels that connected the Atlantic world, developing economic and cultural programs capable of integrating diverse linguistic and cultural communities into a shared model of colonial design, and studying eastern and western empires within and without the Americas would ultimately help to define the aims and ends of the English Empire in its slow and uneven development over the course of the seventeenth century.

NOTES

1. Richard Hakluyt, *A Particulier Discourse Concerning the Greate Necessitie and Manifolde Commodyties That Are Like to Growe to This Realme of Englande by the Westerne Discoueries Lately Attempted, Written in the Yere 1584 by Richarde Hackluyt of Oxforde; Known as Discourse of Western Planting*, ed. David Beers Quinn and Alison Moffat Quinn, 28, 16 (London: Hakluyt Society, 1993).

2. James I/IV, "Letter to the Lords Lieuteteuants [sic] of the Several Shires of *England*, for the increasing of Mulberry-Trees, and the breeding of Silk-Worms, for the making of Silk in *England*," in *Samuel Hartlib His Legacy of Husbandry: Wherein Are Bequeathed to the Common-wealth of England, Not Onely Braband, and Flanders, but Also Many More Outlandish and Domestick Experiments and Secrets (of Gabriel Plats and Others) Never Heretofore Divulged in Reference to Universal Husbandry: with a Table Shewing the General Contents or Sections of the Several Augmentations and Enriching Enlargements in This Third Edition*, ed. Samuel Hartlib, 59-63 (London: Printed by J.M. for Richard Wodnothe, 1655); John Bonoeil, *Obseruations to Be Followed, for the Making of Fit Roomes, to Keepe Silk-wormes in as Also, for the Best Manner of Planting of Mulbery Trees, to Feed Them. Published by Authority for the Benefit of the Noble Plantation in Virginia*, EEBO (London: Felix Kyngston, 1620), 7, 15-16; Charles E. Hatch, "Mulberry Trees and Silkworms: Sericulture in Early Virginia," *Virginia Magazine of History and Biography* 65, no. 1 (January 1, 1957): 3-61; Joseph Ewan, "Silk Culture in the Colonies," *Agricultural History* 43, no. 1 (January 1, 1969): 129-42. The amount of land required for mulberry tree planting fluctuated in the early years of cultivation. The 1636 edict to plant "white Mulberry Trees, and attend Silk Worms" was repealed in 1641 and reinstated in 1642. Throughout the years preceding the publication of the Hartlib circle treatises, the Crown's interest in silkworks was revealed both in its carrots and its sticks: disobedient colonial planters were fined ten pounds of tobacco for noncompliance, while silk growers were compensated with tobacco.

3. John Smith, *Generall Historie of Virginia, the Somer Iles, and New England*, in *The Complete Works of Captain John Smith (1580–1631)*, 3 vols., ed. Philip L. Barbour (Chapel Hill: Published for the Institute of Early American History and Culture, Williamsburgh,

Virginia, by the University of North Carolina Press, 1986) 2:108; Robert Child, "A large Letter concerning the Defects and Remedies of English Husbandry, written to Mr. Samuel Hartlib," in *Samuel Hartlib His Legacy of Husbandry* ed. Samuel Hartlib, 58 (London: J.M. for Richard Wodnothe, 1655); Antonio Barrera Osorio, "Experts, Nature, and the Making of Atlantic Empiricism," *Osiris* 25, no. 1 (2010): 129–48.

4. Michael Lloyd Ferrar, "The Ferrar Papers: At Magdalene College, Cambridge (Continued)," *Virginia Magazine of History and Biography* 11, no. 1 (July 1, 1903): 42.

5. For an account of English agricultural habits, see Joan Thirsk, "Farming Techniques," in *The Agrarian History of England and Wales*, vol. 4, *1500–1640*, ed. H. P. R Finberg and Joan Thirsk, 161–99 (London: Cambridge University Press, 1967). For an excellent overview of New World technologies like tree girding and methods of planting maize under tree covers, see Louis Menard, "Colonial America's Mestizo Agriculture," in *The Economy of Early America: Historical Perspectives & New Directions*, ed. Cathy D. Matson (University Park: Pennsylvania State University Press, 2006), 107–23. On the languages of planting and the iconography of agricultural science in the eighteenth-century British Empire, see Jill H. Casid, *Sowing Empire: Landscape and Colonization* (Minneapolis: University of Minnesota Press, 2005).

6. Richard Dunn, *Sugar and Slaves* (Chapel Hill: The Institute of Early American History and Culture by the University of North Carolina Press, 1972), esp. chap. 5, "Jamaica," 149–87, and chap. 6, "Sugar," 189–223; Raymond Stearns, *Science in the British Colonies of America* (Urbana: University of Illinois Press, 1970).

7. Charles Webster, *The Great Instauration: Science, Medicine, and Reform, 1626–1660* (London: Duckworth, 1975); Mark Greengrass, Michael Leslie, and Timothy Raylor, *Samuel Hartlib and Universal Reformation: Studies in Intellectual Communication* (Cambridge: Cambridge University Press, 1994). For a comparison of the discursive and practical dimensions of these two different industries, see Erica Mae Olbricht, "Made Without Hands: The Representation of Labor in Early Modern Silkworm and Beekeeping Manuals," in *Insect Poetics*, ed. Eric Brown, 223–41 (Minneapolis: University of Minnesota Press, 2006).

8. Carolyn Merchant, *The Death of Nature: Women, Ecology, and the Scientific Revolution* (San Francisco: Harper & Row, 1980); Carolyn Merchant, "The Scientific Revolution and the Death of Nature," *Isis* 97, no. 3 (2006): 513–33; Evelyn Fox Keller, *Reflections on Gender and Science* (New Haven, CT: Yale University Press, 1985); Sandra G. Harding, *The Science Question in Feminism* (Ithaca, NY: Cornell University Press, 1986). Much of the debate over Merchant's thesis is reviewed and responded to in *A House Built on Sand: Exposing Postmodernist Myths about Science*, ed. Noretta Koertge (Oxford: Oxford University Press, 1998), esp. Soble (195–215) and Newmann (216–26).

9. Mauro Ambrosoli, *The Wild and the Sown: Botany and Agriculture in Western Europe, 1350–1850*, trans. Mary McCann Salvatorelli (Cambridge: Cambridge University Press, 1997); David Grigg, *English Agriculture: An Historian's Perspective* (New York: Basil Blackwell, 1989); Joan Thirsk, *Agricultural Regions and Agrarian History in England, 1500–1750* (Houndsmills, UK: Macmillan, 1987); G. E. Fussell, *The Farmer's Tools: The History of British Farm Implements, Tools, and Machinery, AD 1500–1900* (London: Bloomsbury, 1985); G. E. Fussell *Farming Technique from Prehistoric to Modern Times* (London: Pergamon, 1966).

10. Steven Shapin, *Never Pure: Historical Studies of Science as if it was Produced by People with Bodies, Situated in Time, Space, Culture, and Society, and Struggling for Credibility and Authority* (Baltimore: Johns Hopkins University Press, 2010); Deborah E. Harkness, *The Jewel*

House: Elizabethan London and the Scientific Revolution (New Haven, CT: Yale University Press, 2007); Paula Findlen and Pamela H. Smith, *Merchants and Marvels: Commerce, Science, and Art in Early Modern Europe* (New York: Routledge, 2002).

11. Hugh Plat, *The Jewell House of Art and Nature* ([London: 1594], Facsimile ed. (Amsterdam: Theatrum Orbis Terrarum; 1979), 15–16; Gervase Markham, *The Booke of the English Husbandman. Contayning the Ordering of the Kitchen-garden, and the Planting of Strange Flowers: The Breeding of All Manner of Cattell. Together with the Cures, the Feeding of Cattell, the Ordering Both of Pastures, and Meddow-ground: With the Use Both of High Wood, and Underwood. Whereunto Is Added a Treatise, Called Good Mens Recreation: Contayning a Discourse of the Generall Art of Fishing, Together with the Choyce, Ordering, Breeding, and Dyeting of the Fighting-cocke*. EEBO (London: John Norton for William Sheares, 1635), 192.

12. Merchant, *Death of Nature*, and the historiographical review in Pierre Hadot, *The Veil of Isis: An Essay on the History of the Idea of Nature* (Cambridge: Belknap Press of Harvard University Press, 2006). On pronominal resiliency and changing ideas of animacy, see Anne Curzan, *Gender Shifts in the History of English* (Cambridge: Cambridge University Press, 2003).

13. John Evelyn, *A Philosophical Discourse of Earth, Relating to the Culture and Improvement of It for Vegetation, and the Propagation of Plants, &c. as It Was Presented to the Royal Society, April 29. 1675. By J. Evelyn Esq; Fellow of the Said Society* (London: John Martyn, printer to the Royal Society, 1676), 192.

14. Thomas Browne, *Religio Medici*, EEBO (London: R. Scot, T. Basset, J. Wright, R. Chiswell, 1682), 88; Paul M. Tuskes, Michael M. Collins, and James P. Tuttle, *The Wild Silk Moths of North America: A Natural History of the Saturniidae of the United States and Canada* (Ithaca, NY: Comstock, 1996), 4, 52–54.

15. Karen Ordhal Kupperman, "The Behive as a Model for Colonial Design," in *America in European Consciousness, 1493–1750* (Chapel Hill, NC: Omohundro Institute of Early American History and Culture, University of North Carolina Press, 1995), 272–94.

16. Bonoeil, *Observations*, 8 (real p. 6); Women's Silk Culture Association, *An Instruction Book in the Art of Silk Culture* (Philadelphia: Women's Silk Culture Association, 1882), 8.

17. Xinru Liu, *The Silk Road in World History* (Oxford: Oxford University Press, 2010), 1, 10; Hatch, "Mulberry Trees and Silkworms," 53–56.

18. Promoters like Edward Williams hoped that some of these native moths would be tried "in divers particulars, more consenting to the Country and Climate of Virginia" (*Virginia Richly and Truly Valued . . . The Second Edition*), 28.

19. Smith, Books 2, "The Sixt Voyage. 1606," and 5, "The Generall Historie of the Bermudas," in *Generall Historie of Virginia*, 108, 356; Wyatt's instructions are summarized in Hatch, "Mulberry Trees and Silkworms," 23–24.

20. Well into the nineteenth century, Anglophone projectors continued to read native mulberry trees as natural signs of silk. In a meeting of September 28, 1842, growers in New England resolved "that inasmuch as in America and China the mulberry tree is found in the native forests, it is a manifest indication of Divine Providence, that this country, as well as China, was designed to be a great silk growing country." Report of the New England Silk Growers' Convention, September 28, 1842, qtd. in Jacqueline Field, Marjorie Senechal, and Madelyn Shaw, *American Silk, 1830–1930: Entrepreneurs and Artifacts* (Lubbock: Texas Tech University Press, 2007), 1. In southern California, meanwhile, female sericulturalists hired

by female patrons to instruct "women in their homes who desire to add something to the family income" promised that the long growing season and good climate of Los Angeles would "embody a mine of as yet untold wealth for this favored region." Carrie Williams, *Mulberry Trees: The Silk Worm Market for Cocoons* (Minneapolis Beach, CA: Martin B. Van Antwerp, 1895), 3, 10.

21. On Harper's vexed relationship with Parliament and state censors, see Randy Robertson, *Censorship and Conflict in Seventeenth-Century England: The Subtle Art of Division* (University Park: Pennsylvania State University Press, 2009), 73–74.

22. Edward Williams, *Virginia, More Especially the South Part Thereof, Richly and Truly Valued*, EEBO (London: Thomas Harper for John Stephenson, 1650); Edward Williams, *Virgo Triumphan, or Virginia in Generall but the South Part thereof in Particular*, EEBO (London: Thomas Harper for John Stephenson, 1650); Edward Williams, *Virginia's Discovery of Silke-wormes with their benefit, And Implanting of Mulberry Trees*, EEBO (London: Thomas Harper for John Stephenson, 1650). Although Williams appears as the sole author, he explains in the preface "To the Reader" of the first text that "there is little of mine in this, but the Language," for the "Substance" comes from "Mr. *John Farrar* of Goding in Huntingdonshire," fleshed out with "some few additionall collections" from "my own experience of the place."

23. Jeffrey Knapp, *An Empire Nowhere: England, America, and Literature from Utopia to The Tempest* (Berkeley: University of California Press, 1992).

24. Ralph Waldo Emerson, "The Poet," in *Essential Writings of Ralph Waldo Emerson*, intro. Mary Oliver (1849; New York: Modern Library, 2000), 296.

25. Samuel Hartlib, *The Reformed Common-Wealth of Bees. Presented in severall Letters and Observations.* EEBO (London: Giles Calvert, 1655); Charles Butler, *The feminine monarchie or a treatise concerning bees, and the due ordering of them wherein the truth, found out by experience and diligent observation, discovereth the idle and fondd conceipts, which many haue written anent this subiect*, EEBO (London: Joseph Barnes, 1609). The text went through an additional four editions in the seventeenth century.

26. Bonoeil, *Observations* (1620), and John Bonoeil, *His Maiesties Gracious Letter to the Earle of South-Hampton, Treasurer, and to the Councell and Company of Virginia Heere Commanding the Present Setting Vp of Silke Works, and Planting of Vines in Virginia. And the Letter of the Treasurer, Councell, and Company, to the Gouernour and Councell of State There, for the Strict Execution of His Maiesties Royall Commands Herein. Also a Treatise of the Art of Making Silke, Together with Instructions How to Plant and Dresse Vines, and to Make Wine, and How to Dry Raisins, Figs, and Other Fruits, Set Foorth for the Benefit of the Two Renowned and Most Hopefull Sisters, Virginia, and the Summer-Ilands. By Iohn Bonoeil Frenchman, Seruant in These Imployments to His Most Excellent Maiesty of Great Brittaine, France, Ireland, Virginia, and the Summer-Ilands. Published by Authority*, EEBO (London: Felix Kyngston, 1622); Jean-Baptiste Letellier, *Memoirs et instructions pour l'establissement des meuriers* (Paris, 1603), trans. William Stallenge [?] as *Instructions for the Increasing and Planting of Mulberry Trees*, EEBO (London: Eleazar Edgar, 1609); Olivier Serres, *Théâtre d'Agriculture et mesnage des champs*. (Paris: Abraham Saugrain, 1600). Partially trans. Nicholas Geffe, *The Perfect Use of Silke-Worms and their Benefit*, EEBO (London: Felix Kyngston, 1607).

27. William Dugdale, *History of Imbanking and Draying of Divers Fenns and Marshes, Both in Foreign Parts and This Kingdom: And Improvements Thereby: Extracted from Records,*

Manuscripts, and Other Authentick Testimonies (London: Alice [Norton] Warren, 1662), 146–48; Mary Schoeser, *Silk* (New Haven, CT: Yale University Press, 2007), 49.

28. Hartlib, *Reformed Virginian Silkworm*, 9, 26; Williams, *Virginia Richly and Truly Valued . . . The Second Edition*, 34–38.

29. Hartlib, *Reformed Virginian Silkworm*, 10; William Potter, "A Bank of Lands," in Hartlib, ed. *Samuel Hartlib*, 289–300, 292.

30. Ewan, "Silk Culture," 130; Tuskes, Collins, and Tuttle, *Wild Silk Moths*, 4; Janice Neri and Danielle Skeehan, "The Mystery of the Silk Worm: Conversations in the Reading Room and Beyond." Found at the *JCB*: Online Journal of the John Carter Brown Library, August 2012. I thank Lisa Voigt for the reference. The passages have been generously digitized at http://www.brown.edu/Facilities/John_Carter_ Brown_Library/foundjcb.

31. Douglass R. Cope, *The Limits of Racial Domination: Plebeian Society in Colonial Mexico City, 1660–1720* (Madison: University of Wisconsin Press, 1994), 10; Woodrow Borah, *Silk Raising in Colonial Mexico* (Berkeley: University of California Press, 1943); Woodrow Borah, "The Indians of Tejupan Want to Raise Silk on Their Own," in *Colonial Lives: Documents on Latin American History, 1550–1850*, ed. Richard E. Boyer and Geoffrey Spurling, 6–10 (Oxford and New York: Oxford University Press, 2000); Schoeser, *Silk*, 53–55; Hatch, "Mulberry Trees and Silkworms," 5, 38–41.

32. E. G. R. Taylor, "Gerard Mercator, a.d. 1512–1594," *Geographical Journal* 128, no. 2 (June 1962): 201–2; Williams, *Virginia Richly and Truly Valued . . . The Second Edition*, B3v.

33. William Bullock, *Virginia Impartially Examined, and Left to Publick View, to Be Considered by All Iudicious and Honest Men*. EEBO (London: J. Hammond, 1649); Peter Thompson, "William Bullock's 'Strange Adventure': A Plan to Transform Seventeenth-Century Virginia." *William and Mary Quarterly*, 3rd ser., 61, no. 1, (January 1, 2004): 107–28, doi:10.2307/3491677: 16-page web suppl., 2–3 [Bullock, 9]. The dashes indicate line breaks in the marginalia.

34. Williams, *Virginia Richly and Truly Valued . . . The Second Edition*, 39; Richard Ferrar, "From a *Virginia*-Planter in *England*, to the *Virgin*-Lady *Virginia*," in *A Rare and New Discovery of Silkworms*, ed. Samuel Hartlib. EEBO. (London: Richard Wodenothe, 1652), 5–5v.

35. Akinobu Kuroda, "What Was Silver *Tael* System? A Mistake of China as Silver 'Standard' Country," in *Moneta: Three Conferences on International Monetary History*, vol. 156, ed. Georges Depeyrot, Catherine Brégianni, and Marina Kovalchuk, 391–97 (Wetteren, Belgium: Agence Nationale de la Recherche-Dépréciation de l'Argent Monétaire et relations Intérnationales, 2013). For an account of the environmental factors that influenced imperial monetary policy, see Timothy Brook, *The Troubled Empire: China in the Yuan and Ming Dynasties* (Cambridge, MA: Belknap Press of Harvard University Press, 2010).

36. Dennis O. Flynn and Arturo Giráldez, *Metals and Monies in an Emerging Global Economy* (Aldershot, UK: Ashgate, 1997), xix–xx; Schoeser, *Silk*, 13.

37. Modesto Bargalló, *La amalgamación de los metales de plata en hispanoamérica colonial* (Mexico City: Compañía Fundidora de Fierro y Acero de Monterrey, 1969); John Elliott, *Empires of the Atlantic: Britain and Spain in America, 1492–1830* (New Haven, CT: Yale University Press, 2006), 94; Hatch, "Mulberry Trees and Silkworms," 43.

38. Potter, "Bank of Lands," 292.

39. Hartlib, *Reformed Virginian Silkworm*, 30.

40. The fragmentary documentary record on this "Esquire Ferrar" is complicated by John Ferrar's use of the term "Esquire" to refer both to lettered correspondents ("Esquire Hartlib") and formally educated practitioners of the law. As such, "Esquire Ferrar" might refer to Virginia Ferrar's cousin Richard, who signed his verse epistle "ex AEde Trinitaris: Junior" or, according to Lyon Gardiner Tyler, as William Ferrar (1594–1637), Virginia Ferrar's uncle who died in Jamestown. It is also possible, however, that she exchanged silkworm and leaf samples with relatives of her own age, like William's Virginia-born sons William (1626–1678) or John (1631–1685), who fought against indigenous communities and ultimately served as sheriff, justice, and burgess toward the end of his life. A final possibility, suggested by Reid Barbour, is that "her kinsman" refers to Mary Ward, whose brother Ferrar Mapletoft lived in close proximity to the Wards in Virginia. Tyler, *Encyclopedia of Virginia Biography* (New York: Lewis Historical Publishing, 1915), 93; Barbour, email message to author, July 23, 2012.

41. In the archival records of Lower Norfolk County, near Yorktown, Edward Hatch has also found evidence of Sarah Willoughby's participation in this transatlantic community of growers. Hatch, "Mulberry Trees and Silkworms," 53.

42. The definition of empire in the early modern era is a large and ever-expanding area of study, and a full review of the literature far exceeds the scope of this essay. Two recent comparative studies of empire that provide excellent orientations to the field are *Empires in World History: Power and the Politics of Difference*, ed. Jane Burbank and Frederick Cooper (Princeton, NJ: Princeton University Press, 2010), and *Rereading the Black Legend: The Discourses of Religious and Racial Difference in the Renaissance Empire*, ed. Margaret Rich Greer, Walter Mignolo, and Maureen Quilligan (Chicago: University of Chicago Press, 2007). Joseph Miller engages and contextualizes these very questions in his introduction to the recently published *Princeton Companion to Atlantic History*, ed. Vincent Brown, Laurent Dubois, Jorge Cañizares Esguerra, and Karen Kupperman (Princeton, NJ: Princeton University Press, 2015).

"THE CONFINES AND BOUNDARIES OF THE LAND"

The Struggle for Fort King George and the Southern Frontiers, 1721–1725

Alejandra Dubcovsky

In 1721 South Carolina constructed a fort on the mouth of the Altamaha River called Fort King George.[1] The English had great expectations for this small, understaffed, and poorly supplied outpost. They hoped to court new Indian allies, improve tense relations with the Lower Creeks, and counter the threats posed by French traders venturing east from Louisiana. But the fort's power proved more symbolic than practical.[2] Fort King George did not help recruit new native allies, and most Lower Creeks remained wary of English initiatives in the wake of the Yamasee War (1715–1717). The garrison did even less to intimidate the French. French traders continued making inroads and alliances in a territory the English considered theirs. Captain Edward Massey, the second commander of the fort, commented wryly that the garrison was so "incapable of defence" and so incapable of monitoring "any part of its trade [that] it might as usefully have been place in Japan."[3]

Massey was right, for the most part. The fort's defense and military capacity were truly deplorable. But the garrison was not "in Japan." It had been built on the Altamaha River. Envisioned as a display of strength, not as a precipitator of conflict, the fort had nevertheless been erected on land claimed by both the Spaniards and the Yamasees—in the very heart of this debated and "debatable land."[4]

Fort King George was part of a new South Carolina foray into a well-trudged terrain.[5] Intended to curve the nascent French influence, the fort did more to reignite old tensions. Spain, not France, and Spanish soldiers, not French traders became the garrison's biggest challenge.[6] Officials in both Spain and Florida decided to fight the construction of this outpost. Their staunch opposition triggered an intense diplomatic dispute between English South Carolina and Spanish Florida. Where did South Carolina end and Florida begin? What were the boundaries of the Spanish and English empire in North America? How could these borders be controlled? Who was part of Florida? Who belonged in South Carolina? The negotiations over Fort King George demanded answers to these questions.

Both colonial officials and imperial agents became embroiled in the fate of this outpost. In London, Spanish and English diplomats met to fight over the legality of the garrison. As they debated over maps and royal edicts, their talks moved away from this meager outpost and turned to English and Spanish imperial traditions, projections, and anxieties. Speaking through the fort rather than about it, metropole diplomats sidestepped the issue of the garrison itself and focused on resolving or, at the very least, better articulating their rivalries. In Charles Town, Florida and South Carolina officials did the same. Fort King George became a proxy, a way to discuss more urgent predicaments, such as the ongoing Indian raids and the growing number of runaway slaves living in Spanish Florida. In London the conversations focused on charters and legal precedent, while in Charles Town the negotiations dealt with the consequences of the recently concluded Yamasee War and the rising power of African slavery. The goal of this essay is to make sense of these distinct, yet connected debates, and show how Fort King George became a complex point of convergence for both the imperial rivalries of England and Spain and the colonial contests of South Carolina and Florida. By doing so, the struggle for Fort King George moves beyond the banks of the Altamaha River and becomes a larger story about how empires in the colonial South functioned, developed, and competed.[7]

• • •

Colonel John Barnwell, known as "Tuscarora Jack" for his role and success during the Tuscarora War (1711) a decade earlier, spearheaded the petition for and construction of Fort King George.[8] His scheme for a military cordon on the southern frontier was met with resounding support in Charles Town. He then traveled to London with Joseph Boone, South Carolina's agent to

England, to present their plan before the Board of Trade. Once again, their proposal was eagerly received.[9] Barnwell and Boone unhappily discovered, however, that enthusiasm and interest did not translate into funds. In South Carolina, the construction of Fort King George became enmeshed in a contentious power struggle between the House of Commons and the governor. While this quarrel had nothing to do with the garrison itself—this debate was about the need and fate of printed currency in the colony—the bitter tensions between the two political bodies made it unclear who was supposed to pay for the garrison's construction, its weaponry, or its soldier's salaries.[10] In London issues of money also loomed large. The economic crisis caused by the South Sea Bubble had wrecked the government's finances, and Barnwell found his proposal for a series of outposts to guard South Carolina's frontier reduced to one, strategically located garrison.[11]

After pleading for men and supplies, Barnwell received the Forty-First Independent Regiment of Foot, a regiment of invalids.[12] The physical handicap of these men was simply the inauspicious start to the company's many woes. After delays at port and an exceedingly difficult ocean voyage, most of the regiment's already weak soldiers fell sick, probably with scurvy. Illness and fatigue led the Forty-First regiment to spend nearly one year recuperating in South Carolina's hospitals, postponing their duty even further. Unsure of who (or how) was to pay his salary and uncertain of the number of men at his disposal, Barnwell decided to take matters into his own hands. He recruited local men to construct and defend the future Fort King George. He found twenty-six men willing, or perhaps simply desperate enough, to head down to the mouth of the Altamaha River in the agonizing, humid heat of summer. More than half of these men would be dead within the year; disease—probably malaria and dysentery—bore most of the blame.[13]

The colonel proved unsympathetic to the plight of the motley crew he had assembled.[14] He recalled how at the start of his journey from Charles Town one of these men, "pretending to carry me [Barnwell] onto my boat, fell down with me & duck'd me, over head in the water."[15] After having to endure a rather cold night in his wet clothes, Barnwell fell gravely ill. The actions of this unidentified man almost cost the colonel his life. The only excuse for this soldier's behavior was that he had been inebriated—an all too common predicament among the local regiment. Most of his men, Barnwell bemoaned, "were as drunk as beasts." This small incident set the tone for the rest of the expedition. Disorder, drunkenness, and unruly behavior, including constant threats of mutiny and desertion, characterized Barnwell's march to the Altamaha River. Eventually on the evening of July 7, 1721, Barnwell and seven scouts reached the intended site for the fort; the remaining party arrived with the supply sloop a short while later.[16]

Fort King George, built like most colonial blockhouses, was small, with crowded quarters, and designed for defense, not comfort. In spite of Barnwell's complaints, his men completed the fort relatively quickly. By October of that year, the three-story wooden structure watched over the waters of the Altamaha, St. Simons Island to the east, and the vast marshes that seemed to engulf the garrison. The emptiness of the region surprised Barnwell.[17] He had reconnoitered the area less than five years earlier during the end of the Yamasee War, but now the land surrounding the Altamaha appeared different. It seemed unkempt, even deserted. Barnwell noted that the "Indian field [had] gown [sic.] up with Small Bushes," and he could not find any Indian towns or their residents.[18] The colonel realized then that he had established Fort King George not only far away from English towns, but also removed from any Indian settlement. The fort's relative isolation did not perturb Barnwell, for he was certain that the construction of the garrison would draw Indians back to the region (see Figure 2.1).

Indian support proved harder to secure than Barnwell had anticipated. The six Creek Indians hired to guide Barnwell's expedition abandoned the South Carolinians soon after leaving Charles Town. The colonel was flustered, convinced that Creek Indians could not be trusted for they had an inconsistent and unpredictable temperament. In all fairness, however, the Creeks' departure probably had more to do with the South Carolinians' temperament than with their own.[19] Barnwell and his men had done little to recommend themselves. A disorderly and drunken group of twenty local recruits had failed to impress the six Creek guides or to provide assurances that this particular endeavor—unlike previous English promises to construct garrisons, trade houses, and even towns in this region—would actually materialize.

But with each cypress beam Barnwell and his men placed, they signaled South Carolina's commitment to the project and to the region. It did not take long for neighboring Indians to take note. The Creeks, perhaps even some of the same Creeks who had originally dismissed Barnwell's efforts, began discussing the possibilities afforded by Fort King George. Already forging relations with French traders from Louisiana and Spanish soldiers from San Marcos de Apalachee, Creeks saw an English fort on the Altamaha River as another potential ally and, more importantly, as another supplier of European commodities. "The Indians can be expected," lamented Florida's governor Antonio de Benavides, to "become partial [to whoever supplies them] since they are lacking, as they usually lack, weapons and ammunitions

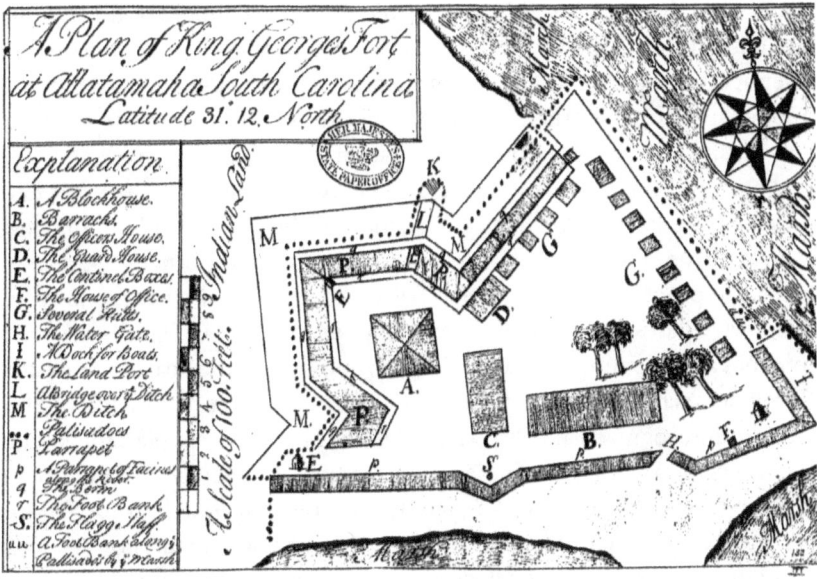

Figure 2.1. "A Plan of King George's Fort at Allatamaha, South Carolina [now Georgia]. Latitude 31°12′ North." Anonymous, 1722 in Colonial Office 700/Georgia 4/1. Courtesy of the National Archives, Kew.

which are the goods they mostly covet."[20] It seemed that Barnwell had been right. Building a garrison had attracted Indian attention, for even before Fort King George was fully functioning as a garrison or as a trading outpost, it had generated support for the English among the local native populations.

Barnwell was pleased, but wary. He was convinced that too much Indian involvement in the affairs of Fort King George would do more harm than good. Late in the summer of 1721, a small Creek party offered to help the destitute and half-finished garrison. The Creeks had approached the fort eager to demonstrate their new loyalty to South Carolina and, in the process, to secure a better (more privileged, and perhaps even exclusive) access to the trading goods that were going to be distributed and sold from Fort King George. But Barnwell refused. The colonel's decision to turn away Indian aid infuriated the garrison's starving soldiers and dumbfounded officials in Charles Town. Members of South Carolina's government had been trying, with limited success, to establish better relations with the Creeks since the end of the Yamasee War. Charles Town officials could not understand why Barnwell had rejected the support of an Indian group they were trying to court. The colonel stuck by his decision and explained that he already had two Indians in his service—one Tuscarora and one Creek—but "did not much Care, that they [the Tuscaroras] and the Creeks Should be much more acquainted then they are."[21] Barnwell argued that Fort King George was intended to help spread English influence in the region, not to serve as a hub for intertribal partnerships. Barnwell thus sought to regulate or, at the very least, keep tabs on Indian participation.

Fort King George was to serve as a beacon of English power. But first Barnwell needed to complete construction of the garrison. Having turned away aid from the Creeks, the colonel had to find an alternative source of labor. He proceeded to hire two African slaves from the nearby town of Beaufort.[22] Slaves, like these two men identified only as "Mr. Duvall's sawyers," were not an uncommon feature of English outposts, trading parties, and early Carolina ranches.[23] Though the risks of using black slaves in the backcountry were both recognized and regulated, Barnwell offered a simple explanation for choosing African over Indian labor: control. While Creeks could have (and in the past had) served as scouts, interpreters, as well as fort builders, their employment fostered relations that Barnwell could not properly monitor. Creek autonomy, evidenced by their earlier and untimely departure, compromised English authority. Barnwell thus restricted Indian involvement and favored a source of labor he thought he could better control.[24]

The Spanish moved to challenge both this control and Fort King George. Though continuous Spanish presence in La Florida began in 1565, when the *adelantado* Pedro Menéndez de Avilés successfully and violently expelled the French Huguenots from the region, Spanish hold on Florida was tenuous. Spanish officials had attempted to establish towns and forts throughout the North American South, but Franciscan missions were by far the largest and most successful Spanish endeavor in La Florida. In the mid-seventeenth century, at the height of mission activity, there were about 70 Franciscan friars, who operated around 40 mission sites that served over 26,000 Indian converts.[25] But all that changed in the 1670s with the founding of Charles Town. Spanish missions quickly buckled under English pressure. Indian slaving raids, supplied and encouraged by South Carolina, decimated Spanish holdings in the Southeast.[26] Spanish missions and towns in Timucua and Guale were targeted first, and then a series of devastating raids at the start of the eighteenth century left Apalachee destroyed. Within thirty years of English settlement in the region, Spanish Florida had lost significant influence over lands and people they had once considered under their control.

This spiraling pattern of loss slowed during the Yamasee War. Powerful Indian groups, like the Yamasees and the Lower Creeks, fled English aggression and sought Spanish protection. With suddenly burgeoning Indian alliances, Spanish Florida had a newfound source of strength.[27] Governor Benavides believed that the "Yamasees, people who are much feared by the English," could help Florida better position itself within the changing geopolitics of the region.[28] It had been almost twenty years, since the first English slaving raids against the Guale missions, that the San Agustín presidio, the main Spanish hold in Florida, had any sort of buffer or Indian ally between its northern lands and South Carolina's advances.[29] Benavides hoped that by encouraging the settling of refugee Yamasee towns to the north of San Agustín, the Spaniards would gain a tactical advantage. Though the governor envisioned the Yamasees serving as a powerful barrier between English and Spanish territory, the Yamasees never saw themselves as a mere buffer.[30]

Many Yamasees relocated to Spanish lands, but the vast majority chose to settle near Creek towns or in Apalachee, over 150 leagues from San Agustín. Most Yamasees did not "embrace the Holy Faith." A census collected by Joseph Primo de Rivera in 1717 revealed that the Yamasees refused to live "close to the presidio" or in Spanish missions.[31] The Yamasees had become Spanish allies, as Benavides had wanted, but only on Yamasee terms. Far more autonomous than the governor had anticipated or hoped, the Yamasees became an important new ally of Spanish Florida. Not only were they vehemently anti-English, but their decision to embrace Spanish protection also gave credence to Florida's efforts to secure native allies.[32]

Determined to maintain and protect Yamasee friendship, Benavides became enraged by the construction of Fort King George. This garrison jeopardized the safety of the recently relocated Yamasees and undermined Spanish ability to protect their new Indian allies. Governor Benavides decided that the fort could not stand, and with that decision he sparked a complicated debate about who was under Spanish protection, where English authority ended, and what the stakes of both were.

In its short tenure, Fort King George served in no battles, provided no immediate relief, and did little to counter the growing influence of French traders. Yet the debates over this garrison spanned an ocean and involved two rival powers. Spanish and English agents debated the legality of Fort King George in London at the same time as a diplomatic expedition departed San Agustín and headed for the garrison on the Altamaha River. One of the most remarkable aspects of these parallel debates is how strikingly different they are. Fort King George brought together the interests of Spain, England, Florida, and South Carolina, only to reveal how truly distinct imperial and colonial realities were.

• • •

In London, Fort King George became a symbol for the long-standing imperial rivalry between England and Spain in North America. Old injuries, planned invasions, rumored attacks, land disputes, and contested alliances could all be subsumed under the diplomatic negotiations over this garrison. For the English, Fort King George demonstrated the increased and, more importantly, the growing influence of South Carolina; the fort was the first step in the colony's new push for southern expansion. For the Spaniards, this lonely outpost was nothing of the sort. Fort King George was a brash, intrusive, and most importantly, illegal transgression by South Carolinian rogues. The English were attempting to claim by right of conquest a territory that the Spaniards argued was legally theirs.

Though it is not too surprising that Spain would oppose English incursions into La Florida, the manner in which Spanish officials articulated their displeasure is revealing. Before traveling to London to present his arguments against Fort King George, the Spanish ambassador, Andrés del Coro Barrutia y Cupide, commissioned Francisco Antonio de Ayala, agent in the Royal Archives of Simancas (the future Archivo General de Indias), to conduct a careful archival search for old Spanish titles to Florida.[33] By order of a royal Cédula (decree), Ayala surveyed all the documents from 1660 to 1685 "relating to the province of San Agustín de la Florida and Apalachee in the particulars of Carolina and S. Jorge [Charles Town]."[34] Ayala scoured the archives for evidence that Fort King George had been built within Spanish jurisdiction. He found plenty. With letters, decrees, and maps in hand, Barrutia y Cupide felt certain he could prove Spain's rightful ownership of the Altamaha River and demonstrate that Fort King George was an illegal incursion into Spanish lands. These arguments, based on Ayala's archival work, reflected a traditional Spanish concern with procedure and legality.[35]

The English officials, including the Duke of Newcastle, showed little regard for arguments based on old treatises. England had entered the colonial race significantly later than Spain; English colonists, including South Carolinians, believed in a right by settlement and control.[36] As Barrutia y Cupide cited Florida's original charter, Newcastle pointed to Spain's inability to occupy the area that divided Florida and South Carolina. The English believed that Barrutia y Cupide's legal claims amounted to nothing if Spain could not settle or at least regulate the region. The English argument was far simpler than the Spanish one and required no trips to the archive. Fort King George could stand because South Carolinians could settle and take the land, and the Spanish could not. As the English explained to Barrutia y Cupide, "Whereas it is notoriously known that the Spaniards have never maintain'd or kept possession of any in those parts except St. Augustine; And your Majesty might with as much reason contest their title to that Settlement as they dispute your Majty's. right to Fort King George, which was neither settled by the Spaniards, nor any other European Nation."[37] Arguing that the Spaniards had no legal claim to the fort for they had not "maintain'd or kept possession" of the land, the English diplomats turned a blind eye to the precedents Barrutia y Cupide cited.

The negotiations in London seemed doomed from the start. Neither the Spanish nor the English diplomats could, to the satisfaction of the other, place Fort King George on a map. The first problem was the Altamaha River. Spain and England had different names for this river. It took some for the Spanish and English agents to realize that they were in fact discussing the same waterway. Then the origin and course of the Altamaha River became a point of contention. The Spanish diplomats placed the Altamaha near San Agustín, but according to the English, this river was far closer to Charles Town. Arthur Middleton, interim governor of South Carolina, explained that South Carolina had control of the lands, "which lyes within the Degrees of 36 and 30 minutes northern latitude, the River Allatamahaw, upon which Fort King George is Erected, [which] lyes in the Latitude above 31 degrees and a halfe, so that it lyes two degrees and a halfe to the northward of the Extent of the said Charter to the Southward."[38] The river's bends and location depended on who was speaking, and both sides argued that the Altamaha River conclusively fell within the boundaries of their colonies.

If placing the Altamaha River on a map proved troublesome, agreeing on where Fort King George had been erected became next to impossible. In spite of arriving with detailed documentary evidence, Barrutia y Cupide could not persuade the English diplomats of where the fort presently stood. The Spanish diplomat got even more upset by the map the English intended to use during the negotiations. This map, Barrutia y Cupide indignantly explained, "supposed that the fort [King George] located at the mouth of the Ylatamaha [sic] . . . was clearly found within the line that the Carolina had established in the direction of Florida, which included [in its borders] the mouth of the Ylatamaha." Barrutia y Cupide could not hide his anger. He dismissed the English map as blatantly inaccurate. "Said map was made in England in the year 1721 and for that reason its demarcations of Carolina could be suspicious since in other maps with that same motive . . . one could not find similar demarcations."[39] The map was merely a political tool argued Barrutia y Cupide. Spanish and English diplomats could not agree on where to place (or what to call) the Altamaha River, where the garrison had been built, or even which map to use to begin discussing the issues they could not agree on in the first place. Fort King George was not so much the issue at hand as was finding a common vocabulary for the unfolding imperial struggle.

As the debate dragged with little progress, the Spanish ambassador began to recognize that Whitehall was purposefully stalling. The fort was already in place, and the English had little to gain from expediting their case. By carrying out these tortuously slow diplomatic talks, the English could keep the garrison in place and, much to the annoyance of the Spanish, continue acting as the champions of peace and "good communications." The Spanish ambassador saw through this façade, but since his own arguments rested on the restoration of legal claims, Barrutia y Cupide was bound to obey the current amity between the two Crowns. At one point during the course of the talks, the Spanish ambassador received word that the South Carolinians in Fort King George were arming Indians and launching attacks against Spanish settlements.[40] Whereas the news of English aggression made the immediate removal of Fort King George an utmost priority in San Agustín, Barrutia y Cupide did little to change his diplomatic strategy in London. The ambassador continued believing that if he could prove that Fort King George was built in Spanish lands then the English would be forced to acknowledge their transgression and abandon the outpost.[41] But they never did.

In London the discussions about Fort King George revolved around imaginary lines, names, and rivers whose flow seemed politically predetermined. The fort itself was not what mattered. It was almost immaterial. This garrison became a way for English and Spanish diplomats to address with new terms their well-established rivalry. Though the debates reached no clear conclusion, the quarrel over this meager outpost showed the importance of England and Spain in each other's colonial worlds. It also revealed the difficulty both empires faced when trying to discuss, let alone understand, colonial contests.

• • •

The fate of Fort King George was also hotly debated in South Carolina. Unlike the diplomatic talks of Whitehall, the debates in Charles Town turned to local matters. Leaving behind maps and latitude lines, Florida and South Carolina agents used Fort King George to discuss the land and people who lay between the two colonies. Yamasee Indians and the growing problem of runaway African slaves quickly dominated the conversation that, in theory, was about the legality of a small garrison on the Altamaha River. As in London, the debates in Charles Town quickly became about something larger, or perhaps simply different, than the fort itself. The outpost was once again relegated to the backdrop.

The construction of Fort King George did not come as a surprise to Spanish officials in Florida. They had known for some time about English efforts to build a garrison on the Altamaha River. Waiting perhaps for the haphazard project to implode without interference, Governor Benavides had taken his time deciding on the best way to attack this fort. Rumors circulated in Charles Town that a joint Spanish, French, and Yamasee force intended to attack and destroy the outpost. But in the end, the Spanish governor opted for a quieter approach. Benavides sent a small party of armed and experienced men directly to the fort to demand its surrender. Much to the surprise of the English soldiers stationed in Fort King George, the Spanish party managed to march undetected to the very entrance of the garrison.[42] Sometime in the first weeks of February 1724, Don Juan Mexia, Don Juan de Ayala, Juan de Sandoval, Don Josef Rodriguez Menéndez, Don Alonzo de Avila Saavedra, and Don Francisco Menéndez Marqués entered the English garrison.[43] A fort designed to counter or, at the very least, warn against foreign presence had let a small Spanish party basically within its gates.

The Spanish presence at Fort King George was an embarrassing oversight. Even if the Spanish party failed in its diplomatic mission, it had already succeeded in obtaining valuable information about the garrison. The Spanish soldiers had gotten a firsthand look at the fort, its rotting beams, inattentive infantry, and the desolate condition of the lands that surrounded the outpost—both between San Agustín and the Altamaha River and between Fort King George and Charles Town. This overland expedition had been as much about espionage as it had been about diplomacy.

South Carolina's governor, Francis Nicholson, understood Florida's tactics. In his correspondence with San Agustín, Nicholson seemed more furious by the route that the Florida soldiers had taken than by that the message they carried. Nicholson chastised Benavides not for sending a diplomatic party, but rather for sending an *overland* diplomatic party. In a biting letter to the Spanish governor, Nicholson explained "that for the future I will Receive no Message but what comes directly over the Barr to Charles Town."[44] But the damage had been done. While future diplomatic missions would travel by sea, as Nicholson had requested, San Agustín officials had used this diplomatic venture to learn vital information about both the garrison and the state of South Carolina.[45]

The South Carolina soldiers stationed at Fort King George wasted no time in apprehending, disarming, and jailing the Spanish soldiers. Benavides had probably guessed that Fort King George would not simply surrender at the sight of six armed Spaniards. Imprisonment, however, was far from the ideal way to start negotiations. After a hurried march to Charles Town and an equally hasty welcome by the English governor, the Spanish diplomats presented three demands. First, the English needed to dismantle Fort King George. Second, South Carolina had to remove all other military and trading outposts from Spanish territory—none was specifically mentioned, so this point was probably about curbing and protesting English incursions into Spanish lands. And third, a clear, mutually recognizable boundary had to be drawn between South Carolina and Florida.

Echoing the diplomatic efforts and arguments taking place in London, the Florida soldiers began the negotiations by presenting official documents. Menéndez Marqués, the leader of the Spanish party, gave Governor Nicholson letters from the king of Spain, the Duke of Newcastle, and the governor of San Agustín. Governor Benavides had assumed that these documents would help establish the legitimacy of the diplomatic party; but they had the opposite effect. They failed to impress the South Carolina governor (like the archival charters and maps had failed to impress English diplomats in Whitehall) and, rather than establishing Spanish claims, these letters made Nicholson question the sincerity and the intentions of the Spanish party.

Menéndez Marqués had presented Nicholson with a letter from the Duke of Newcastle, ordering that Fort King George needed to be "dismantled if an agreement cannot be reached to the satisfaction of his Catholic Majesty."[46] Nicholson had his own letters and instructions from the Duke of Newcastle, and none had ever proven as sympathetic to the Spanish. Nicholson believed that the Spanish were trying to deceive him and declared the letter a fake. It is possible that Barruita y Cupide had purposefully misconstrued this letter in order to aid the Spanish cause in Florida; it is equally as conceivable that the Duke of Newcastle wrote such letter to appease or stall the Spanish efforts in Whitehall but not as a guideline for policy to be enacted on the ground. Instead of validating the Spanish demands, the documents carried by Menéndez Marqués had muddled a debate that had not even started.

But if the letter from the Duke of Newcastle had troubled Nicholson, the epistle from Governor Benavides left him nonplussed. The Florida governor had imbued this small diplomatic party with the authority to "settl[e] the boundaries of the two governments and they had likewise . . . proves [proofs] on that affair."[47] In presenting their demands, the Spanish diplomats argued that establishing a clear boundary between Florida and South Carolina would not only resolve the debate over Fort King George, but would also help avoid similar contests in the future. Nicholson was suddenly placed in a difficult position. In principle he agreed with the Spanish diplomats, but Nicholson knew that unlike Florida, South Carolina benefited greatly from the ambiguity produced by a fluid boundary. A well-demarcated border, Nicholson feared, would hurt South Carolina and transform any English expansion into a punishable transgression. Unsure of how to proceed, Nicholson took a page from the Spanish diplomatic guidebook and argued that since he lacked the appropriate documents and authorization, South Carolina could not and would not engage in boundary disputes at this time.

As for Fort King George, Nicholson simply argued that the removal of the outpost was not an option.[48] Arthur Middleton, then serving as a deputy on the Proprietary Council of Carolina and one of the earliest advocates for Fort King George, lauded South Carolina's "refusal to have the fort demolished." The "service that fort [provides] is to the safety of this province," Middleton explained, "and [he feared] the dangerous consequence that will attend for giving up of the same. "Quit[ing] possession [of the fort]," Middleton argued, "will tend to the utter ruin of this colony."[49] While his predictions that without Fort King George "utter ruin" would befall South Carolina were nothing short of hyperbole, there was more to Middleton's claims than mere theatrics. "Quitting possession" of the fort would make South Carolina appear weak, subject to the demands of Spain. Fort King George needed to stand.

South Carolina officials thus decided to attack any opposition to the project. In a diplomatic stroke of brilliance, Governor Nicholson placed the creation of Fort King George on Spanish shoulders. Selectively forgetting that the garrison had been erected to counter French threats and develop better trading relations with the Creeks, Nicholson argued that the fort had been a necessary precaution against Florida. After all, it was Spanish colonists who had harbored and supported the dangerous Yamasee renegades. It was Florida officials who helped strengthened Creek-Yamasee relations and thus blocked English efforts to secure an alliance with the powerful Lower Creeks. The Spaniards were the ones turning the Indians against South Carolina. Through this reasoning, Nicholson, who had personally ordered the construction and armament of an outpost deep inside Spanish territory, argued that Fort King George was a defense measure against Spanish aggressions. Nicholson circumvented entirely the issue of the fort and began accusing the flabbergasted Spanish diplomats of acting against "the peace accords between the two Crowns."[50]

With this charge, Nicholson overstepped his ground. The Spanish delegation was comprised of soldiers who had devoted their military careers to Florida. They had witnessed firsthand the destruction and violence carried out by South Carolina and its Indian allies. Four of the six men—Juan Ruiz de Mexía, Alonso Davila Saavedra, Don Rodriguez Menendez, and Juan de Sandoval—had been stationed on Santa Catalina Island when a joint English-Indian force slowly engulfed and attacked Spanish holdings on the island. As soldiers, these men had seen Spanish missions burned, the towns of Christian Indians destroyed, and their compañeros killed. Now as diplomats, these men had come face to face with the executioner of such policies, only to discover that the English governor blamed Spanish Florida for his hostile course of action. Menéndez Marqués found the irony of Nicholson's accusations deeply disconcerting. The Spanish diplomats questioned South Carolina's declarations of peace by simply pointing to Fort King George. The armed and garrisoned fort, located a mere fifty miles from San Agustín, did not seem like a commitment to peace. Menéndez Marqués accused South Carolina of supplying and launching Indians raids into Florida from Fort King George.[51] This garrison was not a defensive tool against potential warfare as Nicholson had argued. Fort King George was an act of war.

South Carolina and Florida were at an impasse. With each side accusing the other of inciting violence, the talks could have ended there. But they did not. Nicholson suddenly turned his attention to a seemingly tangential topic: runaway slaves. Instead of discussing the contested garrison, Nicholson used Fort King George to demand the return of escaped slaves. "Some of our runaways from Fort King George and other places are now Entertained at St. Augustine," explained Nicholson, "therefore I hope and Expect your Excellency will cause all those people to be Sent hither by Sea, or Secured till wee can send for them."[52] The governor even gave the diplomats "a paper with the names of seven slaves who have fled said government and also [the names] of their masters who demand their return."[53] Menéndez Marqués was unsure of how to proceed. He had been instructed to remove the fort on the Altamaha, eradicate illegal English settlements, and establish a border. Governor Benavides had not mentioned fugitive slaves.[54]

The first impulse of the Spanish diplomat was to argue that he did not have the authority to deal with the issue of fugitive slaves, which was true. But Menéndez Marqués decided to seize the moment. If Nicholson was going to reprimand the Spanish for harboring English property, then the Florida delegates would do the same. The Spanish diplomats began scolding the South Carolinians for supplying and encouraging attacks against Florida settlers and their Indian allies, in particular the Yamasee. "In that same council," in which the fate of the fugitive slaves was addressed, Menéndez Marqués and Nicholson also "discussed the hostilities by Uchises Indians and other who take actions against this [Spanish] jurisdictions carrying out English goals."[55] Nicholson used Fort King George to ask for the return of fugitive slaves; Menéndez Marqués used it to demand protection for Indians living in Spanish lands.

The negotiations continued for over a month. But weary of entertaining and paying for the Spanish diplomatic party, Nicholson finally ended the talks. He issued "clear orders . . . so that no damage whatsoever would befall this [San Agustín] presidio" or Spanish Indians.[56] The governor hoped that these assurances would persuade the Spaniards to return the escaped slaves back to South Carolina.[57] But Nicholson's promises as well as his expectations fell short. A year after Menéndez Marqués's diplomatic party had left Charles Town, little had changed. Fort King George still watched over the Altamaha River. South Carolina and its Indians allies continued attacking Yamasee towns in Florida. And runaway slaves not only remained in San Agustín, but new fugitives had arrived in the Spanish presidio.[58]

In September 1725, Benavides decided to send a second delegation, this time directly to Charles Town. Though Fort King George was, once again, the reason behind these diplomatic overtures, it was perfectly clear to both parties involved that the outpost itself was only an excuse for conversation. This fact became all too clear when a fire consumed the garrison in 1725, but the debates continued.[59] The demands of the second diplomatic party were similar to those of the first. Once again Spanish officials demanded that South Carolina dismantle Fort King George, remove English settlements from Spanish lands, and establish a boundary between Florida and South Carolina. But Benavides had given this second delegation an additional task: discuss the fate of the fugitive slaves refuged in San Agustín.[60] The Spanish diplomats vowed to keep and even free all the fugitive slaves from South Carolina if the English continued attacking Yamasees or other Spanish Indians. Benavides, like most Florida governors before him, had struggled to protect Spanish Indian allies from ongoing English incursions. The first bout of negotiations over Fort King George had shown him a way.[61] By protecting fugitive slaves, Spanish Florida could help shape how and where South Carolina expanded.

Though South Carolina's construction of Fort King George had undermined the core Indian alliances Florida had carefully tried to rebuild after the Yamasee War, the Spanish runaway slave policy articulated during the negotiations showed that Florida officials had learned how to retaliate. Nicholson targeted Florida's new Yamasee allies; Benavides targeted the slave plantation system that fueled South Carolina's economy and growth.[62] The negotiations over Fort King George exposed the interconnected, yet distinct policies, priorities, and fears of these neighboring colonies.

• • •

The quarrels over Fort King George intertwined an international, imperial rivalry with a deeply local, colonial debate. This garrison, constructed in the land between San Agustín and Charles Town, granted officials in Florida, South Carolina, Spain, and England a way to represent their competing ambitions and efforts. Both of these deliberations—the geopolitical debate in London and the fight over Indians and slaves in Charles Town—intersected in this small, ill-equipped outpost. Fort King George offers a way into the messiness and confusion of these multi-tiered contests that characterized the colonial South. But the point is not merely that Spanish and English relations were messy and confusing, although at times they certainly were. Only by examining how all these players, with their own perspectives and objectives, intersected and differed, can the seemingly inexorable forces of colonialism and imperialism be understood. The struggle over Fort King George was about a small garrison on the Altamaha River. It was also about how empires in the colonial world worked.

Notes

Early versions of this essay were presented at the California American Studies Association Conference at the University of California at Santa Barbara in April 2009 and at the Graduate Student Conference, Intersecting Histories: Transforming Identities, Places and Beliefs, of Claremont University, in May 2009. Special thanks to Jennifer Spear for her comments as well as to audience members of both venues.

1. Larry E. Ivers, *Colonial Forts of South Carolina, 1670–1775*, South Carolina Tricentennial Commission (Columbia: University of South Carolina Press, 1970). For a more general overview, see Daniel Patrick Ingram, *Indians and British Outposts in Eighteenth-Century America* (Gainesville: University Press of Florida, 2012).

2. For the importance and rise of a French presence, see Daniel H. Usner Jr. *Indians, Settlers, and Slaves in a Frontier Exchange Economy, the Lower Mississippi Valley before 1783* (Chapel Hill: University of North Carolina, published for the Institute of Early American History and Culture, Williamsburg, Virginia, 1990), 30–31.; and Verner W. Crane, *The Southern Frontier, 1670–1732* (Durham, NC.: Duke University Press, 1929), 206–12.

3. Edward Massey to "Sir," April 26, 1727, Journals of the Commons House of Assembly (hereafter JCHA), vol. 12, *1725-1727*, 247-50, South Carolina Department of Archives and History (hereafter SCDAH), Columbia, South Carolina.

4. Herbert E. Bolton and Mary Ross, *The Debatable Land: A Sketch of the Anglo-Spanish Contest for the Georgia Country* (Berkeley: University of California Press, 1925), 4-5.

5. For more on the war, see Steven J. Oatis, *A Colonial Complex, South Carolina's Frontiers in the Era of the Yamasee War, 1680-1730* (Lincoln: University of Nebraska Press, 2004), 113-55; William L. Ramsey, *The Yamasee War: A Study of Culture, Economy, and Conflict in the Colonial South* (Lincoln: University of Nebraska Press, 2008), 101-218.

6. For the interconnection of Spanish and English colonial projects, see John Huxtable Elliott, *Empires of the Atlantic World: Britain and Spain in America 1492-1830* (New Haven, CT: Yale University Press, 2006); Jorge Cañizares-Esguerra, *Puritan Conquistador, Iberianizing the Atlantic, 1550-1700* (Stanford, CA: Stanford University Press, 2006). For the particulars of the Southeast see, J. Leitch Wright, *Anglo-Spanish Rivalry in North America* (Athens: University of Georgia Press, 1971); Timothy Paul Grady, *Anglo-Spanish Rivalry in Colonial South-East America, 1650-1725*, Empires in Perspective (London: Pickering & Chatto, 2010); Robbie Ethridge, *From Chicaza to Chickasaw: The European Invasion and the Transformation of the Mississippian World, 1540-1715* (Chapel Hill: University of North Carolina Press, 2010).

7. Arredondo, *Demostracion Historiographica* . . . *March 20, 1742*, 175.

8. For Barnwell's experiences in the Tuscarora War see "The Tuscarora Expedition, Letters of Colonel John Barnwell," *South Carolina Genealogical Magazine* 9, no. 1 (1908): 28-54; Joseph W. Barnwell, "The Second Tuscarora Expedition," *South Carolina Genealogical Magazine* 10, no. 1 (1908): 33-48.

9. Crane, *Southern Frontier, 1670-1732*, 187-235; M. Eugene Sirmans, *Colonial South Carolina, a Political History, 1663-1763* (Chapel Hill: University of North Carolina Press, 1966), 131-66.

10. For the debates on printed currency, see Robert M. Weir, *Colonial South Carolina: A History*, (Millwood, NY: KTO Press, 1983), 93-104, 107-111.

11. Anne L. Murphy, *The Origins of English Financial Markets: Investment and Speculation before the South Sea Bubble* (Cambridge: Cambridge University Press, 2009), 1-10.

12. William A. Foote, "The South Carolina Independents," *South Carolina Historical Magazine* 62, no. 4 (1961): 195-99.

13. "Fr Nicholson to the Right Honble The Lords Commrs for Trade and Plantations," November 28, 1727, vol. 12, 1725-27, 247-50, in *Records in the British Public Record Office Relating to South Carolina* (hereafter PRO), accessed in the SCDAH.

14. Ivers, *Colonial Forts of South Carolina, 1670-1775*, 54.

15. "Fort King George, Journal of Col John Barnwell (Tuscarora) in the Construction of the Fort on the Altamaha in 1721," *South Carolina Genealogical Magazine* 27, no. 4 (1926): 195.

16. Ibid., 194.

17. Jeannie Cook, *Fort King George: Step One to Statehood* (Darien, GA: The Darien News, 1990), 5; Bessie Lewis, *Old Fort King George: The First English Settlement in the Land Which Is Now Georgia* (Brunswick, GA: Glover Printing, 1973); William L. Ramsey, "'Something

Cloudy in Their Looks': The Origins of the Yamasee War Reconsidered," *Journal of American History* 90, no. 1 (2003): 44–75.

18. "Fort King George, Journal of Col John Barnwell (Tuscarora) in the Construction of the Fort on the Altamaha in 1721," *South Carolina Genealogical Magazine* 27, no. 4 (1926): 196.

19. Philip Levy, *Fellow Travelers: Indians and Europeans Contesting the Early American Trials* (Gainesville: University Press of Florida, 2007), chaps. 1 and 2.

20. Letters of Benavides, April 21, 1722, AGI-SD, bnd 5035 58–1-29/32, Reel 38, Stetson Collection, P. K. Yonge Library of Florida History, Gainesville, Florida (hereafter PKY).

21. "Fort King George, Journal of Col John Barnwell (Tuscarora) in the Construction of the Fort on the Altamaha in 1721," 196.

22. Ibid.

23. "To Mr. John Bee in Charles Town in South Carolina with Care Deliver from Ocheese River These," July 30, 1723, vol. 10, 128–32, PRO, SCDAH. For slave activities in early Carolina, see John Lawson, *A New Voyage to Carolina* (London, 1709). The electronic edition is a part of the UNC-CH digitization project, Documenting the American South. Jane Landers, "Gracia Real De Santa Teresa De Mose: A Free Black Town in Spanish Colonial Florida," *American Historical Review* 95, no. 1 (1990): 9–30; Gary S. Dunbar, "Colonial Carolina Cowpens," *Agricultural History* 35 (1961): 125–31; Peter Wood, *Black Majority, Negroes in Colonial South Carolina from 1670 through the Stono Rebellion* (New York: W. W. Norton, 1974), 29–32.

24. Wood, *Black Majority*, 157; S. Max Edelson, *Plantation Enterprise in Colonial South Carolina* (Cambridge, MA: Harvard University Press, 2006), 96–129.

25. There are lots of reasons to believe this number is an exaggeration. But even if there were only half of that number of converts, that is still tenfold the Spanish population of San Agustín. For mission activities, see Jerald T. Milanich, *Florida Indians and the Invasion from Europe* (Gainesville: University Press of Florida, 1995); Jerald T. Milanich, "Franciscan Missions and Native Peoples in Spanish Florida," in *The Forgotten Centuries: Indians and Europeans in the American South, 1521–1704*, ed. Charles M. Hudson and Carmen Chaves Tesser (Athens: University of Georgia Press, 1994). John E. Worth, *The Timucuan Chiefdoms of Spanish Florida*, vol. 1, *Assimilation* (Gainesville: University Press of Florida, 1998). For Indian uprisings, see J. Michael Francis, Kathleen M. Kole, and David Hurst Thomas, *Murder and Martyrdom in Spanish Florida: Don Juan and the Guale Uprising of 1597*, vol. 95, American Museum of Natural History Anthropological Papers (2011).

26. Alan Gallay, *The Indian Slave Trade, the Rise of the English Empire in the American South 1670–1717* (New Haven, CT: Yale University Press, 2002), 37–97. See also Denise I. Bossy's work in this volume.

27. Letters of Benavides, April 21, 1722, AGI-SD, bnd 5035 58–1-29/32, Reel 38, Stetson Collection, PKY.

28. Friar Pulido Report, March 11, 1723, AGI-SD bnd 5070 58–2-16/9, Reel 38, Stetson Collection, PKY.

29. John E. Worth, *The Struggle for the Georgia Coast: An 18th-Century Spanish Retrospective on Guale and Mocama* (Athens: American Museum of Natural History; distributed by the University of Georgia Press, 1995); Paul Kelton, *Epidemics and Enslavement: Biological Catastrophe in the Native Southeast, 1492–1715* (Lincoln: University of Nebraska Press, 2007), esp. chap. 3.

30. Worth, *Struggle for the Georgia Coast*.

31. "Captain Joseph Primo de Rivera," April 28, 1718, Reel 37, Stetson Collection, PKY; John H. Hann, "St. Augustine's Fallout from the Yamasee War," *Florida Historical Quarterly* 68, no. 2 (1989): 181–201.

32. Herbert Eugene Bolton, "Documents Concerning Property Rights in Florida 1716–1764; Fray Joseph Ramón Escudero to Marqués De Monteleón, Spanish Ambassador at London," in Bolton Papers, Bancroft Library, Berkeley, CA.

33. The English make note of another ambassador: Marquis de Pozo Bueno. The marquis seems to have been the official ambassador; Barrutia y Cupide was brought in specifically to debate Fort King George.

34. "Cédula Real," June 24, 1723, AGI-SD, bnd 58-1-24/723, PKY.

35. Bolton and Ross, *Debatable Land*, chap. 3, and Wright, *Anglo-Spanish Rivalry in North America*, 62. While the diplomats in Florida did not conduct archival research, they still attempted to gather the appropriate factual as well as historical (more anecdotal) evidence to back their claims. See Arredondo, *Demostracion Historiographica . . . March 20, 1742*, 172–73.

36. For comparison of English and Spanish practices, see Patricia Seed, *Ceremonies of Possession in Europe's Conquest of the New World* (Cambridge: Cambridge University Press, 1995), 1–16, 69–100. For a general overview, see Elliott, *Empires of the Atlantic World*, 29–56, 88–115.

37. "Council of Trade and Plantations to the Duke of Newcastle," June 21, 1728, in *Calendar of State Papers Colonial, America and West Indies*: vol. 36, *1728-1729*, ed. Cecil Headlam and Arthur Percival Newton (London, 1937), *British History Online*, 21–30.

38. "A. Middleton to Francis Nicholson." September 10, 1725, vol. 11, 1723–1725, 335–37, PRO, SCDAH.

39. "Consejo de India relative to the English in Carolina," December 13, 1723, AGI-SD bnd 58-1-24, Reel 38, Stetson Collection, PKY.

40. "Antonio de Benavides to Andres de Pes," August 18, 1723, AGI-SD bnd 5095 58-1-29/57 Reel 38, Stetson Collection, PKY; "Andrés del Coro Barrutia," November 23, 1724 AGI 58-1-20/196 bnd 5125, Reel 38, Stetson Collection, PKY.

41. Arredondo, *Demostracion Historiographica . . . March 20, 1742*, 175.

42. A letter from Fort King George by Charles Huddy, February 9, 1723/4, vol. 11, *1723–25*, 36, PRO, SCDAH.

43. Arredondo, *Demostracion Historiographica . . . March 20, 1742*, 172–73.

44. "Fr. Nicholson to the Governor of San Agustín," n.d., 1723, vol. 11, *1723–25*, 35, PRO, SCDAH.

45. "Benavides dealing with Fort King George," September 22, 1727, AGI-SD, bnd 58-1-31/10, Reel 39, Stetson Collection, PKY.

46. Documento 14, Testimonio de los autos y demás diligencias . . . June 10 and August 18, 1724, in Manuel Serrano y Sanz, *Documentos Historicos De La Florida Y La Luisiana, Siglos Xvi Al Xviii* (Madrid: Librería General de Victoriano Suárez, 1912), 243–60.

47. "A. Middleton to Francis Nicholson." September 10, 1725, vol. 11, *1723–25*, 338–41, PRO, SCDAH.

48. Documento 14, Testimonio de los autos y demás diligencias . . . June 10 and August 18, 1724, in Serrano y Sanz, *Documentos Historicos De La Florida Y La Luisiana, Siglos Xvi Al Xviii* (Madrid: Librería General de Victoriano Suárez, 1912), 248.

49. "A. Middleton to Francis Nicholson." September 10, 1725, 338–41; "A. Middleton to His Grace the Duke of Newcastle," December 10, 1725, vol. 11, *1723–25,* 360–61. PRO, SCDAH.

50. November 2, 1725, AGI-SD AGI 58-1-31/3 bnd 5158, Reel 39, Stetson Collection, PKY.

51. Ibid.

52. Letter by Francis Nicholson," February 24, 1724, vol. 11, *1723–25,* 32. PRO, SCDAH. For more on Captain Watson, see "John Cockran and John. Drake Committee of the Assembly to Mr. Boone," March 8, 1718, PRO, vol. 7, *1717–1720,* 98–99 (SCDAH), and for more on Cherekleecheee, a Yamasee armed by the Spanish against the English, see Mark F. Boyd, "Diego Peña's Expedition to Apalachee and Apalachicola in 1716," *Florida Historical Quarterly* 28, no. 1 (July 1949): 1–27.

53. November 2, 1725, AGI-SD AGI 58-1-31/3 bnd 5158, Reel 39, Stetson Collection, PKY.

54. Jane Landers, "Spanish Sanctuary: Fugitives in Florida, 1687–1790," *Florida Historical Quarterly* 62, no. 3 (January) (1984): 297–314; Jane Landers, *Black Society in Spanish Florida* (Urbana: University of Illinois Press, 1999).

55. November 2, 1725, AGI-SD AGI 58-1-31/3 bnd 5158, Reel 39, Stetson Collection, PKY.

56. Ibid.

57. Bessie Lewis, *The Story of Old Fort King George: The First English Settlement in the Land Which Is Now Georgia* (n.p.: n.p., 1932), discusses how South Carolinians had to pay the cost of lodging the Spanish party.

58. Irene A. Wright, "Dispatches of Spanish Official Bearing on the Free Negro Settlement of Gracia Real De Santa Teresa De Mose, Florida," *Journal of Negro History* 9, no. 2 (April 1924): 164.

59. "Edward Massey to Sir,'" April 26, 1727, vol. 12, *1725–27,* 247–50, PRO, SCDAH. After an investigation, it was concluded that there had been no arson or foul play. The only problem had been that the soldiers manning the fort had not gone to the aid of the garrison quickly enough. Massey reported that "the men were not so active as they might have been in extinguishing the fire in hopes by the destruction of the fort." Massey had sympathized with the plight of the soldiers stationed in the dilapidated Fort King George and none were prosecuted for misconduct.

60. Documento 14, Testimonio de los autos y demás diligencias . . . June 10 and August 18, 1724, in Serrano y Sanz, *Documentos Historicos De La Florida Y La Luisiana, Siglos Xvi Al Xviii* (Madrid: Librería General de Victoriano Suárez, 1912), 243–60.

61. Ibid. For the intersection of Indian trade and plantation slavery, see Matthew Jennings, *New Worlds of Violence: Cultures and Conquests in the Early American Southeast* (Knoxville: University of Tennessee Press, 2011), 119–20.

62. "Robert Johnson, Francis Yonge, Small Wragg to My Lords," May 28, 1728, vol. 13, *1727–8,* 51–54, PRO, SCDAH.

3

NEGOTIATING SLAVERY AND EMPIRE

Yamasee Indians in the Early Southeast

Denise I. Bossy

The early colonial Southeast was a place where three very different cultures of slavery met, interacted, and at times clashed dramatically. From the sixteenth to the eighteenth century, southeastern Indians, the Spanish, and the British practiced discrete types of slavery. The Spanish and British believed slavery to be central to their efforts to establish, expand, or just hold onto their fragile empires. Scholars have deeply examined the fundamental importance of slavery to the establishment and growth of British South Carolina and, to a lesser extent, Spanish attempts to destabilize Carolina by proffering freedom to runaway slaves from British plantations. Yet relatively little attention has been paid to the ways in which southeastern Indians shaped British and Spanish colonial practices of slavery in the Southeast. A number of southeastern Indian communities, most notably the Yamasees, had extensive knowledge of each system of slavery and were just as deliberate as the Spanish or British in using slavery as a tool to promote their geopolitical ambitions. For thirty years, the Yamasees were one of the most powerful slave-raiding communities in the Southeast and, as with the British, slavery was the foundation of their economy. But in stark contrast to the British or Spanish, the Yamasees were also the victims of the transatlantic system of racialized slavery.[1]

By meaningfully putting Yamasees at the center of contestations between European colonies and Indian nations over what slavery meant in the colonial South, this essay contributes to studies of early America that emphasize the negotiated nature of empire. Atlanticists have, for the past several decades, examined how the periphery (colonies, and particular experiences in specific colonies) shaped and structured early modern empire.² Many scholars contend that local peoples and conditions tempered and limited imperial ambitions, institutions, and ideologies.³ Ethnohistorians have increasingly taken the lead in this regard by deeply examining how Indian communities and spaces determined how European empires functioned in shared spaces. Such works move beyond teleological narratives that seek the origins of modern nations; instead, they presume that "in building new empires and nations on the sites of those that had come before, European societies took their form and shaped from the Indian spaces they inhabited (and often shared with them)."⁴ Heeding the call to "Face East," these scholars have put Indians at the center of imperial analyses, examining those places where Indians dominated and Europeans were incorporated into Native systems and others where accommodations between Indians and colonizers led to innovative and flexible geopolitical and economic interactions. Yet they have not lost sight of the violence and scale of European colonization in the process.⁵

By focusing on Indian and African slavery, this essay responds to another important historiographical development in the study of the early South: the emergence of Indian slave trade studies. For the past fifteen years, scholars have increasingly focused on the Indian slave trade that swept across the South between 1656 and 1715, destroying hundreds of Indian communities and prompting surviving communities to establish large confederacies. As historian Alan Gallay has demonstrated, Indian slavery was the first economic engine of colonial South Carolina and paved the way for the rise of plantation slavery in the colony.⁶ Ethnohistorian Christina Snyder has argued that slavery also played a critical role for Indians, enabling them to weather colonialism and American expansionism in the South. By dramatically changing their practices of slavery, southern Indians were able to negotiate their way through population losses and changing geopolitical and economic conditions. In the seventeenth century, this meant becoming commercial slavers of other Indians; by the late eighteenth century this would entail adopting racialized slavery and owning African slaves.⁷ At present archaeologists and ethnohistorians of Indian slavery in the South are turning to the interpretive framework of the shatter zone to understand the effects of the Indian slave trade on Indian communities across the South.

While this work on the shatter zone collectively recognizes the agency of Indians who participated in the commercial slave trade and the creative responses of Indian victims to the slave trade, it often fails to appreciate the extent to which Indians participated in and actively shaped several systems of slavery in the early South. Most of these scholars construe the participation of southeastern Indians in the Indian slave trade that swept across the

South from 1650 to 1715 as purely reactive, an effort by Indians to survive colonization by becoming commercial slave traders and integrating into the emerging Atlantic economic system.[8] And these studies largely ignore Africans and systems of African slavery. A similar lacuna also exists in the literature on southern slavery where scholars continue to overlook the Indian slave trade. Despite repeated calls for historians of the South to place Indians at the center of narratives about the region's past and a rich body of scholarship upon which they could draw, Indians (and Indian slavery) remain largely the purview of specialists in southern ethnohistory.[9] My work shows that the practices and the ideologies of slavery in the early South were shaped by complex interactions between Indian, African, British, and Spanish peoples. It focuses on not only how conditions at the periphery shaped slavery in the early South, but also how slavery varied, often at the same time and even in the same place. It argues that the Yamasees played an active role in shaping Indian and African slavery in the early Southeast.

We follow the experiences of the Yamasees from 1650 to 1715, a period during which they moved from interior Georgia to Spanish Florida to British South Carolina. A series of slave raids sparked the coalescence of the Yamasees in the 1650s and 1660s, and they became an unusually mobile community willing to move hundreds of miles to protect their freedom and sovereignty. The Yamasees had uncommon firsthand knowledge of each slave system and played an important role in shaping slavery across the Southeast. As one of the most active slave trading communities, they made the commercial trade in Indian slaves possible. But they also helped many enslaved Africans to escape from South Carolina and seek freedom in Spanish Florida. And when faced with their own enslavement, they repeatedly mobilized their communities and sought out new political allies and trading partners. They played a crucial role in bringing the Indian slave trade to a dramatic end. By following their involvement in each culture of slavery we can compare southern slaveries and recognize not only the importance of slavery to the region's political and economic history but also the mutability of slavery in the region. In the early South, slavery was often shaped by social behavior and practices as much as by ideologies.[10]

• • •

The Yamasees displayed a particularly flexible approach to slavery, engaging in each system when it suited their goals, and this flexibility was grounded in their ability to understand and manipulate the nuances and differences between their own slave practices and those of the Spanish and British.[11] This flexibility was a function of the Yamasees' remarkable mobility. The Yamasees were a coalescent society that began to form along the Georgia coast in the mid-seventeenth century and encompassed a number of ethnic groups who joined the confederacy at different points in time. Archaeologists believe that the core of the Yamasees were Indian communities from the interior of Georgia who migrated from the Ocmulgee-Oconee region to the coast in the mid-seventeenth century to escape slave raids by Westo Indians. Over the course of the period under study, the Yamasees actively moved in and out of Spanish and British colonial spaces, becoming intimately familiar with the types of slavery practiced by these aspiring empires. The Yamasees also moved in and out of Indian spaces—Apalachicola (Lower Creek), Guale, Timucuan, and Apalachee—creating a broad network of alliances with other southeastern Indian communities, alliances that were often created and consecrated through kinship ties.

At the heart of these Indian alliances lay a shared indigenous construction of slavery that was fundamental to diplomacy and war in the Native South. Slavery was the inversion of kinship. Southeastern Indian communities placed a great deal of weight on the balance of opposites: war and slavery were balanced by diplomacy and kinship.[12] Yamasee alliances with other southeastern Indians are not only important to understanding Yamasee mobility and involvement in southern slaveries, they are also important to the methodology of this essay. Because the Yamasees appear intermittently in scattered British and Spanish sources, it has been necessary to also use sources that deal with other southeastern Indians with whom the Yamasees had cultural affiliations or direct contact.

Before the Spanish and British tried to establish colonies in the Southeast, the Yamasees and other southeastern Indians had a long history of taking enemy captives in battle. Our understanding of the roles and fates of captives in southeastern Indian communities prior to contact is quite limited. In the chiefdoms of interior Georgia from which the Yamasees descended (Altamaha, Ocute, and Ichisi), micos (chiefs) displayed their spiritual and worldly power through their control over territory and labor (including slave labor), the distribution of local and rare objects, and the collection of tribute. Archaeological evidence suggests that the ancestors of the Yamasees and other Indians from the Southeast killed most of their enemies regardless of gender or age. Some captives were kept alive to give as gifts or for future sacrifice at important rituals, particularly the deaths of micos and other elites.[13] As the Spanish conquistador Hernando de Soto moved into the Ocmulgee-Oconee region during the first spring of his long trek across the South in 1540, he was immediately exposed to the ritualized diplomacy of the Yamasees' progenitors in the region—a diplomacy that included the gifting of male slaves who served the Spanish as burdeners. Though elsewhere Soto and his men had been forced to extort and kidnap Indians as slaves, the mico of Ichisi "was the first who came in peace." To signify that he wanted to engage in diplomacy, Ichisi sent his principal men to greet Soto with deerskins. Several days later, Ichisi then personally provided Soto with "very good food and fifteen Indians to carry the burdens."[14] Deerskins, food, and slaves symbolized Ichisi's hopes for an alliance with the Spanish.

Several days after Ichisi had provided Soto with Indian slaves, the mico of Ocute—who was the paramount chief in the region—also gave the Spanish "as many Indian burdeners as they wished." But the circumstances under which Ocute did so were quite different. Ocute and Soto had a falling out which made Soto "angry." To appease the conquistador, Ocute's people then brought him food and burdeners.[15] It seems likely that the source of their conflict was Ocute's reaction to the demands that Soto made through his recitation of the Requirimiento, a Spanish legal document that all conquistadores were required to read to each and every Indian community they encountered. A description of Soto performing that reading at Ichisi survives. First developed in 1512, the Requirimiento was, as one scholar describes it, a "protocol for conquest" that offered Indian micos a terrible ultimatum: either acknowledge the Catholic Church as supreme and submit to Spanish religious and political authority or suffer war and the enslavement of their wives and children.[16] As the region's paramount, Ocute was the one who usually issued demands. Hearing Soto's angry tirade through an interpreter, the mico of Ocute reportedly "trembled with fear." After that came a hard capitulation, for in addition to providing food and slaves, the Indians of Ocute also had to genuflect before a cross that the Spanish planted in the ground.[17]

Soto and other Spanish conquistadores who ventured to La Florida in the sixteenth century planned to enslave Indians, anticipating that slaves would serve as porters to carry their supplies, interpreters, and guides to help them navigate the new cultural and physical landscape and also to serve as sex objects to gratify their baser needs. In fact, Spanish slavers from Hispaniola were in all likelihood the first to make contact with Indians in the Southeast. Records of early Spanish slave raids survive from the 1510s. For example, one Spanish slave raid resulted in the enslavement of approximately five hundred Indians from the "Island of Giants" probably in present-day South Carolina sometime between 1514 and 1516. Around the same time, Spanish raiders also began to skirt the Gulf Coast in search of Indian slaves.[18] By the time Soto arrived in the Southeast, Indians on both coasts had almost thirty years of experience with Spanish slaving expeditions and the Spaniards had honed their strategies for taking Indian slaves. Soto not only brought along iron chains and collars with which to restrain the Indians he abducted and enslaved, but he also perfected the art of extorting slaves from Indian communities unwilling to give them voluntarily; he took elite Indians hostage and then wrested porters and sex slaves from micos and communities desperate to save their leaders, kin, or children.[19]

Though Soto and other Spanish conquistadores acquired the majority of Indian slaves through violence and extortion, there were circumstances under which the sixteenth-century ancestors of the Yamasees and other southeastern Indians offered the Spanish slaves of their own accord—as was the case in Ichisi. Southeastern Indian and Spanish leaders had a loosely shared understanding of the relationship between authority and labor, epitomized in both societies by a master or mico's control over slaves. But there was a significant difference between Spanish and Indian constructs of slavery: southeastern Indians did not sell or buy slaves. Although exchange networks connected Indian communities across the South in the centuries prior to European contact, there is no archaeological or documentary evidence that points to the existence of commercial slave trading in the South prior to the mid-seventeenth century. The distinction is an important one; it reveals that southeastern Indians dehumanized captives but did not commodify them. In the Native South, slaves had a currency that was political and social but not economic.[20]

For the Ichisi, Ocute, Altamaha, and other southeastern Indians, slavery was deeply connected to the male realms of warfare and diplomacy. The French, who attempted to establish a permanent settlement in northeast Florida (1564–1565), described the captivity culture that was integral to the warfare complex of the Timucuans. The French put their Fort Caroline settlement in territory under the control of Saturiwa. As part of their diplomatic negotiations, they agreed to aid Saturiwa in a battle against his old enemy Outina, paramount of the Thimogonas (from whom the name Timucua derives). In preparation for this battle, the Saturiwa Indians engaged in an elaborate ritual that climaxed in the dramatic (but nonfatal) stabbing of Saturiwa's favorite son. The torture inflicted on him served as a mnemonic device, vividly reenacting the pain that the Saturiwas had experienced in losing their loved ones to the Thimogonas. The ritual also elicited a gendered response from the community: a "company of young girls" wept in mourning for two hours and male warriors were incited to avenge the loss of their relatives by bringing back captives and the scalps of their enemies.[21]

Blood revenge and captivity were pivotal to Indian warfare in the South from the sixteenth through the eighteenth centuries, and British traders later described similar motives for Indian wars even when Yamasees and other southeastern Indians began to sell some of their captives in a commercial market economy with the British.[22] In the seventeenth and eighteenth centuries, clan matriarchs played a critical role in instigating war parties across the Southeast, doing so not only to avenge losses suffered earlier but also to bring peace to the souls of the dead—a process later termed Crying Blood by the Cherokees.[23] The controlling and gifting of captives were important displays of power on the part of chiefs. At the same time, warriors acquired prestige by bringing captives to their clans and chiefs. Thus the warriors who returned to the Saturiwa chiefdom with Thimogona captives or scalps in 1564 fulfilled their clan obligations to the living and departed while also garnering honor that could translate into personal political advancement. Their prowess in war was signified through goods, titles, and names that commemorated their successes.[24]

Slavery was also central to political affairs in the Native Southeast. Ichisi, Ocute, Altamaha, and other Indian micos across the Native Southeast ritually gifted war captives with their new and old allies to promote political alliances. The Spanish noted in 1573, for example, that the cacique (chief) of the Ais in southeast Florida sent two Spanish captives to the Tequesta cacique "as a present."[25] The Tequestas promptly executed these Spanish captives, but the exchange strengthened their relationship with the Ais even as their decision to kill the captives symbolized their enmity toward the Spanish. Just as taking captives was a central motive for warfare, returning captives was often a vital and early step in the peace process between southeastern Indian communities. When the Tocobagas of the present-day Tampa region sought to establish peace with their Calusa enemies in 1567, their first gesture was to return twelve Calusa captives. The Spanish became deeply familiar with the politics of ransoming captives from Indian communities and also engaged in this practice to promote their political alliances with Indian chiefdoms in La Florida. Pedro Menéndez de Avilés, St. Augustine's founder and La Florida's first governor, was in fact partly motivated to establish the colony because his only son had shipwrecked along the southwestern coastline. Though he never found Juan, Menéndez did secure the release of a number of captives from the Calusa cacique Carlos, including an African named Luis who would prove to be an invaluable translator for La Florida's first Spanish governor.[26] In 1565 Menéndez also ransomed the Tequesta chief's young daughter from the Calusas, hoping to use her redemption to establish an alliance with the Tequestas.[27] Similarly, when Franciscan missionary Martin Prieto first attempted to establish contact with the Apalachee Indians in 1608, he sent two Apalachee captives ahead whom he had redeemed from the Timucuans to ensure that the Apalachees understood his was a peaceful mission before he tried to enter their region.[28]

Captive redemption was once again center stage as the Guales and Spanish tried to rebuild their alliance in the wake of the Guale Revolt (1597–1598). When Spanish governor Gonzalo Méndez de Canzo demanded that the Guales release a Franciscan missionary from captivity, Guale micos from coastal Georgia countered that they would do so only if the Spanish returned a number of young boys then being held in St. Augustine: "all chiefly heirs and sons of caciques." Not only this, but the Guales also provided the Spanish with an itemized list of prestige goods required to complete the exchange: six knives with yellow handles, three bundles of beads, six hatchets, twelve axes, and one white blanket (perhaps a substitute for the white eagle feathers and wings which southeastern Indians often used with one another to sanctify peace treaties). Though the Spanish gave the requisite gifts and the Guales freed the friar, Governor Canzo reneged on the agreement, instead keeping his Guale hostages and then capturing another seven children to punish the Guales.[29]

Canzo believed that only slavery and other such displays of Spanish power could keep Indians in check. After establishing La Florida, the Spanish had periodically entertained the notion of enslaving Indians, but royal prohibitions on the enslavement of Indians limited the ambitions of some colonial officials. In the late sixteenth century, there was a small-scale enslavement of Indian women, some of whom were the sex slaves and wives of Spanish soldiers.[30] And a number of Spanish governors—most notably Menéndez and Canzo—had aspirations to use enslavement as a punitive measure against Indians who openly resisted Spanish colonization. A very small number of Indians were condemned to hard labor as *forzados*, but not to the extent that these Spanish governors had hoped.[31] In 1573 Menéndez requested Crown permission to use war and slavery to subdue the southern Indians (southward from Daytona around to Tampa Bay) who frequently killed or enslaved shipwrecked Spaniards and Spanish soldiers. Enraged that these Indians boasted they were "the masters of the Christians and hold them as slaves," Menéndez planned to export Indian slaves to Cuba, Santo Domingo, and Puerto Rico.[32] But the Royal Council of the Indies rejected Menéndez's petition, concluding that "there is no ground for decreeing at the present."[33]

In 1600 Governor Canzo put Menéndez's strategy for dealing with Indians south of St. Augustine into action. Without waiting for Crown approval,

Canzo enslaved seventy-eight Surruque and Ais Indians. While Menéndez had intended to export Indian slaves, Canzo kept them in the presidio of St. Augustine where they were briefly forced to provide domestic and agricultural labor for soldiers.[34] Canzo erred in using slavery to assert Spanish dominance over Florida Indians and was soon compelled by royal order to free the enslaved Indians. Even if the royal council had authorized Indian enslavement in this or other instances, it seems unlikely that the Spanish could have sustained such a project.

It was not only royal proclamations or orders that inhibited the development of an Indian slave trade in Florida but local conditions. La Florida was a poor colony, dependent on financial support from the Spanish Crown for its survival. Though the Spanish did engage in commercial trade with Indians, particularly in Apalachee, colonists simply did not have the goods sufficient to create and sustain a slave trade. In sharp contrast, merchants and traders in colonial South Carolina tapped into a vast transatlantic network that provided the credit and goods to build this costly slave trade. Even more importantly, Indians in La Florida expressed no interest in participating in a commercial slave trade. While they continued to take war captives during the seventeenth century, they captured and kept slaves for traditional, geopolitical reasons. As a result, the Spanish extracted labor from the Indians living in or near Franciscan missions through a system of tribute instead of relying on Indian or African slaves.

• • •

From the mid-sixteenth century until the 1650s, southeastern Indians practiced indigenous slavery—a profoundly political form of slavery grounded in the notion that slaves were enemies captured in war or outsiders who did not have kinship ties in their community. But beginning in the 1650s, Indians in the Ocmulgee-Oconee region increasingly suffered under wars led by Westo Indians who sold Indians from interior Georgia, Florida's missions, and elsewhere to English colonists in Virginia and later Carolina. Seeking refuge from Westo slave raids, the chiefdoms of Altamaha, Ocute, and Ichisi fissioned. The majority moved to the coast and regrouped in Santa Elena between 1659 and 1665, there beginning the process of Yamasee ethnogenesis.[35] The Yamasees moved again in the 1660s when the Westos began to attack their new coastal settlements; many Yamasees relocated to Spanish missions in the Guale-Mocama region, staying for only twenty years and then moving north again, to the interior and the coast and ultimately returning to the Port

Royal region of South Carolina in the 1680s and 1690s.[36] Slavery prompted each of the Yamasees' early migrations, establishing a pattern that is evident in the historical record: the Yamasees moved hundreds of miles at a time to preserve their freedom (see Map 3.1).

The Westos are widely regarded by scholars as one of the first Indian commercial slave-raiding communities in the Southeast. According to a number of scholars, the Westos established a "well-honed predatory strategy" in response to British colonization that other southeastern Indian communities later adopted: engaging in large-scale often long-distance wars for captives whom they exchanged with British colonists for trade goods, most notably firearms.[37] It is true that the Westos would later become powerful slavers and trading partners of the English colonies of Virginia (1670) and South Carolina (1674). But this singular focus on their commercial slaving often obscures the reality that Westo captive taking in the 1650s and 1660s was initially driven by demographic and political motives—namely, to replace or increase their population and to establish their place in the region. In 1661 the Spanish first began to report Westo attacks on coastal Indian mission settlements in the Guale region. The Spanish managed to capture four of the retreating Westos and a subsequent interrogation offers a glimpse into Westo motives. The Westo captives described themselves as the victims of Virginians ("gente blanca") who warred on them from their fortified town. In fact, in 1657 the Virginians (with the Pamunkey Indians) had driven the Westos south of the colony.[38] The Westos had then traveled from Virginia ("Jacan") down into interior Georgia and Alabama, and from their new bases launched attacks on Indians in the interior and coastal regions.[39] They soon adopted a predatory form of captive taking, providing Virginians with a new source of bound labor at a time when colonists struggled to procure enough indentured servants or enslaved Africans. It seems likely that many of the Yamasees' ancestors found themselves laboring in Virginia's tobacco fields.[40] Slavery became integral to Westo survival and soon was a tool for their geopolitical expansion, a tool that the Yamasees would later embrace as well with even greater success than the Westos.

As Westo raiders moved against the Santa Elena region in the 1660s, the Yamasees fled farther south, most settling in or near Spanish missions in the Guale-Mocama mission province, some in the missions of Apalachee and Timucua, and still others choosing to find refuge with their Indian allies the Apalachicolas.[41] But the majority of the Yamasees only lived in La Florida for roughly twenty years.[42] One of the main sources of tension between the Spanish and Yamasees was the *repartimiento*—an exploitative labor system

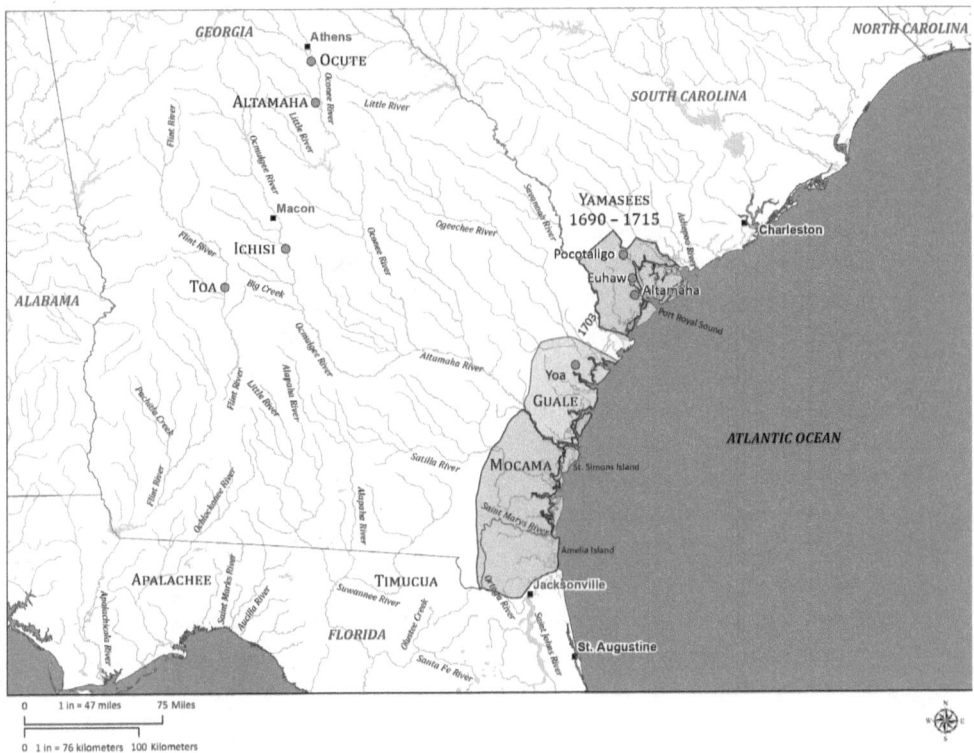

Map 3.1. Yamasee Sites, 1500 to 1715. Map by David W. Wilson, Center for Instruction and Research Technology, University of North Florida.

first implemented by the Spanish in La Florida around 1600 whereby Indian caciques and cacicas from mission communities selected young men to travel to St. Augustine or other key sites for four to seven months of the year. Repartimiento laborers performed work that was essential to the colony's functioning, including building public works (most notably the Castillo de San Marcos), running ferries, constructing roads, growing food crops for the presidio and missions, and carrying burdens. In exchange for this annual tribute of laborers, the Spanish paid Indian caciques and cacicas in goods that reinforced their chiefly power.[43]

Seventeenth-century Spanish La Florida was far from a slave society. It was a society with few slaves due to the lack of a commercial Indian slave trade, the long-standing royal ban on Indian slavery, and the relative dearth of African slaves in the colony.[44] In fact, there were far more Spanish captives and slaves held by Indian communities than African slaves in sixteenth- and seventeenth-century La Florida. Pedro Menéndez believed that the Indians of southwest Florida alone had taken captive some 230 Spaniards in the twenty years before he set foot in La Florida.[45] African slaves, on the other hand, were quite rare and were generally either royal slaves owned by the Spanish Crown or privately owned slaves brought into the colony by a few wealthy officials.[46] There were likely less than fifty African slaves in the first settlements. By 1606 that numbered had doubled, and there were one hundred African slaves in La Florida, sixty owned by private individuals and the rest by the Crown. But this was the high watermark of African slavery until the mid-eighteenth century. By 1618 disease had killed all but eleven of the royal slaves. In the 1650s the total number of African slaves in St. Augustine ranged between five and seven, and the number of Indian forzados (convict laborers) was often greater during the same period.[47] Though free and enslaved Africans were essential to La Florida's economy, society, and military, the Indian repartimiento was by far the most significant source of labor in the colony. Writing in 1647, treasury officials explained that "this presidio cannot be preserved except with the service of these natives."[48]

Severe population declines in the major mission provinces during the seventeenth century left the Spanish desperate for more Indian laborers, and the arrival of hundreds of Yamasees in Guale-Mocama in the 1660s seemed like a promising solution. The Spanish increasingly relied on these newly arrived Yamasee immigrants, who were largely "pagan," and they soon provided close to half of the repartimiento labor force from the Guale-Mocama missions. This development reflected the very real demographic changes occurring; by 1675 there were 350 pagan and 326 Christian Indians in the province and twenty-four of the fifty repartimiento laborers were Yamasee.[49] It also reflects a strategy devised by Guale-Mocama leaders and Spanish officials to shift some of the burden of the repartimiento onto Yamasee shoulders. In 1636, long before the Yamasees migrated into Guale-Mocama, the Guale alone had provided fifty-four laborers for the repartimiento.[50] But flight from the missions, epidemics at midcentury, and chronic Spanish abuses of the repartimiento system had made it difficult for the Spanish to draft sufficient Indian laborers.[51] Writing to cacica of the Mocama Indians, Cacica Merenciana, to encourage her to promote good relations with the Yamasees who had settled in her territory, Governor Juan Marquéz Cabrera explained that doing so could "be to your own self interest" because the Yamasees could help in defending her community, tilling agricultural fields and also "relieve your own subjects in other tasks that come up in the service of His Majesty."[52]

Yamasee repartimiento laborers became all the more important to the Spanish in 1672, when they began construction of the Castillo de San

Marcos to protect the city against the threat of invasion from the newly established English colony of South Carolina. A formidable fortification made out of coquina that still stands in St. Augustine today, the Castillo took over twenty years to build. Its construction was so labor-intensive that the Spanish increased the repartimiento drafts. Yamasee and other repartimiento laborers suffered under grueling work conditions, through illness and food deprivation. In 1674 Spanish governor Nicolás Ponce de León II, desperate for more workers to replace Indians who had died during service, requested fifty African slaves from Cuba—but none came.[53] When a Spanish war party returned from an attack on Scottish, Yamasee, and English settlements south of Charleston in 1686, the governor promptly commandeered the eleven African slaves who had been seized and put them to work on the Castillo.[54] The Yamasees disproportionately suffered from the intensified repartimiento demands that the Castillo's construction created. In 1673 the Yamasees living in Guale-Mocama contributed approximately 20 percent of their adult male population to the repartimiento while the Christian Indians contributed only 14 percent. The table below suggests part of the reason for this difference. Only *unmarried* adult men over the age of twelve were eligible for the repartimiento draft and the Catholic Church did not recognize Yamasee pagan marriages. All Yamasee men were therefore categorized as single. This drain of men stressed Yamasee clans and towns, leading many to resist the repartimiento and to contemplate leaving La Florida. The Yamasees had not abandoned their homelands in interior Georgia to become virtual servants to the Spanish.

The repartimiento had long been a source of tension between Indian and Spanish communities, and many Indians equated the repartimiento system with slavery. This proved to be a rallying point in the Timucua Revolt (1656). When the western Timucuans launched a small-scale war against the Spanish, they did so partly in response to their experiences with the repartimiento labor system. Virtually the entire repartimiento labor force (almost two hundred men) had recently died of starvation as they made their way to St. Augustine. When the Spanish governor Diego de Rebolledo then demanded that elite and chiefly Indian men carry corn on their backs like common men, the Timucuans responded in word and deed "saying they were not slaves."[55]

The Yamasees understood their participation in the repartimiento system as an exchange of labor for Spanish protection from their enemies, harkening back to the arrangement between micos and their tributaries in the ancestral chiefdoms.[56] But problems were apparent from the start. In 1668 "a quantity

Mission Name (Location)	1669 Repartimiento	1673 Repartimiento	1681 Total Adult Population	Married Men	Single Men	Married Women	Single Women
Yamasees (Sapelo)	—	—	67	—	44	—	23
Yamasees (St. Simons)	—	12	73	0	50	0	23
Yamasees (San Pedro)	—	—	11	—	?	—	?
Yamasees (Amelia)	—	12	101	—	72	—	29
Colones (Asao)	—	—	17	—	9	—	8
Totals	—	24	269	0	(>175)	0	(>83)
Christians (Sapelo)	16	16	186	68	19	68	31
Christians (St. Simons)	9	8	126	41	21	41	23
Christians (Cumberland)	4	2	71	23	5	23	20
Christians (Fort George)	—	—	37	14	3	14	6
Totals	29	26	420	146	48	146	80

Table 3.1. Repartimiento Records for Guale-Mocama Region. Repartimiento Order to Adjutant Francisco de Aizpiolea, 1669; Repartimiento Order to Adjutant Diego Diaz Mejia, 1673; Census of Guale and Mocama, 1681. All in Worth, *Struggle for the Georgia Coast*, 80–81. 187, and 100–103.

of" Yamasees "fled from the fields" of St. Augustine, leaving those fields "impossible to cultivate" and the presidio struggling (once again) to feed its Spanish soldiers. While the Spanish expected Yamasees to bow to their authority, Yamasee men were not subjects of the Crown.[57] When the Spanish proved incapable of protecting the Yamasees, the Yamasees left. Beginning in 1680, the Yamasees and other Indians in Guale-Mocama began to suffer from attacks, most notably a series of raids in 1680 by Indians allied with the English, namely the Westos accompanied by some Uchizes (ancestors of the Lower Creeks) and Chiluques (from Santa Elena).[58] Unhappiness with the repartimiento and these attacks prompted most of the Yamasees to leave. They would soon make their way back to Port Royal in what was now South Carolina, becoming a powerful force in the region. Having been the victims of Westo slave raids on several occasions and the target of an exploitative labor system in Spanish Florida, the Yamasees once again sought to protect their communities by moving. But they also implemented a new strategy. For the first time, the Yamasees engaged in commercial slave raiding.

• • •

In 1683, the Yamasees moved to the southern frontiers of South Carolina. There they became commercial slave raiders, targeting Spanish mission Indians in the regions that many among them had just left and exchanging their war captives with Scottish and English colonizers. Commercial slave raiding played a critical role in the Yamasees' mobilization of geopolitical power. Through their direct access to British trade goods, the Yamasees fostered alliances with select Indian communities in the region, pursuing the white path of peace as well as the red path of war to promote their survival and geopolitical expansion.[59] By 1715 the Yamasee population had grown to 1,220 people living in at least ten distinct towns.[60] But growth had come at a price.

Living in southern Carolina, the Yamasees witnessed (and experienced) the rise of a colonial plantation economy based on racialized slavery for the first time. While the Spanish had established a chain of Indian missions to extend their geopolitical control over the region, the British engulfed South Carolina in successive waves of plantations and ranches that moved inland. The Spanish had converted Indians into Catholics laborers, but the English largely purchased their slaves not only by importing Africans but also by buying southeastern Indians who were far cheaper and relatively easier to acquire than Africans until the 1710s.

By the 1680s, both the Spanish and the English had begun to see slavery as geopolitically significant to their imperial ambitions in the Southeast. The English sought to dismantle the Spanish by enslaving their Indian allies, fostering and sometimes launching slave raids against the Spanish missions. Meanwhile, the Spanish actively encouraged enslaved Africans and Indians to run away from Carolina plantations and seek sanctuary in La Florida. Critical to these colonial policies was the participation of Yamasees and other southeastern Indians. Select southeastern Indian clans and towns captured and sold Indians from La Florida and also guided runaway slaves to the Spanish. In these ways, southeastern Indians did more than facilitate colonial policies: they also shaped English and Spanish cultures of slavery. Without southeastern Indians, the English could not have created a commercial Indian slave trade and the Spanish could not have established a slave sanctuary policy.

Soon after moving to Port Royal, the Yamasees launched their first slave raid against the Timucuan mission of Santa Anhoica in February 1685. They returned with captives: twenty-two women and two men. The Scottish settlers who had established a colony in Port Royal just the previous year encouraged the Yamasee raid, providing arms and other incentives. The raid would prove Yamasee intentions to ally with the Scots, who had witnessed the sudden surge of Yamasees near their colony with alarm. The mico of Altamaha had recently led his people out of the Spanish Guale-Mocama missions after Governor Cabrera abused him for not providing enough repartimiento laborers. The Scots worried that it might be "a design of the Spaniards" to send the "thousand or more Yamasees . . . from the Cowetas and Kuscetaws" and "three nations of the Spanish Indians that are Christians, Sapella, Soho, and Sapickays." What the Scots were witnessing was a new coalescence of Yamasees and Guales from the Savannah River region, Spanish missions, and Apalachicola Lower Creek towns. Perhaps as many as two thousand Yamasee and Guale people coalesced in Port Royal. But they did so of their own volition, not as agents of the Spanish.

Now Altamaha not only led the Yamasee coalescence but also a group of fifty men to burn Santa Catalina de Ahoica, including the church and convent. The Yamasees returned with "a great booty" of slaves—which the Scots promptly purchased—and also church ornaments and Catholic texts. The Scots took this as a sign that they could trust the Yamasees in the fight against the Catholics and start a lucrative partnership in commercial slave trading.[61] But the Spanish soon retaliated in kind in 1686 and 1687, destroying the Scottish and Yamasee settlements in Port Royal and briefly driving the Yamasees physically and politically closer to the English in Charleston. Despite these retaliatory attacks, the Yamasees used the commercial slave trade much as the Westos before them: to promote their demographic, economic, and geopolitical expansion.

For two decades the Yamasees, with their allies the Apalachicolas (Lower Creeks), became the main suppliers of Indian slaves seized from Spanish La Florida. These slave wars had a devastating impact on Spanish missions, leading to the enslavement of as many as thirty thousand Indians from La Florida and the collapse of the Guale-Mocama, Timucua, and Apalachee missions.[62] The English played an active role in encouraging and at times directing these Indian slave raids, most notably in the 1702 attacks on the coastal missions and the siege of St. Augustine and again in the virtual destruction of Apalachee in 1703–1704. But Yamasees and Apalachicola Creeks led the majority of the raids that preceded and followed these attacks.[63] Only a few hundred mission Indians remained in northern La Florida by 1704, and they were primarily concentrated around St. Augustine. The Yamasees began to look farther afield for slaves, carrying on a long-distance war against the

Calusas and moving deep into southern Florida to extract slaves.⁶⁴ Yamasees also fought alongside South Carolinians in the 1712 and 1713 campaigns of the Tuscarora War, motivated to seek slaves elsewhere by their oppressive debts to British traders and the near depopulation of La Florida.⁶⁵

By the 1710s, the Yamasees faced a number of escalating problems. Though their involvement in the Indian slave trade had enabled the Yamasees to grow in size and regional power, they were outpaced by the expansion of British South Carolina. Two major branches of the economy fueled the colony's expansion: first, the Indian trade in slaves and animal hides, and second, the local productions of forest products, animal and agricultural foodstuffs, and rice. Both branches of the economy rested on slavery. South Carolinians had intended from the very start to establish a slave society where the predominant labor was to be supplied by African (and Indian) slaves.⁶⁶ By 1708 South Carolina's slaves outnumbered its white citizens, and Indians comprised 25.5 percent of the slave population: 1,400 of 5,500 slaves.⁶⁷ In five short years, the Indian slave population had tripled, largely because of the Yamasee- and Lower Creek–led slave raids.

Yet the irony of slavery as practiced by South Carolinians was that they enslaved not only enemies and outsiders but also the very people with whom they were allied. British trader and Indian agent John Wright owned at least forty-seven slaves, almost half of whom were Indian and included at least one Yamasee Indian, a girl named Maria. Wright likely used some of his Indian slaves as interpreters, guides, and burden carriers when he traveled to Indian communities. But other enslaved Indians probably labored alongside enslaved Africans, cultivating rice and raising livestock at Wright's Goosecreek plantation.⁶⁸

While Wright's plantation was in the core zone of Carolinian settlement, where planters established agricultural plantations worked by large groups of slaves, Port Royal—where the Yamasees lived—was a frontier settlement that particularly attracted British traders who complemented their work in the Indian trade with raising livestock and small-scale agriculture.⁶⁹ The location was ideal for the Indian trade and pulled colonial traders into the region. In fact, this was why the Yamasees had first chosen to settle in Port Royal—it lay at the nexus of a major trading route that ran north to Charleston. Just to the south was the Savannah River, the gateway to the major Indian trading hub at Savano Town (present-day Augusta) and to the inland roads to the Creeks and Cherokees. The area was also attractive to colonial ranchers because the region's many small waterways served as natural fences for free-range livestock. By the late seventeenth century, colonists had begun to settle closer to the Yamasee confederacy in Port Royal, and Yamasees increasingly found their lands overrun by British cattle and pigs as well as colonists and traders. In 1707 the South Carolina General Assembly took measures to protect Yamasee lands, establishing the colony's first Indian reservation, but colonial settlers trespassed with alarming frequency.[70]

The presence of the Yamasees and the proximity to inland trade routes to other Indian slaving communities meant that Indian slaves were easier and cheaper to acquire than Africans in Port Royal. Anecdotal evidence suggests that many of the region's British settlers owned Indian slaves. And the Yamasees quickly came to understand the centrality of slavery to British colonial expansion. All they had to do was look to the colonial traders they knew best to see how participation in the Indian slave trade could enable ambitious and well-connected traders to become plantation owners. Thomas Nairne, for example, was both a trader and the first agent appointed by the colony to oversee affairs with the Yamasees. He had moved to Port Royal in 1698, settling on St. Helena Island. He became both one of the colony's main Indian traders and a large landowner, expanding his holdings to over 3,600 acres. To work that land, Nairne had at least twenty-seven slaves, five of whom were Indian. He had probably purchased at least some of those Indian slaves from the Yamasees. We do not know whether the Yamasees were concerned about the fate of their captives—there would be no reason to expect that they would be. But they were concerned about the spread of colonists across their lands, an expansion that was directly fueled by both the Indian and African slave trades. In 1712 the Yamasees expressed their great anxiety that Thomas Nairne "would cause theire Lands to be taken from them."[71]

The commercial slave trade had been empowering for the Yamasees, fostering their demographic growth while also promoting their geopolitical and economic expansion. The Yamasees controlled pivotal trade routes and were allied with the powerful Lower Creeks. Attracted to the power and protection the Yamasees could offer, more Yamasees, Guales, and other southeastern Indians joined the confederacy in the early eighteenth century. But the Indian slave trade and their proximity to colonial settlements also proved to be terribly destabilizing for the Yamasees.[72] Not only did colonists encroach on Yamasee lands, but also the Yamasees themselves became the target of enslavement (once again), as British traders seized their adopted captives, wives, and children to repay debts. This was becoming a problem already by the late seventeenth century, less than a decade after the Yamasees moved to South Carolina. For example, in 1692 an English trader kidnapped and enslaved the nephew of the Altamaha mico, and the mico was forced to ask the South Carolina Grand Council to intervene.⁷³ Not even the most powerful of Yamasee leaders was safe. By the 1710s, the relationship between the Yamasees and the British was at a breaking point. South Carolina officials generally attempted to prohibit or limit the enslavement of Indian allies. But the sharp decrease in the availability of Indian slaves after the collapse of the Spanish mission system prompted British traders (who were under intense financial pressure to repay their debts to Charleston merchants) to abuse and enslave their Indian clientele in larger numbers.⁷⁴

Having experienced the repartimiento labor system and participated in the expansion of British slavery, the Yamasees now became extremely vulnerable to enslavement in the British colonial world. British traders who enslaved their Yamasee clients drew on an older English tradition of debt peonage. But in colonial South Carolina, Yamasee and other southeastern Indians who were enslaved were governed by the same statutes as enslaved Africans and experienced the same horrors of slavery. On occasion the governor or assembly might redeem an Indian whose community was politically important to the colony. But the vast majority of Indian slaves were funneled into the racialized system of slavery practiced by the British.⁷⁵

Together and separately, enslaved Indians and Africans sought to escape the bonds of slavery. There were several routes to freedom, and the Yamasees played a primary role in helping enslaved people find freedom in their communities or in Spanish St. Augustine.⁷⁶ Slaves from South Carolina began to seek sanctuary in La Florida in 1687, shortly after the Yamasees moved from Florida to South Carolina. When this first group of eleven slaves converted to Catholicism, Spanish governor Diego de Quiroga decided not to return them to the English and instead offered to compensate their masters. More runaways soon followed and Spanish officials asked the Crown to develop an official policy. That 1693 policy—to refuse to return runaways to the English but instead encourage them to seek sanctuary in La Florida—was driven primarily by geopolitical motives. The Spanish did not by any means oppose slavery, and Catholic baptism was not a route to freedom for slaves owned by the Spanish. Still, the policy proved effective. More than a hundred slaves had successfully escaped to St. Augustine by 1738, and even more attempted to do so. In 1724, for example, a small group of slaves traveling in one canoe coordinated their escape from three different plantations. The group included one African man, two Indian men, and two Indian women, one of whom carried her two-year-old child.⁷⁷

While some individual Yamasees fled enslavement, the confederacy saw the rising threat of enslavement as a community-wide problem by the 1710s.

The South Carolina General Assembly had tried to anticipate the problems that enslaving allied Indians could cause, freeing Indians whose enslavement was contested by Indian allies and issuing an important restriction that traders had to wait three days in Indian towns before buying slaves—in effect, recognizing the rights of Indian matriarchs and warriors to determine the fates of their captives.[78] But colonial traders violated these restrictions with impunity. The Yamasees initially tried to preserve peace, loudly complaining to the commissioners of the Indian trade and their Indian agent and demanding redress. But distracted by internal political quarrels, the colony did not listen attentively to what were increasingly the sounds of war.[79]

Near midnight on May 27, 1715, four Yamasee and Lower Creek leaders arrived in St. Augustine carrying an emblem of southeastern Indian commitment to refashioning what slavery meant in the region. Eight belts of deerskins held one hundred and sixty-one knots, together representing not a centralized Indian nation but rather the shared discontent of so many southeastern Indian towns. Fearing their own enslavement and marginalization, the Yamasees and Lower Creeks wished to renew their friendship with the Spanish in order to offset the growing oppression of British traders and slavers. Precisely six weeks earlier, the Yamasees had killed a peace party of British traders and officials sent by Carolina in a last ditch effort to put back the pieces of a crumbling relationship wrent asunder by deep conflicts over slavery. Among those killed were John Wright and Thomas Nairne. Many other southeastern Indian communities soon did the same, killing ninety traders and four hundred colonists over the course of what would become known as the Yamasee War, a moniker that masks the participation of other southeastern Indians in the war, namely the Lower Creeks, Apalachees, Savannahs, Upper Creeks, Choctaws, Cherokees, and piedmont Indians.[80]

Though Indian communities fought for what were often different or at least discrete goals and though their motives for war were many, they shared a common fear of their own enslavement. For several years, word had reached the Yamasees that South Carolinians had begun to enslave the children of their Indian allies to the north (likely in Savano Town). Soon British traders began to demand that Yamasee men pay for trade goods in slaves or they would enslave their children, wives, and even the men themselves. The problem was that Indian slaves were increasingly scarce in La Florida, and British traders were experiencing their own severe credit crunches as a result, facing numerous lawsuits from their merchant creditors and (even worse) the possibility of losing the credit lines on which they relied to acquire the trade goods without which they simply could not work.[81] The Yamasees and Lower

Creeks took these threats seriously and when the South Carolina peace party arrived, rather than giving the Indian leaders some hope, they believed their worst fears were about to be realized. One of the South Carolina agents fueled these fears when—driven by his own looming debts—he threatened that the "white men" would "hang four of their headmen and take all the rest of them for Slaves."[82] The Yamasee Indian leaders believed that this had been the British governor's plan all along.

Another group of people capitalized on the dislocating effect of the war on Carolina. Enslaved Africans joined the Yamasees, living in their towns and joining in the fight to stop the enslavement of their people. By 1715 the Yamasees and enslaved Africans shared many of the same grievances against the British. Most notably, both had suffered under the expansion of Carolina's plantation slave economy. After the Yamasee War, many Africans and Yamasees moved into Spanish territory and joined in Spanish policies to destabilize that same slave economy. In 1724 a Yamasee mico Cacique Jorge appeared before the governor of La Florida in order to support the petition of thirty-one Africans seeking their freedom. Four of the group had fought under the mico against the British during the Yamasee War and had subsequently spent several years living with the Yamasees.

Most notable among the Africans was Francisco Menéndez, who went on to serve as the captain of the slave militia in La Florida and the "cacique" of the free black settlement Gracia Real de Santa Teresa de Mose, established in 1738 two miles north of St. Augustine. Along with the Yamasee cacique and his people, the thirty-one Africans had retreated to St. Augustine after the Yamasee War, where the Yamasees settled into an Indian mission community.[83] The Africans expected that they, too, would find freedom in La Florida. They must have been more than dismayed when Yfallaquisca (Mad Dog) sold them instead to Governor Juan de Ayala y Escovar. Possessing few slaves of their own, these Spaniards were desperate for new laborers. And Yfallaquisca had threatened to kill the Africans if the Spanish did not purchase them. However, as Mico Jorge (and Francisco Menéndez) reminded Governor Antonio de Benavides, the Spanish governor had violated an important Spanish slave policy.[84] In 1693 (and again in 1733), the Spanish Crown issued edicts that guaranteed freedom to slaves who successfully ran away from their British owners in Carolina and sought sanctuary in Spanish La Florida. The Crown's intention was clear: vastly outnumbered by the British, the Spanish wished to check South Carolina's rapid geopolitical and economic expansion by striking at the heart of its plantation economy. The move stirred alarm among the British; in dangling the promise of freedom to South Carolina's enslaved population, were the Spanish not threatening to destabilize the entire British Southeast?[85]

Perhaps no one involved in this controversy understood southern slavery in all of its forms better than Mico Jorge. His astute testimony shows us that the Yamasees had acquired a firsthand knowledge of all three slave systems in the eighteenth-century Southeast. By 1724 the Yamasees had been alternately accomplices in and victims of three different systems of slavery that were respectively Yamasee, Spanish, and British. In his testimony supporting the Africans' bid for freedom, Mico Jorge demonstrated a shrewd understanding of how the Spanish constructed slavery and implicitly drew a sharp distinction between Spanish and Yamasee practices. One of the conditions that the Spanish placed on runaway slaves seeking freedom in La Florida was that they convert to Catholicism. The African petitioners had fulfilled that requirement. In his testimony supporting the Africans' bid for freedom, Mico Jorge reminded the Spanish of their own policy and charged that the Spanish were acting illegally; contrary to their own Crown's proclamation, they had re-enslaved the African runaways. Yfallaquisca's situation was different, however; as Mico Jorge contended, Yfallaquisca was a "heathen" who did not abide by the same slave codes and practices. He could not be accused of breaking the Spanish statutes on slavery.[86]

• • •

This was not the first time that Yfallaquisca had renegotiated slave practices in the South. An important Yamasee war captain, Yfallaquisca had been part of the Creek-Yamasee delegation that appeared before the Spanish in 1715. It was Yfallaquisca who had been entrusted with carrying the knotted strands of deerskins to the Spanish. Just months earlier, he had also been present at the important meeting at the Yamasee town of Pocotaligo, where he had helped to launch the Yamasee War itself. When he appeared before the Spanish that May, he did so as a spokesman for the most powerful Lower Creek mico, the Emperor Brim. Yfallaquisca pointedly explained to the Spanish that the war had started because the English threatened to enslave their wives and children. The Yamasees and Lower Creeks now sought to relocate their families near St. Augustine, and they intended to bring the runaway Africans who had joined them.[87]

How could Yfallaquisca help to end the Indian slave trade and then attempt to sell Africans who had allied with the Yamasees and Lower Creeks during the war—a war fought with the express purpose of changing what slavery meant? The answer is that Yfallaquisca was not opposed to slavery.

His ancestors had engaged in captivity before European colonization and, as a war captain, he had engaged in traditional captivity practices while also participating in the British commercial slave trade. Putting an end to the Indian slave trade had been necessary, but it had also made it more difficult for Yfallaquisca and other Indian men to acquire trade goods, especially guns. Having spent so much time in South Carolina, perhaps Yfallaquisca increasingly associated slavery with Africans. Perhaps this was also a calculated move. Over the course of the eighteenth century, many (but not all) southeastern Indians increasingly participated in the enslavement of Africans not only for economic gain but also to demarcate themselves in a South that was rapidly becoming black and white. By becoming slave owners, Indians protected their status as free people. But the cost, once again, was great.

Scholars mark the Yamasee War as the tipping point in South Carolina's slave system, leading to the rapid demise of the Indian slave trade and the colony's wholesale commitment to African slavery and racialized slavery. It also marked a period in which Indians and Africans pushed back. Yamasee Indians led the charge to end the Indian slave trade, teaching Carolinians that they could not ignore the politics of slavery and showing many Africans the way to freedom in La Florida.

The Yamasees moved again during the war. Some went to St. Augustine, but others went to the Lower Creeks to live again as a people who understood that war had to be balanced by peace, that captivity had to be balanced by kinship—something they had strayed from but not forgotten. Cacique Jorge's 1724 testimony reminds us of a number of things about southern *slaveries* in this period. Slavery was complex, highly situational, and contested. It was about geopolitics as much as it was about economics. It also led to what we might think of as unlikely allies and enemies. It was rarely ideologically driven. It was always messy.

Notes

1. While the English and Spanish were also the victims of enslavement during this period, they were not targets of the transatlantic slave trade. For Ottoman enslavement of Europeans, see Robert C. Davis, *Christian Slaves, Muslim Masters: White Slavery in the Mediterranean, the Barbary Coast and Italy, 1500–1800* (New York: Palgrave Macmillan, 2004). On Britons in particular, see Linda Colley, *Captives: Britain, Empire, and the World, 1600–1850* (New York: Pantheon, 2003), 23–136.

2. See the forum in response to Steve Pincus's essay on mercantilism in the *William and Mary Quarterly*, esp. the essay by Christian J. Koot, "Balancing Center and Periphery," *William and Mary Quarterly*, 3rd ser., 69 (January 2012): 41–46.

3. Christine Daniels and Michael V. Kennedy, eds., *Negotiated Empires: Centers and Peripheries in the Americas, 1500–1820* (New York: Routledge, 2002); Koot, "Balancing Center and Periphery," 41–46.

4. Juliana Barr and Edward Countryman, eds., *Contested Spaces of Early America* (Philadelphia: University of Pennsylvania Press, 2014), 23.

5. Daniel K. Richter, *Facing East from Indian Country: A Native History of Early America* (Cambridge, MA: Harvard University Press, 2003); Kathleen DuVal, *The Native Ground: Indians and Colonists in the Heart of the Continent* (Philadelphia: University of Pennsylvania Press, 2006); Robert Michael Morrissey, *Empire by Collaboration: Indians, Colonists, and Governments in Colonial Illinois Country* (Philadelphia: University of Pennsylvania Press, 2015).

6. Alan Gallay has been at the forefront of this field. See Alan Gallay, *The Indian Slave Trade: The Rise of the English Empire in the American South, 1670–1717* (New Haven, CT: Yale University Press, 2002). Alan Gallay, ed., *Indian Slavery in Colonial America* (Lincoln: University of Nebraska Press, 2009). For a recent review of the field, see Denise I. Bossy, "The South's Other Slavery: Recent Research on Indian Slavery," *Native South* 9 (2016): 27–53.

7. Christina Snyder, *Slavery in Indian Country: The Changing Face of Captivity in Early America* (Cambridge, MA: Harvard University Press, 2010).

8. Robbie Ethridge has been the major proponent of the "shatter zone," and her work is currently inspiring a whole generation of scholarship. See esp. Robbie Ethridge and Sheri M. Shuck-Hall, eds., *Mapping the Mississippian Shatter Zone: The Colonial Indian Slave Trade and Regional Instability in the American South* (Lincoln: University of Nebraska Press, 2009). For a recent assessment of this subfield, see Denise I. Bossy, "Shattering Together, Merging Apart: Colonialism, Violence, and the Remaking of the Native South," *William and Mary Quarterly*, 3rd ser., 71 (October 2014): 611–31.

9. These divisions between scholars of Indians and scholars of Africans are problematic in other regional fields, too. For a recent and successful effort to address this problem in the French Atlantic world, see Brett Rushforth, *Bonds of Alliance: Indigenous and Atlantic Slaveries in New France* (Chapel Hill: University of North Carolina Press, 2012). For a response to this lacuna in Andean scholarship, see Rachel Sarah O'Toole, *Bound Lives: Africans, Indians, and the Making of Race in Colonial Peru* (Pittsburgh: University of Pittsburgh Press, 2012). [Andrew Frank recently organized a symposium featuring presentations by preeminent scholars directly aimed at offering new Indian-centered narratives for southern historians. Titled "Indians as Southerners, Southerners as Indians," the symposium was held at Florida State University in Tallahassee during September 2014. Four of the symposium presenters (Kristofer Ray, Angela Pulley Hudson, Rose Stremlau, and Daniel H. Usner Jr.) then organized a panel titled "The Native South: A Critical Intervention," at the 7th Annual Native American and Indigenous Studies Association Conference at Washington, DC, in May 2015].

10. I pay little attention to European ideologies of slavery not because they were unimportant, but because they have received much more scholarly attention elsewhere. For important studies that include relevant discussions of British slave ideology and culture in early South Carolina, see Peter H. Wood, *Black Majority: Negroes in Colonial South Carolina from 1670 through the Stono Rebellion* (New York: W. W. Norton, 1974); Philip D. Morgan, *Slave Counterpoint: Black Culture in the Eighteenth-Century Chesapeake and Lowcountry* (Chapel

Hill: University of North Carolina Press, 1998); Ira Berlin, *Many Thousands Gone: The First Two Centuries of Slavery in North America* (Cambridge, MA: Harvard University Press, 1998); Robert Olwell, *Masters, Slaves, and Subjects: The Culture of Power in the South Carolina Low Country, 1740-1790* (Ithaca, NY: Cornell University Press, 1998); Jennifer Morgan, *Laboring Women: Reproduction and Gender in New World Slavery* (Philadelphia: University of Pennsylvania Press, 2004); and S. Max Edelson, *Plantation Enterprise in Colonial South Carolina* (Cambridge, MA: Harvard University Press, 2006). For Spanish ideologies of slavery and culture in Florida, see Jane Landers, *Black Society in Spanish Florida* (Chicago: University of Illinois Press, 1999).

11. In her illuminating study of changing captivity practices from the Mississippian era (950–1600 C.E.) through the nineteenth century, Christina Snyder argues that southern Indians displayed a particularly flexible approach to slavery and that "the practice's adaptability explains its longevity." Christina Snyder, *Slavery in Indian Country: The Changing Face of Captivity in Early America* (Cambridge, MA: Harvard University Press, 2010).

12. Joseph M. Hall Jr., *Zamumo's Gifts: Indian-European Exchange in the Colonial Southeast* (Philadelphia: University of Pennsylvania Press, 2009); Robbie Ethridge, *From Chicaza to Chickasaw: The European Invasion and the Transformation of the Mississippian World, 1540–1715* (Chapel Hill: University of North Carolina Press, 2010).

13. Ethridge, *From Chicaza to Chickasaw,* 52–55; "Adelantado Pedro Menéndez Reports the Damages and Murders Caused by the Coast Indians of Florida, 1573–4," *Colonial Records of Spanish Florida,* vol. 1: *1570–1577,* ed. Jeannette Thurber Connor, 39 (Deland: Florida Historical Society, 1924).

14. Rodrigo Rangel, "Account of the Northern Conquest and Discovery by Hernando de Soto," trans. John E. Worth, in *The De Soto Chronicles: The Expedition of Hernando de Soto to North America in 1539–1543,* vol. 1, ed. Lawrence A. Clayton, Vernon James Knight Jr., and Edward C. Moore, 270–73 (Tuscaloosa: University of Alabama Press, 1993).

15. Ibid.

16. Patricia Seed, *Ceremonies of Possession* (New York: Cambridge University Press, 1995), 69–99.

17. Rangel, "Account of the Northern Conquest," 272–73.

18. Paul E. Hoffman, "A New Voyage of North American Discovery: Pedro de Salazar's Visit to the 'Island of Giants,'" *Florida Historical Quarterly* 58 (April 1980): 415–26. Hoffman, *A New Andalucia and a Way to the Orient: The American Southeast during the Sixteenth Century* (Baton Rouge: Louisiana State University Press, 1990), 7–20.

19. Charles Hudson, *Knights of Spain, Warriors of the Sun: Hernando de Soto and the South's Ancient Chiefdoms* (Athens: University of Georgia Press, 1994), 142–311.

20. Susan M. Alt, "Unwilling Immigrants: Culture, Change, and the 'Other' in Mississippian Societies," in *Invisible Citizens: Captives and Their Consequences,* ed. Catherine M. Cameron, 205–22 (Salt Lake City: University of Utah Press, 2008). For a recent effort by archaeologists to ask comparative questions about practices of captivity and slavery, see Lydia Wilson Marshall, ed., *The Archaeology of Slavery: A Comparative Approach to Captivity and Coercion* (Carbondale: Southern Illinois University Press, 2014).

21. René de Laudonnière, *Three Voyages,* trans. Charles Bennett (Tuscaloosa: University of Alabama Press, 2001), 79–84.

22. For more on southeastern Indian constructions of slavery, see Denise I. Bossy, "Indian Slavery in Southeastern Indian and British Societies, 1670–1730," in *Indian Slavery in Colonial America*, ed. Alan Gallay (Lincoln: University of Nebraska Press, 2009), 207–50.

23. James Adair, *The History of the American Indians*, ed. Kathryn E. Holland Braund (Tuscaloosa: University of Alabama Press, 2005), 184.

24. Cameron Wesson, *Households and Hegemony: Early Creek Prestige Goods, Symbolic Capital, and Social Power* (Lincoln: University of Nebraska Press, 2008), 35–36. Writing about the Cherokees in the 1720s, Alexander Long described the practice of chiefs rewarding warriors who returned from battle with the scalps of their enemies by exchanging those scalps for beads and deerskins from the town storehouse. Alexander Long, "A Small Postscript on the Ways and Manners of the Indians Called Cherokees, 1725," ed. David Corkran, *Southern Indian Studies* 21 (October 1969): 46–47.

25. "Adelantado Pedro Menéndez Reports," 39.

26. John H. Hann, *Indians of Central and South Florida, 1513–1763* (Gainesville: University Press of Florida, 2003), 153–54.

27. Hann, *Indians of Central and South Florida*, 105–7.

28. John H. Hann, *Apalachee: The Land Between the Rivers* (Gainesville: University Press of Florida, 1988), 10.

29. Report of Governor Gonzalo Méndez de Canzo, July 1, 1598, in *Murder and Martyrdom in Spanish Florida: Don Juan and the Guale Uprising of 1597*, by J. Michael Francis and Kathleen Cole (New York: American Museum of Natural History, 2011), 105.

30. Paul E. Hoffman, *Florida's Frontiers* (Bloomington: Indiana University Press, 2002), 70. On cross-cultural sexual and marital relationships in early St. Augustine, see Kathleen Deagan, "Mestizaje in Colonial St. Augustine," *Ethnohistory* 20 (Winter 1973): 55–65.

31. John E. Worth, *Timucuan Chiefdoms of Spanish Florida*, vol. 1, *Assimilation* (Gainesville: University Press of Florida, 1998), 189.

32. "Adelantado Pedro Menéndez to the King, Madrid 1573," in *Colonial Records of Spanish Florida: Letters and Reports of Governors and Secular Persons*, vol. 1: *1570–7*, ed. Jeanette Thurber Connor (Deland: Florida State Historical Society, 1925), 30–35.

33. "Royal Council of the Indies, July 19, 1574," in *Colonial Records of Spanish Florida*, vol. 1, 76-77.

34. Auto of Gonzalo Méndez de Canzo about the liberty of Indians, January 31, 1600, trans. John Hann, Miscellaneous Translations (1574–1716), John H. Hann Collection, University of Florida, Gainesville. The Ais had recently killed a Spanish solider, sent by Canzo to promote the Catholic conversions of the Ais. Canzo had made a grave miscalculation, selecting for the job a man who had been involved in a war against allies of the Ais. Hoffman, *Florida's Frontiers*, 87. Hall Jr., *Zamumo's Gifts*, 61–63.

35. The Spanish mentioned the Yamasees for the first time in 1663. Fray Carlos de Anguiano, April 6, 1663, in *The Struggle for the Georgia Coast: An 18th-Century Spanish Retrospective on Guale and Mocama*, by John E. Worth (Athens: American Museum of Natural History; distributed by the University of Georgia Press, 1995), 92.

36. John E. Worth, "Yamasee," in *Handbook of North American Indians: Southeast*, vol. 14, ed. Raymond D. Fogelson, 245–53 (Washington, DC: Smithsonian Institution, 2004). Fray Carlos de Anguiano, April 6, 1663, in Worth, *Struggle for the Georgia Coast*, 92; David McKivergan, "Migration and Settlement among the Yamasee in South Carolina" (PhD diss.,

University of Maine, Orono, 1989), 219–20. Worth, *Struggle for the Georgia Coast*, 24–30. William Green, Chester B. DePratter, and Bobby Southerlin, "The Yamasee in South Carolina: Native American Adaptation and Interaction along the Carolina Frontier," in *Another's Country: Archaeological and Historical Perspectives on Cultural Interactions in the Southern Colonies*, ed. J. W. Joseph and Martha Zierden (Tuscaloosa: University of Alabama Press, 2001), 15–18.

37. Ethridge, *From Chickaza to Chickasaw*, 98–100. For the best explanation of Westo ethnogenesis, see C. S. Everett, "'They shalbe slaves for their lives:' Indian Slavery in Colonial Virginia," in *Indian Slavery in Colonial America*, ed. Alan Gallay, 78–80 (Lincoln: University of Nebraska Press, 2009). Gallay, *The Indian Slave Trade*, 41–42, 68-69. Eric Bowne, *The Westo Indians: Slave Traders of the Early Colonial South* (Tuscaloosa: University of Alabama Press, 2005).

38. There is some scholarly disagreement about the origins of the Westoes. The most current research suggests that they were a coalescent community established in Richmond, Virginia, in 1656 and included a number of different refugees including Iroquoian-speakers from the Great Lakes, Indians from Virginia, and possibly from La Florida. C. S. Everett, 'They shalbe slaves for the lives': Indian Slavery in Colonial Virginia," in *Indian Slavery in Colonial America*, ed. Alan Gallay, 72.

39. Governor Alonso Arganquiz y Cotes, September 8, 1662, AGI-SD 225. Governor Alonso Arganquiz y Cotes, November 15, 1661, in Worth, *Struggle for the Georgia Coast*, 15.

40. Bowne, *The Westo Indians*, 61–65. On the Westos, see Maureen Meyers, "From Refugees to Slave Traders: The Transformation of the Westo Indians," in *Mapping the Mississippian Shatter Zone*, 81–103; William A. Fox, "Events as Seen from the North: the Iroquois and Colonial Slavery," in *Mapping the Mississippian Shatter Zone*, 63–80.

41. Worth, *Struggle for the Georgia Coast*, 21–22.

42. Ibid., 35.

43. Worth, *Timucuan Chiefdoms of Spanish Florida*, 1:188–96. Bushnell, "Republic of Indians," 203–4. The Guales first consented to a labor tribute system in the wake of the Guale revolt. Hoffman, *Florida's Frontiers*, 85.

44. For the distinctions between slave societies and societies with slaves see Ira Berlin, *Many Thousands Gone: The First Two Centuries of Slavery in North America* (Cambridge, MA: Harvard University Press, 1998), 1–14.

45. "Adelantado Pedro Menéndez Reports," 34–35. Spanish reports from this and other regions suggest that tens of Spaniards were taken captive each year. Many, but certainly not all, came from shipwrecks along the southern coastline.

46. Jane Landers, *Black Society in Spanish Florida* (Chicago: University of Illinois Press, 1999), 157–58. In 1580, for example, four African girls accompanied the wives of the new governor, Dona Maria de Solid, and the wife of Rodrigo de Junco. Hoffman, *Florida's Frontiers*, 70.

47. Landers, *Black Society in Spanish Florida*, 19–20. Worth, *Timucuan Chiefdoms of Spanish Florida*, 1:189.

48. Quoted in Hoffman, *Florida's Frontiers*, 119.

49. Worth, *Struggle for the Georgia Coast*, 27–28.

50. Worth, *Timucuan Chiefdoms of Spanish Florida*, 1:192.

51. Hoffman, *Florida's Frontiers*, 121–24, 128–35.

52. Don Juan Marquéz Cabrera to Cacica Merenciana, January 30, 1681, in "A Letter to Merenciana, Indian Chieftainess," trans. Charles Arnade and Louis Arana, *Georgia Historical Quarterly* 45 (December 1961): 410.

53. Jason B. Palmer, "Forgotten Sacrifice: Native American Involvement in the Construction of the Castillo de San Marcos," *Florida Historical Quarterly* 80 (Spring 2002): 448.

54. Hoffman, *Florida's Frontiers*, 157–59.

55. Council of the Indies, June 15, 1657, Mary Ross Papers, Georgia State Archives, Morrow, folder 20, no. 18. For a particularly fine reinterpretation of Timucua relations with the Spanish and French, see Jonathan DeCoster, "Entangled Borderlands: Europeans and Timucuans in 16th-Century Florida," *Florida Historical Quarterly* 91 (Winter 2013): 375–400.

56. Worth, *Struggle for the Georgia Coast*, 27–28.

57. "Commission to Captain Antonio de Argüelles, 1668," in *Struggle for the Georgia Coast*, 77.

58. Worth, *Struggle for the Georgia Coast*, 27–35. A pirate attack in 1683 seems to have been the final straw for the Yamasees and the many Guales who joined them.

59. The recent emphasis on the shattering effect of Indian slave raids has left relatively unexplored the ways in which southeastern Indians also actively pursued peace in this period, as Joseph Hall argues. Because the slave trade created a virtual "shatter zone" of unprecedented violence, depopulation, and dislocation, exchange and diplomacy were crucial to survival for southeastern Indians. Even Indians who became slave raiders "devoted many of the proceeds of war to the ceremonies of peace." Hall, *Zamumo's Gifts*, 96.

60. Governor Johnson of Carolina to the Board of Trade, July 12, 1720, in Records in the British Public Record Office Relating to South Carolina (hereafter RBPROSC), microfilm, South Carolina Department of Archives and History, Columbia, 10: 237–38.

61. Caleb Westbrooke, February 21, 1685, *Calendar of State Papers. Colonial Series, America and West Indies, 1685–1688*, ed. John William Fortescue, vol. 12 (London: HMSO, 1860), no. 28. Hereafter CSP. Information of several Yamasee Indians, May 6 1685, *CSP 1685–1688*, no. 174. For Scottish suspicions of Yamasee coalescence see Lord Cardross, March 25, 1685, *CSP 1685–1688*, no. 174.

62. Governor Francisco Córcoles y Martinez to the King, January 14, 1708, in *Here They Once Stood: The Tragic End of the Apalachee Missions*, ed. Mark F. Boyd, Hale G. Smith, and John W. Griffin (Gainesville: University Press of Florida, 1951), 90. Gallay, *Indian Slave Trade*, 288–99.

63. Steven C. Hahn, *The Invention of the Creek Nation, 1670–1763* (Lincoln: University of Nebraska Press, 2004), 48–65. Gallay, *Indian Slave Trade*, 294–99.

64. Report of Joseph Xavier Alana and Joseph Maria Monaco [1743], trans. R. Wayne Childers, *Florida Historical Quarterly* 82 (Summer, 2003): 62–66. Hann, *Indians of Central and South Florida*, 179–82.

65. John Barnwell, "The Tuscarora Expedition: Letters of Colonel John Barnwell," *South Carolina Historical and Genealogical Magazine* 9 (January 1908): 28–54. "Letter from Colonel Moore to President Pollock, March 27, 1713," *South Carolina Historical and Genealogical Magazine* 10 (1909): 39.

66. Morgan, *Slave Counterpoint*, 1–26.

67. Governor and Council of Carolina to the Council of Trade and Plantations," *CSP*, September 17, 1709, no. 739.

68. June 15, 1714, Miscellaneous Records 1715–1717, South Carolina Department of Archives and History, film ST 0459, 19–21 and 42–47.

69. Edelson, *Plantation Enterprise*, 126–33.

70. Lawrence S. Rowland, Alexander Moore, and George C. Rogers Jr., *The History of Beaufort County, South Carolina*, vol. 1, *1514–1861* (Columbia: University of South Carolina Press, 1996), 80–94.

71. June 20, 1712, *The Journals of the Commissioners of the Indian Trade: September 20, 1710-August 29, 1718*, ed. W. L. McDowell (Columbia: South Carolina Archives Department, 1955), 27. Inventory of the Estate of Elizabeth Nairne, March 3, 1721, *Charleston County Will Book, 1721–1722*, SCDAH, 20–21. One of Nairne's neighbors, Robert Graham, owned three African and ten Indian slaves. May 15, 1714, Miscellaneous Records 1715–1717, 211–14.

72. Hahn, *Invention of the Creek Nation*, 52–55.

73. August 11, 1692, in *Journal of the Grand Council of South Carolina, April 11, 1692-September 26, 1692*, ed. A. S. Salley (Columbia, SC: The State Co., 1907), 55.

74. In 1711, for example, trader Cornelius Macarty kidnapped the wife and child of an Indian man from the Yamasee town of Euhaw, and trader George Wright seized the wife of an Indian man from Tomatley. McDowell, ed., *Journals of the Commissioners of the Indian Trade*, 11, 37. For an analysis of these crimes from Native perspectives, see William L. Ramsey, *The Yamasee War: A Study of Culture, Economy, and Conflict in the Colonial South* (Lincoln: University of Nebraska Press, 2008), chap. 1.

75. Ramsey, *Yamasee War*, 33–37; Morgan, *Laboring Women*, 144–65.

76. A few Indian and African women found freedom through marriage with their masters and some African men through military service for the colony. Ramsey, *Yamasee War*, 42–43.

77. Landers, *Black Society in Spanish Florida*, 24–28. September 9, 1725, *South Carolina Council Journals, No. 3*, SCDAH, 1121h.

78. July 31, 1711, *Journals of the Commissioners*, 12.

79. Ramsey, *Yamasee War*, 79–100.

80. Ibid., 101–56.

81. Denise I. Bossy, "Godin & Co.: Charleston Merchants and the Indian Trade, 1674–1715," *The South Carolina Historical Magazine* 114 (April 2013): 96–131.

82. Huspaw King to Charles Craven, 1715, in Ramsey, *Yamasee War*, 228.

83. Yamasees began to move near St. Augustine during the Yamasee War; by 1717 there were ten Indian communities in the area, including at least three that were Yamasee. Spanish census records indicate that the 1724 migration under Mico Jorge contributed to a brief demographic rise in the Indian population near St. Augustine. "Visitation of Governor Antonio de Benavides, December 1–11, 1726," AGI-SD 866, in *Missions to the Calusas*, trans. John H. Hann, 363–68 (Gainesville: University Press of Florida, 1991). John H. Hann, "St. Augustine's Fallout from the Yamasee War," *Florida Historical Quarterly* 68 (October 1989): 180–200.

84. "Memorial of Cacique Jorge, 1724," AGI-SD 844, microfilm reel 15, Stetson Collection, P.K. Yonge Library of Florida History, University of Florida, Gainesville (hereafter PKY). Jane Landers, "Africans and Native Americans on the Spanish Frontier," in *Beyond Black and*

Red: African-Native Relations in Colonial Latin America, ed. Matthew Restall (Albuquerque: University of New Mexico Press, 2005), 58–59.

85. Royal Decree, November 7, 1693, SD 58-1-26, SC. Royal Decree, October 4, 1733, SD 58-1-24, and Royal Decree October 29, 1733, SD 58-1-24, SC, PKY.

86. For Francisco Menéndez's petition see "Memorial of the Fugitives, 1724," SD 844, microfilm reel 15, folio 530, SC, PKY. For an insightful biography of Menéndez, see Jane Landers, "The Atlantic Transformations of Francisco Menéndez," in *Biography and the Black Atlantic,* ed. Lisa A. Lindsay and John Wood Sweet, 209–23 (Philadelphia: University of Pennsylvania Press, 2013).

87. "Testimony of the four caciques," July 5, 1715, AGI-SD 843, microfilm reel 36, SC, PKY. For an analysis of the Creek political and information networks revealed by this meeting, see Alejandra Dubcovsky, "One Hundred Sixty-One Knots, Two Places, and One Emperor: Creeks Information Networks in the Era of the Yamasee War," *Ethnohistory* 59 (Summer 2012): 489–513.

4

THE SELLER KING

Revisiting Control and Authority in French Louisiana

Alexandre Dubé

On the levee that served as the marketplace of French New Orleans, one could find poultry raised and vegetables grown by the Ouacha nations of the Mississippi Delta and purchase a handkerchief sold by a woman from Senegambia. Deer meat made its way from hunters campaigning along the Mississippi River. The bear fat they also processed was stored in pots boasting Mexican patterns. Deerskins, traded with Choctaws, Quapaws, and Caddos for French shirts and knives, piled up in waterfront warehouses, waiting for ships to take them to La Rochelle—but also perhaps to Mobile and from there to the Carolinas, loaded on pack mules bought from New Spain. A merchant could sell notebooks of Dutch paper, handkerchiefs from India, perhaps even some delicate teacups from China—all on offering for some silver dollars brought by officers of Spanish Pensacola. A soldier, detached from his post at Fort Toulouse, may have brought his gun with him—a French weapon from Tulle, now repaired with British fittings. In the thicket of vegetation surrounding the town, that soldier may have bought—no questions asked—a piece of jewelry left, or stolen, by the sailor of a ship from Curaçao.[1]

Such was the Louisiana that eighteenth-century commerce had wrought. Recent works have profoundly renewed our understanding of the French Empire in the American South. Or rather, they have turned their attention to the socioeconomic world that made the French Mississippi Valley a crossroads of the Atlantic World and a marginal imperial space.[2] The Mississippi colony, rooted in the Caribbean world and the North American interior, has long been portrayed as the object of deleterious imperial neglect by an earlier historiography concerned with the weakness of the ties between Versailles and New Orleans. It is no longer simply that. Metropolitan disinterest has been transfigured into full participation in a "self-organized" Atlantic World. It was a world where goods went where they were needed, almost casually crossing frontiers, ceaselessly making the foreign into the familiar. In the Mississippi colony, as elsewhere in the Atlantic World, the behavior of entrepreneurial settlers, corrupt local officials, defiant marginal populations, expansive and commercial Native polities, and eventually emerging republics, delineated spaces of liberty—of nevertheless considerable inequality—from imperial regulatory ambitions.[3]

Historians followed closely early modern political thinkers themselves when they ascribed such intimate connection between the regulation of commerce and their assertion of political dominion. Eighteenth-century observers increasingly put the "mercantilist" injunction of commercial exclusivity (the obligation to buy goods from the metropole, carry colonial productions to the metropole, all of which sailed on metropolitan ships) at the heart of the colonial relation.[4] Faced with the rising tides of commerce and consumption, European monarchs played the part of King Canute. Their curses took the form of the usual and expected rules and regulations attempting in vain to control the flow of goods across the ocean and into the inland roads. The apparent centralization of France's imperial administration, under the auspices of a single institution, the Ministry of the Navy, made the contrast between the highly documented pretentions of control of the metropole, and their perpetual thwarting in colonial polities, a defining feature of Louisiana, and perhaps even of the whole empire.[5]

The movement of things, and people—fundamental paradigms of Atlantic history—across, and often despite, the political boundaries of empire, gave a new interpretative potency to French Louisiana. The world of foreign goods unearthed from the archives or retrieved from Louisiana's damp soil contributed powerfully to stories of humbled empires contained in their ambitions by the many material impediments to imperial power. Colonists fending for themselves in "opportunistic" and "entrepreneurial" ways were engaging in intercoastal trade, smuggling, and a "frontier exchange economy" made of countless daily transactions far from the gaze of officials.[6] Yet the *presence* in Louisiana, and in its archives, of these goods, of indigenous staples, and of illicit traders masks the fundamental role of the French Crown in gathering them in the colony. A considerable number of those goods traded in New Orleans, legally or not, may have been subsidized by the king, or may even have begun their Mississippi lives as the king's own. The role of direct royal intervention upon the Louisiana trade cannot be traced through the usual regulatory framework that has attracted, by the many transgressions it suffered, the attention of scholars. Neither is it wholly to be found in the shadows of government corruption and patronage that often serve as the best illustration of the permeability of official policy to local interests.[7] While scholars have rightly reminded us that the blurriness between official sanction, tacit acceptance, and illicit behavior was a generative force of imperialism, we should avoid making the material world the mere texture of larger sociopolitical struggles, resources to be bargained and exchanged. Early modern polities mobilized numerous nonmaterial, normative resources that shaped the form, distribution, material of goods, which in turn served to crystallize political and ideological expectations. This may have been especially sensitive in marginal spaces of the Atlantic World such as Louisiana, where a few key actors—importers, merchants, local retailers—could dominate trade by securing access to goods and controlling their distribution. Control over access and prices in turn sparked conflict over the administration of justice and political influence.[8] In the Mississippi Valley, the French Crown was one such dominant actor. Royal administrators were empowered to mobilize the monarchy's intellectual resources and had the capacity to lay claims to its potentially considerable material means. Indeed, in Louisiana, the French Crown was involved in the direct purchase and sale of an astonishing diversity of goods—from reams of paper to silks, from copper kettles to coarse linens. Such state commerce coexisted, and indeed, shaped profoundly trades of necessity such as interimperial smuggling and the frontier exchange economy. All were reflections of an economy of scarcity.

Scarcity

New Orleans may have stood at the crossroads of many different licit and illicit circuits of trade, but it never truly seemed to have transcended the anxieties of scarcity. The high retail prices in New Orleans—a constant remarked by all observers and travelers, in turn appalled or enticed—hint at a world of recurring dearth. Yet the assessment of scarcity—of its very existence—in Louisiana, and in the Atlantic World, remains a delicate exercise, caught between a healthy suspicion for the theatrics of official rhetoric and the normative character inherent in all judgments of lack. In the study of illicit trade, the former has often dominated over the difficulties of the latter. If scarcity, however defined, is real, it is assumed to explain the existence of illicit trades developed to counter it. But if the illicit economy is thriving, complaints of scarcity are often assumed to be nothing more than self-serving official discourse meant to extract additional resources from the imperial state.[9] Both assumptions rely on a specific intellectual operation of abstraction, which requires envisioning trade as a series of substituting fluxes—of interchangeable goods, capital, or credit. Goods and people lose their individuality, assumed to be replaced by other nondescript goods, carried by anonymous merchants. The illicit trades would carry whatever need the licit commerce would not.

Difficulties in assessing scarcity, it turns out, is not limited to historians of the Atlantic World. In 1731 the Company of the Indies (Compagnie des Indes, the Company), which had hitherto held the official monopoly over the Louisiana trade, relinquished its dominion over the Mississippi and returned it to the direct administration of the royal government. It left the new caretaker, the Ministry of the Navy, with an urgent problem. Goods which had previously been supplied by the Company would now have to reach New Orleans from a different source, and quickly. It was a time of dire need. The Natchez and the French had been waging war since 1729, and the terrorized inhabitants of New Orleans required food, weapons, and goods that would convince their powerful neighbors—the Choctaw, the Creeks, the Caddos, the Quapaws, the Illinois—to either continue their friendship or, at least, ensure their neutrality. Faced with the problem of scarcity, faced with the challenges of creating, ad hoc, the conditions of supply for a small, but still sizeable settlement such as New Orleans itself, eighteenth-century administrators had to ponder both the reality of scarcity and the frustrating indeterminacy of its contours. How much *should* men and women consume? What should be considered *truly* necessary? Contemporary discussions over the frustrating indeterminacy of the superfluous and the necessary echoes the uneasiness of later historians.[10] And, much like them, eighteenth-century administrators poured their hope into a disembodied, collective commerce, capable to supply each need as it arose. Yet the situations they faced prevented them from sharing in the *longue durée* the inevitability of organic commercial response.[11] The recent past had given them the illustration of both the tragic consequences of scarcity and the logistical challenges of a single imperial supplier. Between 1717 and 1721, at the height of the colonization frenzy that fueled the Mississippi Bubble, perhaps as many as seven thousand settlers, sometimes gathered by promises of prosperity and sometimes rounded up by the Parisian police, arrived en masse in Louisiana. Ill-equipped, ill-organized, thousands died on the beaches of the Gulf of Mexico amidst crates of supplies. Supplies of everything, that is, except food.[12]

Administrators thus had to answer colonial needs first and the birth of new commercial ties second. What *their* assessment of scarcity showcases, however, is that its politically generative capacity stemmed precisely from the contrast between the fine grain of commerce, with observable lacks in specific goods, and the smoothened abstraction of its theory.

Company Supplies

Whatever the answer of royal administrators would be to the challenges of supplying Louisiana in 1731, it would have to contend with the immediate past, the supplying practices of the Company of the Indies. This Company was the latest incarnation of a series of Company-States that the French king had entrusted with a host of potential jurisdictions over colonists, goods, indigenous nations, and foreigners in the Mississippi Valley. After the debacle of the Mississippi Bubble, the newly reorganized Company had emerged as a consolidated monopoly over a variety of Atlantic and Pacific trades and direct political administration of the Mascarene Islands, the East Indian factories such as Pondichéry, and Louisiana.[13] In the Mississippi Valley, the directors of the Company had attempted to enforce a dual monopoly. First, they established the Company as the sole purchaser of colonial goods produced by African and indigenous captives or obtained by European settlers. Indigo, tobacco, skins and furs, and Spanish silver traded with Pensacola and New Spain, which the Company required for its Asian trade, were to be channeled to the small posts of Biloxi (1699), Mobile (1702), and eventually New Orleans (1718) before being shipped back to France on the Company's vessels. Second, the Company of the Indies maintained the exclusivity over the supplies of all goods sold in Louisiana. Every tool, every piece of cloth, every bottle of wine—even every human being kept in bondage—required for the settlers' plantations, or demanded for their workshops and households, would have to be bought at the Company's warehouses. Whatever merchandise settlers may have needed, the Company could supply thanks to an extensive supplying network covering much of northern Europe.[14]

The types of goods supplied to the colony were quite varied, comprising dozens of types of cloth (painted cloth, Morlaix, bretagne, blankets, and so on), hardware (earthenware, china), ironware (hoes, pickaxes, iron sheets, steel, nails), and foodstuffs (vinegar, olive oil, wine, brandy, spices). Some of these goods were clearly intended for the Spanish trade. The garrisons of Pensacola and Los Adaes, as well as passing ships at the mouth of the Mississippi River, supplied precious silver from their species-rich economies. Other goods were set aside for the wide variety of indigenous trades of Louisiana. The Company traded with the Caddos, the Creeks, the Quapaws, the Illinois, the Petites Nations of the Delta, and especially the numerous and powerful Choctaw confederacy. It also settled on Natchez territory.[15]

Trade by itself did not guarantee harmonious relations. When the Natchez killed the French inhabitants of Fort Rosalie in 1729, the survival of the small French settlements of the Mississippi appeared to be in jeopardy. This, the fourth conflict to erupt between the French and the Natchez, prompted a brutal and frenzied retaliation from French troops and militia.[16] Royal troops were sent to supplement the Company's own soldiers, adding to the costs of what the directors, in Paris and Lorient, were already considering a dubious venture. They thus entered discussion with the comptroller-general of finances, Philibert Orry, and the secretary of state for the navy, Jean-Frédéric Phélypeaux, comte de Maurepas, asking if the king would agree to the "retrocession" of Louisiana.

The negotiations took some time while the fighting continued in the Mississippi Valley. Ministers and directors reached an agreement during the last months of 1730, and by a decree of the royal council, dated January 23, 1731, Louis XV officially accepted the return of Louisiana to his administration.[17] Local Company officials became local royal officials, thereafter reporting back to the minister of the navy and its clerks in Versailles.[18] Everything the Company owned in the Mississippi Valley was to be immediately transferred to the king's own possession—except for the settlers' debts. The king had inherited a war, along with thousands of "settlers, soldiers and slaves" and their needs.

The Weight of the Company

The retrocession did not come cheap for the Company. Its directors agreed to pay to the royal treasury 1.45 million *livres tournois* (hereafter *livres*) for relinquishing the Company's titles to the Mississippi colony. Still, the directors of the Company felt the payment of such a substantial sum was preferable to being saddled with a more onerous obligation: supplying the colonists' needs. The question of supplies proved to be one of the major contentious issues of the negotiations. Directors of the Company used their ships and networks of suppliers as a bargaining chip to secure their claims to settlers' debts; ministers of the king used the threat of the legal obligation to supply to extract money from the Company.

The transfer of Company property to the king required determining the fate of the considerable amount of money owed to the Company by the settlers of Louisiana. Over the years, the Company had sold goods and captives at credit, slowly repaid at the Company's warehouse with colonial staples. The directors of the Company had been eager to maintain their claims over this debt and had initially suggested retaining elements of the Company's commercial monopoly, possibly as a fee for metropolitan merchants who would eventually trade in the colony, perhaps as a duty levied on Louisiana goods sent to France. To secure guarantees from the king, the Company's directors threatened to divert the vessels that were already being outfitted for Louisiana to another, more lucrative, destination, leaving the settlers without supplies if their terms were not met.[19]

That this was seen as a credible threat by the royal ministers suggests that the smuggling which took place in New Orleans was not believed sufficient to provide for the colony in the short term. The Company could hardly ignore the existence of such contravention to its monopoly. Its own employees had continuously engaged in numerous instances of illegal retail trade.[20] Small vessels plying the waters of the Gulf of Mexico were also able to dock illegally at New Orleans, Mobile, and sometimes Île Dauphine (Dauphin Island). One energetic trader, Laurent-Patrice MacMahon, a merchant from Nantes, claimed, for instance, to have sold 2,100 *livres* worth of cloth and brandy in one such venture. The Company did its best to integrate illicit ventures into its fold; MacMahon was thus laying claims to expertise as a merchant capable of developing the Spanish trade in Louisiana, an object of much interest to the Company. MacMahon joined the Company's colonial administration.[21]

Assessment of the weight of such trade in the colony's economy remains notoriously difficult. The Company's employees may have been able to bring goods illegally on board of the Company's ships with the complicity of the captains or supercargoes, but these may not have been more than a few bales or a few casks at a time.[22] More threatening perhaps for the Company's monopoly was the competition from well-connected planters, who lobbied directors for the right to import goods for their own use. They then dispatched servants or slaves to sell those goods on the levee. Some of these influential planters had only meager funds. Charles Pradel, an officer in the troops, required the help of his brother in foraging silver in southern

France that allowed him to purchase a cargo worth 2,000 *livres*. Others drew from vaster pools of resources. Jean-Daniel Kolly, a Swiss financier who was attempting to rebuild his fortune in Louisiana, was able to import 80,000 *livres* worth of goods at the time of his immigration. His wife later assembled two cargoes valued at 60,000 *livres*.[23]

These amounts are by no means insignificant, but they remain dwarfed by the estimates of goods imported by the Company itself. Between 1720 and 1731, the Company claimed to have brought about 20 million *livres*—in goods, money, and African captives—into Louisiana.[24] While such claims, made during the negotiations for the retrocession, were politically motivated exaggerations, the lists of ships sent by the Company to Louisiana during those years does reveal a trade conducted by huge vessels, laden to the brim. Between 1721 and 1731, the average tonnage of the Company's Louisiana vessels was nearing 315 tons. As a comparison, the ships sent to New Orleans by private merchants from La Rochelle and Bordeaux between 1731 and 1764 averaged between 150 and 160 tons; Caribbean traders, who could attempt to circumvent the Company's monopoly usually sailed ships much smaller than 100 tons, making it unlikely they carried large quantities of diverse goods.[25] During the years of feverish Mississippi speculation, the worth of European goods sent to the 380 to 400 households of New Orleans may have neared one million *livres* per year.[26] Even if we allow this amount to account for the high value of the African captives sold by the Company (priced at one thousand *livres* per enslaved man), its shipping represented a considerable amount of goods in the relatively unencumbered houses of the Atlantic World.[27] That most of the smuggling taking place in New Orleans was made up of goods loaded on company ships, rather than on passing vessels, suggests it would have required an extremely large number of illegal ships to supply an equivalent to the sheer amount of goods sent by the Company annually.

Supplying the Needy

These evaluations may have been unavailable to Orry and Maurepas, but the Company's threat to cut supplies to the colony nonetheless appeared dangerous in the immediate time and problematic for the future. The war with the Natchez, which threatened to develop into conflict with the Chickasaws, made the retrocession of the colony to the king an urgent matter. The survival of the colony was at stake. The established settlers, the colonial militia, and the recent reinforcements all required material support. But once the danger had passed—if indeed it had—the colony would still need to be supplied. Settlers would need access to what was generally termed "their needs."[28]

What those needs were, however, remained an uncomfortably ill-defined notion, both for the Company's directors and the royal ministers. Somehow the word was tied to "necessity," which, in a society of dearth was frequently synonymous with "food," but Louisiana and the other Atlantic colonies proved it could be much more capacious. Needs could relate to what one couldn't *decently* part with, according to one's status. Such was, for instance, the necessity of the colony's administrative elite to host officers daily and visiting dignitaries infrequently. Needs could also, more generally, refer to the capacity to participate in one's community. Wine and bread were required for the Eucharist, for instance. And bread was also, along with certain types of dress and food, a blurry yet ultimately powerful marker of Frenchness.[29] Needs could, more vaguely still, refer to those goods required to accomplish certain activities and duties—weapons and ammunition for soldiers, paper and ink for royal clerks. For royal officers, the ubiquitous use of the expression "the needs of the service" could justify requesting a wide variety of material and financial resources.[30] It is perhaps in that latter sense that the Company included the supply of African captives as a necessity for Louisiana: the desire for a plantation economy needed, they argued, human bondage.[31]

Circumscribing the specific needs of Louisiana from general propositions could only be learned from experience. It was costly knowledge. Some goods sent by the Company had been left to rot in its warehouse for lack of demand. Some types of cloth disappeared almost overnight. Supplying the colony also required a formidable logistical effort. Provisioning a whole society, however small it may have been, from the Company's own port of Lorient in Brittany, entailed coordinating purchases, production, and transportation with the difficult and capricious rhythms imposed by the weather. Lastly, the political cost of failing to supply the colony could be high. Quite apart from military conflict with indigenous nations, privileged access to certain goods—either legally from the Company's warehouse or from turning a blind eye to illicit trade—could create destructive factionalism as parties competed around redistributive practices. One such conflict had prompted the Company to order a general inquiry in 1723. It eventually led to the recall of Jean-Baptiste Lemoyne de Bienville, the founder of New Orleans, back to Paris in 1726. It may also have explained why the Company was willing to include influential or enterprising newcomers, such as MacMahon, into its own local government.[32]

In short, there was an implicit threat in the notion of settlers' needs: it had the potential to expand unpredictably to an increasing variety of goods and merchandise, some of which could be bulky and of low value (iron sheets, for instance) and others of high technical specificity and hard to come by (such as goods for the indigenous trades). The association of such goods with the notion of need in turn made them the object of contentious political claims. It was such claims that made it an "infinitely onerous" burden to the directors of the Company of the Indies and the satisfaction of the "settler's needs" an endeavor which went "well beyond the strengths of a company." It threatened to be an onerous burden to the Crown, too, and Maurepas shrewdly toyed with the idea of imposing a legal obligation on the Company, forcing it to continue supplying the Louisiana settlers their unspecified "needs." The directors escaped that requirement by offering nearly 1.5 million *livres* to the royal treasury.[33] It freed the Company from any future responsibility and preserved its claims over the settlers' debts. The *Gironde*, which left in May 1731, would be the last of the Company's ships bound for New Orleans.[34]

The king would have to find the strength to carry "the onerous burden" for the following years. Afterward, it would be up to the "commerce of France" to bear that weight.

The King's Encouragements

The pre-industrialized world of the eighteenth century knew intimately the threats of famine and the pangs of hunger.[35] France's fatherly king often offered succor to his beleaguered subjects. The theory of the benevolent monarch, as well as more pragmatic concerns over urban disorders, often led the Crown to purchase and distribute bread and flour in times of need. The emergency relief to Louisiana planned in 1731 may have been understood as an iteration of this larger conception of royal concern, though very few discussions of the meaning of such acts seem to survive. Existing routines seem to have taken care of ratiocinations over the nature of necessity and the superfluous.

To supply Louisiana, the navy borrowed extensively from the knowledge amassed over the years by the Company of the Indies. It first requested lists and inventories of yearly supplies. Some of the material they contained could easily be procured through the regular channels of the ministry itself. Flour, alcohol, and guns, which fleets consumed in great quantities, could be obtained from the usual syndicate of navy suppliers. Other commodities frequently used by navy personnel (leather belts, paper, paint, etc.) could also easily be purchased from local French merchants who usually supplied the arsenal of Rochefort. But the settlers of Louisiana also consumed goods that never made it to the navy's warehouses. The lists sent by the Company of the Indies comprised agricultural implements, luxury goods, and ordinary wares: silk stockings, wooden combs, blankets for cribs, dog bells, and so on. It was the ordinary consumption of a society of plantations, a society that also needed to trade with indigenous neighbors to survive. Maurepas thus requested the list of the Company's past suppliers and manufacturers from small towns in Brittany; from textile centers like Montpellier, Rennes, Rouen, and Montauban and from the European entrepôt of Amsterdam.

The list was then forwarded to Maurepas's agent, Léon Dupérier de Saint-Léon. A curious man, the son of Molière's manservant, Saint-Léon was a former child actor in the famed playwright's troupe and was now frequently lending his name to secret government operations. Saint-Léon managed from Paris the logistics of transportation, contacting the suppliers sufficiently in advance to produce or assemble the required amounts in time for shipment.[36] All goods were to be channeled to Rochefort, on the western coast of France, there to be loaded on royal ships bound for the Mississippi, or offered as lucrative freight contracts to private traders of La Rochelle and, more rarely, Bordeaux.[37]

But much like emergency bread supplies in metropolitan France, such relief was conceived as a temporary measure. The king infrequently bought and sold bread; no one imagined the king operating royal bakeries. Louis XV was not about to become a merchant either.[38] Maurepas's objective was to make Louisiana an attractive destination for metropolitan merchants which, for the minister, required "free trade" for all French merchants originating from one of the thirteen ports authorized for colonial commerce.[39] The potential of the colony needed to be communicated to merchants. Maurepas knew their initial forays needed to be profitable to incite repeat ventures; their goods needed to be adequate to avoid the dire consequences of undersupply. Only by nurturing tentative endeavors would the colony be able, in time, to sustain bigger trade, an evolutionary view of commerce increasingly shared among merchant circles and political philosophers—not least amongst them Montesquieu.[40] This process would take time.

In order to set it in motion, Maurepas began by writing to representatives of chambers of commerce in the major ports of France to inform them of the upcoming end of the Company's monopoly. While the minister insisted that "only experience can give them [the merchants] the knowledge of the resources one can gain from [Louisiana commerce]," he sought to accelerate the pace by forwarding the lists he had received from the Company.[41] To ensure merchants would find in Louisiana a lucrative return cargo, Maurepas also negotiated with the Fermiers-Généraux, monopolists of the tobacco trade, a guaranteed floor price for the Louisiana leaf sold in France.[42] To minimize the risks of unprofitable venture and encourage the supply of European goods to the Mississippi, Maurepas also offered a direct subsidy. The royal treasury would pay 40 *livres* per ton of European goods brought to New Orleans.[43]

These were not inconsequential sums. The *Saint-Paul* was the first merchant ship to reach Louisiana after 1731: royal subsidy reached 14 percent of the invoice value of the cargo.[44] As an additional enticement, the owners of the *Saint-Paul* were awarded a freight contract from the ministry to carry flour bought by the king, worth 5 percent of the invoice value of the total cargo. Profits on transatlantic trades are notoriously difficult to assess, but if they hovered, as G. Daudin suggested, between 2 percent and 30 percent, such "encouragements," as they were called, could make the difference between a profitable voyage and a costly one. They may also have been instrumental in the decision to send ships to Louisiana in the first place by offering the guarantee of a return paid in France, rather than a later debt to collect in New Orleans.[45]

Timing also provided a challenge. Navigating seasons offered relatively limited windows of opportunity for transatlantic ships if they were to arrive in the colony before hurricane season in the fall. The arrival in New Orleans of multiple ships in short succession would adversely impact their sales. While the first vessel to arrive in colonial ports could generally command extremely high prices, the initial demand was rapidly satisfied. Subsequent traders could be left with their unsold wares for many costly months, forced to pay for warehousing or selling at bulk in order to depart quickly. This created the fluctuations that contemporaries referred to as "price revolutions."[46] Thus, in 1734, when a merchantman from Saint-Malo appeared at the mouth of the Mississippi while a ship from La Rochelle was already docked in New Orleans, the new royal *commissaire*, Edme-Gatien Salmon, tried the utmost to divert it to Mobile, hoping the even smaller market of that town would at least mitigate the inevitable losses.[47] The paradox was apparent: Maurepas's policy had to be *slowly* successful. Early disappointments could discourage European captains from attempting the Louisiana trade.

Securing a return cargo to avoid an unproductive voyage on ballast was always a challenge in colonial trade. It would be one in Louisiana as well:

the production of tobacco, indigo, and furs of the colony had never struck observers as particularly bountiful. The entire annual tobacco and indigo harvest could often fit in a single ship.[48] Furs and skins were reputed delicate, suffering from months of warehousing. The colony also offered bricks and lumber, bulky cargo of low value that would eventually find a market in Saint-Domingue. But that lay in the future. More immediate prospects included the highly desirable silver left in New Orleans and Mobile by the Spanish trade. To these, Maurepas added yet another incentive. The various iterations of paper currency that circulated in Louisiana could be remitted—in priority—by metropolitan merchants at the colonial treasury for letters of exchange on the royal treasury. These provided the guarantee of a quick and somewhat liquid return. The king's credit might not have been impeccable (some of these letters of exchange would lose quite a bit of value in times of war and royal bankruptcy), but the credit of Louisiana's inhabitants was, at best, untested and, at worst, assessed from the settlers' considerable debts towards the Company of the Indies.

Shared knowledge, floor price, direct subsidies, and guaranteed returns were all ways through which the Crown lowered the risk, and thus the transaction costs, for would-be initial Louisiana traders. These provided, in Maurepas's word, "encouragement" that would nurture the nascent Louisiana trade into a fruitful commerce. Only then could a multitude of merchants fulfill the settlers' current needs, those included in the Company's lists, and future desires, which remained unspecified in some future horizon. In the meantime, the navy still had to provision the Mississippi Valley. What Maurepas did not envision, however, was how such royal encouragements would modify the subsequent shape of that commercial growth.

The King's Trade

Routines of purchasing, transporting, and warehousing naval stores were essential components of the navy's daily activities both in France and the colonies. Goods purchased by Dupérier de Saint-Léon for Louisiana thus easily entered administrative practice as they reached Rochefort. They were received by the navy's warehouse keepers who oversaw storage. Scriveners kept track of their movements on and off board their ships. Navy comptrollers signed orders of payments to suppliers. The naval intendant of Rochefort, chief officer of the arsenal, supervised the whole.[49] The colonies, modeled in part after the arsenals, replicated this organizational structure.

Once the goods reached New Orleans, the local equivalent of the intendant, the *commissaire-ordonnateur*, signed the official paperwork confirming the arrival of the goods, turning them over to the general warehouse keeper in New Orleans. They would later be dispatched to the local warehouses of the colony, from the Arkansas to the Illinois, where they were similarly registered and inventoried. Iron from Sweden, glass beads from the Netherlands, woolens from Normandy and Languedoc, silks and guns from Lyonnais: all could be bought at royal warehouses whether at Fort Toulouse amongst the Alabamas or at Natchitoches amongst the Caddos.

Sales

The scale of the operation—and its coordination—certainly proved difficult and costly for the colonial administration, but the real novelty was the selling. The king of France did not usually sell things. The monarch was, first and foremost, a spender, a redistributor of graces. Through the spectacle of his largesse, the monarch was in fact removed from the world of mercantile exchange. He stood amidst an economy of the gift, as befit powerful leaders, or gave its frame to the concept of taxation, which was more properly associated with the res publica.[50] Still, there were anomalies, again when it came to flour and bread. During the dearth of 1725, agents of Louis XV bought grain for the provisioning of Paris, which was then resold to millers and bakers at a reduced price. In Canada a series of bad harvests similarly led colonial intendants to order the seizure of flour surpluses from bourgeois households. Such seizures were treated as forced sales, and the owners were compensated. The flour was subsequently redistributed to bakers and poorer households.[51] In France as in Canada, it seemed politically impossible to conceive of grain as outright gifts to the population. Gifts from the king were appropriate only in exceptional moments of rejoicing. Trying times in Paris, Quebec, or New Orleans could not fully capture the charity or the majesty of the king. Thus, when it came to goods sent to Louisiana, they would have to be sold.

The Warehouse

Admittedly, for the colonists, little had changed. Settlers who previously bought their goods from the Company of the Indies' warehouses, who purchased on credit with the Company and often failed to repay their debts to the Company now went to the same buildings to get access to the same goods—and again failed to repay. For colonial administrators, selling things only required minimal adjustment from usual routines. In an arsenal warehouse, the keeper received an order from the military commander to deliver a certain amount of specific goods—a blanket, a uniform, a bayonet—to the bearer, whether a soldier, a carpenter, or a scribe. The warehouse keeper would dutifully release the goods, ask for a receipt, and register the transaction. In the colony, sales would be treated similarly: the keeper would receive payment, deliver the goods, consign the sale in his registers (or, as seems more frequent, on scraps of paper),[52] and report the corresponding revenue to his superior in New Orleans. The messiness of inventory management and the less-than-ideal bookkeeping probably entailed verbal orders, preferential treatments, and possible coercion that rarely made it to either account book or letter. Still, sales of the king's goods became part of the tracking and classifying apparatus of the navy, for which some lists and accounts have survived.

• • •

While most of the sale records for the warehouses are lost, a few monthly accounts, established in 1744, 1747, 1749, and 1751 by *commissaire-ordonnateurs* Sébastien-François-Ange Lenormant de Mézy and Honoré-Gabriel Michel, have survived—all for the New Orleans warehouse. They record 167 named individuals, eleven of whom were women, for a town that had a population of about 1,700, free and unfree—perhaps 350 households in all.[53] The presence of "the so-called" *Andrée* as well as the *dame Favrot* suggests people of varied conditions bought from the king's warehouse. Between 10 and 50 percent of the sales of 1747, 1749, and 1751 did not bear the name of buyers. Rather, the amount was recorded under the catchall rubric of "retail." The accounts for June 1747 also show 4,113 *livres* in sales by auction, a procedure usually followed for spoiled goods or goods threatening to spoil.[54]

The different labels—names, retail, and auction—may hint at a difference in scale of purchases: there are no recorded purchases belonging to a named account below 48 *livres*, an amount representing the monthly wages of a skilled New Orleans hunter. "Retail" may thus aggregate numerous transactions worth a few *sols*. But named accounts may also indicate an ongoing commercial or sociopolitical relationship, which may explain the variety in status between clients. Some were likely individuals providing services to the administration—like the blacksmith Lorrain, who could find specialized tools and Swedish iron plates to work at his forge, or the baker *dame* Picquery, who transformed the king's flour into bread and biscuit. Magdeleine Le Roy, a seamstress, probably fashioned suits as gifts to indigenous war and peace leaders. Some of these leaders bought goods themselves, such as the otherwise anonymous "Biloxi chief" (two separate occurrences) or "the Pascagoula chief." Some were likewise individuals who could more easily extract credit from the warehouse keeper or his superiors; nearly a quarter of the buyers were military officers and administrators. Their purchases amounted to 35 percent of the total value of goods sold. The most frequent customers, with seven individual purchases, were Étienne de Bénac, the major of New Orleans, and Balthazar Ponfrac de Mazan, lieutenant of the troops. The first operated a canteen for soldiers, which he could supply from the warehouse, while the latter was quite active in trade. Mazan's purchases at the warehouse are contemporary with his purchase and outfitting of a ship, amounting to 20,000 *livres*—which he bought with silver coins.[55]

By 1744 the king was sending annually between 150,000 and 300,000 *livres* worth of merchandise, which represented between a third to more than half of the colonial budget.[56] The influx of royal goods in Louisiana was substantial. The scale of the operation was, by Louisiana's standards, staggering, making Louis XV the biggest single retailer of Louisiana. General accounts established from time to time indicate that the amount of goods held in the king's warehouses could even reach 650,000 *livres*.[57] By comparison, the estate of Widow Gervais, a private retailer, had an inventory of 34,000 *livres*. A portion of the king's goods thus valued would no doubt be used, rather than sold, consuming their estimated value. Still, the monarch was far and away the biggest merchant in the Mississippi Valley, with 1 million *livres* in goods being sold by the monarch between 1731 and 1744.[58] The annual sales at the New Orleans warehouse alone in 1744 reached 110,600 *livres*. Nearly 60 percent of the value was sold at retail. This represented as much as twice the value of goods sent yearly from La Rochelle by one of the biggest import-export partnerships of the colony.[59] By 1753 the value of royal exports to the colony rose to nearly 400,000 *livres*.

Yet simultaneously to the king's shipments, the colony's trade was growing. From hesitant beginnings in 1731—with three French ships docking in New Orleans—the Louisiana trade succeeded in attracting thirty ships in 1744.[60] Whether through subsidies, the regularization of intercolonial trade, government contract, or simply through the dissemination of knowledge about the colony's potential amongst transatlantic and Caribbean merchants, New Orleans was now a trade destination capable of regularly sustaining dozens of voyages annually. The persistence of the king's "temporary" relief in Louisiana for more than thirty years after the return of the colony to royal dominion thus needs to be accounted for.

Pressures of Price Practice

Clients of the warehouse—as far as we can tell—needed to pay for their purchases with money, for the king would not take colonial goods.[61] French coins were rare, and Spanish silver was a valuable export commodity. The royal warehouse, therefore, proved to be a good use for the various notes, *billets*, and card money that were circulating in the colony. Yet fur and deerskin traders, as well as artisans and planters, needed to have access to tools and trade goods before they could convert the product of their labor (or that of their captive workforce) into those forms of paper currency. Warehouse keepers seemed to have been hard-pressed to refuse advancing goods on credit, creating nightmares for the *commissaire-ordonnateur*. The main financial administrators were told by the minister, in no uncertain terms, that the sales of goods were supposed to sustain the colonial treasury. Yet the colonial government's needs—such as repairing buildings, paying troops, supplying war parties—arose at various times during the year, whereas the sales from the warehouse were heavily conditioned upon the coming and going of royal ships. The demands of pressing payment from the colonial government's suppliers, usually in letters of exchange, does not combine well with the necessity of extending credit to clients of the royal warehouse, who themselves had little coin to spare. In such a situation, the colonial government had to rely on the issuing of a paper currency. It could be used for payment at the warehouse or converted into letters of exchange at the colonial treasury in the fall, when ships brought French goods.[62]

It is here that the warehouse's twin status—as a retail shop and as a government depot, had unexpected effects. The warehouses stocked weapons, copper kettles, and various utensils that could both be sold to any passing buyer and at other times be used for the service of the king by soldiers, officers, and clerks. Some of these men (and a few women paid by the colonial administration) received goods, rather than money, for their services.[63] Soldiers, in fact, may have received most of their salaries in merchandise rather than coin and food ration. This also meant that the use of the warehouse was integrated in the colonial administration's hierarchical structures. Warehouse keepers could be caught between the duties of obedience to a hierarchy and the task of managing the goods. In 1744 warehouse keeper

Alexis-Philippe Carlier was jailed at Fort Tombecbé for failing to deliver, free of charge, garden implements for his commanding officer.[64] The same tools that could be requisitioned by the commander in the name of the king needed to be paid if they were to be used for the commander's garden. As Carlier's case suggests, it was a delicate distinction to impress upon one's superior officer. Only the *commissaire-ordonnateur*'s intervention succeeded in freeing the warehouse keeper. Other influences upon sales can be discerned in the archives; colonial authorities admitted to sometimes ceding goods at lower prices to the poorer inhabitants of the colony.[65] The moral requirements of charity, it turned out, also exerted pressures upon the price and use of the king's goods. Indeed, it was difficult even for Maurepas to avoid entirely the language of kingly generosity. The supply of Louisiana, he often insisted, was proof of gracious, fatherly concern from Louis XV.[66] The fact that succor was a temporary measure reinforced the belief that it fell to each and every one to feed themselves—for the suspicion of idleness was never far. Maurepas kept an eye on levels of goods being sent to Louisiana. When the minister deemed that the quantity of alcohol sent to New Orleans seemed unseemly high, he could only ascribe the settlers' "considerable" consumption either to luxury or to vice.[67]

In Louisiana the warehouse thus added to the colonial administration's repertoire of tools. Warehouses enabled the governor, the *commissaire-ordonnateur*, and, to some extent, post commanders and warehouse keepers themselves to tinker with the prices of goods or even choose the buyers they preferred. Such practices could then, if needed, channel goods at specific points, or into specific hands, without ever resorting to recognizable regulatory practices such as market regulations or trading licenses. This was especially the case in the colony's indigenous trades.

Warehouses and the Deerskins Trade

While the needs of the settlers remained ill-specified, there was, in the Company of the Indies' lists, a subset of goods that had a very clear use and answered a very specific political need: maintaining Louisiana's alliances with indigenous people.

Historians insist rightly that indigenous trades were paramount for the survival of the Louisiana colony. Such an assessment was already the Company's own before the retrocession of the colony to the king. After all, the Company had followed in the footsteps of the early adventurers and explorers. René-Robert Cavelier de La Salle, the Lemoyne brothers, and Antoine Laumet *dit* Lamothe Cadillac had all been heavily schooled in the Canadian fur trade, from which they understood the value of indigenous alliances to ensure the survival of their early expeditions and, later, of their small settlements.[68] They also benefited personally, and aggressively, from the trade. All of them savvy political operators, La Salle, Lemoyne, and Cadillac had used the trade to reward friends and partisans and secure patrons amongst the French. Whereas companies of commerce, such as the Company of the Indies, came and went, these early adventurers and their companions remained, sometimes marrying indigenous women to strengthen their position. It made them difficult to ignore and hard to oppose.[69]

In any case, the companies' policies were rooted in the necessity of good diplomatic relations between their small settlements and their powerful neighboring nations. Alliance was sustained with gifts and trade. However, from the earliest moments of settlement, the companies had directly encouraged settlers, rather than licensed traders, to engage in a daily sustenance trade. Trading goods for foodstuff maintained "good friendship," hopefully guaranteeing the settlers from the threats of both hunger and violence, if not providing abundance. The Company of the Indies' directors reasoned that armed conflict, and the logistical costs of operating, centrally, a variety of indigenous trades on the vast territory it claimed, would be too costly to sustain by the Company alone.[70]

Again, this policy suggests that directors of the Company of the Indies felt capable of enforcing at least enough of the Company's commercial monopoly and supply the settlers with goods required by their allies. There was, however, at least one notable exception: the Choctaw trade.

The populous Choctaw confederacy held, for observers in the Mississippi Valley, in Paris, and in Versailles, the survival of the coastal settlements in its hands. It forcefully maintained its own borders and could allow or deny access to New Orleans and Mobile to the British of Georgia and the Carolinas. The Choctaws requested French traders in their many villages, requiring the costly transportation of large quantities of goods.[71] Early in the 1720s, the Company's local administrators recommended that the trade be subcontracted to some chosen individual. By 1726 that individual was the military commander of Mobile, who used the trade, and the status it conferred upon him among both Choctaws and the French, to buttress his own political ambitions.[72] This made him a dangerous subordinate to Governor Étienne Périer, who disliked this influential rival.[73] But not for long. Périer's bumbling conduct of the war with the Natchez eventually brought his recall to France in 1733 and signaled the return to Louisiana of the founder of New Orleans, Jean-Baptiste Lemoyne de Bienville.[74]

The Prices of Bienville

Bienville's return to the Mississippi, after his recall to France in 1726, signaled a crucial opportunity to rethink trade and diplomacy in the Mississippi Valley. Minister of the Navy Maurepas was willing to listen. In 1733 the immediate threat to Louisiana had receded as the French and the Choctaws captured, burned, and reduced to captivity the Natchez. However, the panicked, brutal reaction of Governor Étienne Périer had threatened to bring into the conflict other indigenous nations. This was a situation the Ministry of the Navy was keen to avoid.

Throughout his Parisian exile from 1726 to 1731, Bienville had skillfully managed his reputation as a former colonial governor. His return to Louisiana was in fact predicated on the notion that he was more suited for dealing with the "Natives" than Périer had been.[75] Bienville was thus more than ready to oblige with an analysis of the immediate conflict.

For the once and future governor, the last iteration of the Natchez War (1729–1731) served both as a bloody cautionary tale and a vindication of his own past practices of alliance in the Mississippi Valley. The government of Louisiana should, Bienville believed, aim to directly court only a few war leaders who would commit to French interest. This required the skillful distribution of goods. For Bienville (and others who came to similar conclusions), the Natchez War had been caused by a fatal combination of unskillful diplomacy, the misplaced greed of a colonial official, and the misguided thrift of the Company of the Indies. Similar mishandling with the Choctaws could lead to ominous rupture with the confederacy. In a series of much-quoted letters, Bienville offered what has now become part of the standard historical analysis of the Choctaw polity. The confederacy, he claimed, had the capacity to play European rivalries to its own advantage. Any French loss was a British gain. The way to the self-interested Choctaw hearts was therefore trade while the commercial ruthlessness of the Carolina merchants meant they were able to outmaneuver their French counterparts and pose a veritable risk to Louisiana.[76]

Bienville's analysis relied upon the extension of self-interest to British, French, and Choctaw traders equally. French merchants would abandon the Choctaw trade if it was not profitable. Now, however, having direct control over the warehouse and its numerous trade goods, the king, or rather, his governor, had everything he could need to ensure the profitability, and continuity, of the trade. French traders would have to buy their goods from the royal warehouse. The administrators would handpick the buyers and decide upon the quantity of goods they would receive. They would even modulate the prices of the trade goods. Thus, the price of trade goods sold at the royal warehouse, for the Choctaw trade and only for the Choctaw trade, should be lowered.

The question of prices at the royal warehouse had not been seriously examined. The king was, after all, just substituting for the Company of the Indies, even in the company's mercantile activities. But what price was *just* for a king who could not expect to be motivated by profit? Company practice provided a model that prevented too close an investigation into the matter. The navy would just follow the Company of the Indies' precedent by adopting its pricing model. All goods sold in Louisiana were thus subjected to a tariff, conceived rather similarly as those of private merchants. A percentage increase was applied over the "price of the invoice"—the purchase price in France. Goods sold in New Orleans and Mobile would therefore be priced at 50 percent above the price of France; elsewhere, the increase would vary between 70 percent (Natchez) and 100 percent (the Illinois country).

Now, however, prices *did* matter, and greatly. Bienville argued the point: while private traders expected a "gain" that made the trade in the first place, the king did not. Not truly. Only a just compensation.[77] Of course, Bienville's analysis reduced Choctaws, traders, British, and the king to terms that made the political situation of Louisiana understandable to his readers in Versailles. But his proposals arrived on Maurepas's desk at the same time as did reports on the costs of the Second Fox War (1728–1733) in the Pays d'En Haut, as well as the initial accounts on the costs of the Natchez War.[78] As the budget of the navy was perennially tight, Maurepas initially resisted Bienville's suggestions of lowered prices. More revenues stemming from sales in the Louisiana warehouse, the ministers hoped, would mean less transfer of funds from France. Bienville, however, timed his suggestions and reports skillfully. He first confessed he had *already* lowered the price of trade goods, only seeking ministerial approval ex post facto. Bienville had ordered goods for the Choctaw trade sold at 33 percent above the invoice price, rather than at the 50 percent prescribed in the official tariff. By 1735 they were sold at 25 percent above the invoice price. Bienville admitted he had even sold certain goods at a lower price still. By 1736 Maurepas had relented. He admonished Bienville only to do what he could to preserve the tariff.[79]

Bienville, it turns out, was willing to do very little. By 1744 goods for the Choctaw trade were sold in Louisiana at the same price paid by the navy in France. Not only was there no profit to be had for the king, but the royal retailing business of Louisiana was now operating at a loss, having paid the costs of warehousing, transportation, and the inevitable spoilage and theft that ensued. This, then, was the shape royal control took in the Louisiana deerskins trade. Control over the fur trade was managed not by license, but simply by being authorized to purchase at cost. The amounts of goods delivered annually to the Choctaw traders subsequently rose from 45,000 to 60,000 *livres*, in addition to 40,000 *livres* already set aside for diplomatic gifts. Goods that made their way to the Choctaw represented nearly half the value of a typical annual royal supply. As Daniel Usner has remarked, French soldiers were an intrinsic part of the fur trade economy of Louisiana; indeed, their role was fully integrated in the colonial government's policies.

Soldiers (and other government officers) received their salary's worth in goods taken from the royal warehouse, goods which they could then either trade with the Choctaws or, if they lacked the skills, connections, or desire, trade with French merchants for alcohol. These French merchants then resold these European goods to fur traders and collected the furs in payment. Commanding officers also participated in this commerce. In addition to the influence they exerted upon the warehouse keepers, they also probably retained part of their men's wages for various "advances," as was the case elsewhere in the Atlantic World. As in Canada, officers could also partner with skilled traders; throughout the 1740s and 1750s, all the commanders of Fort Tombecbé, the central hub of the Choctaw trade, engaged in fur and skins trading. Warehouse keepers, as we have seen, were evidently poorly equipped to resist orders from post commanders when it came to prices and flow of goods. They were also often part of the trading scheme themselves. Lalande, the warehouse keeper of Tombecbé in the 1740s and the official trading partner of the post commander, was said to understand Choctaw "better than the interpreter himself."[80]

The royal government also continued the Company's policy of selling to the population of New Orleans the flour imported for the soldiers' rations, forcing the troops to provision themselves amongst the Choctaws and the Creeks. The frontier exchange economy thus had a strong government component.

The example of the Choctaw trade, with its merchandise offered at cost to authorized deerskin traders, must have influenced practices at other posts. A sustained attempt by a *commissaire-ordonnateur*, Sébastien-François-Ange Lenormant de Mézy, to enforce the original pricing model inherited from the Company led to angry protest from soldiers or, rather, from their officers. Higher prices for goods amounted to reducing the soldiers' and the officers' pay.[81]

• • •

In the words of one official, the sales at the warehouse "have been very detrimental to the French trade with the colony, by interfering with merchant ships that come [to the colony] and can never sell their goods at the same price as those sold in the king's warehouse."[82] Indeed, the erosion of the sale price for trade goods seems to have yielded the market to the king. Subtle indications gleaned from the archives suggest that indigenous trade goods were not an ordinary component of private vessels' cargo.

Could the smuggling trade supply the colony with much-needed indigenous goods? When envisioning the supply of indigenous allies and neighbors, both the Company of the Indies and Minister Maurepas did not make the mistake of believing trade goods would be easily found. Neither should we. Early modern goods were not easily interchangeable. The impressive variety of cloth identified by countless names, which historians are now struggling to recognize themselves, led merchants, and officials, to value highly the legibility of their goods on a scale of social and political reference provided by the marketplace. A white, "two-points" blanket from Rouen—a usual component of the Choctaw trade—was a specific good, identified by provenance and quality (the "point" system), both inscribed on bills of laden. Even prices located blankets within a recognizable hierarchy of textiles. Even in the best conditions, most of these goods were not easily substituted by others; white blankets from Rouen were compared with other white blankets from Rouen for defects, quality of tincture, density of weaving, and so on. In 1717 the Company of the Indies itself had attempted to find substitute goods for its Canadian beaver monopoly by working with a cloth maker to produce imitations of the British red strouds requested by New France's allies. They proved unpopular. The Company had quickly learned that "[the Indians] are as discriminating about cloth as the most clever merchants." When the Company took over Louisiana, it had therefore contracted directly with manufacturers to ensure the conformity of its Louisiana goods to indigenous trade.[83] Caribbean smugglers may have been hard-pressed to find replacements for these sorts of goods in the markets of Saint-Domingue, Vera Cruz, or Jamaica.

This may explain why, even as the Louisiana trade slowly rose, the colony remained dependent upon the king to be supplied with strategic, highly specialized goods. Even Maurepas's encouragement had the effects of allowing French merchants to focus on carrying the least differentiated types of goods—"flour, wine, spirits, salted meats are assured sales and should form the basis of every cargo."[84] Indigenous trade goods were a riskier trade than foodstuffs and, in any case, merchants would have to compete with the king's lowered prices. Thus, even as the docks of New Orleans harbored dozens of ships, colonial administrators could still lack some, if not all, of the necessary goods upon which they may feel the security of the colony depended. In 1755 the acting *commissaire-ordonnateur* had to report to the commander of Natchitoches that

> as for trade goods, we are lacking them now more than ever, but if our ships arrive this month, or before the 15th of January, we would still have time to supply you with goods we ordinarily have in the warehouse; for the others comprised in your list, you would do well to buy them here from some merchants, such as linen shirts, trade guns, mirrors, belts, silk handkerchief, horse saddles, horse pistols, cotton cloth (*indienne*) earrings and rings, although I would give you with pleasure mirrors and belts should we receive enough of them.[85]

Clearly, the all-important blankets and *limbourg*—the "goods we ordinarily have in the warehouse"—were missing from those goods made available by private merchants. Traders from Georgia and the Carolinas could, and did, provide suitable goods for the Choctaw and Creek trade, but they may have preferred to trade directly with the indigenous population rather than risk imprisonment as smugglers in New Orleans, as happened with four traders from Charleston in 1739.[86] When war with Britain threatened metropolitan supply, fears over the solidity of Louisiana's Native alliances soared. It is probably no coincidence that Governor Vaudreuil, during the War of the Austrian Succession (1740–1748), thought it wise to encourage Choctaw factionalism. Fewer goods in fewer hands could perhaps create a stronger pro-French faction rather than dilute a few goods throughout an entirely disgruntled nation, ready to embrace British interests and attack the colony.[87]

Conclusion

In Louisiana, Louis XV was a retailer. Or rather, the Magasins du Roi, the royal warehouses of the French Mississippi Valley, were operated in his name. It was an incongruous role, one that a king was never truly intended to play.

Perhaps that is the reason why it has gone unnoticed. None of the considerable range of his agents, from exalted minister in Versailles to warehouse keeper in Tombecbé, could have entirely foreseen that role, for the warehouses were neither part of a plan destined to exalt the monarchy nor were they intended to centralize all commercial operations in the Mississippi Valley. It had emerged, in this very specific form, as a product of circumstances, afterthoughts, routines, expediencies, and historical precedents. Merchants and ministers reacted to the end of the Company of the Indies' monopoly and the Natchez War out of ill-defined notions of needs, of the ordinary course of commerce, and of the necessary responsibilities of a king. From these concerns, and from the precedents of logistical and hierarchical routines, emerged the blurry figure of the seller king, so much a creature of routine that few of the administrators who came after Bienville thought it worthy of mention.

Tempting as it may be to constantly measure the inadequacy of empires to meet their considerable rhetorical pretentions, the material lives of things can also illuminate the unexpected forms of control that imperial polities *did* produce and shape in distant and marginal colonies. The sheer concentration of material resources made possible by the routines of the ministry of the navy had effects that went well beyond the utterances of law and official correspondence. However limited they can appear, such resources were out of the reach of most individual merchants. And yet these goods came to Louisiana embedded within a number of claims that pertained to the specific nature of the monarch that allowed many to speak for them, to make them instruments of diplomacy, of paternalistic concern, and of barely disguised self-interest.

The seller king was a conglomerate of voices that certainly did not speak with the intended clarity of purpose found amongst apologists of the French monarch or with the orthodoxy of regulatory texts. Imperial polities could be captured, claimed by many, precisely because it was *made* to be captured, twisted, and transformed. The so-called failures of imperial policy—a heuristic device that has seen much use in the historiography of the French Empire—may be less meaningful than the constraints that emerged from imperial practices. Unforeseen generative effects of policy could constrain both populations and royal agents having to contend with the results. It is through aggregation and channeling of the unexpected that imperial polities insinuated themselves into the interstices of colonial spaces. Permeable to the discourses their institutions produced about themselves, polities made up of aggregates of individual actions and collective effects could enact forms of control that were not wholly located in laws and their apparatus of judicial repression.[88] This may have been especially true in the small society of French Louisiana, confronted as it was with the question of supply and survival. In doing so, imperial polities reorganized lines and interests, forcing actors to redefine what could be, and should be, done. Sometimes despite the wishes of actors located at their heart, imperial polities proposed and produced the conditions of what was commercially and politically possible.

Notes

I would like to thank Joseph Ward, Kathleen DuVal, and my fellow presenters for their comments, critiques, and patience regarding this chapter. It has also benefited from the discerning eye of H. V. Nelles, Anne-Marie McManus, and Juliana Barr. I am also grateful for Catherine Desbarats, who has helped enormously to shape this project over the years.

1. These examples, taken from the following works, give a sense of the past and present historiographical interest in the material culture of French Louisiana: Daniel H. Usner Jr., *Indians, Settlers, and Slaves in a Frontier Exchange Economy* (Chapel Hill: University of North Carolina Press, 1992), 149–74, 197–204; Sophie White, "Slaves' and Poor Whites' Informal Economies in an Atlantic Context," in *Louisiana: Crossroads of the Atlantic World*, ed. Cécile Vidal, 89–102 (Philadelphia: University of Pennsylvania Press, 2014), and Sophie White, *Wild Frenchmen and Frenchified Indians: Material Culture and Race in Colonial Louisiana* (Philadelphia: University of Pennsylvania Press, 2012); N. M. Miller Surrey, *The Commerce of Louisiana during the French Régime, 1699–1763* (New York: Columbia University, 1916); Shannon L. Dawdy, *Building the Devil's Empire: French Colonial New Orleans* (Chicago: Chicago University Press, 2008), 109–10; Richard White, *The Roots of Dependency, Subsistence, Environment and Social Change among the Choctaws, Pawnees, and Navajos* (Lincoln: University of Nebraska Press, 1988); Kathleen DuVal, *The Native Ground: Indians and Colonists in the Heart of the Continent* (Philadelphia: University of Pennsylvania Press, 2006), 75–88; Helen Sophie Burton and F. Todd Smith, *Colonial Natchitoches: A Creole Community on the Louisiana-Texas Frontier* (College Station: Texas A&M University Press, 2008), 105–27; Marcel Moussette and Gregory A. Waselkov, *Archéologie de l'Amérique coloniale française* (Montreal: Lévesque Éditeur, 2013); and Russell-Aurore Bouchard, *Les armes de traite* (Sillery, Quebec, Canada: Boréal, 1976). On the Curaçao trade, see Records of the Superior Council of Louisiana (hereafter RSCL), July 7, 1747, 1747070701, New Orleans. On the Pensacola trade, see RSCL, 1748120701, New Orleans.

2. On the relationship between political history, imperial history, and Atlantic history, see Alison Games, "Atlantic History: Definitions, Challenges and Opportunities," *American Historical Review* 111, no. 3 (June 2006): 741–57, and Elizabeth Mancke, "Polity Formation and Atlantic Political Narratives," in *Oxford Handbook on the Atlantic World, c.1450–1820*, ed. Philip D. Morgan and Nicholas Canny, 382–99 (Oxford: Oxford University Press, 2011). Cathy Matson, "A House of Many Mansions: Some Thoughts on the Field of Economic History," in *The Economy of Early America: Historical Perspectives and New Directions*, ed. Cathy Matson, 1–70 (University Park: Pennsylvania State University Press, 2006).

3. One of the strongest programmatic versions of the Atlantic World as "decentralized" and "self-organized" is David Hancock, "The Triumphs of Mercury: Connection and Control in the Emerging Atlantic Economy," in *Soundings in Atlantic History: Latent Structures and Intellectual Currents, 1500–1830*, ed. B. Bailyn and P. Denault, 1–42 (Cambridge, MA: Harvard University Press, 2009); Cathy D. Matson and Peter S. Onuf, *A Union of Interests: Political and Economic Thought in Revolutionary America* (Lawrence: Kansas University Press, 1990). For examples of enterprising Native polities, see Pekka Hämäläinen, *The Comanche Empire* (New Haven, CT: Yale University Press, 2009), and Kathleen DuVal, *The Native Ground: Indians and Colonists in the Heart of the Continent* (Philadelphia: University of Pennsylvania Press, 2007). For the classical study linking political demands and mercantilism in the French Empire, see Charles Frostin, "Histoire de l'autonomisme colon de la partie française de St. Domingue aux XVIIe et XVIIIe siècles: Contribution à l'étude du sentiment américain d'independance" (PhD diss., Service de Reproduction des Thèses, Université de Lille, 1973).

4. This short definition, useful for France, is borrowed from Jean Tarrade, *Le commerce colonial de la France à la fin de l'Ancien Régime: L'évolution de 'l'Exclusif' de 1763 à 1789* (Paris: PUF, 1972), 87. For a panoramic view of mercantilism and the perennial difficulty of its definition, see Lars Magnusson, *Mercantilism: The Shaping of an Economic Language* (London: Routledge, 1994). See also Pernille Roge and Sophus Reinert, "Introduction: The Political Economy of Empire," in *The Political Economy of Empire in the Early Modern World*, ed. P. Røge and S. Reinert, 1–7 (Basingstoke, UK: Palgrave-Macmillan, 2013).

5. See remarks by Mark G. Hanna, "Smuggling," in *Oxford Bibliographies in Atlantic History*, http://www.oxfordbibliographies.com. See also Wim Klooster, "Inter-Imperial Smuggling in the Americas, 1600–1800," in *Soundings in Atlantic History: Latent Structures and Intellectual Currents, 1500–1830*, ed. B. Bailyn and P. Denault, 141–80 (Cambridge, MA: Harvard University Press, 2009). On the French Empire, J. Pritchard, *In Search of Empire: The French in the Americas, 1670–1730* (Cambridge: Cambridge University Press, 2004), and the remarks by Brett Rushforth and Chris Hodson, "Absolutely Atlantic: Colonialism and the Early Modern French State in Recent Historiography," *History Compass* 7 (2009): 1–17.

6. For examples of "opportunistic," see for Louisiana, Shannon L. Dawdy, *Building the Devil's Empire: French Colonial New Orleans* (Chicago: Chicago University Press, 2008), 244; elsewhere, Michael J. Jarvis, *In the Eye of All Trade: Bermuda, Bermudians and the Maritime Atlantic World, 1680–1783* (Chapel Hill: University of North Carolina Press, 2010), 43. For examples of "entrepreneurial," see Edwin J. Perkins, "The Entrepreneurial Spirit in Colonial America: The Foundations of Modern Business History," *Business History Review* 63 (Spring 1989): 160–86 and, for Louisiana, Robert M. Morrissey, *Empire by Collaboration: Indians, Colonists and Governments in Colonial Illinois Country* (Philadelphia: University of Pennsylvania Press, 2015), 144. The concept of "frontier exchange economy" is from Usner Jr., *Indians, Settlers, and Slaves*, 5–9, 147–50. See also Ralph Lee Woodward, "Spanish Commercial Policy in Louisiana, 1763–1803," *Louisiana History* 44, no. 2 (Spring 2003): 133–64.

7. See the remarks by Steve Pincus in "Reconfiguring the British Empire," *William and Mary Quarterly*, 3rd ser., 69, no. 1 (2012): 63–70. For an overview of the "negotiated empires" paradigm, see Christine Daniels and Michael V. Kennedy, eds., *Negotiated Empires: Centers and Peripheries in the Americas, 1500–1820* (New York: Routledge, 2002).

8. See, for instance, Alan Taylor, *William Cooper's Town: Power and Persuasion on the Frontier of the Early American Republic* (New York: Vintage Books, 1996), 80–100; Douglas M. Bradburn and John C. Coombs, "Smoke and Mirrors: Reinterpreting the Society

and Economy of the Seventeenth-Century Chesapeake," *Atlantic Studies* 3, no. 2 (October 2006): 131–57.

9. Despite a growing number of studies on the matter, there remains a split between the cultural study of consumption of specific goods "on the spot" and the manner in which these specific goods were shipped. See Jan de Vries, "Between Purchasing Power and the World of Goods: Understanding the Household Economy in Early Modern Europe," in *Consumption and the World of Goods*, ed. John Brewer and Roy Porter, 85–132 (London: Routledge, 1993).

10. A concise presentation of the enormous historiography over the question of luxury can be found in Maxine Berg, "Luxury, the Luxury Trades, and the Roots of Industrial Growth: A Global Perspective," in *The Oxford Handbook of the History of Consumption*, ed. Frank Trentmann, 173–91 (Oxford: Oxford University Press, 2012). See also Istvan Hont, "The Early Enlightenment Debate on Commerce and Luxury," in *The Cambridge History of Eighteenth-Century Political Thought*, ed. Mark Goldie and Robert Wokler, 377–418 (Cambridge: Cambridge University Press, 2006).

11. Matson, "Some Thoughts," 31–40; Hancock, "Triumph of Mercury," 112–40.

12. On the Mississippi "Bubble," the speculative and colonial frenzy that presided upon the first considerable effort to settle Louisiana, see Edgar Faure, *La banqueroute de Law: 17 juillet 1720* (Paris: Gallimard, 1977), and François Velde, "Was John Law's System a Bubble? The Mississippi Bubble Revisited," in *The Origins and Development of Financial Markets and Institutions: From the Seventeenth Century to the Present*, ed. Jeremy Atack and Larry Neal, 99–120 (Cambridge: Cambridge University Press, 2009). Marcel Giraud estimates the number of migrants at 6,760, of whom as many as 3,500 may have died during the crossing and after their arrival. Marcel Giraud, *Histoire de la Louisiane française*, 5 vols (Paris: Presses Universitaires de France / L'Harmattan, 1953–2012), 4:168–82.

13. On Company-States and their jurisdictional claims, see Philip J. Stern, *The Company-State: Corporate Sovereignty and the Early Modern Foundations of the British Empire in India* (London: Oxford University Press, 2011). The canonical narrative of company rule in French Louisiana is Marcel Giraud, *Histoire de la Louisiane française*, 5 vols. For a general overview of the Company of the Indies, see Philippe Haudrère, *La Compagnie des Indes*, 2nd ed. (Paris: Les Indes Savantes, 2005).

14. Gérard Le Bouëdec, "Les approvisionnements de la Compagnie des Indes (1737–1770): L'horizon géographique lorientais," *Histoire, économie et société* 1, no. 3 (1982): 377–412.

15. "État des prix des marchandises qui ont esté fournies par la Compagnie des Indes avec la notte des lieux d'où ces marchandises doivent estre tirées pour les avoir de première main, et les noms des Correspondants de ladite Compagnie...," Archives Nationales d'Outre-Mer (France) (hereafter ANOM) F1^A, 30, 349.

16. Arnaud Balvay, "The French and the Natchez: A Failed Encounter," in *French and Indians in the Heart of North America, 1630–1815*, ed. Robert Englebert and Guillaume Teasdale, 138–58 (East Lansing: Michigan State University Press, 2013); Sophie White, "Massacre, Mardi Gras and Torture in Early New Orleans," *William and Mary Quarterly*, 3rd ser., 70, no. 3 (July 2013): 497–538.

17. Arrêt du 23 janvier 1731, ANOM C13^A, 13, 247.

18. Étienne Périer to Jean-Frédéric Phélypeaux, comte de Maurepas, December 10, 1731, ANOM C13^A, 13, 57.

19. Giraud, *A History of French Louisiana*, 5:431; Thomas Wien, "Selling Beaver Skins in North America and Europe, 1720–1760: The Uses of Fur-Trade Imperialism," *Journal of the Canadian Historical Association* 1, no. 1 (1990): 298–300.

20. See, for instance, the testimony of company employee Marc-Antoine Caillot in *A Company Man: The Remarkable French-Atlantic Voyage of a Clerk for the Company of the Indies*, ed. Erin M. Greenwald, trans. Teri F. Chalmers, 123 (New Orleans: The Historic New Orleans Collection, 2013).

21. Dawdy, *Devil's Empire*, 123–25. For a different view of MacMahon, see Giraud, *History of Louisiana*, 5:111–12.

22. Haudrère, *Compagnie des Indes*, 1:391–401.

23. Charles Pradel to his brother, September 1, 1729, Historic New Orleans Collections, New Orleans, Collection Pradel; Giraud, *History of French Louisiana*, 5:149.

24. Procès-verbal de délibération de l'assemblée générale d'administration de la Compagnie des Indes, ANOM, C13^A, 13:249.

25. While tonnage is not always possible to determine, the name given to the vessels (*barque, goëlette, bateau*) all hint at the small crafts ordinarily used for the inter-Caribbean trade. See, for some mentions, see the goëlette *Aimable Thérèse* (seventy tons), RLSC 1763122001; the bateau *Notre-Dame-de-Conception* (seventy tons) RLSC 1763041402; the bateau *Nuestra Señora de Guadalupe* (bought from Campeche, seventy tons), RLSC 1758042401; the bateau *Saint-Joseph* (forty tons), RLSC 1759042301, and the bateau *Nouvelle-Orléans* (sixty tons), RLSC 1758031502). Shannon Dawdy's characterization of the legal transatlantic trade as only a minority of New Orleans' ordinary commercial liaisons relies on a measure of *frequence* (the number of times ships of varying origins docked in New Orleans) rather than worth (the value of the cargo) or tonnage (the carrying capacity of these ships). Ships plying the Caribbean were notably smaller than transatlantic vessels and carried fewer amounts of goods on average. Until we have a better estimate of the content of inter-imperial traders, it seems difficult to ascribe such evaluation based on the number of voyages rather than on value.

26. This average (n=53) is calculated from Mémoire des hommes, Armement des navires de la Compagnie des Indes, http://www.memoiredeshommes.sga.defense.gouv.fr/fr/article.php?larub=28&titre=armements-des-navires (last accessed June 27, 2016). The estimate of "metropolitan" ships sent from France is based, for La Rochelle, on Archives Départementales de Charente-Maritime, B 245 to B 259 (n=147), from Bordeaux, on Archives Départementales de Gironde, 6B 93 to 6B 103 (n=45).

27. Bed and linen, valued anywhere from 50 to 600 *livres*, consistently represented the most valued item in households of the French Atlantic World. These are only crude indications in the current absence of a systematic treatment of inventories scattered in the many repositories of Louisiana archives. For an overview, see J. A. Dickinson, C. Dessureault, and T. Wien, "Living Standards of Norman and Canadian Peasants, 1690–1835," in *Material Culture: Consumption, Life Style, Standard of Living (16th-19th Centuries)*, ed. A. Schuurman and L. S. Walsh, 95–114 (Milan: Università Bocconi, 1994). Lois Green Carr and Lorena S. Walsh, "The Standard of Living in the Colonial Chesapeake," *William and Mary Quarterly*, 3rd ser., 45, no. 1 (January 1988): 135–59; and Carole Shammas, "Changes in English and Anglo-American Consumption from 1550–1800," in *Culture and Consumption: The World of*

Goods, ed. John Brewer and Roy Porter, 177–205 (London: Routledge, 1993). The wealthiest households of Paris were valued at 50,000 *livres*. Annick Pardailhé-Galabrun, *La naissance de l'intime: 3000 foyers parisiens, XVIIe-XVIIIe siècles* (Paris: Presses Universitaires de France, 1988). The majority of analyses of inventories in Louisiana concern the Illinois Country. See Cécile Vidal, "Les implantations françaises au pays des Illinois au XVIIIe siècle, 1699–1765" (PhD diss., École des Hautes Études en Sciences Sociales, 1995), esp. 589–600. According to G. M. Hall's estimates, 5,761 African men, women, and children were sent to Louisiana by the Company of the Indies. G. M. Hall, *Africans in Colonial Louisiana: The Development of Afro-Creole Culture in the Eighteenth Century* (Baton Rouge: Louisiana State University Press, 1992), 60–63.

28. See the description of the news of royal retrocession in Marc-Antoine Caillot, *A Company Man: The Remarkable French-Atlantic Voyage of a Clerk for the Company of the Indies*, ed. Erin M. Greenwald, 123 (New Orleans: The Historic New Orleans Collection, 2013).

29. Colin Jones and Rebecca Spang, "Sans-culottes, sans café, sans tabac: Shifting Realms of Necessity and Luxury in Eighteenth-Century France," in *Consumers and Luxury: Consumer Culture in Europe, 1650–1850*, ed. Maxine Berg and Helen Clifford, 37–62 (Manchester, UK: Manchester University Press, 1999). See also the important reminders about cultural notions of comforts in Daniel Vickers, "The Northern Colonies: Economy and Society, 1600–1775," in *The Cambridge Economic History of the United States*, vol. 1, *The Colonial Era*, ed. S. L. Engerman and R. E. Gallman, 209–48 (Cambridge: Cambridge University Press, 1996). On Frenchness, see White, *Wild Frenchmen*, and Cécile Vidal, "'Nos ancêtres les Gaulois' ou la francité dans le laboratoire colonial (XVIe-XIXe siècle)," in *Français? La nation en débat entre colonies et métropole*, ed. Cécile Vidal, 1–14 (*XVIe-XIXe siècle*) (Paris: Éditions de l'EHESS, 2014); John E. Crowley, *The Invention of Comfort: Sensibilities and Design in Early Modern Britain and Early America* (Baltimore: Johns Hopkins University Press, 2001).

30. Alexandre Dubé, "Les biens publics: Culture politique de la Louisiane française, 1730–1770" (PhD diss., McGill University, 2010), 504–71; Hervé Drévillon, *L'impôt du sang. Le métier des armes sous Louis XIV* (Paris: Taillandier, 2005).

31. On the need for captives, see *Mémoire* in ANOM DFC 12; *Mémoire*, ANOM C13^C, 1. See also Extrait, December 6, 1730, ANOM C2, 24.

32. O'Neill, *Church and State*, 153–58; Dawdy, *Devil's Empire*, 123–24.

33. Délibération de la Compagnie concernant la retrocession faite au Roi de la concession de la Louisiane, 22 janvier 1731, in *Recueil ou collection des titres, édits, déclarations, arrêts, règlements et autres pièces concernant la Compagnie des Indes orientales établie au mois d'août 1664*, ed. Dernis (Paris: Boudet, 1755), 4:187–89.

34. Giraud, *History of Louisiana*, 5:494.

35. Florent Quellier, "Culture de la faim et pratiques alimentaires à l'époque moderne," in *Profusion et pénurie: Les hommes face à leurs besoins alimentaires*, ed. Martin Bruegel, 85–101 (Rennes, France: Presses Universitaires de Rennes, 2009).

36. Georges Monval, *Le Laquais de Molière* (Paris: Stock, 1887), 90–91; Inventaire après-décès, M. de Saint-Léon, Archives Nationales (France), Paris, Minutier Central, MC/ ET/LIII/304.

37. État des prix des marchandises qui ont esté fournies par la Compagnie des Indes avec la notte des lieux d'où ces marchandises doivent estre tirées pour les avoir de première main, ANOM F1^A, 30, 349; Compte que rend le Sieur de Saint-Léon, ANOM F1^A, 30, 369;

Soumission pour la fourniture des effets destinez pour la Colonie de la Louisiane pendant 1732, June 10, 1732, ANOM F1^A, 30, 382. Government freight contract also meant that the weight of the king in Louisiana's economy cannot be detected simply by tracking the movement of the king's flûte.

38. Steven L. Kaplan, *Bread, Politics and Political Economy in the Reign of Louis XV* (The Hague: Martinus Nijhoff, 1976); Judith A Miller, *Mastering the Market: The State and the Grain Trade in Northern France, 1700–1860* (Cambridge: Cambridge University Press, 1999).

39. Calais, Dieppe, Le Havre, Rouen Honfleur, Saint-Malo, Morlaix, Brest, La Rochelle, Nantes, Bordeaux, Bayonne, and Sète, *Lettre patentes du roy portant règlement pour le commerce des colonies françoises*, April 1717 (Paris: Veuve Muguet, Hubert Muguet, and de la Tour, 1717).

40. Maurice Filion, *La pensée et l'action coloniales de Maurepas vis-à-vis du Canada, 1723–1749: L'âge d'or de la colonie* (Montreal: Leméac, 1972); Catherine Larrère, "Montesquieu: Commerce de luxe et commerce d'économie," in *Lectures de l'Esprit des lois*, ed. Céline Spector and Thierry Hoquet, 467–84 (Bordeaux: Presses Universitaires de Bordeaux, 2004).

41. Jean-Frédéric Phélypeaux, comte de Maurepas to d'Abbadie, April 30, 1731, ADCM, 41 ETP, 6. Economists would qualify Maurepas's actions as lowering transaction costs, one of the main functions of state institutions according to its foremost thinker, Douglass North. See his "Institutions, Transaction Costs, and the Rise of Merchant Empires," in *The Political Economy of Merchant Empires: State Power and World Trade, 1350–1750*, ed. James Tracy, 22–40 (Cambridge: Cambridge University Press, 1991); Classen to the Chamber of Commerce of La Rochelle, August 24, 1731, Archives Départementales de la Charente-Maritime [ADCM], Chambre de Commerce de La Rochelle, 41 ETP 79, 1263; and John G. Clark, *New Orleans, 1718–1812: An Economic History* (Baton Rouge: Louisiana State University Press, 1970), 68–69.

42. Jacob M. Price, *France and the Chesapeake: A History of the French Tobacco Monopoly, 1674–1791* (Ann Arbor: University of Michigan Press, 1971), 329–57.

43. Employ des fonds dûs au Roy par la Compagnie, August 28, 1736, ANOM C13^A, 21. Numerous orders of payment for this subsidy can be found in ANOM F1^A, 39–48. The subsidy was later split between 20 livres per ton of European goods brought to the colony, and 20 livres per ton of colonial goods brought back to France.

44. On the *Saint-Paul*, see Jean-Frédéric Phélypeaux, comte de Maurepas to Edme-Gatien Salmon, September 13 1731, ANOM B 55; Maurepas to Beauharnois, September 15 1731, ANOM B 55; Maurepas to Philibert Orry, August 12, 1732, ANOM B 56; and Maurepas to Morat, August 12, 1732, ANOM B 56.

45. On various estimates of profitability, see the useful analysis of Guillaume Daudin, *Commerce et prospérité: La France au XVIIIe siècle* (Paris: Presses de l'Université Paris-Sorbonne, 2005). On the character of eighteenth-century accounting and the measure of profit, see Pierre Gervais, "A Merchant or a French Atlantic? Eighteenth-Century Account Books as Narratives of a Transnational Merchant Political Economy," *French History* 25, no. 1 (March 2011), 28–47; Pierre Gervais, "Crédit et filières marchandes au XVIIIe siècle," *Annales: Histoire, Sciences sociales* 67, no. 4 (October–December 2012), 1011–48; Khalil Saadani, *La Louisiane française dans l'impasse, 1731–1743* (Paris: L'Harmattan, 2008), 137–38.

46. On the dynamics of prices in the Caribbean markets, see Dale Miquelon, *Dugard of Rouen: French Trade to Canada and the West Indies, 1729–1770* (Montreal: McGill-Queen's University Press, 1978), 91.

47. Crémont to Jean-Frédéric Phélypeaux, comte de Maurepas, February 24 1734, ANOM C13^A 18; J. G. Clark, *New Orleans*, 72–75.

48. Price, *France and the Chesapeake*, 338.

49. James Pritchard, *Louis XV's Navy, 1748–1762: A Study of Organization and Administration* (Montreal: McGill-Queen's University Press, 1987); Paul W. Bamford, *Forests and French Sea Power* (Toronto: University of Toronto Press, 1956); Jean-François Claverie, *Les marchés de fournitures et de travaux dans la marine royale au XVIIIe siècle, au port de Rochefort* (Villeneuve-d'Ascq, France: Presses Universitaires du Septentrion, 2002).

50. Alain Guéry, "Le roi dépensier: Le don, la contrainte et l'origine du système financier de la monarchie française d'Ancien Régime," *Annales: Histoire, Sciences Sociales* 39, no. 6 (1984): 1241–69; Natalie Zemon Davis, *The Gift in Sixteenth-Century France* (Madison: University of Wisconsin Press, 2000), 142–66.

51. Steven L. Kaplan, "Lean Years, Fat Years: The 'Community' Granary System and the Search for Abundance in Eighteenth-Century Paris," *French Historical Studies* 10, no. 2 (Autumn 1977): 197–230; Louise Dechêne, *Le Partage des subsistances au Canada sous le régime français* (Montreal: Boréal, 1994), 117.

52. See the description of the process in Dumont de Montigny, *The Memoir of Lieutenant Dumont, 1715–1747: A Sojourner in the French Atlantic*, ed. Gordon M. Sayre and Carla Zecher, trans. Gordon M. Sayre, 374–76 (Chapel Hill: University of North Carolina Press, 2012). On the existence of billets from the warehouse keeper, see Mémoire sur la Louisiane, c. 1750, Bibliothèque Nationale (France) (hereafter BNF), Joly de Fleury, 1726, 125–27.

53. This crude estimate is based on the comparison of the census of 1737 (1,722 inhabitants for New Orleans) and the 1763 census, which records 383 households for New Orleans, respectively, for a population of 2,524. For the 1763 census, see Archivo General de India, Santo Domingo, Legajo 2595. Paul Lachance, "The Growth of the Free and Slave Populations of French Colonial Louisiana," in *French Colonial Louisiana and the Atlantic World*, ed. Bradley G. Bond, 204–43 (Baton Rouge: Louisiana State University Press, 2005).

54. For the following analysis, see the *bordereaux* in ANOM C13^A, 31, 213–247; 33, 251–92; 35, 228–51; 36, 201–05. My thanks to Pierre Gervais for the observation about the possible meaning of names included in the *bordereaux*. "État des rations extraordinaires délivrées à divers officiers . . . pour l'année 1744," December 26, 1744, ANOM C13^A, 28: 309; for the identification of Picquery: Pierre de Rigaud de Vaudreuil to Antoine-Louis Rouillé, January 28, 1752, ANOM C13^A, 36: 49.

55. Transaction between André Gerbe and Balthazar de Ponfrac, chevalier de Mazan, May 8, 1747, RSCL 1747050805.

56. The following amounts were recorded for these years: 1733: 144,610 *livres*; 1744: 190,599 *livres*; 1752: 393,567 *livres*. Jean-Frédéric Phélypeaux, comte de Maurepas to Edme-Gatien Salmon, August 25, 1735, ANOM C13^A, 20: 237–37v; Sébastien-François-Ange Lenormant de Mézy to the minister, December 30, 1744, ANOM C13^A, 28; "La Louisiane," ANOM F1^A, 37.

57. Colonial accounts, 1731–1744, ANOM F3 159.

58. Memorandum by Lenormant de Mézy, March 21 1747, ANOM C13^A, 31; Lenormant to the minister, December 30, 1744, ANOM C13^A, 28; BNF Joly de Fleury 1726, 127. For examples of colonial retail and bulk merchants, see J. G. Clark, *New Orleans*, 100–105; Sophie White, "'A Baser Commerce': Retailing, Class, and Gender in French Colonial New Orleans," *William and Mary Quarterly*, 3rd ser., 63, no. 3 (July 2006): 517–50.

59. These were Maurice Testar and Augustin Chantalou. J. G. Clark estimates the value of their monthly cargos between 3,000 *livres* and 5,000 *livres* per month. J. G. Clark, *New Orleans*, 101.

60. From the estimates of J. G. Clark, *New Orleans*, revised by S. L. Dawdy, "La ville sauvage: 'Enlightened' Colonialism and Creole Improvisation in New Orleans, 1699–1769" (PhD diss., University of Michigan, 2003), 133.

61. Except perhaps in deerskins, often accepted for payment. Vaudreuil to Frédéric Phélypeaux, comte de Maurepas, March 20 1748, ANOM C13^A, 32:37.

62. Lenormant de Mézy, BNF Joly de Fleury, 1726, 125. For an example of term payment upon "the arrival of the ships," Vaudreuil to Frédéric Phélypeaux, comte de Maurepas, Vaudreuil Papers, November 4, 1745, Huntington Library, San Marino, CA.

63. Frédéric Phélypeaux, comte de Maurepas to Fagon, October 17 1742, ANOM B, 75:167; Lenormant de Mézy to Maurepas, December 26, 1744, ANOM C13^A, 28:304.

64. Lenormant de Mézy to Frédéric Phélypeaux, comte de Maurepas, October 22, 1745, ANOM C13^A, 29:142.

65. Jean-Baptiste Lemoyne de Bienville and Edme-Gatien Salmon to Frédéric Phélypeaux, comte de Maurepas, March 25, 1742, ANOM C13^A, 27:19; d'Abbadie to Étienne-François de Choiseul, June 6, 1764, ANOM C13^A 44. These sales at discounted price cannot be easily traced through the nominative accounts and may have been recorded under "retail."

66. Jean-Frédéric Phélypeaux, comte de Maurepas to Jean-Baptiste Lemoyne de Bienville and Edme-Gatien Salmon, March 24, 1738, ANOM B, 66: 7; Maurepas to Fagon, October 29, 1742, ANOM B, 75: 181.

67. Marginalia in Maurepas's hand in Dossier La Fontaine, April 1735, ANOM E 246. In Canada, indeed, wheat was reputed to be loaned to the inhabitants, and hence to be repaid at the following harvest. Dechêne, *Partage des subsistances*, 112–18.

68. Richard White, *The Middle Ground: Indians, Empires and Republics in the Great Lakes Region, 1650–1815* (Cambridge: Cambridge University Press, 1991), 50–142.

69. Charles Edwards O'Neill, *Church and State in French Colonial Louisiana: Policy and Politics to 1732* (New Haven, CT: Yale University Press, 1966), 185–218.

70. "In order to preserve their alliance and friendship in favor of the settlers who would establish their residence next to theirs," Procès-verbal de délibération de l'assemblée générale, ANOM C13^A, 13:249.

71. Journal du sieur Régis du Roullet, Newberry Library (hereafter NL), Ruggles Collection, Chicago, IL, 417.

72. Bernard Diron d'Artaguiette to Frédéric Phélypeaux, comte de Maurepas, January 10, 1731, ANOM C13^A, 13.

73. See entries for September 1729 from the Journal du sieur Régis du Roullet. . . , NL, Ruggles 417. See also Jean-Baptiste Lemoyne de Bienville and Edme-Gatien Salmon to Frédéric Phélypeaux, comte de Maurepas, September 16, 1736, ANOM C13^A, 20.

74. Étienne Périer to Frédéric Phélypeaux, comte de Maurepas, April 6, 1732, ANOM C13^A, 14.

75. Mémoire du Roi for Jean-Baptiste Lemoyne de Bienville, September 2, 1732, ANOM B, 57:796. See also "La Louisiane," Dossier Lemoyne de Bienville, July 1, 1742, ANOM E 977.

76. This paragraph and the following draw from Bienville's and Maurepas's letters: Maurepas to Jean-Baptiste Lemoyne de Bienville, 1732, ANOM, B, 57:853; Bienville and

Edme-Gatien Salmon to Maurepas, May 13 1733, ANOM C13^A 16: 68–70; Bienville and Salmon to Maurepas, April 5, 1734, ANOM C13^A 18:63; Bienville to Maurepas, August 1734, ANOM C13^A, 18:180; Bienville and Salmon to Maurepas, April 2, 1735, ANOM C13^A, 20:25; Bienville to Maurepas, June 26, 1736, ANOM C13^A, 21:175; Maurepas to Bienville, November 11, 1736, ANOM B 64:529v; Bienville and Salmon to Maurepas, April 12, 1735, ANOM C13^A, 20:25v; Bienville and Salmon to Maurepas, April 5, 1734, ANOM C13^A 18:63–64; Bienville and Salmon to Maurepas, June 14, 1736, ANOM C13^A 21:41; Maurepas to Bienville and Salmon, August 17, 1736, ANOM B 64:514.

77. Jean-Baptiste Lemoyne de Bienville and Edme-Gatien Salmon to Frédéric Phélypeaux, comte de Maurepas, April 5, 1734, ANOM C13^A:18, 63; Bienville and Salmon to Frédéric Phélypeaux, comte de Maurepas, June 14, 1736, ANOM C13^A 21:41.

78. R. David Edmunds and Joseph L. Peyser, *The Fox Wars: The Mesquakie Challenge to New France* (Norman: University of Oklahoma Press, 2014); Frédéric Phélypeaux, comte de Maurepas to Jean-Baptiste Lemoyne de Bienville, 1734, ANOM B, 61:655.

79. Jean-Baptiste Lemoyne de Bienville and Edme-Gatien Salmon to Frédéric Phélypeaux, comte de Maurepas, April 5, 1734, ANOM C13^A, 18:63–64; Bienville and Salmon to Maurepas, April 12, 1735, ANOM C13^A, 20:25v; Bienville and Salmon to Maurepas, June 14, 1736, ANOM C13^A, 21:41; Maurepas to Bienville and Salmon, August 17, 1736, ANOM B, 64:514.

80. Vaudreuil to de Pierre Annibal de Velle, February 29 1744, Vandreuil Papers, Huntington Library, San Marino, CA.

81. Vaudreuil to Frédéric Phélypeaux, comte de Maurepas, January 6, 1746, ANOM C13^A, 30: 15–15v; Lenormant de Mézy to Maurepas, April 9 1747, ANOM C13^A, 31: 125.

82. BNF Joly de Fleury 1726, 127. See also various commentators agreeing on this point: AN Marine G56, folio 180; Fabry de Bruyère, BNF Ms Fr 12 224; Governor Kerlérec, ANOM C13^A, 56: 249. Certainly, prices do not tell the whole story. The king's 25 percent may not be different from the merchant's 25 percent. Yet the king was dealing directly with the manufacturers of many of these goods, whom he usually forced to absorb the cost of transportation to the arsenal. This may have reflected a higher invoice price for goods sold to the navy than for goods sold to merchants.

83. On the "convention economics" of the ancien régime, see Jean-Yves Grenier, *L'économie d'Ancien Régime: Un monde de l'échange et de l'incertitude* (Paris: Albin Michel, 1996); Grenier, "Une économie de l'identification: Juste prix et ordre des marchandises dans l'Ancien Régime," in *La qualité des produits en France, XVIIIe—XXe siècle*, ed. Alexandre Stanziani, 25–53 (Paris: Belin, 2004); Philippe Minard, "Facing Uncertainty: Markets, Norms and Conventions in the Eighteenth Century," in *Regulating the British Economy, 1660–1850*, ed. Perry Gauci (Farnham, UK: Ashgate, 2011). On indigenous demand and consumption, see Laura Johnson, "Goods to Clothe Themselves: Native Consumers and Native Images on the Pennsylvania Trading Frontier, 1712–1760," *Winterthur Portfolio* 43, no. 1 (2009): 115–40; Daniel K. Richter, *Facing East from Indian Country: A Native History of Early America* (Cambridge, MA: Harvard University Press, 2001), 177–79; Peter Mancall, Joshua Rosenbloom, and Thomas Weiss, "Indians and the Economy of Eighteenth-Century Carolina," in *The Atlantic Economy during the Seventeenth and Eighteenth Centuries: Organization, Operation, Practice, and Personnel*, ed. Peter Coclanis, 297–322 (Columbia: University of South Carolina Press, 2005).

84. AN Marine G 51 fol. 454. Shannon Dawdy suggests that colonial officials were rather seeking to extract more goods from the imperial administration as a manipulation rather than as a structural problem, as I am suggesting here. Shannon Lee Dawdy, "La Nouvelle-Orléans au XVIIIe siècle: Courants d'échanges dans le monde caraïbe," *Annales: Histoire, sciences sociales* 62, no. 3 (2007): 663–85.

85. Vincent-Guillaume Le Sénéchal d'Auberville to César de Blanc, December 15, 1755, Historic New Orleans Collections, d'Auberville Papers, Folder 5, New Orleans.

86. Vaudreuil to Frédéric Phélypeaux, comte de Maurepas, December 29, 1744, Vandreuil Papers, Huntington Library; "True Relation of Godfrey Harding and Florence Eggin," NL, Ayer 271.

87. Patricia Galloway, "Choctaw Factionalism and Civil War, 1746–1750," in *Practicing Ethnohistory: Mining Archives, Hearing Testimony, Constructing Narrative* (Lincoln: University of Nebraska Press, 2006); Vaudreuil to Frédéric Phélypeaux, comte de Maurepas, February 12, 1744, Vandreuil Papers, Huntington Library.

88. Catherine Desbarats, "La question de l'État en Nouvelle-France," in *Mémoires de Nouvelle-France. De France en elle-France*, ed. Ph. Joutard and Thomas Wien, 187–98 (Rennes, France: Presses Universitaires de Rennes, 2005). See for instance, Brett Rushforth, "Insinuating Empire: Indians, Smugglers, and the Imperial Geography of Eighteenth-Century Montreal," in *Frontier Cities: Encounters at the Crossroads of Empire*, ed. J. Gitlin, B. Berglund, and A. Arenson, 49–65 (Philadelphia: University of Pennsylvania Press, 2012).

"A WELL GROUNDED CHRISTIAN COMMONWEALTH"

Nicholas Trott of South Carolina and Britain's Atlantic Empire

Travis Glasson

Nicholas Trott (1663?–1740) served as chief justice of South Carolina for sixteen years in the early eighteenth century. Trott was closely identified with the province's increasingly disliked proprietary government and was a conspicuously divisive figure in local politics. Best known for his place in South Carolina history, this chapter situates Trott's career in a wider frame. It considers, first, Trott's family and his emergence from a seventeenth-century milieu shaped by transatlantic commerce and political contestation. The Trotts, who had interests in London, Bermuda, the Bahamas, and South Carolina, managed to weather the political storms of the second half of the seventeenth century to build economic and political networks that spanned the Atlantic Ocean. Second, it traces Trott's connections to a group of like-minded Anglican activists who hoped to make the Church of England a stronger presence in the colonies after 1688. While Trott's devotion to Carolina's proprietary government seems primarily due to careerism, his attachment to the Church of England was apparently sincere and manifested in multiple forms. Trott's partisan religious activism, like other aspects of his career, was also based on the careful cultivation of transatlantic networks. Trott's career illustrates the ways that early Carolina politics echoed and intersected with Restoration-era disputes about the nature of imperial governance and then with wider efforts to reform the English Empire on political and religious lines following the Glorious Revolution.

Nicholas Trott was born, according to a published obituary, on January 19, 1662/3 and died in South Carolina on January 21, 1740.[1] He began his career as a colonial officeholder in 1693, when he was appointed as Bermuda's attorney general and then as secretary to that colony's council.[2] He arrived in South Carolina in 1699 to take up the offices of attorney general, advocate general in the local Admiralty court, and naval officer in charge of registering shipping in and out of Charleston.[3] Carolina's proprietors may have dispatched Trott to remedy endemic problems with record keeping in the province, which were revealed in 1697 and 1698 when the newly created Board of Trade twice demanded written information on the laws in force in the colony.[4] After his arrival, Trott quickly became involved in the factional politics of the young colony, and Governor Joseph Blake temporarily suspended Trott from office for challenging his authority. Restored to his offices in 1702, he was promoted to chief justice by the proprietors in 1703.[5]

Over the course of the ensuing decade, Trott became a staunch supporter of the proprietors' interests, the most important legal authority in South Carolina, and one of the most prominent members of a pro-Church of England political faction that obtained a strong Anglican establishment and aimed to limit the political participation and power of Carolina's dissenters. In addition to the chief justiceship, Trott served at points as judge in South Carolina's vice admiralty court, a member of the provincial council, secretary and register of the colony, and in other offices. In 1714, at the height of his influence, Trott traveled to England and the proprietors granted him unprecedented powers: there could be no quorum at a Carolina council meeting without his presence, and all laws passed in the colony had to receive his personal approval. Unsurprisingly, Trott's sweeping new authority angered the colony's governor and many colonists, and the proprietors were forced to withdraw these extraordinary powers in 1716. Nevertheless, Trott remained a key supporter of their authority in the colony.[6]

The high point of Trott's career as a judge came in 1718, when he presided over the admiralty trials of the pirate Stede Bonnet and his alleged crew. Accounts of the trial were subsequently published in London and Trott's explication of the law of piracy, in which he characterized pirates as "Brutes" and "Beasts of Prey" with whom "neither Faith nor Oath is to be kept," became well-known and frequently cited in legal circles.[7] Trott's abrasive religio-political partisanship, stranglehold on so many of the colony's offices, and close ties to the London-based proprietorship made him a polarizing figure in South Carolina. Trott's many local opponents accused him of abuse of power and rapacious fee collecting and complained loudly to the proprietors about his activities.[8] Trott retained the proprietors' support, but his fate, and that of their increasingly unpopular government, became intertwined. According to one early Carolina historian, the last proprietary governor, Robert Johnson, "perceived that although he was called Governor, yet Trott ruled the province and therefore resolved to do nothing without his advice."[9] With the fall of the proprietary government in 1719, Trott was expelled from his offices. While some other proprietary appointees returned to power once South Carolina became a royal colony, Trott never regained any of his posts, despite making efforts on both sides of the Atlantic to do so. In his later years, he spent time in England and Carolina, devoting himself to publishing several works and practicing law. At his death, he possessed a large library and substantial wealth in land, slaves, and cash.[10]

As this précis suggests, Trott's activities in South Carolina are well documented in an array of manuscript and printed sources. In addition, a substantial quantity of his own writings, including three works he published during his lifetime and other manuscript materials, survive. However, details about Trott's early life remain murky. Neither his obituary nor his writings provide any direct information about his parentage, siblings, birthplace, or early life, but it is clear that he was part of an extended Trott family that had roots in London's merchant class and flourished by taking advantage of the opportunities emerging in Restoration Britain's Atlantic empire. Some members of the family remained in London while others became established overseas, especially in Bermuda. These family connections provided the context in which Trott's career developed and suggest his early immersion in circumatlantic controversies touching on the nature and governance of England's empire.

It has been claimed that while his mother's name is uncertain, Trott was the son of Samuel Trott, merchant, and the grandson of Perient Trott, merchant of London. It is also held that Trott was educated as a boy at the Merchant Taylor's School in London and that he became a member of the Inner Temple at the age of thirty-two. He was married twice, first to Jane Willis in Bermuda in 1694 and second to Sarah Rhett, the widow of a longtime friend and political ally in South Carolina, in 1727.[11] Definitive conclusions about Trott's early life have proven elusive in part because the extended Trott family was conspicuously mobile; its members had the inconvenient tendency to be born and die in different places. The extended family also favored the same small group of male names (including Perient, Nicholas, and Samuel) across and even within successive generations, making it difficult to distinguish between sons, brothers, uncles, and cousins. Early historians of South Carolina identified Nicholas Trott of South Carolina with the Nicholas Trott who served as governor of the Bahamas between 1694 and 1697. This identification has been proven incorrect; the two men are clearly distinguished from each other in seventeenth- and eighteenth-century documents. The Bahamian governor is now regularly identified as Nicholas Trott the elder (1658–1730). The chief justice of South Carolina, the primary subject of this chapter, is identified as Nicholas Trott the younger (1663?–1740).[12] The pair were clearly related and cooperated on several legal matters. Current biographic references identify Nicholas Trott of South Carolina as the nephew of Nicholas Trott, governor of the Bahamas, but it also seems possible that they were cousins.

• • •

Trott's career in South Carolina built on the wealth and influence that members of his family aggressively pursued in Britain's Atlantic Empire in the seventeenth century. Nuala Zahedieh has observed of Britain's seventeenth-century colonial merchants that "the best returns were made by those who could combine political power on both sides of the Atlantic and secure economic advantages through a range of rackets, restrictive practices, and government contracts."[13] The Trott family prospered in this environment. The key figure in the family's rise to prominence was the London-based merchant Perient Trott (1614–1679), who had ties to Bermuda and to Virginia's tobacco trade by the 1640s.[14] Bermuda was initially colonized by the Virginia Company and had much in common with Virginia in the early seventeenth century. In 1615, control of Bermuda passed to the Somers Islands Company, a newly chartered joint stock company legally separate from the Virginia Company but initially controlled by many of the same investors. Tobacco cultivation was the key to the early development of both colonies, with Bermuda's settlers actually producing more of the crop than their Virginia counterparts until 1625. However, by the 1630s Bermuda's tobacco trade was in dire straits. The expansion of tobacco cultivation in the Chesapeake and in other newly established colonies like Barbados flooded the market with the crop. Bermudan settlers responded by diversifying their economy, but London-based shareholders were hurt by the collapse of the colony's staple trade and many began selling their stakes in the company.

Over the ensuing decades, most shares in the Somers Islands Company were transferred to settlers resident in Bermuda, as under the company's structure shareholding was the key to owning freehold property in the colony, but the London-based Perient Trott also began investing. In 1644 he was serving in the salaried office of "husband," responsible for keeping accounts for the company's ships' voyages.¹⁵ In 1658 Perient purchased the twenty shares of the puritan Earl of Warwick, a prominent figure in the early years of the company. Perient seems to have ably negotiated the political turmoil of the Civil Wars and the Restoration in England. By 1663, the probable year of Nicholas of South Carolina's birth, Perient was the company's single largest investor and owned twice as much land in Bermuda as anyone else: 716 acres that he leased to twenty-seven tenants.¹⁶ As a whole, Bermuda's tobacco trade was floundering, but in the 1660s Perient was making substantial profits through it and other business ventures in the colony.¹⁷ On the back of Perient's success, more family members became involved in Bermuda. Most significantly, while Perient Trott Sr. seems to have remained based in London, his sons Samuel Trott (1646–1699) and Perient Trott Jr. (d. 1691) moved to Bermuda permanently as their father acquired land there. Like other Bermudians, the Trotts' economic activities became quite varied, and they profited from trading, planting, logging cedar, leasing out land, whaling, slave owning, and anything else to which they could turn their hands. While not big merchants or planters by the standards of London and the sugar islands, the Bermuda Trotts did well. When he died in 1691, for example, Perient Trott Jr. was wealthy enough to will ten slaves to family members and to leave instructions that three other enslaved Indian people that he owned should be put out to work for wages and then freed after fifteen years.¹⁸ Other Trotts also became either long-term residents or frequent visitors; both Nicholas the elder and Nicholas the younger lived in Bermuda in the 1690s.

The family also benefited from some good marriages. Most importantly, in 1659 Martha, a daughter of Perient Trott Sr., married Robert Clayton of London. Although the match was not initially an earth-shattering one—Martha's dowry was one share of Somers Islands Company stock while Robert was only an ambitious apprentice scrivener—over the course of the ensuing decade Clayton amassed a spectacular fortune as co-founder of a banking partnership. The firm he established with another former scrivener's apprentice, Robert Morris, flourished in the 1660s by providing landowners with innovative loans that were secured through mortgages on property; Clayton and Morris prospered whether their clients repaid their loans or defaulted. By 1670 the Claytons were living in palatial splendor and Robert had embarked on a political career. He served for long stretches as a London alderman, was knighted and served as sheriff, was elected as the city's Lord Mayor, and served as a Whig MP between 1679 and his death in 1707, playing a prominent, Williamite part in the events of the Glorious Revolution. His wealth, connections, and financial acumen led to Clayton's appointment as an assistant to the Royal African Company, commissioner of customs, and in 1702 as a director of the Bank of England.[19] Martha's marriage to Clayton, which produced no children, gave the Trotts connections to London's highest financial and political circles. They exploited these ties extensively. Clayton became involved in Bermuda affairs and Perient brought other extended family members into the Somers Islands Company as shareholders and allies. Perient's brothers-in-law Robert Stevens and Nathaniel Smith, both Merchant Taylors in London, and his son-in-law John Wyse, a "merchant in Smyrna trading in buffalo hides," were active alongside him in the company and Bermuda business ventures.[20] Perient's trading and networks evidently allowed him to amass considerable capital and further diversify his activities. By 1666 he had the wherewithal to partner with two other City merchants and make a successful bid to farm Charles II's despised Hearth Tax, obligating Trott and his partners to make annual payments starting at £145,000 per year to the government.[21]

While Perient prospered in London, Samuel, his eldest son and perhaps Nicholas of South Carolina's father, became the most influential figure in the family's operations in Bermuda, appearing in island records by 1669. Samuel married there twice, and while he may have spent periods at sea and in England, Bermuda seems to have consistently remained his primary home. The long-term presence of Samuel and other Trotts on the island meant that the family was more closely tied to Bermuda than the other London-based shareholders in the Somers Islands Company. In 1671, in an apt illustration of this dynamic, a consortium of Bermuda–connected London investors, including Perient Trott and other family members, backed a joint-stock venture to conduct whaling out of Bermuda. Samuel Trott was the investors' Bermuda-based partner; he was to undertake the whaling and split the proceeds evenly with the London financiers.[22] At his father's death in 1679, Samuel inherited seventy-five acres in Bermuda, part of which he was already occupying. By the 1690s, Samuel also held the office of collector of customs on Bermuda and was a member of the island's council.[23] He likely owed at least the first position to his powerful brother-in-law, Robert Clayton, who was one of the royal commissioners of customs between 1689 and 1697.[24] Samuel's brother Perient Trott Jr. also wielded influence on the island, serving as a member of the Bermuda council between 1687 and his early death in 1691.[25] The clan's collective influence on Bermuda proved enduring, with two Trotts serving as speakers of the Bermuda assembly between 1726 and

1748.[26] Individual members of the family certainly had disputes with each other—for example, Bermuda records suggest a bitter 1691 dispute between Nicholas Trott the elder and Mary, the widow of Perient Trott Trott Jr., over his will—but mutual support seems to have been more typical and essential to their fortunes.[27]

The transatlantic Trott family's interests in Bermuda embroiled it in multigenerational disputes touching on the constitution of the Restoration empire. The charter of the Somers Islands Company vested its shareholders with extensive monopoly rights over Bermuda's trade. One expression of this was the mercantilist "magazine ship" system established by the company, which required islanders to sell their tobacco on the London market and to ship it there via a company-controlled vessel. This system guaranteed that the company's stockholding landowners would not be cheated by their sharecropping tenants and also ensured that shareholders would profit from freight fees, the sale of goods to the islanders, and a duty levied on each pound of tobacco shipped. Islanders chaffed at how this system limited their abilities to diversify their economy, ship their tobacco to other locations, and profitably time London's tobacco market. While most of the company's London-based shareholders were content with the relatively small but steady and low-risk profits that this system produced for them, the Trott family was more directly engaged in the tobacco trade and other business with Bermuda. As a leading shareholder, Perient Trott Sr. increasingly claimed the right from the 1660s on to send his own trading ships to Bermuda, sell his tobacco when and where he saw fit, and in general to actively manage his business in pursuit of larger profits. Moreover, the Bermuda-based Trotts frequently sympathized with their fellow islanders who sought more control over the political and economic affairs of the colony and looked to evade the company's regulations.

The Trotts' independent streak brought them into conflict with other shareholders in the Somers Islands Company, who were anxious to retain control over their fractious colony and considered the Trotts' operations as a fundamental threat to their monopolistic privileges. In 1670 the company sought to crack down on Trott's private trading with the island through a court order declaring forfeit all the tobacco that he had shipped in the previous year, preventing his ships from entering Bermuda's harbor, and seizing some of his Bermuda property. Challenges were also launched to the legitimacy of Trott's earlier purchase of the Earl of Warwick's shares in the company. In response Perient Trott Sr., supported by Samuel in Bermuda, launched an effort to gain control over the company, and failing in that effort, mounted a legal and public relations attack on the company's practices and the colony's governor, Sir John Heydon. This included the publication of a series of pamphlets claiming that his fellow shareholders' treatment of him and the people of Bermuda amounted to a violation of the company's 1615 charter.[28] In increasingly expansive language, these pamphlets moved from airing Trott's personal grievances to challenging the very existence of the company. Copies of Trott's writings were publicly burned in Bermuda as his opponents attempted to prevent colonists from taking up such incendiary arguments. Perient Trott Sr. died in 1679, but his family, other Bermudians, and a Tory London "fortune hunter" Francis Burghill, built on the arguments that Trott laid out in his pamphlets to call for direct Crown intervention in the dispute. Such appeals to the Crown were timely in that they intersected with wider late Stuart efforts to rein in corporate privilege and to assert more authority over their overseas subjects. In 1684 these events culminated in the conclusion of a five-year *quo warranto* trial in which the company's charter was revoked and Bermuda became a Crown colony. When the news reached Bermuda, Samuel Trott and his friends held a drunkenly festive mock funeral for the company.[29]

The Trotts and their Bermuda allies countenanced the prospect of Crown governance primarily as a way to circumvent their opponents in the Somers Islands Company. They believed that constitutional change would leave them freer to pursue their own trade. The intersection of local disputes with wider conflicts between Crown and Parliament meant that these were tumultuous times in both Bermuda and the wider empire.[30] However, neither the coming of royal authority to the island during the reign of James II nor the subsequent Glorious Revolution made the Trotts any more quiescent in defense of their interests. In 1690 Samuel Trott clashed with Governor Robert Robertson over Trott's position as collector of customs.[31] The family also feuded bitterly with Roberston's successor as governor, Isaac Richier.[32] According to Richier, the Trotts repeatedly challenged his authority and boasted that their familial connection to Robert Clayton made them the real power on the island. Richier complained to the Lords of Trade that "after Sir Robert's promotion to the Custom-House" a member of the family "told the people of Sir Robert's sense of their sufferings, and that they might depend on him for relief, with promises of mighty matters that he would do for the good of the common men if they would rely on him and his relatives, but that on the contrary not the Governor himself could escape if Sir Robert were offended, such were his riches and his interest."[33] According to Nicholas Trott the elder, who became his particular enemy, Richier was guilty of a variety of crimes including abusing his authority in search of bribes, refusing to let Samuel Trott take up the office of collector, and being "disaffected to the present Government."[34]

Nicholas Trott the younger's initial foray into colonial politics appears to have occurred against this backdrop. In December 1692, he appeared in person alongside Nicholas Trott the elder before the Lords of Trade and Plantations in London, where both Trotts "swore that they had often heard Governor Richier speak disrespectfully of their Majesties," a dangerous charge in the aftermath of the revolution.[35] The Trott clan outmaneuvered Richier, as they had his predecessor Robertson, and by 1695 they were pursuing the prosecution of a deposed Richier for smuggling and other crimes committed during his governorship.[36] Nicholas the younger also appears to have continued the family tradition of falling out with Bermuda's governors. While he was initially on good terms with Richier's successor, John Goddard, who appointed him Bermuda's secretary in 1693, by 1697 their relationship had become intensely acrimonious. Goddard briefly had Trott jailed for using "very villainous language" toward him and sent affidavits to the Duke of Shrewsbury, Charles Talbot, attesting that Trott had slandered Shrewsbury and two other Lords of Trade by claiming that they had accepted bribes, perhaps in connection with the prosecution of Richier. "If any fellow deserves to be hanged," Goddard wrote of the future chief justice, "he does."[37] Trott would display a similar ability to enrage his opponents in South Carolina.

The Trotts' successive disputes with the Somers Islands Company and Bermuda's governors were not the only way that they entered into controversies centered on the governance of the English Empire. Elsewhere in the Atlantic, they pursued similar mixtures of political power and commercial opportunity. Bermuda's early settlement, small size, and dense population meant that its seventeenth-century residents frequently looked to other colonies for new trade and lands. From the 1670s, the new English colony of South Carolina was attracting particular attention from Bermudians. In 1679 Samuel Trott, his brother Perient Trott Jr., and a third partner, John Pristo, were granted 770 acres of land on the Stono River in the new colony. Although this land was inherited by other relatives after Samuel's death in 1699, this familial connection to South Carolina was probably part of the background to Nicholas the younger's decision to emigrate there.[38]

Nicholas Trott the elder likewise participated in this push out from Bermuda, becoming governor of the Bahamas in 1694.[39] Puritan migrants from Bermuda had established the initial permanent European settlement in the Bahamas on the island of Eleuthera in 1648; in 1666 another group of Bermudians established a settlement on the island of New Providence. The Crown, seeking to regularize the administration of the islands as part of its wider effort to exercise tighter supervision over the empire, awarded control over the Bahamas to the Carolina proprietors in 1670. There were dense webs of connections between the various groups that controlled and invested in the Restoration empire. Links between Bermuda, the Bahamas, and South Carolina were particularly strong. The Trotts had cultivated alliances within these circles for decades and Nicholas Trott the elder seems to have owed his appointment as Bahamian governor to a thicket of familial and business relationships. The power of his brother-in-law Clayton in this period may well have been critical. Other Trotts also sought their fortunes in the Bahamas. One of Nicholas the elder's nephews—another Perient—was named to the Bahamas council during his governorship and occupied a position in the vice admiralty court established in the colony.[40]

Nicholas Trott the elder's governorship proved highly controversial, and he gained an apparently well-earned reputation for unscrupulousness. His three years in office were marked by some significant accomplishments, including a major attempt to reform and regularize property holding on the island, refounding the newly christened town of Nassau, constructing and arming a fort there, and rebuilding the first Anglican church in the colony. Like many colonial governors, he aimed to profit from his time in power and claimed ownership of the entirety of Hog Island, a cay that forms part of New Providence's main harbor.[41] The proprietors subsequently approved this unpopular land grab, but his other activities became more problematic. His governorship became best known for multiple accusations that he used his office to illegally line his pockets.[42] They included the charge that in 1695 he orchestrated the plundering of a Dutch ship stuck on a Bahamian reef by detaining its crew to prevent them from salvaging the vessel's cargo. Worse, it was claimed that he then extorted money from the shipwrecked men before allowing them to leave the colony. One Dutch sailor claimed that Governor Trott had threatened him that "I shall make you know I am King of Providence."[43]

While these were serious charges, Governor Trott's transatlantic reputation was most harmed by the claim that he was in league with pirates. It is an ironic testament to the Trott family's ability to adapt to changing times that while his kinsman became notorious as an abettor of pirates in the Bahamas, Nicholas of South Carolina became most famous for his rigorous judicial treatment of Stede Bonnet and his pirate crew. The Bahamas' location, thin population, many small islands, and light governance made the colony a notorious pirate haven. The Bahamians and several of their proprietary-era governors were seen as overly friendly towards pirates, too willing to resupply their ships and to help them dispose of stolen goods in exchange for payoffs. Trott's governorship coincided with a broader crackdown on piracy by the Board of Trade, and fairly or not, he became seen as the embodiment of the Bahamas' depravity in this regard.[44] Richard Coote, the Earl of Bellamont and a colonial governor who had his own ties to pirates, claimed that "Trott is the greatest pirate-broker that was ever in America".[45] The most damaging specific accusation was that in 1696 Trott allowed the ship of Henry Every, infamous for his piratical exploits in the Indian Ocean, to come in to port in New Providence in exchange for a large bribe in money and stolen cargo including elephant tusks. Safely ashore, the pirates shared out the huge fortune they were said to have amassed in the East Indies and then later split up, with Every and nearly all his men managing to permanently disappear. Trott subsequently defended himself by insisting that he did not know that the ship's captain was the infamous Every and by claiming that he feared that the more than one hundred heavily armed men who made up the ship's crew posed a serious threat to the small population of Nassau if they were not granted permission to come ashore. His protestations of innocence were not sufficient, and the proprietors removed him from office in 1697 while the Board of Trade recommended to the king that he be prosecuted.[46]

This public humiliation did not dampen Nicholas the elder's enthusiasm for political infighting. In 1695, at the height of his power, he had unsuccessfully inquired about buying a share of the Carolina proprietorship.[47] Despite being subsequently dismissed as Bahamian governor by the Carolina proprietors, Nicholas the elder launched a new attempt to elbow his way into their ranks after 1700. In that year he married Anne, the daughter of Thomas Amy, a London druggist. A relative of the proprietary Colleton family, Amy initially served as a recruiter of settlers for Carolina, later became a trustee for a share of the proprietorship, and finally became a proprietor in his own right. Amy in turn settled his proprietary share on Nicholas the elder as his daughter's marriage portion. However the other proprietors seem to have disputed Trott's title to this share and never "admitted him to its possession or profits."[48] In this period, in an echo of the family's self-interested support for royal authority in Bermuda, Trott the elder and Amy were also said to have been "floating various unsavory bargains for giving up Carolina to the Crown in exchange for either the governorship for themselves or for their personal profit."[49] Nicholas the elder named Nicholas the younger as his Carolina resident proprietary deputy in 1702, but the proprietors' confidence in Nicholas the younger does not appear to have been adversely affected by their disputes with his relative.[50] Nicholas the elder's close but contentious connection to the proprietorship culminated in his years' long engagement in an English lawsuit, *Danson v. Trott*. The case encompassed, on the one hand, a claim that Nicholas the elder and his wife had attempted, after Thomas Amy's death, to dishonestly gain full ownership of the proprietary share for which Amy had served as a trustee and, on the other hand, the Trotts' counterclaim that they were owed compensation for Amy's years of expenditure and work on behalf of the Carolina proprietors. This byzantine chancery case, which has been likened to the fictional *Jarndyce v. Jarndyce* of Dickens's *Bleak House*, wound its way through English courts for years, ultimately reaching the House of Lords in 1729, where Trott's claims were finally rejected. Nicholas the younger served for at least some time after the fall of Carolina's proprietary government as counsel for his relative in this case.[51] At times allying himself with local people, at times with factions in the proprietorship, and at times with neither, Nicholas Trott the elder looked to the main chance while keeping one foot in the colonies and one in London. As a whole, the Trott family flourished by identifying and exploiting the opportunities present in seventeenth-century England's multipolar Atlantic Empire. Their extensive business and political networks gave Nicholas the younger connections to the interest groups engaged in empire building while their successive disputes gave him an early education in the intimate and bare-knuckled world of colonial politics.

• • •

Nicholas Trott the younger's office holding in Bermuda and Carolina seems a natural extension of his family's activities, but his known biography offers few clues to the roots of the support for the Church of England that was the other essential feature of his career. The Trotts do not seem to have had an explicitly religious agenda in Bermuda. The foundation of that colony had strong connections to seventeenth-century Puritanism, but it was never a bastion of politicized Anglican High Churchmanship like that espoused by Nicholas the younger in South Carolina. In fact, Samuel Trott of Bermuda, sometimes cited as Nicholas's father, was said in the mid-1670s to be a dissenter.[52] Nevertheless, Nicholas signaled his status as a committed churchman soon after his arrival in South Carolina, becoming one of the commissioners for the Charleston library created in 1700 through the efforts of the Reverend Thomas Bray (1658–1730). Bray's libraries, established in England and around the empire in this period, were intended to put edifying and orthodox religious literature into the hands of the clergy and laity. Bray's first foray into strengthening the colonial Church of England was his term of service as the bishop of London's commissary for Maryland, and in this capacity he was at the forefront of a lobbying effort in Maryland to solidify and expand Anglicanism's legal establishment in the colony in the mid-1690s. As the subsequent founder of three voluntary religious organizations active in Britain and the colonies—the Society for Promoting Christian Knowledge (SPCK), the Society for the Propagation of the Gospel in Foreign Parts (SPG), and the Associates of Doctor Bray—Bray was the central figure in the creation of a politically engaged Anglican activism in Britain's Atlantic Empire in the years around 1700. Bray and his lay and clerical allies launched a multipronged campaign to strengthen the legal position of the Church of England elsewhere in the colonies, supply colonial communities with properly trained and ordained Anglican clergymen, improve lay and clerical devotion and religious knowledge, and to bring more of the colonies' religiously and racially diverse populations into the Church of England.[53] Trott became one of the most prominent lay supporters of this agenda resident in Britain's colonies.

While the origins of his churchmanship are uncertain, the aggressive strategies that Trott used to promote imperial Anglicanism are strongly resonant of those employed by his kinsmen around the Atlantic. Crucially, Trott sought to make the Church of England stronger in Carolina by diligently cultivating alliances with like-minded people in England and America. In 1702 Trott became, through Bray's nomination, a member of the SPG. While the commitment of colonial SPG members varied, Trott became an assiduous local informant on Carolina for the society's London-based leadership. Likewise, Trott made connections with those members of the Anglican hierarchy most interested in the colonies, writing to Archbishop of Canterbury Thomas Tenison and the successive bishops of London John Robinson and Edmund Gibson. Nor, in keeping with family tradition, did Trott hesitate to use such contacts to advance his individual interests, seeking church leaders' support for his publishing projects and, after the fall of the proprietary government, trying to enlist them in his campaign for reinstatement as chief justice.[54] In Carolina, Trott also created alliances in pursuit of his politico-religious agenda. He became a strong supporter of the missionaries that the SPG sent to Carolina and they in turn praised him when they wrote to their London superiors.[55] Likewise, Trott allied himself with political figures including Nathaniel Johnson, who was also elected an

SPG member in 1702 and served as governor between 1703 and 1709, and the prolific proprietary officeholder William Rhett (1666–1722), whose widow Trott would later marry.

The most important political expression of Trott's network building and Anglican partisanship was his part in the passage of a series of laws that established the Church of England as Carolina's official church and, for a time, curtailed the political rights of dissenters. In the first thirty years of its history, colonial Carolina was largely a friendly place for religious dissenters, and the proprietors regularly appointed non-Anglicans to offices, including the governorship. By 1700, however, with staunch churchmen among the proprietors and Anglicans becoming more assertive throughout the English Empire, partisans of the Church of England began to become more strident in Carolina. The elevation of James Moore to the governorship in 1700 over two dissenting rivals marked the beginning of a period of "bitter conflict between Anglicans and dissenters in which religion became the primary divisive force in South Carolina politics."[56]

Trott, by virtue of his evidently extensive education and legal training, was a prominent figure in the Anglican Church party. In an intricate series of maneuvers redolent of Trott family members' earlier bids for power in London, Bermuda, and the Bahamas, in 1704 Carolina's Church party, operating under Moore's successor as governor, Nathaniel Johnson, secured the passage of two laws. The first, which was passed in a thinly attended emergency session of the provincial assembly, excluded elected dissenters from that body by requiring delegates to swear that they took communion in the Church of England or that they conformed to that church and had not taken communion in any other church within the past year. The second, known as the Church Act, was speedily passed by the rump assembly created by this test. It established the Church of England as the colony's official church; laid out seven parishes; provided salaries for ministers appointed to them; and among other provisions, created a body of commissioners to oversee the affairs of the church in the colony. This commission was made up of Johnson's political allies, including Trott, and its extensive powers included the authority to suspend clergymen from their pulpits for misconduct. Dissenters were enraged by their exclusion from political participation and the Church Act, and they launched an ultimately successful English lobbying effort to have the measures disallowed by the proprietors. In objecting to the Church Act, dissenters found unlikely temporary allies in the SPG, which objected to the law's provision that empowered commissioners to suspend ministers, believing it threatened the dignity and independence of clergymen and infringed on the authority of the bishop of

London to superintend the colonial church. A revised Church Act was passed to respond to SPG objections and, while the measure was subject to successive acts altering and clarifying its specific terms, the Church of England was now securely established in South Carolina. The political exclusion of dissenters was ended in 1706, but they were unable to undo the Church Act's core provisions, and the Church of England remained state-supported in the province throughout the colonial period.[57]

The preamble to the Church Act held that "in a well grounded Christian Commonwealth, Matters concerning Religion and the Honour of God" ought to be given attention because doing so was "the best Way and Means to obtain his Mercy and a Blessing upon a People and Country."[58] While it was the most sweeping and controversial of the laws pushed through by Trott and his allies, it was part of a larger bundle of measures designed to give the Church of England a larger role in the province and to compel respect for religion. In the period between 1700 and 1712, when the Church party was at its most powerful and assertive, laws were introduced or reenacted in Carolina for the suppression of "blasphemy and prophaneness," the punishment and prevention of bastardy, the promotion of the Christianization of slaves, the funding of the construction of Charleston's imposing St. Philip's Church, the tighter regulation of taverns and punch houses, the creation of a Free School for the religiously infused education of children, and the "better observance of the Lord's Day."[59] Many of these laws were paternalistic and intrusive, but several contained measures intended to make early Carolina's culture less aggressively individualistic and perhaps even more humane. The law on bastardy, for example, fined women who had children out of wedlock, but it also mandated that those children's fathers were responsible for their financial support. The law promoting slave Christianization never challenged masters' rights to own people, but it did consider the enslaved as human beings with souls capable of salvation. The law regulating the Sabbath closed inns and other sites of recreation on Sundays and threatened fines for anyone absent from church without a "reasonable or lawfull Excuse," but it also sanctioned fines against any "Master, Mistress, or Overseer" who forced his or her slaves or servants to work on the day.

Trott's cooperation with other Carolina churchmen in the passage of such laws augmented his power and served their mutual political interests, but his religious convictions were apparently sincere and deeply held. Trott saw the law as a tool for making Carolina more Anglican and godly, but he did not view it as sufficient in and of itself. So he looked for other ways to act on his religious convictions. In 1703, for example, Trott wrote to Archbishop of

Canterbury Thomas Tenison requesting five hundred copies of pamphlets that he could distribute to counter the arguments of the large numbers of Anabaptists with which Carolina was "swarming."[60]

The ultimate expression of his deep interest in religious matters was Trott's little appreciated but decades-long commitment to researching and writing an analysis of the original Hebrew of the Old Testament. Trott's modern reputation rests on his legal and political career, but religious scholarship was an integral part of his life's work and connected him to like-minded people in Europe, Britain, and elsewhere in the empire. He remained engaged in his biblical researches for decades, even at times of intense political and legal activity. In 1703 Trott told Archbishop Tenison that he had recently completed an "explication of the Hebrew of the Bible" and, in a continuation of his network building, reported that he had requested Thomas Bray to share the work with leading Hebraicists.[61] Anglican missionary Francis Le Jau mentioned Trott's work on "a New Sort of Hebrew Lexicon" to the SPG soon after Le Jau's arrival in South Carolina in 1706.[62] Nearly a decade later, in 1715, Trott wrote to Bishop of London John Robinson and mentioned his continuing work on the project. Trott's efforts resulted in the 1719 publication at Oxford of what became known as his *Clavis Linguae Sanctae*, a relatively short Latin-language explication of the Book of Psalms based on the Hebrew roots found in it.[63] Trott envisioned this as just the first volume of a wider philological study of the Hebrew Bible, which he continued to work on after his removal from office in South Carolina. Trott's subsequent work on the subject was not published, and it has been stated that it "has apparently been lost."[64] However, it seems that Trott ultimately produced two further substantial manuscripts—amounting to some 1,500 pages—that were donated in the late 1740s to Oxford's Bodleian Library, where they remain.[65] In the words of a nineteenth-century account, the manuscripts amount to an "explanation of all the Hebrew, and some Chaldee, roots found in the Old Testament." According to Thomas Frankland, who conveyed the manuscripts to the Bodleian and was married to Trott's granddaughter, Trott "desired on his death bed that his forty years' labour relating to the Hebrew root might be sent as a present to the Publick Library at Oxford."[66]

As his sending the work to Thomas Bray and seeking the support of Anglican bishops suggests, Trott was as assiduous in forging transatlantic networks to promote his scholarship as he was other aspects of his career. For example, the published portion of it includes a brief endorsement by the Oxford orientalist John Gagnier. Similarly, in 1724 Trott, or a supporter of his, sent a copy of the work to the rector of the University of St. Andrews in

Scotland, who instructed three members of the university to review it. One of the assigned reviewers, Hebrew professor Gabriel Johnston, praised the work extensively, claiming "the performance of the author is as exact as (I am persuaded) the design of it was pious."[67] Trott's attempts to gain recognition for his work bore fruit. He was awarded honorary degrees by Oxford and the University of Aberdeen, to which a copy of the book was also sent, in recognition of his linguistic and legal work.

In light of his subsequent transatlantic reputation as a legal figure, it is notable that Trott's religiously inflected philological interests directly intersected with his practice as a judge. His affinity and reverence for the Hebrew scriptures was, for example, at the root of his interest in and belief in witchcraft. In a judge's charge that Trott delivered to a South Carolina grand jury in 1706, he defended the existence of witches while preparing jurors to consider an accusation of witchcraft against a South Carolina woman. Trott's belief in witches seems to have rested squarely on a faith in the literal truth of the Bible and he called jurors' attention to biblical passages mentioning witches before deploying his linguistic knowledge to argue, contra skeptics, that the English translations of them present in the King James Version accurately reflected the original sense of the Hebrew. Trott's subsequent discussion of the evidence necessary to secure a conviction for witchcraft set a relatively high standard—he rejected the concept of spectral evidence and insisted on the necessity of either a confession or two witnesses to an act of witchcraft—but he did believe that witches were active in Carolina. Despite Trott's obvious support for issuing an indictment, the grand jury failed to charge the accused witch and in 1707 there was a "riot provoked by Trott's apparent zeal in the matter."[68] Francis Le Jau, who shared Trott's beliefs, lamented that "a notorious Malefactor evidently guilty of Witchcraft, & who has kill'd several Persons by the Devils help was lately return'd Ingoramus by the Grand Jury" and was amazed that "men call open Witchcraft Imagination and no more."[69]

More generally, Trott's religious convictions are evident throughout texts related to his judicial career. Trott's speeches in which he condemned the pirate Stede Bonnet and members of his crew to death are largely exhortations to repent taken from scripture.[70] The collection of charges that Trott delivered to grand juries between 1703 and 1708, which provides a window onto his political and legal thinking, is replete with references to the Bible, classical authors including Aristotle and Cicero, influential expositions of the common law by Edward Coke and Matthew Hale, civil law collections and treatises by John Cowell, Denis Godefroy, and Thomas Wood, and works on natural law by Richard Cumberland, the Jesuit Francisco Suarez, Pufendorf, and others. While these references demonstrate the breadth of Trott's education and reading, his charges are also notable for the use they make of leading Anglican theorists including Thomas Bennet, Richard Hooker, Robert Sanderson, John Sharp, Jeremy Taylor, and John Tillotson. Trott deployed Sanderson and Tillotson, for example, alongside Thomas Aquinas and the Bible in attempting to impress on grand jurors that the oaths they took as part of their service were a "Religious Act" that imposed on them a "Sacred Obligation" to inquire diligently into the accusations that they would hear.[71]

Besides frequently relying on influential Anglican divines to frame his legal arguments, Trott envisioned the courts that he controlled as interventionist sites for a religiously inspired reformation of manners. When introducing his arguments on witchcraft, Trott claimed that "we live in an Age of Atheism and Infidelity," and he clearly saw his role as a judge, in part, as countering this zeitgeist.[72] In the final grand jury charge included in his collection, Trott urged the jurors to be willing to "punish Vice & Immorality, and to inform the Magistrates against such Offenders." He approvingly noted the creation in England of "several Societies all over the nation for the Reformation of Manners" and the support they received from "Persons of the best Rank & Quality" and Queen Anne.[73] Trott's charge cited Josiah Woodward's laudatory 1699 account of the founding of the Societies for the Reformation of Manners in England, while in this same period Francis Le Jau was unsuccessfully attempting to create such a society in his Carolina parish after being urged to do so by the SPG's secretary.[74] In this too, then, Trott was partaking in the wider currents of transatlantic Anglican activism.

The best expression of the symbiotic relationship between Trott's legal work and his religious preoccupations was his 1721 publication *The Laws of the British Plantations in America, Relating to the Church and Clergy, Religion and Learning*. Published after Trott had returned to England following the fall of the proprietary government, the volume was a systematic and comparative compilation of laws on the establishment of religion and religious matters more broadly conceived. The work cast the Atlantic Empire as a coherent entity, attempting to comprehensively catalog legislation enacted across Britain's Caribbean and continental American colonies. Arranged first by colony and then thematically, rather than chronologically, the collection was designed to enable the reader to understand the laws on a given subject operative in a particular colony, and then to compare them with those in force elsewhere. Its form and content amounted to an implicit argument: Britain's Atlantic Empire could and should be made more godly by being made more Anglican.

Assembling these materials was a major challenge, and both travel and Trott's transatlantic connections were essential to the project. The editions of various colonies' laws produced by London and colonial printers were key sources. He reported, for example, obtaining a locally printed edition of Virginia's laws during a visit there. Contacts helped him obtain others: he thanked Alexander Skene, former secretary of Barbados and a religiously minded South Carolina planter, for providing a copy of a law passed there and the strongly Anglican colonial governor Francis Nicholson for giving him a copy of the College of William and Mary's charter. He drew on his personal manuscript collections of the laws of Bermuda and South Carolina and a manuscript collection of Pennsylvania laws "which I procured from thence." The Trotts' long-standing ties to imperial administrators also helped. He was able to transcribe laws from several colonies—Virginia, Rhode Island, New Hampshire, Antigua, Nevis, and others—while in London, where "thanks to the Favour of William Popple," secretary to the Board of Trade, and the "Assistance of the Clerks there" he "had the Perusal of the Records of the Laws of the British Plantations in America."[75]

The work capitalized on Trott's legal expertise to further what he recognized to be a shared transatlantic religio-political agenda. Trott intended the work primarily for the "use and service," of his fellow members of the SPG. He hoped the book would "not only be of Use to them in the Management of those Works of Piety they are engaged in" but also a tool in the service of remaking colonial law, a "Means they may see what *Laws* are wanting, or need to be altered in any Province."[76] Other like-minded Anglicans hoped to wield the law in support of their religious agendas in this period. One prominent example is provided by Edmund Gibson, who became the bishop of London in 1723, soon after the publication of Trott's *Laws of the British Plantations*. Gibson, best known as a political ally of the Walpole regime, was also the most influential bishop within the SPG for several decades and a key figure in the effort to strengthen Anglicanism in the colonies. Gibson first rose to prominence as a compiler and interpreter of canon, common, and statute law related to the Church of England. Satirized by his dissenting and political opponents as Dr. Codex after the title of his 1713 treatise on the subject, Gibson argued that his work was primarily for the benefit of the clergy and "in Support of the Rights and Privileges of the Church."[77] Although Trott made no direct reference to Gibson's work in his own *Laws of the British Plantations,* Trott's scholarship can be understood as an extension of similar sentiments to the more vexed issue of the Church's position in the empire. As Trott noted in the manuscript of his grand jury charges, quoting the fifteenth-century jurist John Fortescue, he believed that English law was not "for Prince & People only as they be in a Body Politic, but also for the singular benefit of the Church of God, the Rights & Liberties whereof, the Common Law maintaineth inviolably."[78] Likewise, the lay and clerical churchmen who made up the SPG's membership not only paid scrupulous attention to the varied legal status of the Church of England in different colonies, they also believed it proper and necessary to use the law and their political influence in other ways to further their religious aims.[79]

• • •

L. H. Roper has argued that the most influential early South Carolinians, including Nicholas Trott, should be regarded as they regarded themselves: "more as inhabitants of an Anglo-Atlantic world rather than as denizens of an 'Old World' or a 'New.'"[80] This characterization is even more useful for the Trott family as a whole. Neither entirely "colonial" nor entirely English, individual Trotts moved regularly from place to place while the family as a whole strategically maintained representatives in London and in the colonies. When it suited their individual or collective interests in relationship to a particular issue, family members could ally with one or more of the various metropolitan groups concerned in imperial governance: other merchants, the Crown and agents of royal centralization and control, the Somers Islands Company's shareholders, the Carolina proprietors, or the Society for the Propagation of the Gospel. At other moments, Trotts could and did ally with colonial settlers and argue for more local autonomy vis-à-vis the imperial actors present in the metropole. Chief Justice Nicholas Trott shared this family identity, moving easily between Bermuda, Carolina, and London, building a career based on the careful maintenance of local and long-distance networks and seeing his own possibilities as bounded only by the limits of England's Atlantic possessions.

Trott's career was also shaped by the rise of an assertive Anglican activism in the late seventeenth and early eighteenth century. Figures like Thomas Bray, Edmund Gibson, and many others associated with the SPCK, SPG, and other networks of churchmen were troubled by the power of dissenters in English dominions abroad, convinced that the colonies were particularly irreligious and immoral and anxious to use their learning, political influence, and the law to effect change. Most of these figures were also supporters of stronger, more centralized, and ultimately royal authority over the colonies. Trott shared some of his religious allies' wider interests in tightening the ties between England and its colonies. He was, for example, interested in bringing early Carolina's inchoate law code into closer conformity with English law, in which he was trained and for which he had deep respect.[81] Yet, Trott was also, by virtue of his self-interest and family background in the multipolar empire of the Restoration, committed to upholding the privileges and power of Carolina's proprietors.

It is indicative of the way the Britain's Atlantic Empire was changing that Trott ultimately became a bitter enemy to Francis Nicholson, appointed by the Crown as governor of South Carolina in 1720. Nicholson was a key proponent of royal authority around the empire in the early eighteenth century, a commitment born of his military service in Flanders, Tangiers, and New England and expressed across a career that saw him serve as lieutenant governor or governor in the Dominion of New England, Virginia, Maryland, and Nova Scotia before arriving in South Carolina.[82] Nicholson opposed Trott's reappointment to any of the judicial offices that he had held under the proprietors, and Trott was among just a small number of Carolinians who did not quickly reconcile themselves to the new administration.[83] Yet, Nicholson, like Trott, was a committed Anglican activist and a member of the SPG. Indeed, Nicholson was the single most influential layperson in the missionary organization in its first several decades and one of the most generous financial supporters of the colonial Church of England. Nicholson shared Trott's view that the problems of the colonial church might best be viewed and addressed by looking at Britain's Atlantic Empire as a whole, but he combined this with an unswerving commitment to the maintenance and expansion of royal authority.

In ensuing decades, most supporters of colonial Anglicanism would share Nicholson's perspective and see devotion to the Church of England and the Crown as a natural pairing. Indeed, in the decades preceding the American Revolution, this combination of Anglican activism with royalism would come to alarm some colonists who feared it amounted to a two-pronged attack on their religious and political liberty. Trott's career, though, with its roots in his family's seventeenth-century activities and its combination of dedication to Anglicanism and proprietary power, suggests some of the flexibility and variability still present in the English Empire in the two decades immediately following the Glorious Revolution. If Nicholson's activities contributed to the emergence of a more homogenous and centralized British Empire over the course of the eighteenth century, Trott's career serves as a reminder that this process was gradual and long uneven in its effects.

Notes

The author would like to thank Philip Stern for his comments and Andrew Baylay of the Bermuda Archives for his generous research assistance.

1. *South-Carolina Gazette*, February 9, 1740. For overviews of Trott's career, see L. Lynn Hogue, "Trott, Nicholas," *American National Biography Online* (hereafter *ANBO*) (New York: Oxford University Press, 2000); and Alexander Moore, "Trott, Nicholas (1663-1740)," *Oxford Dictionary of National Biography* (hereafter *ODNB*) (Oxford: Oxford University Press, 2004).

2. Trott's career in Bermuda is best detailed in Henry Campbell Wilkinson, *Bermuda in the Old Empire: A History of the Island from the Dissolution of the Somers Island Company until the end of the American Revolutionary War: 1684-1784* (London: Oxford University Press, 1950), 36-43, 80-83, 260.

3. A. S. Salley, ed., *Commissions and Instructions from the Lords Proprietors of Carolina to Public Officials in of South Carolina, 1685-1715* (Columbia: Historical Commission of South Carolina, 1916), 113-18. Trott was appointed to the office of Advocate General by the proprietors but on arrival found it already occupied by a royal nominee and did not take it up.

4. Charles H. Lesser, *South Carolina Begins: The Records of a Proprietary Colony, 1663-1721* (Columbia: South Carolina Department of Archives and History, 1995), 238-39.

5. Salley, *Commissions and Instructions*, 162-63.

6. Ibid., 264-66.

7. *The Tryals of Major Stede Bonnet and Other Pirates . . .* (London, 1719), 3; L. Lynne Hogue, "An Edition of 'Eight Charges Delivered At So Many Several General Sessions, & Gaol Deliveries: Held at Charles Town . . . In the Years 1703. 1704. 1705. 1706. 1707. . . . By Nicholas Trott Esq; Chief Justice of the Province of South Carolina'" (PhD diss., University of Tennessee, 1972), 28-33. On Trott's activities as an admiralty judge, see Randall Bridwell, "Mr. Nicholas Trott and the South Carolina Vice Admiralty Court: An Essay on Procedural Reform and Colonial Politics," *South Carolina Law Review* 28 (1976): 181-218.

8. Francis Yonge, South Carolina's agent in London during the late proprietary period, wrote a defense of the 1719 overthrow of the proprietary government that was particularly focused on and critical of Trott. See Francis Yonge, *A Narrative of the Proceedings of the People of South-Carolina in the Year 1719 . . .* (London, 1726).

9. [Alexander Hewatt], *An Historical Account of the Rise and Progress of the Colonies of South Carolina and Georgia*, 2 vols. (London, 1779), 1:258-59.

10. Hogue, "Trott, Nicholas," *ANBO*; Moore, "Trott, Nicholas (1663-1740)," *ODNB*.

11. The most authoritative and current account of Trott's life is Hogue, "Trott, Nicholas," *ANBO*. Houge's account of Trott's parentage is followed in Moore, "Trott, Nicholas (1663-1740)," *ODNB*. Despite Hogue's careful efforts, there are some pieces of evidence that raise questions about whether Nicholas of South Carolina was actually the son of the merchant Samuel Trott and about other aspects of his early life. (1) In his will, dated May 6, 1699, Samuel Trott mentions five sons by name, designates his son Nicholas Trott as his "youngest son," and leaves him a legacy to be given to him "when he shall attaine the age of twenty one yeares." This strongly suggests that Samuel's son Nicholas Trott was too young to have been the Nicholas Trott who became chief justice of South Carolina. Nicholas Trott of South Carolina would have been thirty-six years old at this point, according to his published

obituary. See Will of Samuel Trott (d. 1699), Bermuda Archives, Hamilton, Bermuda, Book of Wills #2.1, 172–77. (2) There is also some evidence that Samuel Trott, the son of Perient Trott (d. 1679), was born in 1646. If that is correct and Nicholas Trott of South Carolina was born in 1663, then Samuel would have had to have fathered at least five sons by the age of eighteen. For Samuel Trott's birth in 1646, see Charles J. Robinson, *A Register of the Scholars Admitted into the Merchant Taylor's School* . . . 2 vols. (Lewes, UK: Farncombe, 1882), 1:250. (3) The published records of the Merchant Taylor's School, which Nicholas of South Carolina is said to have attended, state that the Nicholas Trott who was a student there in 1672 was born April 16, 1666. Nicholas Trott of South Carolina is said in his published obituary to have been born on January 19, 1663. See Robinson, *Register of the Scholars Admitted into the Merchant Taylor's School,* 1:277. This seems to raise the possibility that the Nicholas Trott educated at Merchant Taylor's was not the future chief justice of South Carolina. (4) The records of the Inner Temple state that the Nicholas Trott, who was admitted there in 1695, was the son of Nicholas Trott, merchant of London, http://www.innertemplearchives.org.uk/detail.asp?id=6686 (accessed January 24, 2013). The same statement is made in Joseph Foster, *Alumni Oxonienses: The Members of the University of Oxford, 1715–1886,* 4 vols. (Oxford: Parker, 1891) 4:1441. It is therefore difficult to identify Nicholas of South Carolina as both Samuel Trott's son and as the Nicholas Trott who trained at the Inner Temple. (5) It is reflective of these difficulties that Hogue, who has given the most sustained attention to Trott's career, has changed his view of Trott's precise lineage several times. Compare Hogue, "An Edition of 'Eight Charges,'" 7; with Hogue, "Nicholas Trott: Man of Law and Letters," *South Carolina Historical Magazine* 76, no. 1 (January 1975): 28; and with Hogue, "Trott, Nicholas," *ANBO*. While it is clear that Nicholas of South Carolina was part of this extended family, I too have found it difficult to reach definitive conclusions about his parentage and early life.

12. See Hogue, "An Edition of 'Eight Charges,'" 3–7.

13. Nuala Zahedieh, *The Capital and the Colonies: London and the Atlantic Economy, 1660–1700* (Cambridge: Cambridge University Press, 2010), 129.

14. J. H. Lefroy, *Memorials of the Discovery and Early Settlement of the Bermudas or Somers Islands, 1515–1685,* 2 vols. (London: Longmans, Green, 1877), 1:590; Michael Jarvis, *In the Eye of All Trade: Bermuda, Bermudians, and the Maritime Atlantic World, 1680–1783* (Chapel Hill: University of North Carolina Press, 2010), 57.

15. Lefroy, *Memorials,* 1:197, 590.

16. Richard Dunn, "The Downfall of the Bermuda Company: Restoration Farce," *William and Mary Quarterly,* 3rd ser., 20, no. 4 (October 1963): 494.

17. Jarvis, *In the Eye of All Trade,* 58.

18. Will of Perient Trott (d. 1691), Bermuda Archives, Book of Wills #3.1, 119–28; Virginia Bernhard, *Slaves and Slaveholders in Bermuda, 1616–1782* (Columbia: University of Missouri Press, 1999), 120. Bernhard may conflate Perient Trott (d. 1691) of Bermuda with his father (d. 1679).

19. Frank T. Melton, *Sir Robert Clayton and the Origins of English Deposit Banking, 1658–1685* (Cambridge: Cambridge University Press, 2002), 69; Melton, "Clayton, Sir Robert (1629–1707)," *ODNB*.

20. Lefroy, *Memorials,* 2:195, 2:213, 2:357–58, 2:511. For the identification of Smith, Stevens, and Wyse as Perient Trott's relations by marriage, see Will of Perient Trott, August 6, 1679, National Archives, Kew, England, Prob/11/360; and Melton, *Sir Robert Clayton,* 69.

21. Melton, *Sir Robert Clayton*, 69; C. D. Chandaman, *The English Public Revenue, 1660-1688* (Oxford: Clarendon Press, 1975), 92. This venture seems to have gone poorly and resulted in legal disputes between the farming partnership and the government. See Lydia M. Marshall, "The Levying of the Hearth Tax, 1662-1688," *English Historical Review* 51, no. 204 (October 1936): 628-29.

22. Lefroy, *Memorials*, 2:357-60.

23. J. W. Fortescue, ed., *Calendar of State Papers, Colonial Series, America and West Indies, January, 1693-14 May, 1696. Preserved in the Public Record Office* (London: His Majesty's Stationery Office, 1903), 613-14.

24. Melton, "Clayton, Sir Robert (1629-1707)," *ODNB*; Wilkinson, *Bermuda in the Old Empire*, 35-37.

25. Wilkinson, *Bermuda in the Old Empire*, 439.

26. Ibid., 441.

27. Nicholas Trott the younger may have also been involved in this dispute on Nicholas the elder's side. See Bernhard, *Slaves and Slaveholders in Bermuda*, 205-6.

28. See [Perient Trott], *A True Relation of the Just and Unjust Proceedings of the Somer-Islands-Company*... (London, 1676); [Perient Trott], *A True Relation of the Illegal Proceedings of the Somer-Islands-Company in their Courts at London*... (London, 1678); [Perinent Trott], *The Strange Actings of Sir John Heydon, Kt. and Governour in the Somer Islands*... (London, 1678). (London, 1678).

29. On the end of the Somers Island Company and the Trott family's place in its destruction, see Jarvis, *In the Eye of All Trade*, 50-61; Dunn, "Downfall of the Bermuda Company," 487-512. Also see the various sources printed in Lefroy, *Memorials*.

30. Owen Stanwood, *The Empire Reformed: English America in the Age of the Glorious Revolution* (Philadelphia: University of Pennsylvania Press, 2011), 40-47.

31. J. W. Fortescue, ed. *Calendar of State Papers, Colonial Series, America and West Indies, 1689-1692. Preserved in the Public Record Office* (London: His Majesty's Stationery Office, 1901), 283, 298, 319, 329.

32. Jarvis, *In the Eye of All Trade*, 70-73.

33. Fortescue, ed. *Calendar of State Papers, Colonial Series . . . 1689-1692*, 554-58.

34. Ibid., 739-40.

35. Ibid., 748-49; Fortescue, ed. *Calendar of State Papers, Colonial Series . . . January, 1693-14 May, 1696*, 159.

36. Fortescue, ed. *Calendar of State Papers, Colonial Series . . . January, 1693-14 May, 1696*, 501, 542, 613-14.

37. Fortescue, ed. *Calendar of State Papers, Colonial Series, America and West Indies, 15 May 1696-31 October 1697. Preserved in the Public Record Office* (London: His Majesty's Stationery Office, 1904), 525-26.

38. Noel Salisbury and J. W. Fortescue, eds. *Calendar of State Papers, Colonial Series, America and West Indies, 1677-1680. Preserved in the Public Record Office* (London: Her Majesty's Stationery Office, 1896), 464. Julia E. Mercer, *Bermuda Settlers from the Seventeenth Century: Genealogical Notes from Bermuda* (Baltimore: Genealogical Publishing, 1982), 218-21.

39. Wilkinson, *Bermuda in the Old Empire*, 7, 37.

40. Ibid., 79; Cecil Headlam, ed., *Calendar of State Papers, Colonial Series, America and West Indies, 1701. Preserved in the Public Record Office* (London: His Majesty's Stationery Office, 1910), 384–86.

41. Michael Craton and Gail Saunders, *Islanders in the Stream: A History of the Bahamian People*, 2 vols. (Athens: University of Georgia Press, 1992–1998), 1:100–101.

42. On Nicholas Trott the elder and piracy, see Douglas R. Burgess Jr. "Piracy in the Public Sphere: The Henry Every Trials and the Battle for Meaning in Seventeenth☒Century Print Culture," *Journal of British Studies* 48, no. 4 (October 2009): 893–904; Craton and Saunders, *Islanders in the Stream*, 1:100–106.

43. Cecil Headlam, ed., *Calendar of State Papers, Colonial Series, America and West Indies, 1699. Also Addenda 1621–1698. Preserved in the Public Record Office* (London: His Majesty's Stationery Office, 1908), 164–65.

44. For the Board of Trade's wider crackdown on piracy, see Ian K. Steele, *Politics of Colonial Policy: The Board of Trade in Colonial Administration, 1696–1720* (Oxford: Clarendon Press, 1968), 42–59.

45. Wilkerson, *Bermuda in the Old Empire*, 80.

46. Headlam, ed. *Calendar of State Papers, Colonial Series . . . 1699*, 307–8.

47. Fortescue, ed. *Calendar of State Papers, Colonial Series . . . January, 1693–14 May, 1696*, 572–73.

48. Edward McCrady, *The History of South Carolina under the Proprietary Government, 1670–1719* (New York: Macmillan, 1897), 270–71, 387.

49. Lesser, *South Carolina Begins*, 45.

50. Salley, *Commissions and Instructions*, 170.

51. Hogue, "Nicholas Trott: Man of Law and Letters," 31–32. A synopsis of *Danson v. Trott* is in *English Reports*. See 3 *Eng. Rep.* 173, 1694–1865.

52. [Perient Trott], *A True Relation of the Illegal Proceedings of the Somer-Islands-Company*, 14.

53. On Bray's career, see Leonard W. Cowie, "Bray, Thomas (bap. 1658, d. 1730)," *ODNB*.

54. For Trott's correspondence and connections with religious figures in England, see William Manross, *The Fulham Papers in the Lambeth Palace Library: American Colonial Section Calendar and Indexes* (Oxford: Clarendon Press, 1965), 130–31, 141–42; William Manross, *S.P.G. Papers in the Lambeth Palace Library: Calendars and Indexes* (Oxford: Clarendon Press, 1974), 142, 144, 146.

55. On Trott's relations with Carolina's Anglican clergymen, see Frank J. Klingberg, ed., *Carolina Chronicle: The Papers of Commissary Gideon Johnston 1707–1716* (Berkeley: University of California Press, 1946), and Frank J. Klingberg, ed., *The Carolina Chronicle of Dr. Francis Le Jau 1706–1717* (Berkeley: University of California Press, 1956).

56. M. Eugene Sirmans, *Colonial South Carolina: A Political History, 1663–1763* (Chapel Hill: University of North Carolina Press for the Institute for Early American History, 1966), 76.

57. An account of the political disputes surrounding the Church Act can be found in ibid., 86–96.

58. Nicholas Trott, *The Laws of the British Plantations in America, Relating to the Church and the Clergy, Religion and Learning* (London: Cowse, 1721), 5.

59. For these laws, see Nicholas Trott, *The Laws of the Province of South Carolina . . .* , 2 vols. (Charleston, SC: Lewis Timothy, 1736), 1:91–234.

60. Manross, *Fulham Papers*, 130. This request was forwarded to the SPG. See *Archives of the United Society for the Propagation of the Gospel in Foreign Parts*, Bodleian Library of Commonwealth and African Studies at Rhodes House, Oxford, England. *Journal* 1:191.

61. Manross, *Fulham Papers*, 130.

62. Klingberg, ed., *Carolina Chronicle of Dr. Francis Le Jau*, 18.

63. Nicoloa Trotio, *Mafteah leshon hakodesh Clavis linguæ sanctæ* (Oxford, 1719).

64. Hogue, "Trott, Nicholas," *ANBO*.

65. William Dunn Macray, *Annals of the Bodleian Library Oxford with a Notice of the Earlier Library of the University*, 2nd ed. (Oxford: Clarendon Press, 1890), 154–55. The Trott manuscripts are listed as part of the Fell Collection in the published catalog of Hebrew manuscripts held at Oxford. See Adolf Neubauer and Arthur Ernest Cowley, *Catalogue of the Hebrew Manuscripts in the Bodleian Library*, 2 vols. (Oxford: Clarendon Press, 1906), 2:419.

66. Macray, *Annals of the Bodleian Library*, 155.

67. Trott's *Clavis* also received a favorable contemporary review in a French language journal. See Hogue, "An Edition of 'Eight Charges,'" 28, 256–58. On Trott and Johnston, see *Library Bulletin of the University of St. Andrews* 5, no. 46 (April 1912): 72–77, which suggests their contact "may have led to the latter's advancement" as Johnston's career subsequently took a surprising turn. He resigned his university position and, after several years in the London household of Whig politician Spencer Compton, Johnston was appointed royal governor of North Carolina in 1733. On Johnston's career, see Max R. Williams. "Johnston, Gabriel," *ANBO*, and William S. Powell, "Johnston, Gabriel (1698–1752)," *ODNB*.

68. Hogue, "An Edition of 'Eight Charges,'" 39–40, 52–56.

69. Klingberg, ed., *Carolina Chronicle of Dr. Francis Le Jau*, 25.

70. *Tryals of Major Stede Bonnet and Other Pirates*, 34–36, 41–43.

71. Hogue, "An Edition of 'Eight Charges,'" 126–32.

72. Ibid., 142.

73. Ibid., 176.

74. Klingberg, ed., *Carolina Chronicle of Dr. Francis Le Jau*, 69, 74, 78, 81, 87–88.

75. Trott, *Laws of the British Plantations*, i–vi.

76. Ibid., viii–ix.

77. Edmund Gibson, *Codex Juris Ecclesiastici Anglicani* . . . (London, 1713), i.

78. Hogue, "An Edition of 'Eight Charges,'" 186–88.

79. I have written elsewhere about the ways, for example, in which early eighteenth-century Anglican activists' interests in harnessing the law for their religious ends impacted the development of the law on slavery in the British Empire. See Travis Glasson, "'Baptism doth not bestow Freedom': Missionary Anglicanism, Slavery, and the Yorke-Talbot Opinion, 1701–30," *William and Mary Quarterly*, 3rd ser., 67, no. 2 (April 2010): 279–318.

80. L. H. Roper, *Conceiving Carolina: Proprietors, Planters, and Plots, 1662–1729* (New York: Palgrave Macmillan, 2004), 7.

81. Trott probably played a central part in the creation of South Carolina's 1712 "reception statute," which made more than 160 designated English statutes operative in South Carolina and which explicitly made the common law of England, with the exception of those parts relating to ancient forms of land tenure and ecclesiastical issues, "in full force" in the province. See Harold Simmons Tate Jr., "South Carolina's Reception of English Law" (PhD diss., University of South Carolina, 2008).

82. Accounts of Nicholson's career include Kevin R. Hardwick, "Nicholson, Sir Francis (1655–1728)," *ODNB*; Jacob Judd, "Nicholson, Francis," *ANBO*; Randy Dunn, "Francis Nicholson's Empire," in *English Atlantics Revisited: Essays Honouring Professor Ian K. Steele*, ed. Nancy L. Rhoden (Montreal: McGill-Queen's University Press, 2007), 59–80; Stephen Saunders Webb, "The Strange Career of Francis Nicholson," *William and Mary Quarterly*, 3rd ser., 23, no. 4 (October 1966): 514–48; and Bruce T. McCully, "Governor Francis Nicholson, Patron 'Par Excellence' of Religion and Learning in Colonial America," *William and Mary Quarterly*, 3rd ser., 39, no. 2 (April 1982): 310–33.

83. Sirmans, *Colonial South Carolina*, 132.

6

THE EMPIRE, THE EMPEROR, AND THE EMPRESS

The Interesting Case of Mrs. Mary Bosomworth

Joshua Piker

Connoisseurs of empire would do well to turn their eyes to Savannah, Georgia, in August 1749, when over one hundred Creeks visited Georgia's capital. The colony's leaders had not invited them, but Georgians could not afford to ignore so many Native allies, especially since they were led by Malatchi, the Creeks' most powerful headman. The Creeks were in town at the invitation of Mary Bosomworth and her husband, Thomas. The visitors expected to see the Bosomworths off on a trip to Britain and to receive a large parcel of presents from Britain's king. Georgia's leaders disliked and distrusted the Bosomworths, and the colony's Powers That Were believed that Mary and Thomas had invited the Creeks down so as to pressure the colony into granting Mary both a portion of the king's gifts and a large chunk of Georgia real estate. The clash of agendas that ensued led to parades and riots, speeches and shouted arguments, ceremonial dinners and hastily written affidavits—to say nothing of gunfire (possibly as a salute, possibly as a threat), reports of an Indian attack, a standoff between Creeks and militiamen, personal insults, foaming at the mouth (by Malatchi), tendentious mischaracterizations (by Georgia's leaders), a night in jail (for Mary), and a tearful apology (by Thomas). The Creeks eventually left Savannah loaded down with presents and bad feelings. Thomas was then thrown in jail for debt, and while Mary unsuccessfully sought bail money, Savannah's officials retreated to their writing desks to churn out long, self-justifying reports aimed at convincing London that somehow this fiasco had been all for the best. As a dark comedy, the Savannah incident is hard to beat, but the incident moves into the realm of historical significance when we realize that all involved were arguing about empire. In essence, three imperial projects clashed on the streets of Savannah, and all three involved Mary Bosomworth.[1]

The first such project was British. In the late 1740s, British officials were taking steps to make their empire imperial in the modern sense: centralized, regularized, hierarchical, and militaristic. Both the colony of Georgia and Mary herself, though, were creatures of Britain's old, pre-modern empire. Georgia was founded in 1732, at a time when imperial aims could be outsourced to a private group, the Trustees, who ruled Georgia with little oversight. Mary came to prominence primarily because the old-model empire left its colonists to rely on local brokers like her for everything from connections with indigenous powers to food. Mary's rise, in short, was facilitated by imperial neglect and colonial weakness. British efforts at imperial reform would change both Georgia's and Mary's status, with Georgia becoming a royal colony in 1752 and Mary becoming a nonfactor by the early 1760s. Before that point, though, Georgia's impotence and Mary's importance serve as a rough index of the success of Britain's imperial project. The 1749 Savannah incident demonstrates that imperial reform still had a ways to go.[2]

British plans for imperial reform notwithstanding, the only emperor in Savannah during the 1749 incident was Creek. Malatchi, the leader of Savannah's Creek visitors, had started calling himself emperor in 1747: "I am now Emperor of the Creek Nation" with "2000 fighting Men under my Command" and "the Care of their Wives and Children." Since his late father was frequently called emperor, Malatchi came by the title honestly but not legitimately. Malatchi, it turns out, was not the first emperor in a nation that was not a nation and did not have an emperor. As a result, in 1749, Malatchi was attempting to forge the Creeks' disparate collection of regions, ethnic groups, and towns into a coherent nation and to put himself at its head; but this imperial project was very much a work in progress. And Mary was an important part of his plans. She was, thanks to her Creek mother, a cousin, a member of his clan, and a native of Coweta, his hometown and political base. Of equal importance, her British father, her years working with Georgia officials, and her marriages to three British subjects gave her an impressively dense web of British connections. Those ties were critical to Malatchi because he knew that he would first become "Emperor of the Creek Nation" when dealing with non-Creeks. Influence abroad could then be used to create unity and authority at home, but Malatchi needed Mary and her British family for his Creek imperial project to succeed.[3]

Mary was willing to serve as his ally because she had her own imperial project to look after. Much of the unpleasantness during the Savannah incident, in fact, occurred after she declared that she was "Empress and Queen of the Upper and Lower Creeks" and produced an affidavit from Malatchi and ten other Creek headmen acknowledging her as "our Rightful and natural princess" with "full power and Authority . . . to transact all affairs relating" to "Lands Territories dignities or Royalties." Mary was furious when she made these claims—the Savannah meeting was not going as the Bosomworths had intended—and so her claim to be a "Sovereign" in "Alliance" with George II was a bit over the top. But she had been describing herself as the Creeks' "Rightfull and Natural Princess" since 1747, and in 1750 she restated her "full power and Authority" with regards to lands and the like. Her father was a British trader, but her title and its perquisites were based on her "Descent on the Mother's Side, (who was Sister to the Old Emperor), of the Same Blood of the Present Mico's and Chief's now in that Nation." It might have been an open question whether Mary—as the sister's daughter of one emperor and cousin of a second—had a better claim to empire than Malatchi, who was an emperor's son in a matrilineal society where people did not assume that a son would inherit his father's title. But Mary had no intention of challenging Malatchi. Her claims were directed outward, toward Britain, not at the Creek polity; she hoped to win not political authority in her mother's country but wealth in her father's colonial world. Whatever her motivations and whatever her plans, though, we are once again discussing both an imperial project and Mary Bosomworth.[4]

There are, of course, logical questions to be asked: Why was empire on everyone's agenda during the Savannah incident? And what does Mary's ubiquity tell us? Finding answers requires looking in more detail at each imperial project. For now, though, we might simply note that if Alexander Hamilton was right to call "an imperium in imperio" a "political monster" in *Federalist* 15, then early modern mapmakers were right when they filled their maps' margins with monsters. The imperial periphery was a place of political innovation, a place where empire was very much part of the conversation but where empires themselves lacked the power to control the discussion. That reality led to the assertion of imperial claims that seemed monstrous to some but which others saw as—in the words of the Federalists' Constitution—"necessary and proper."

• • •

For twenty-first century Americans, the British Empire is the quintessence of early modern power. That is, after all, what makes the rebels' victory in the American Revolution so impressive. Britons around 1750 might have been gratified by that image, but they also would have thought it was ridiculous. They lived in "a world of insecurity and challenge," "of widespread and often intense fears" that centered on both their enemies' plots and their own weaknesses. The move toward imperial reform emerged in this atmosphere of dread and impotence, and British experiences on the imperial periphery regularly reminded officials that, while the empire's reach was long, its arms were weak.[5] The Georgian leaders who took part in the 1749 Savannah incident certainly knew that all too well. Georgia at midcentury, though, was the periphery's periphery; arguing that its leaders were weak is stating the obvious. More interesting, however, is that Georgia's profound insecurity was shared by British officials in South Carolina, Britain's most prosperous colony on the North American mainland. Thus, in 1751, the colony's governor, James Glen, bemoaned "the situation of this Frontier Province left in the time of War without a single Ship to defend our Trade and extensive Coast from the Neighbouring French and Spanish settlements . . . or from the attempts of their Indians upon our backs." The governor's concerns were well-founded.[6]

Take the ship that Glen mentioned. He had been asking London to station one off South Carolina's coast since 1746. Two years later, the situation was so desperate that Glen hired two private sloops and paid for them out of his own pocket, even though it cost "more than I have saved in the space of almost five Years, that I have been in this Province in the Station of Governor." Or take those Indians whom Glen mentioned. "Their Friendship," Glen wrote in 1748, "cannot be relyed upon, and at best we are . . . in a manner Tributaries to them." Worried about a similar problem a few years earlier, a South Carolina agent had begged London for fifty soldiers, but Glen upped the ante, asking for four forts, two with garrisons of twenty-five men, one with fifty, and the last with one hundred. If two hundred regulars in four small forts does not sound like much in the face of the two thousand warriors that Malatchi claimed to be able to put in the field, recognize that London ignored Glen's "melancholy Account of the misery of this Country"; the forts were never built. To complete South Carolina's misery, its problems were not confined to the ocean or the frontier. Charleston, the colony's economic and political hub, was defended by Fort Frederic and Fort Johnson, both of which the colony's House of Assembly described as being in a "ruinous state." Governor

Glen agreed, writing in May 1752 that he was "most ashamed ... to give" Fort Frederic "the Name of Fort. It is ... a low Wall of Oyster Shells which a Man may leap over! ... [A] Garden Fence is full as a good a Security." Glen went on to sum up the colony's situation at midcentury, and in so doing he provided us with a solid account of British imperial power in colonial North America: "Forts and Fortifications, Batteries and Bastions, Ramparts and Ravelings, sound well; but if they are empty Sounds, they will signify little."[7]

We can hear that empty sound when, less than a month later, Glen asked Mary to resolve a crisis that threatened to bring on "a general Indian War" and endanger the "Safety of this Province." In April 1752, Creeks killed five Cherokees within earshot of Glen's home. The violence promised the further worsening of relations between Britain and the Creeks, and Glen worried that—because the victims had been under British protection at the time of their deaths—the Cherokees would believe the attack could only have happened with "our knowledge and Connivance." Faced with the implosion of his colony's relations with its key Indian neighbors, Glen called upon Mary. After all, she was fluent in Muskogee and English, and she was a kinswoman of Malatchi, the Creek leader whom Glen hoped to pressure into making amends for the attack. Moreover, Mary had a history of working closely with British officials. As she herself noted, one of Glen's predecessors had described her as "a proper Person to be employed in all Negotiations with [the Creek] Nation," and if she was exaggerating when she claimed that the Creek initiatives conducted by Britons in Georgia were "chiefly transacted by my Interest and Influence," then it is also true that she was—in the words of a British colonel—"a most usefull person, and ... May be of Infinite Service to the Crown of Great Britain." It was easy to see why Glen would argue that "Mrs. Bosomworth" was "a very proper Person to be sent into ye Creek nation to demand satisfaction" for the dead Cherokees.[8]

And yet that was far from the whole story. To begin with, Glen picked Mary because he was out of options. He needed an agent; he had approached three other prospects, each of whom thought the job was too dangerous. Glen had no choice but to appoint Mary. Moreover, it would be generous to call Mary's reputation "mixed" in 1752. As Glen searched desperately for an agent, he knew that it had been several years since a British official had a kind word to say about Mary. More recently, the king's representatives had described her as a "pernicious and self-interested" person who was "capable of doing much Mischief" in the service of her "extravagant and idle Claims of Royalty and Lands." In addition, while from one angle her Creek connections offered hope that she could win Malatchi over, from another angle those same connections must have made Glen suspect that Mary would take whatever deal Malatchi offered and present it to Glen as the best she could get.[9]

In fact, that is exactly what happened. Mary colluded with Malatchi to execute an innocent man, leaving Glen no choice but to celebrate an outcome that he knew was unjust; then Mary secretly acquired a Creek affidavit supporting her land claims while doing everything she could to pad her bill for per diem reimbursement. Glen was a smart man, and a knowledgeable one. He could not have been too surprised. But that fact simply leaves us to contemplate a situation in which a seemingly powerful official in a seemingly powerful colony within a seemingly powerful empire felt that Mary Bosomworth was his best option in a dangerous crisis. If Mary was the answer, then the questions confronting the British imperial project at midcentury were powerfully worrisome.[10]

• • •

Malatchi's own imperial project faced equally worrying questions, and once again Mary was very much part of the mix. The central problem that Malatchi confronted was the reality that the Creek nation consisted of dozens of semi-autonomous communities. "Every town," a trader noted, "is independent of another. Their own friendly compact continues the nation." Creek towns were knit together into coalitions by bonds of kinship, friendship, and mutual interest, but there were no coercive institutions—no centralized military, no regularized bureaucracy, no duly constituted constabulary—or legal strictures in place to ensure that communities and their members toed the party line on the issues of the day. Creek towns were free to craft their own geopolitical strategies, and would-be Creek headmen were free to disagree with the course chosen by their own communities.

As a result, leaders in this society relied on persuasion, generosity, influence, and dense and carefully cultivated webs of relationships to produce consensus, and Creeks everywhere accepted the reality that they would inevitably find themselves working at cross-purposes from fellow Creeks. That those disagreements and conflicting agendas did not lead to intra-Creek warfare both testified to the real bonds that held the Creeks together and marked out the limits—if a Creek community went to war against a group they disagreed with, that group was, by definition, not Creek—of the Creek polity. From the perspective of someone habituated to the nation-states of the twenty-first century, the eighteenth-century Creek political system seems chaotic, disorderly, and fundamentally unsystematic. Malatchi and his contemporaries would have disagreed. They were used to thinking locally and building coalitions from there, and they had long since mastered the art of balancing community-based factions and cementing family-inflected alliances. They knew there was method where we might see something verging on madness because they knew the customs, histories, and agendas that mobilized towns and families. The fact that the Creeks were, for much of the eighteenth century, the most powerful polity in the region suggests that they had a point.[11]

Malatchi grew up enmeshed in both this political world and a family that was at the forefront of the Creek effort to create a polity that was larger, more regularized, more powerful, and more enduring than the typical Creek faction or regional bloc. He was born in Coweta, the most powerful town in Creek country, and his father, Brims, was the most influential Creek of his generation. That Brims himself was known as Emperor suggests his commitment to a different mode of Creek leadership and political organization, and the fact that Brims passed both his influence and his "imperial" project to his son—as opposed to his sister's son, as would be typical in a matrilineal society like the Creeks—confirms the family's willingness to experiment socially and politically.[12] That willingness notwithstanding, however, the Creek commitment to community autonomy was not something that could be simply pushed aside. Malatchi, in fact, could not explain his imperial project in Muskogee—the Creeks' lingua franca—without recurring to the town. Thus, when he wanted to say "nation," he said (i)*tálwa*, the same word he used for "town." "Emperor" or "king," in Malatchi's terms, was *mí:kko*, the leader of a town. A literal translation of his word for "kingdom" would be "town leader above a town leader," and the root of "to rule" was, again, *mí:kko*. Put another way, the Spaniard who proclaimed "Language is the perfect instrument of empire" did not speak Muskogee. Malatchi did, and if the title Emperor of the Creek Nation was ever going to be anything but an oxymoron, he would have to overcome the Creeks' ingrained localism.[13]

Malatchi chose to do so by reaching out—way out—to the British. His relationship with South Carolina had gone south in 1746, and his ties with Georgia were, if anything, even more tense, as the 1749 Savannah incident demonstrated. Starting in the late 1740s, therefore, Malatchi began to forge connections with British leaders, not colonists. He first claimed to be emperor, for example, in a 1747 speech to a British officer (not a colonial official) in a British fort (not a colonial capital). That speech began with Malatchi emphasizing that the "Royal King" had sent the officer, who knew better than to credit the colonists' "Lies and bad Talks." Malatchi ended by expressing his eagerness to "have the good Talk from the Great King," who "will always do us Justice and redress our Grievances." He singled out "the Great King's Son" and sent him "this Pipe of Peace with the Arms and dress of my Forefathers." Malatchi was forging a transatlantic "Chain of Friendship," but he was also pushing aside colonial officials.[14]

Creek traditions sanctioned long-distance diplomacy of this sort, but those traditions also emphasized combining words and gifts with personal contacts. For Malatchi, that was where the Bosomworth family came in. In 1747 he sent Abraham Bosomworth, Mary's brother-in-law, "to the Great King with this Talk of mine"; Abraham returned in 1749 bearing large gifts from George II to the Creeks. Mary planned to visit England that summer, a development Malatchi encouraged. He visited Savannah in 1749 to see her off. While there, Malatchi approved a document which "authorized and Impowered" Mary to negotiate the Creeks' land issues with "His Majesty King George or his Great Men and Councellors over the Great Water." A year later, Malatchi signed a similar proclamation, one that began by noting the Creeks' "frequent Complaints . . . to the King's beloved Men here," before going on to say that "the Magistrates of Savannah . . . refused to hear our Talk"; the document then affirmed twice-over that Mary had the power to negotiate with the king "over the Great Water." Because these documents also describe Mary as Creek royalty, historians treat them with a healthy degree of skepticism. Malatchi likely had a similar reaction to Mary's claims, but he also realized that he could use her to advance his larger plan, bypass his colonial neighbors, and forge a direct relationship to London.[15]

Of course, as Malatchi worked the Atlantic angle, he routinely claimed to be emperor, the Creeks' "Rightful and Natural Prince." Doing so made sense—European titles for a European audience. Back home, however, he knew better than to be emperor. After all, as a trader noted, "Indians . . . have no such titles or persons, as emperors, or kings." Instead, in 1746, a year before Malatchi became "Emperor," he took a new Creek title, Opiya Mico. "Mico" refers to the leader of a town. "Opiya" literally means "seeker, one who is looking for something," but it connotes both distance and spiritual power. When combined, the title–Far Off Mico–referenced the widespread tendency among southeastern Indians to reward those with the ability to engage productively with distant and dangerous forces. Malatchi used that title, along with "Emperor," regularly between 1747 and 1752, presenting himself as "Malatchi Opiya Mico Emperor of the . . . Creek Nation," with "prince," "king," or "commanding king" sometimes substituting for "emperor." In other words, variations in phrasing aside, his self-presentation began with his personal name, moved to his Creek title, and ended with a nation-ruling, European-inspired designation. He was banking on the cultural resonance of linking a powerful personal name with a Native title implying that overseas connections buttressed national leadership.[16]

The last reference to Malatchi as Opiya Mico comes from October 1752, at the moment when his willingness to execute someone—albeit not the guilty party—to make amends for the dead Cherokees at Governor Glen's gate allowed him to repair his relations with Charleston. Governor Glen, forced to accept Mary and Malatchi's choice of sacrificial victim, would soon find himself simultaneously declaring victory and praising Malatchi to the skies in his communications with both the Creeks and his superiors back in London: "How glorious is such Behaviour for Malatchi[.] How friendly to the English[.] How Salutory to his own Nation[. H]e therefore deserves to be Esteemed, Valued and Loved by Both English and Creeks." Malatchi was "highly satisfied" with Glen's rhetoric, and he was not shy about spreading the news, calling a meeting of the towns in Coweta's neighborhood where "the Contents of the [governor's] Letter were interpreted Parragraph by Paragraph" and sending a messenger throughout Creek country to "acquaint all the Head Men there what Answer the Governor had given." The newly close relationship with Malatchi's (in Glen's words) "Loving Freind & Brother" in Charleston gave Malatchi the chance to speak and act for an apparently united Creek nation, first in presenting (via the Bosomworths) the Creek consensus about the execution, then in leading a large Creek delegation (accompanied by the Bosomworths) to Charleston in the spring of 1753, and finally in the ensuing conference (at which "Mrs. Bosomworth" was much discussed and her husband ran himself ragged—"heartily tiered"—looking after the Creeks) with Glen. Throughout the Charleston meeting, the documents regularly describe Malatchi as "emperor" or "king." Since he was speaking Muskogee, of course, he was still referring to himself as "mico." But by June 1753, it certainly seemed as if his years as Opiya Mico and the help of the Bosomworths had moved him closer to being "Emperor of the Creek Nation."[17]

By the summer of 1753, thanks to the governor, Britain's rulers back in London would hear of both Malatchi's friendly actions in 1752 and his recent meeting with Glen in Charleston. Britain's leaders learned of the "Dignity" and "Admirable Sense" of "King Malatchi," whose "his very name became a Terror to" his enemies and who "is now looked upon by all his own People as the greatest Leader they ever had." At the same time, devotees of London's periodicals read "King Malatchi's" own description of his efforts to punish those Creeks who had wronged the British, to say nothing of his statement that "I hope, our friendship with the English, will stand upon the same good footing as heretofore."[18]

If they read closely, in fact, both Glen's superiors and London's general public would have been instructed in Malatchi's understanding of imperial politics. As Malatchi demonstrated in a 1753 speech to Glen, he believed that face-to-face relationships could serve as surrogates for long-distance connections: "I have never had the pleasure to see the great King George, nor to hear him talk, but I now see your excellency who are his representative, which I look upon as the same thing." Those relationships were crucial to international harmony: "I have now heard you talk, which is very good, and perfectly agreeable to my own sentiments; and I shall always be careful to observe the treaties between us and our friends the English." And that harmony would bring prosperity: "The great King George has no doubt well considered of the most likely method of establishing a friendship betwixt his subjects . . . and the Indians and wisely concluded, that the most likely way to unite them, and to cement a friendship betwixt them, would be by trade and commerce." As "poor people," the Creeks "had few or no goods to give in exchange for those things they might want from the English," but "it was agreed upon, that skins should be the commodity to be given in exchange." And what might Malatchi himself gain from this imperial relationship? That went undiscussed by the Creek "King," who no longer had to worry about either his ties to Britain or his people's access to British goods.

He could, instead, broaden the reach of his imperial diplomacy. Over the next two years, France's representatives in Louisiana eagerly sought out "the Emperor of the Kawitas," "carressed [him] in an extraordinary Manner," sent him "a Suit of Cloaths . . . that is all covered with gold Lace," and began "treating with him for a private alliance in order to frustrate all the plots of the English." At least one French officer was appalled—"the noble Coweta, whom the French honored with the pompous title of Emperor"—but his superiors viewed Malatchi as a "good and faithful ally of the French." At the same time, of course, Malatchi was asking a British trader about "his Brother the Governor of Carolina" and reminding Glen that "you promised him when he was in Town to let him have whatever he sent for." In response, Glen wrote, "You may readily command every thing in this Province that can procure it," and he pressed Malatchi to "shew your Regard for me your Friend and Brother" and "your Attachment to the English." Even before Glen sealed the letter, though, Malatchi was dead, "depart[ing] this Life, at a hunting Camp, in the Woods" after an extended illness. We have only to think of the goods and services he could command at the time, of the relationships that allowed him to requisition those goodies, of the long-term and long-distance strategies that produced those relationships, and of the memories of (to quote one of Glen's successors) "the late Emperor" to recognize that, while Malatchi may not have died as befits the twenty-first century vision of an emperor, he had successfully leveraged the language to empire. Given the importance of Mary in that success, it was no wonder that Malatchi was remembered after his death not simply as "their [the Creeks'] then Emperor" but also as someone who was "nearly allied to" and "the great friend of the Bosomworths."[19]

• • •

With the exception of the 1749 confrontation in Savannah with which this essay began, that "friend[ship]" appears most clearly in the records surrounding the 1753 conference between the Creeks and Glen. While in Charleston for that meeting, one of the subjects that Malatchi returned to repeatedly was Mary Bosomworth. On May 30, he praised her actions as Glen's agent. On May 31, he described her many services to Georgia, decried the colony's attempts to take her land, and stated clearly that "My Sister, Mrs. Bosomworth, I do not look upon as a white Person. She is an Indian . . . and was entitled to the Lands she possessed." The fact that the daughter of a Creek woman was herself a Creek was a core truth in the kinship system of Malatchi's people, and no Creek at the 1753 conference would have failed to recognize that, in calling Mary his "Sister," Malatchi was invoking not descent from common parents but rather the fact of a shared clan identity. But Malatchi evidently believed his British listeners needed a little remedial instruction in these topics to understand his ties to Mary and her place in the world.

On June 2, though, Malatchi truly warmed to the topic. He started by stating several times that "my Sister Mrs. Bosomworth" had a legitimate claim to the Georgia land; he then denounced Georgian encroachments and said that the Creeks "went to Mrs. Bosomworth, and advised her to go to the great King, and relate the whole Affair to him." Finally, Malatchi turned to the 1749 Savannah incident:

> I came down myself with some of the Head Men to Georgia to see Mrs. Bosomworth embark for England. . . . I was received in a very rude and uncivil Manner, more like Enemies than Friends. . . . They carried Mrs. Bosomworth forcibly from us a Prisoner. The House in which we were was surrounded with armed Men, so that we really began to think that they had

evil Designs against us.... They have taken Mrs. Bosomworth's Land from her, which was given her by the Indians.

Malatchi closed by requesting, in a clerk's words, "that His Excellency the Governor would be pleased to represent the Case of His Sister Mrs. Bosomworth, concerning the Lands, to the Great King. Which the Governor promised to comply with, not only on Account of her own Services but as it was so strongly recommended by [Malatchi]."[20]

For a would-be empress, Malatchi's speech was a godsend. True, Malatchi referred to Mary via a clan term ("my Sister") and a married name ("Mrs. Bosomworth"); he did not call her empress or princess. (It would, in fact, have been impolitic for him to do so since the Creeks in attendance knew that she was neither.) But the Creeks' leading headman did repeatedly take time out of an international conference to attest to the fact that the Creeks saw Mary as one of them, supported her land claims, deplored Georgia's actions, and expected South Carolina's royal governor to let Britain's king know all of this. And better yet, Glen did as requested. He wrote to Georgia's leaders that the Creeks had "complained loudly and publickley of the late Behaviour and Conduct of the Collony of Georgia," and he insisted that "some Remedy must be applied" or peace in the region "will be very precarious." Glen also wrote to London that "King Malatchi" had raised issues that "required Your Lordships particular notice as they appeared to me to be of great importance to the Peace of this Province and of Georgia, I mean the Lands said to be convey'd by the Indians to Mrs. Bosomworth," Malatchi's "near relation."[21]

In other words, by the summer of 1753, Mary had both Malatchi and Glen pressing Britain's leaders on her behalf, an Anglo-Creek lobbying team for an Anglo-Creek empress. Mary had spent the previous two decades repeatedly assembling exactly this sort of Anglo-Creek combination to further her position in the British world. In the 1730s, the Creeks she turned to were Malatchi's predecessors and the Briton was Georgia's de facto leader, General James Oglethorpe; in the 1740s, the Creeks were Malatchi and his allies and the Britons were the Bosomworth family and the British army officers stationed in Georgia. And now, in the 1750s, she deployed Malatchi and Glen. Her imperial project was a relatively late addition to this effort, but that project too was distinctly Anglo-Creek. She first asserted royal status in 1747, proclaiming a British-inspired title only a year after her first print claim to be an Indian; prior to that, she had described herself as a British subject. And the same year that she proclaimed herself empress during the Savannah incident, she also started claiming a Creek name, Coosaponakeesa.

Even Mary's goals were Anglo-Creek. She wanted to get land like a Creek but to own it—and more to the point, to sell it—like a Briton, and she wanted to be reimbursed like a Briton for the goods and services she provided to her Creek kinsmen on Britain's behalf. Living on the margins of two old worlds had its privileges.[22]

In 1754 Mary moved decisively to claim those privileges. That fall, "Coosaponakeesa, Rightful and Natural born Princess of the upper and lower Creek Nations of Indians," arrived in London and requested a meeting with King George. She was turned down, but she and Thomas met with the Lord Commissioners for Trade and Plantations twice, and they submitted petitions to the Board of Trade, the Lord Justices of Council, the Treasury Department, and the Lord Commissioners. Throughout, they played up her royal lineage and authority, requested both reimbursement for past services and confirmation of her land claims, and hinted very broadly that "the Continuance of Friendship & Allaince" with the Creeks and "the defence & protection" of the colonies depended upon the king's answer. The Bosomworths were, in short, employing the imperial equivalent of the full-court press.[23]

British officialdom was unimpressed. The Board of Trade produced a scathing internal report about the Bosomworths, replete with words like "dangerous," "insolent," and "fraudulent"; the Lord Commissioners, for their part, referred to the Bosomworths' "irregular and unprecedented" claims and noted that their actions had produced "great disorders." But unimpressed is not the same thing as unconcerned. British officialdom was, in fact, quite concerned. For the next five years, they were unable to put the Bosomworth matter behind them. Georgia's first royal governor was recalled in disgrace because of his dealings with "Mr. and Mrs. Bosomworth.... Persons interested in Points prejudicial to [the king's] Interests." His replacement repeatedly wrote to London about the Bosomworths: "my Lords it were earnestly to be wished that some expedient might be fallen upon, to put an end to this thorny affair . . . as this Colony in my opinion can never be exempt from apprehensions while it subsists." Finally, in 1758, the Lord Commissioners agreed to settle "The Affair . . . of the Bosomworths" and thereby "induce the Bosomworths to employ that Ascendancy, which they certainly have over some of the Tribes of Indians, to the Good, instead of the prejudice, of His Majesty's Service." In the 1759 deeds that wrapped up the "Affair," Mary was referred to as simply Thomas's "Wife," and coverture and advanced age soon pushed her off Britain's radar screen. But decades later, William Bartram passed along a garbled history about her: "The Crick to this day . . . glory in the name of a widow of their grand chief" who married "Doctor Bosemoth" and received a "dowry" of land. Bartram knew this woman only as "the Queen," a title which suggests the enduring legacy of Mary's imperial project.[24]

• • •

Mary's success seems odd because, of the three imperial projects discussed in this essay, her claims to empire are the ones that appear truly risible. In fact, if we return to Hamilton's comment about empires within an empire, we might even say that Mary's project was monstrous. That is not true of the other two imperial projects. We are, after all, used to discussing the British Empire; it is a historiographical given. Describing Malatchi as an empire builder is not a given, but there is both a long history of labeling Latin American Native polities as empires and a growing interest in seeing colonial-era Native North American peoples as powerful, perhaps even as imperial.[25] So, if we squint a bit, perhaps we can make out a Creek emperor in what is now western Georgia. But Mary Bosomworth as empress? An Anglo-Creek woman who married first an Anglo-Creek trader, then her British servant, and then a chronically indebted and heroically dishonest Anglican minister? A woman who came to prominence first as a trader, interpreter, and go-between, and then as a peddler of (at best) half-truths about her influence and authority? No amount of squinting can make Mary seem imperial. If we stop with that fact, though, then we miss the larger significance of both Mary's claim to empire and her intimate involvement in other imperial projects.

Mary, Malatchi, and their contemporaries in the British government were all speaking the same language, the language of empire. Certainly, they meant different things by "empire," but just as certainly they were all responding in comparable ways to the needs and opportunities of their shared world. It's a commonplace to say that this world was chockablock with empires—British and French, Spanish and Dutch. Like most commonplaces, this one is true but does not do much to enhance our understanding. So, think a bit more deeply about the world that I have been describing. It was a world of connections, of continent-encompassing and ocean-spanning networks, of threats and possibilities from afar—a world, in other words, that was tailor-made for a large-scale entity like an empire. It was a world in which success depended upon bringing others (people from different continents, strange cultures, and foreign nations) into one's plans, ideally in a subordinate position—a world, in other words, that seemed to demand an empire's impulse toward both inclusion and hierarchy. It was a world that was chaotic and disorderly, full of clashing agendas and incompatible visions—a world, in other words, that was open to an empire's structuring habits. Mary and her contemporaries lived in imperial world, not because their world was dominated by any one empire or even by the competition between empires, but rather because empire seemed to provide a solution to so many of life's problems.

And given all of that, Mary's claims to empire point not toward something monstrous and outrageous but rather toward something very human and very ordinary. The nature of life in the early modern world made her claims to empire seem sensible, if not plausible. After all, if the British Empire was not truly imperial yet, and if there was room for a Creek headman to claim to be an emperor, then why shouldn't an ambitious and well-connected Anglo-Creek seek wealth via the language of empire? Mary's imperial claims were at once based upon lies and founded upon a set of core early modern truths—about the nature of empire, about the ubiquity of imperial discourse, and about the possibilities available to a would-be empress when empires were ever-present but never strong. In North America during the middle of the eighteenth century, Mary could claim to be an empress and the most powerful people in Creek country, colonial capitals, and London could not afford to ignore her. In Mary's world, empire was a tool that fit comfortably into some surprising hands.

Notes

1. Because of the rich documentary record associated with the Savannah incident, dozens of historians have written about it. Recent books by John T. Juricek and Steven C. Hahn provide far and away the most thorough and nuanced accounts. See John T. Juricek, *Colonial Georgia and the Creeks: Anglo-Indian Diplomacy on the Southern Frontier, 1733–1763* (Gainesville: University Press of Florida, 2010), chap. six; Stephen C. Hahn, *The Life and Times of Mary Musgrove* (Gainesville: University Press of Florida, 2012), chap. seven. A comment on usage: In what follows, I will frequently refer to Mary Bosomworth as "Mary." Referring to the essay's only woman by her first name—and failing to do so for the men discussed herein—is problematic, but I do so for two reasons. In the first place, the essay features three Bosomworths—Mary, Thomas, and Abraham—and so using "Mary" reduces the risk of confusion. Second, and more important, Mary did not become "Mary Bosomworth" until she married Thomas in 1744. Before that, she was first Mary Griffin, then Mary Musgrove, and finally Mary Matthews; she certainly had Creek names as well. It seems odd to write, e.g., "Mary Bosomworth was doing thus-and-so in the 1730s" when there was no such person. Thus, I have opted to use her first name to identify her.

2. For the ways in which political turnover, cultural developments, and military conflict began re-shaping Britain's empire and Britons' view of the colonies well before 1763, see Stephen Conway, *War, State, and Society in Mid-Eighteenth Century Britain and Ireland*

(New York: Oxford University Press, 2006); Bob Harris, *Politics and the Nation: Britain in the Mid-Eighteenth Century* (New York: Oxford University Press, 2002); David Armitage, *The Ideological Origins of the British Empire* (New York: Cambridge University Press, 2000); Kathleen Wilson, "Empire of Virtue: The Imperial Project and Hanoverian Culture, c. 1720–1785," in *An Imperial State at War: Britain from 1689 to 1815*, ed. Laurence Stone, 128–64 (London: Routledge, 1994); P. J. Marshall, *The Making and Unmaking of Empires: Britain, India, and America, c. 1750–1783* (New York: Oxford University Press, 2005); Timothy J. Shannon, *Indians and Colonists at the Crossroads of Empire: The Albany Congress of 1754* (Ithaca, NY: Cornell University Press, 2000).

3. John T. Juricek, ed., *Early American Indian Documents: Treaties and Laws, 1607–1789*, vol. 11: *Georgia Treaties, 1733–1763* [hereafter GT] (Frederick, MD: University Publications of America, 1989), 151 ("Emperor"). Steven C. Hahn provides the best treatment of Malatchi himself and his family's ambitions in *The Invention of the Creek Nation, 1670–1763* (Lincoln: University of Nebraska Press, 2004).

4. GT, 140 (1747), 176 ("Empress," "Sovereign"), 179–80 (affidavit), 202–3 (1750). See also *The Colonial Records of the State of Georgia* (hereafter CRSGA) 27:16 (vols. 1–28, edited by Allen D. Candler, Kenneth Coleman, and Milton Ready [Atlanta, 1904–1916, 1974–1976], and volumes 29–38 in the microfilm collection of the Georgia Department of Archives and History, Atlanta). Mary's title of choice shifted. "Princess" seems to have become her go-to title, but as late as 1758, British imperial officials back in London remembered that she had claimed "to be rightfull Empress of the Creek Nations"; see ibid., 34: 327. For several 1754 claims that Mary was the Creeks's "princess," see ibid., 28 (part 1): 94; ibid., 26: 466; *Journal of the Commissioners for Trade and Plantations from January 1754 to December 1758* (London: His Majesty's Stationery Office, 1933), 85.

5. I have explored the relationship between Britain's midcentury movement toward imperial modernization and British-Indian relations in Joshua Piker, *The Four Deaths of Acorn Whistler: Telling Stories in Colonial America* (Cambridge, MA: Harvard University Press, 2013), sec. 1. Harris, *Politics and the Nation*, 4 ("insecurity"), 23 ("widespread"), chap. 3. In gesturing at empire's long but weak arms, I paraphrase Frederick Cooper; see David Hancock, *Oceans of Wine: Madeira and the Organization of the Atlantic Market, 1640–1815* (New Haven, CT: Yale University Press, 2009), 423n11.

6. James Glen to the Lord Commissioners for Trade and Plantations, July 15, 1751, Letter Book of James Glen, 128–129, "Dalhousie Muniments: Papers Relating to America, in the Dalhousie Muniments, Scottish Record Office, General Register House, Edinburgh," Huntington Library microfilm #662, San Marino, CA.

7. For ships in 1746, see "Records in the British Public Records Office Relating to South Carolina, 1663–1782," (hereafter BPRO-SC) 22: 207–8, ed. W. Noel Sainsbury, Georgia Historical Society, Savannah; ibid., 23:112–14 (1748). For Indians, see James Glen to the Board of Trade, April 14, 1748, Glen Letterbook, 80–81; The Humble Representation of John Fenwicke late of the Province of South Carolina, [c. 1745], BPRO-SC, 22:40–56, esp. 49 (50–100 men); James Glen to the Lord Commissioners for Trade and Plantations, February 3, 1748, Glen Letterbook, 77–78 (forts); James Glen to the Lord Commissioners for Trade and Plantations, April 28, 1748, BPRO-SC, 22:272–78, quotation ("true") from 275. South Carolina was not left entirely unprotected. Three "Independent Companies"—300 soldiers—were

stationed there off and on from the mid-1740s onward. Larry E. Ivers, *British Drums on the Southern Frontier: The Military Colonization of Georgia, 1733–1749* (Chapel Hill: University of North Carolina Press, 1974), 210–14. *The Colonial Records of South Carolina: The Journals of the Commons House of Assembly* [hereafter SC-JCHA], 12 vols., ed. J. H. Easterby, Nicholas Olsberg, and Terry W. Lipscomb (Columbia: South Carolina Department of Archives and History, 1951–1983), March 11, 1752, 142 ("ruinous"), May 5, 1752, 280 ("ashamed," "Batteries").

8. For the Creek attack and Glen's response, see Piker, *Four Deaths*, preface and sec. 1, SC-JCHA, April 29, 1752, 260 ("Safety"), 262 ("general"); James Glen to the Lord Commissioners, December 16, 1752, BPRO-SC, 25:130–135, quotation ("Connivance") from 132. *The Colonial Records of South Carolina: Documents Relating to Indian Affairs, 1750–1765*, [hereafter DRIA], 2 vols., ed. William L. McDowell Jr. (Columbia: South Carolina Department of Archives and History, 1958, 1970), 1:264 ("proper," "chiefly"); GT, 146 ("usefull"). Journals of South Carolina's Council [hereafter SC-CJ], South Carolina Department of Archives and History, Columbia, May 27, 1752, 259 ("proper").

9. For Glen's difficulty finding an agent, see Piker, *Four Deaths*, chap. 2. CRSGA 25:413 ("pernicious"); SC-JCHA, May 26, 1749, 208 ("Mischief"); CRSGA 36:408 ("capable").

10. For the Bosomworths' agency, see Piker, *Four Deaths*, chap. 8.

11. For the eighteenth-century Creek political system, see Michael D. Green, *The Politics of Indian Removal: Creek Government and Society in Crisis* (Lincoln: University of Nebraska Press, 1982); Kathryn E. Holland Braund, *Deerskins and Duffels: Creek Indian Trade with Anglo-America, 1685–1815* (Lincoln: University of Nebraska Press, 1992); Robbie Ethridge, *Creek Country: The Creek Indians and Their World* (Chapel Hill: University of North Carolina Press, 2003); Joshua Piker, *Okfuskee: A Creek Indian Town in Colonial America* (Cambridge, MA: Harvard University Press, 2004); Hahn, *Invention of Creek Country*.

12. Specialists debate whether Brims was Malatchi's uncle or father. The "uncle" argument relies on two incontrovertible points. First, the Creeks' matrilineal system meant that a son was part of his mother's clan, not his father's, and therefore a man was supposed to inherit from his uncle (mother's brother), not father. Second, the British practiced patrilineal inheritance, assumed that sons inherited from fathers, and were remarkably obtuse when it came to recognizing the implications of other people's kinship systems, especially when dealing with issues of political authority. Therefore, many scholars assume that Creeks referred to Malatchi as Brims's "nephew," but the British heard (and wrote down) "son." We know, in fact, that this sort of mistranslation happened all the time. However, other evidence suggests that we cannot simply assume that "son," in Malatchi's case, meant "nephew." To begin with, some Creeks were gradually moving to a system of patrilineal inheritance during the mid-to-late eighteenth century, and this was especially true of elite Creeks who had intense contacts with Europeans. Malatchi's family certainly fits that bill, and so they may have been slightly ahead of this particular curve. In addition, there are quite literally no references to Brims as Malatchi's uncle. Every time their relationship appears in the records, it is as father-son. Given the number of people who wrote about the men over many decades, I find it unlikely that someone would not have accidently written down "uncle-nephew" if that, in fact, had been their relationship. Even a blind pig will sometimes find an acorn, and for all of their ethnocentrism, the British did sometimes note other uncle-nephew connections among the Creeks. Relatedly, Malatchi's chosen successor was Tagulki, who was, again, invariably

described as his son. Were the British wrong about that too? It seems unlikely that dozens of different observers writing about three generations of a very famous family over the course of more than half a century made exactly the same mistake time and again. My sense, then, is that the "uncle-nephew" argument relies on an ahistorical reading of a Creek kinship system that was, in fact, in flux. Malatchi and his family were at the forefront of some of the eighteenth-century Creeks' most significant political innovations. Historians who accept this point should not be surprised to find that Malatchi and his kinsmen were willing to play with the tenets of the Creek kinship system. Given the intersection of politics and kinship in Creek country, in fact, it seems unlikely that Malatchi's family would seek to alter the former without also modifying the latter.

13. James Adair, *The History of the Americans Indians,* ed. Kathryn E. Holland Braund (Tuscaloosa: University of Alabama Press, 2005), 416 ("independent"); Karen O. Kupperman, *Indians and English: Facing Off in Early America* (Ithaca, NY: Cornell University Press, 2000), 85 ("instrument").

14. For more detail on Malatchi's efforts to reach across the Atlantic, see Piker, *Four Deaths,* chap. 3. For the 1747 speech, see GT, 148–52.

15. GT, 151 ("Great"). For Abraham's status and history, see "The State of the Particular Services of Abraham Bosomworth," in SC-CJ, May 28, 1751, 115–19; Memorial of Abraham Bosomworth, in SC-JCHA, May 31, 1749, 263. For an invoice of the presents, see ibid., May 28, 1751, 110–14; for presents Abraham claimed to have distributed, see Colonial Office [hereafter CO], 5/389, folios 135–148, National Archives, Kew, England. For seeing Mary off, see CRSGA 26:491–92; ibid., 6:252–53, 256–57. For the 1749 document, see GT, 179–80. For 1750, see ibid., 202–5; see also ibid., 211–12.

16. For Malatchi as emperor and related titles, see GT, 148, 151, 154, 155, 157–61, 179, 202–10. Adair, *History,* 415 ("Indians"). Jack B. Martin and Margaret McKane Mauldin, *A Dictionary of Creek/Muskogee* (Lincoln: University of Nebraska Press, 2000), 306 ("seeker"); SC-CJ, October 29, 1746; Hahn, *Invention of the Creek Nation, 1670–1763,* 195–201. Adair, *History,* 118, translates the Chickasaw version of Opiya Mico as "a far-off, or distant chieftain."

17. For the last document to link Malatchi to the title Opiya Mico, see DRIA 1:303–4. For Glen's letter about Malatchi, see SC-CJ, November, 15, 1752, 5–8. For Malatchi's reaction, see DRIA 1:322. For Malatchi between October 1752 and June 1753, see Piker, *Four Deaths,* chap. 4. For the Bosomworths during that same period, see ibid., chap. 8; DRIA 1:409 ("tiered"); BPROSC 25:337 ("Mrs.").

18. James Glen to the Lord Commissioners of Trade and Plantations, June, 25, 1753, BPRO-SC 25:324–30, quotations from 329–330; *The Gentleman's Magazine* 23 (September 1753), 423–26. The quotations in the paragraph that follows are drawn from this periodical. The material published in London originated in a selection of South Carolina Council Journal records that Glen had copied out and mailed to London. One version is published in DRIA 1:387–414. The version Glen had sent to London can be found in CO 5/374, folios 157–86; it was received by his superiors on August 20, 1753. Portions of this material, including several of Malatchi's speeches, were also published in Charleston's newspaper, the *South Carolina Gazette,* in 1753 on July 11, July 23, July 30, and August 6.

19. Mississippi Provincial Archives: French Dominion, collected, edited, and translated by Dunbar Rowland, A. G. Sanders, and Patricia Kay Galloway (Baton Rouge: Louisiana State University Press, 1927-1984), volume 5:157 ("Emperor," "treating"), 171 ("ally"). DRIA

2:55 ("Suit," "promised"), 56 ("Brother"), 68 ("carressed"), 91 ("command"), 103 ("Life"). Jean-Bernard Bossu, *Travels in the Interior of North America 1751–1762*, trans. Seymour Feiler (Norman: University of Oklahoma Press, 1962), 153 ("pompous"). BPROSC, 29:120 ("late"). CRSGA, 28 (part 1): 89 ("friend"), 140 ("then," "allied").

20. N.B.: In this paragraph and the one that precedes it, I quote from, and cite, the more accessible published version of the 1753 conference minutes. However, in the case of a few words, the published version differs from the handwritten version in Britain's National Archives (CO 5/374). In my quotations, I have silently brought the DRIA version into line with the contemporary document. DRIA 1:392 (May 30), 396–97 (May 31), 404–6 (June 2). The clerk's words do not appear in DRIA, but see CO 5/374, folio 181.

21. DRIA 1:462 (Georgia); BPRO-SC, 25: 337–38 (London).

22. For the definitive biography of Mary, see Hahn, *Mary Musgrove*. For her efforts in the 1730s to build ties to both Creeks and Britons, see Piker, *Four Deaths*, chap. 7. For the officers sending positive statements about Mary back to London, see CRSGA 27:16, 17, 196; ibid., 36:252. See also ibid., 27:47–51. For Mary's initial claim of royalty, see GT, 140. Hahn provides the dates for Mary's first claims to an Indian identity and a Creek name in *Mary Musgrove*, 166, 175. My understanding of Mary's land-related initiatives has been shaped most particularly by Juricek, *Colonial Georgia and the Creeks*, chaps. 5–7.

23. CRSGA 26:466–85 ("Coosaponakeesa"), 470 (king). The various petitions are cited in this note, with the exception of the one to the Lord Justices, which is in ibid., 27:66–67. For the meetings, see *Journal of the Commissioners*, 85–87, 103–5. For "Continuance," see "The Humble Petition of Thomas Bosomworth of the Colony of Georgia, Clerk, in behalf of himself and Mary his Wife of Indian Extraction, descended by the Maternal Line from the Sister of the Old Emperor of the Creek Nations; of the same Blood with the present Micos or Chiefs now presiding there; over numbers of which by the Laws and the Voice of the said Nation, she has a Rightfull and Natural Power to Command," February, 4, 1755, T 1/360 (no folio numbers), National Archives, Kew, Great Britain. For "defence," see CRSGA 27:46.

24. For the report, see "State of the Case relative to the Lands reserved by the Creek Indians in Georgia and of the Claims and Pretensions of the Bosomworth's with Respect to Such," 27–62, quotations from 35 ("dangerous"), 36 ("insolent"), 46 ("fraudulent"), vol. 49, folio 7, Shelburne Papers, Clements Library, Ann Arbor, MI. The document is undated and unsigned, but GT, 380n3, provides both pieces of information. *Journal of the Commissioners*, 85–86. CRSGA, 28 (part 1): 23 ("Lords"), 268–77 (deeds; "Wife" appears on 268); ibid., 34:202 ("Persons"), 319 ("Affair"), 329 ("induce"). William Bartram, "Observations on the Creek and Cherokee Indians," in *William Bartram on the Southeastern Indians*, ed. Gregory A. Waselkov and Kathryn E. Holland Braund, 139–86, quotations from 153 (Lincoln: University of Nebraska Press, 1995).

25. The fullest realization of the concept of an indigenous North American empire can be found in the work of Pekka Hämäläinen. See esp. *The Comanche Empire* (New Haven, CT: Yale University Press, 2008), and "The Shapes of Power: Indians, Europeans, and North American Worlds from the Seventeenth to the Nineteenth Century," in *Contested Spaces of Early America*, ed. Juliana Barr and Edward Countryman (Philadelphia: University of Pennsylvania Press, 2014), 31–68. Other notable works in a similar vein include Juliana Barr, *Peace Came in the Form of a Woman: Indians and Spaniards in the Texas Borderlands* (Chapel Hill: University of North Carolina Press, 2007); Kathleen DuVal, *The Native Ground: Indians*

and Colonists in the Heart of the Continent (Philadelphia: University of Pennsylvania Press, 2006); Michael Witgen, *An Infinity of Nations: How the Native New World Shaped Early North America* (Philadelphia: University of Pennylvania Press, 2012). Matthew Bahar's soon to be published monograph, *Storm of the Sea: Indians and Empires at the Heart of the Sea*, will bring the concept of an indigenous empire to the East Coast.

⇜ 7 ⇝

THE AMERICAN SOUTH IN THE FRENCH EMPIRE

Les Étés Longs et Chauds

Christopher Morris

Toward the end of May 1673, Father Jacques Marquette discussed his plan to canoe down the Mississippi River with some Menominee Indians he met in what is now the state of Wisconsin. They warned him that "the great River was very dangerous, when one does not know the difficult Places; that it was full of horrible monsters, which devoured men and Canoes Together; that there was even a demon, who was heard from a great distance, who barred the way, and swallowed up all who ventured to approach him." Most terrible of all was the climate in the southern reaches of the river. "The Heat was so excessive In those countries," they assured the Jesuit, "that it would Inevitably Cause Our death." Marquette brushed off the warnings as the fanciful imaginings of childlike heathens. The horrible monsters turned out to be cliff paintings of mythical horned serpents or underwater panthers that guarded the turbulent, indeed, treacherous waters at the mouth of the Missouri River. The demon proved to be a rock and water formation near the mouth of the Ohio River, which Marquette's paddlers cautiously skirted. However, the warnings about the heat were to be heeded, for it truly was, as Marquette described it, "excessive and Unbearable," all the more so if Marquette continued to wear the heavy black robe that marked his order. In the canebrakes below the mouth of the St. Francis River, Native peoples reclined on scaffolds above smoldering fires, the smoke from which kept mosquitoes away, and beneath awnings that shielded them from the sun. Marquette's men rigged a sail, not to catch the wind, of which there was little, but to provide shade as they drifted southward in the heat of a mid-July day. By the end of summer, he was back in Wisconsin recovering from an ailment contracted while on his southern excursion, very possibly the same ailment he battled all fall and winter, dysentery, and from which he died the next spring. Marquette died in the cold, but it may well have been the heat and humidity of the lower Mississippi River region, conditions conducive to dysentery, that killed him, as the Menominee had predicted.[1]

In the same year that Marquette suffered the heat and humidity of the North American south, his fellow countrymen established two trading posts in even hotter regions of the globe, in India at Chandernagore, on the Hooghly River in present-day West Bengal, and at Pondichéry, on the Coromandel Coast in present-day Tamil Nadu. In West Africa, the French Company of Senegal opened for business at Saint-Louis near the mouth of the Senegal River. The First French Empire may have begun in the cold of the St. Lawrence River Valley, but it soon expanded to include colonies and settlements in the tropics, in India, Africa, and the West Indies.

Strictly speaking, the climate of the Deep South is not tropical. The tropics are by common definition humid and the mean monthly temperature never falls below sixty-four degrees Fahrenheit. The South is sufficiently humid, but even along the Gulf Coast, winter average temperatures are about ten degrees too cool to meet the definition. Nevertheless, summers in the South are hot. The average summer high in southern Louisiana is 90 degrees Fahrenheit, one degree cooler than the summer highs for Calcutta, which is in the tropics. Until the widespread use of air conditioning in the latter half of the twentieth century, the South's long, hot summers were brutal, and they were the subject of much inquiry into the relationship between climate and culture. One thinks of Clarence Cason's critique of southern race and class relations, *Ninety Degrees in the Shade* (1935), or the opening sentence of Ulrich Bonnell Phillips's book, *Life and Labor in the Old South* (1929): "Let us begin by discussing the weather, for that has been the chief agency in making the South distinctive." For the founders of France's colony in the American South, coming as so many of them did from Canada, the weather took some getting used to; it also took some understanding, as participants in the enterprise of empire both on the ground in Louisiana and in the ministries and salons of France struggled to imagine how such a climate could be settled by French people and incorporated by them into the French Empire. Would it be settled as a cultural and economic extension of French

Canada? But perhaps it was too hot. Would it be integrated into the sphere of the West Indies? But perhaps it was too cool.[2]

The French Empire, the Spanish Empire, the United States, the South, the Mississippi Valley, the eighteenth-century Atlantic, the hot and humid southerly extreme of the temperate latitudes: Louisiana has a place within the histories and historiographies of all these spaces. When people and ideas moved between Louisiana and Europe, Canada, Africa, and Asia, they connected these spaces and created new ones. Moreover, without ever moving through geographic space, some people nevertheless moved through and thereby connected historical spaces; for example, those who began their lives within territory contested by French and Native peoples and ended them within the state of Louisiana, within the South, and within the United States. Some people, again without moving through geographic space, began their lives in a densely forested, swampy terrain that had a moderate climate and ended in a cleared drained, and cultivated landscape that had warmed over time. Or cooled. How climate had changed was less certain than that it had changed. As seventeenth and eighteenth century French moved into what is now Louisiana and the Gulf South, they encountered a climate not familiar to them. When they discussed their experiences with Louisiana's climate, comparing and contrasting it with climatic experiences in other geographic and historical spaces and theorizing about its effects on French settlers and the progress of colonization, they brought Louisiana into a transatlantic and early modern scientific discourse on global climate and climate change. They also initiated the ongoing discussion of the relationship between history and climate in the American South.[3]

The heat, humidity, and their effects on health and disease, natural resources including forests, fish, wildlife, soil quality and arability, all figured into French calculations of how they could best live in and profit from their colony in the lower Mississippi Valley. They debated whether the environment was sufficiently similar to that of France to permit them to live within it as French. They also debated how the environment, including the climate, might be transformed into one that was more familiar. Inevitably, such discussions connected the North American South through comparison and analogy to other hot and humid places within the empire, while distancing it from such cold places as Canada. The transatlantic discussion of the nature of Louisiana's climate and whether the colony was best thought of, administered, and developed as an extension of the Antilles or of Canada stemmed in part from uncertainty about a climate that was not quite like either, that was too cool to be like the one, too hot to be like the other. Such ambivalence also stemmed from the fact that Louisiana was founded, settled, and administered by Canadians, who on one hand viewed it as an extension of New France, but who at the same time knew better than anyone just how different the weather was at the southern end of France's North American Empire.

The founder of the Louisiana colony, Pierre Le Moyne d'Iberville, arrived on the Gulf Coast late in 1698. The previous fall, in the midst of a snowstorm and with ice forming on the water near his ship, he had captured the British fort of Port Nelson on the shores of Hudson Bay. His superiors in France demonstrated their approval by tasking him with establishing a permanent French presence at the mouth of the Mississippi River, lest the British or the Spanish get there first, and so he went from the cold of Hudson Bay to the heat of the Gulf of Mexico.

In fact, Iberville never spent a summer in Louisiana. In 1702 he left the colony for France, which was again at war with England. Assigned to the West Indies, he captured the island of Nevis, then died rather suddenly in Havana of either yellow fever or malaria. The exact cause of death was uncertain, but whatever it was, it signified the tropics. Iberville's career, which took him from the snow and ice of a scurvied Canada to the heat and humidity of a feverous West Indies, personified the gulf colony's location at the seam between the temperate and tropical halves of the French Empire.

From its very beginnings, New France was known for scurvy, a disease caused by a deficiency of vitamin C due to a lack of fruits and vegetables but which early modern Europeans associated with particular places. In winter of 1535–1536, scurvy broke out among Jacques Cartier's crew at the Iroquoian village of Stadacona on the St. Lawrence River. It was a disease apparently unknown to Cartier and his men, who therefore assumed it was a New World contagion. By 1609 Stadacona was gone and construction on the settlement of Quebec had just begun when scurvy broke out again, apparently confirming the disease's ties to place. By the seventeenth century, despite the reports of outbreaks onboard ships during long voyages, the French knew scurvy as *mal de terre,* land sickness, and attributed it to cold winters in densely forested places such as Canada and Scandinavia. For example, Marc Lescarbot, who in 1623 wrote in his journal of an outbreak of scurvy at St. Croix, on the present-day border of Maine and New Brunswick, attributed it to the "bad quality of the air by reason of Lakes that be thicke there, and of the great rottenness in the Woods, whose odour the bodies having drawne up, during the raines of Autumn and Winter." Moreover, the logic of medieval medicine suggested to Lescarbot that as the cold of winter drew inward and bound up the body's melancholy black humors—by which Lescarbot meant fluids, black bile in particular—one became more susceptible to scurvy.[4]

Scurvy was thought to be far less common, though not unheard of, in warmer climates, which were associated instead with other diseases. Englishman Thomas Trapham, for example, who in 1679 authored the first publication in the genre that historian Geoffrey Hudson calls hot climate medical literature, attributed the relative infrequency of scurvy in Jamaica to the island's steady salt breezes. However, if cold climates bound up bodily humors, hot climates loosened them so that they moved too freely, as indicated by excessive perspiration, which in theory led to stomach pain, headache, and listlessness, which in turn made one susceptible to "Pestilent Feavours and Calentures," "Frenzies," and "other hot cholerike sicknesses." Durand de Dauphine visited Virginia in 1689 and learned from English settlers that hot weather and salt water, the very conditions thought to alleviate scurvy, brought on fevers and general bad health, an explanation the Frenchman found plausible. Probably no disease was more associated with the tropics than yellow fever, a disease thought to be of African origin that first broke out in the Americas in 1648, in the Yucatan and several West Indian islands, including French Guadeloupe.[5]

The connections between body, place, and climate were taken for granted by the time French Canadians ventured out of the Great Lakes region and down the Mississippi River into the heat and humidity of the North American South, about which many complained. "Very Hot," Jesuit Father Jacques Gravier recorded in his journal during his first trip southward, while somewhere in the vicinity of present-day Memphis. Heat spoiled supplies of meat, which his party had to throw overboard. "The navigation of the Mississipi is very slow and tedious, and very difficult," Gravier wrote, "especially in ascending it. It is also very troublesome on account of the gnats and other insects called Mosquitoes, midges, And black flies; the heavy rains: the excessive Heat." Conditions were somewhat better at Biloxi, where sea breezes helped "temper the Heat, which would otherwise be excessive." Writing in late May, while ascending the Mississippi River from New Orleans to Arkansas, Father Paul du Poisson noted that the heat "was increasing every day. During the whole voyage we had only one entire day that was cloudy; there was always a burning sun above our heads." Once at the Arkansas settlement, Poisson found that "the excessive and extraordinary heat which has prevailed this year, has prostrated all the people with sickness."[6]

Jean-François-Benjamin Dumont de Montigny arrived in Quebec in 1715. It was his first time to New France, where the river froze every winter, carriages were fitted with iron runners and propelled by iron rods, horses wore ice shoes, and soldiers wore ice skates. "I was not used to walking on the ice, and I fell down repeatedly, so many times that the fingers of both hands froze," he recorded in his journal. On this occasion Dumont nearly lost his fingers to frostbite. When at last he arrived at the inn where he was to spend the night, he proceeded straight to the stove to warm his hands, only to be admonished by the innkeeper, who explained that he needed to thaw his hands slowly, in a bucket of cold water. The procedure worked, Dumont acknowledged, though not without considerable pain. "I thanked him kindly and returned to my room, vowing to myself that in such winter weather the entire town could go up in flames, but I would not go out." In 1719, Dumont was reassigned to Louisiana, where the winters were easy, he later recalled. It was the summers he found difficult to bear. The heat of the sun was so strong that if one was not careful it caused "severe headaches and even death to some who have been exposed to its rays. There are some in particular"—fishermen, he observed—"who feel its impact on their skin." "Exposure often causes a fever, and after nine days, their skin peels off in strips."[7]

Not all found the heat of southern Louisiana so unbearable, indeed, some found the climate quite similar to that of France. Writing in October 1727, from New Orleans to her father in Rouen, Ursuline Sister Marie Madeleine Hachard wrote that "we are nearer to the sun here than in Rouen," by which she meant close to the equator, "without, however, having very great heat. The winter is very moderate. It lasts about three months, but there is but a little light frost." If Dumont de Montigny and others expressed concerns about the climate, Hachard was typical of those who were more optimistic, who saw the weather as providing no obstacle, or even better, as facilitating colonization because it was moderate, like that of France. Though located at the same latitude as Egypt and the Barbary Coast of Africa, the climate of Louisiana, claimed Antoine Simon Le Page du Pratz, was more like that of Languedoc, while northern Louisiana summers, he claimed, were like those of La Rochelle.[8]

In fact, that was not the case. The summer temperatures of La Rochelle are similar to those of Montreal and much milder than those of Louisiana, which is warmer even in winter, though not nearly so much warmer as Montreal is colder. Global temperatures were cooler in the seventeenth and eighteenth centuries, during the period of the so-called Little Ice Age, which may have exacerbated the disparity in North America between summer highs and winter lows. It was the extreme cold of Quebec's winters that made Louisiana's hot summers seem unbearable to so many of the Canadians who settled it as an extension of New France, and so tropical, like the West Indies, not only to them but to the officials in France to whom they reported. The climate of Louisiana, reported Jesuit Father Louis Vivier, in 1750, "although infinitely more bearable than that of the islands, seems heavy to one who has recently landed," especially heavy, he might have added, to one who has recently landed from Canada. And lest anyone think the climate was like that of France, Vivier added that it was "too hot for wheat." Without wheat there would be no local source of bread, and without bread, Louisiana could never be like France.[9]

Seventeenth and eighteenth century Europeans formulated abstract theories of climate that predicted global patterns that somehow had to account for anomalies presented by those with firsthand experience and knowledge of specific locales. Geosymmetry was the guiding concept for understanding climate in the abstract and held that locations of similar latitude around the world had similar climates. As Alain Manesson Mallet explained in 1683, parallel climates circled the earth between the equator and the poles and were distinguished by the length of day and exposure to the sun. Moreover, the climatic zones south of the equator mirrored those north of the equator. Global climate was thought to be symmetrical west to east and north to south. Climate and latitude were synonymous. In theory, one could look at a map of the world and without ever leaving Europe, know the climate of any place in the world, and knowing the climate, know what and to some extent who might be found there. "These lands are," wrote Pierre Biard in his description of New France, "parallel to our France, that is to say, at the same climate, and even elevation, and by the law of astrology, they must have the same influences, same inclinations, and temperature." Biard had firsthand knowledge of the North American climate and ought to have known better. However, theory predicted that the climate of the North American South was similar to that of North Africa, Persia, Bengal, and central China, whereas the climate of Canada was like that of northern Europe, and Biard clung to theory.[10]

The concept of geosymmetry persisted through the eighteenth century and well into the nineteenth century, even as evidence of local anomalies mounted, the most obvious of which was that the climate of North America was far more extreme than it should have been. In his entry on climate for the famous *Encyclopédie* he edited with Denis Diderot, Jean le Rond d'Alembert acknowledged that while wind, volcanoes, proximity to sea, and mountains all complicated the action of sunlight upon the land, affecting climates within climatic zones, nevertheless, d'Alembert held that climates encircled the earth in parallel between equator and poles and were distinguished first and foremost by length of day. No quaint notion dreamed up by provincial Europeans at the dawn of their encounters with distant continents, climatic symmetry was a serious theory that survived the scientific revolution, European expansion, and a steady stream of what might have been, but which was not, regarded as contradictory empirical evidence. In 1823 William C. Woodbridge drew a map of world climates that took into account local information collected since the beginning of European expansion, including information on forest cover, water quality, and proximity of Arctic ice but which held true to the theory of geosymmetry. Following a suggestion made by Alexander von Humboldt a few years earlier, Woodbridge replaced the straight latitudinal lines that marked distance from the equator with modulating latitudes that demarcated climatic zones. As the original theory of geosymmetry had predicted, and as the information presented on the map proved, within the climate zones that circled the globe—labeled as frozen, cold, warm, hot—contained between modulating lines of latitude that were no less fixed on the map than the earlier straight lines, could be found similar resources, opportunities, and people. In a concession to more than three centuries of history, the map indicated that whereas Europe ranged from the cold zone of the Baltic states to the warm zone of the Mediterranean states, North America ranged more dramatically, from frozen to hot. Unwilling to surrender the essential idea of geosymmetry, the map sought to rationalize the universal and the particular, by indicating that what could be found in a climatic zone on one side of the world could be found in the same zone on the other side and everywhere in between.[11]

Almost from the beginning of the establishment of New France, there occurred a debate over the source of the extreme cold in a region that was, theoretically, supposed to have a climate similar to that of old France. The most common explanation attributed the cold to the dense forests, which were thought to prevent circulation of warm air and to shade the earth from the sun's warmth. Francesco Giuseppe Bressani, an Italian Jesuit who spent seven years in Canada, disagreed, and instead attributed the cold climate to the dry air. "I do not dispute whether the cold of new France is more intense than that of Countries which are under the same latitude; certain it is, that it is much more acute, and accompanied with much snow and ice, which keep the rivers frozen five and six entire months. But all this may be an effect of the dryness, which is necessary for the snows and ice." He continued, "cold alone, although intense, is not sufficient without either some little body, or exhalation, or dry quality, therefore water, even in its natural state, would be fluid; and where dryness prevails, although the cold is not greater than elsewhere, it contracts or expands itself into snow and into ice." The dryness and Bressani added, the exceptional healthfulness of the Canadian climate was the consequence of its stony and sandy soil, "whence the Sun cannot derive other than very dry exhalations." The rivers and lakes of Canada added no noticeable moisture to the air, according to Bressani. Their bottoms consisted of rock and sand, their surfaces were in a constant state of agitation from wind and current, which restrained the action of the Sun upon them, and their waters were pure and wholesome in quality, which altogether meant they emitted few if any vapors.[12]

The idea that climatic variations were related to land cover dated to antiquity. Theophrastus, a student of Aristotle, had observed that clearing and planting the land around Philippi, by allowing sunlight to reach and even enter the broken ground had over time warmed the local climate. However, he also noted that wetland drainage had cooled the climate in the vicinity of Larissa, in Thessaly, so much so that the olive trees were dying. Whereas water had a moderating effect on local climates, tree cover had a cooling effect. It is likely that observant cultivators ever since Theophrastus had their own ideas regarding land, trees, water, air, and climate, which they may have discussed among themselves without writing about them. Such ideas were discussed more openly following European encounters with the dense forests of North America. In 1664 Englishman John Evelyn wrote, in *Silva: or, A Discourse of Forest-Trees*, that dense forests interfere with the interaction of land, air, and sun, causing excessive and unhealthy humidity and the soil to release noxious vapors. He pointed to North America as an example of a land that was excessively forested, and consequently was cold, damp, and unhealthy. Of course, excessive deforestation could be a problem. Evelyn wrote to address concerns in England of an irreversible timber shortage that would have consequences for the navy and the defense of the realm. Similar discussions took place in France, resulting in the French Forest Ordinance of 1669, Europe's first nationwide conservation regulation.[13]

Bressani returned to Italy and died there in 1672, nearly three decades before the establishment of Louisiana, but had he lived to know of its establishment, he would have been struck by its climate, which contrasted markedly with the rest of France's North American Empire. He would have attributed Louisiana's extreme heat to vapors released from the pervasive, muddy soils and the numerous stagnant marshes with their mucky bottoms and foul waters. Furthermore, he would have expected Louisiana's population to be as sickly as Canada's population was, in his view, healthy.

These were the conclusions drawn by another priest who did visit Louisiana shortly after its establishment. In 1717 Father François Le Maire wrote glowingly of Louisiana in a report he submitted to the Navy Council. Following the theory of geosymmetry, he explained that the colony's climate was similar to that of Persia, India, and China, and that for the most part the air was healthy and the soil fertile. He cautioned, however, that the country near the gulf was prone to deadly diseases of the sort that afflicted other parts of the Americas, most notably the more southerly Spanish colonies. "I admit that even far from the sea, up some 20 miles inland, it is a little unhealthy, but it comes only from the earth that is not cleared, where the sun cannot dry the swamps and bottom lands," which consequently "release vapors harmful to the health and that it is the true cause of the unhealthy air we breathe." Le Maire noted that on the islands, presumably the West Indies, that had been cleared and dried, inhabitants enjoyed constant good health.[14]

The European concept of geosymmetry regarded the Old World of Europe and what Europeans knew of North Africa and Asia as the norm, and the New World of the Americas as the exception, because of its peculiar geophysical features, including its extensive forests and wetlands that in part defined it as a new world, unmodified by people. The word "excessive" conveyed the abnormality of Canada's cold and Louisiana's heat in a way that proved the rule of Europe's normality and the validity of the theory of geosymmetry. But if the excessive cold of Canada and heat of Louisiana were attributable to local conditions, some of those conditions might be altered—perhaps not ocean currents or land elevations, but forests and wetlands most definitely—and the climate might thereby be normalized. Just what Louisiana could become with a little tinkering was the subject of some debate. Le Maire clearly believed that the climate of the colony would be much improved if the forests were cleared and the sun permitted to dry the swamps and reduce the vapors. Similarly, Vivier thought that "if the country were less densely wooded, especially on the side toward the sea, the wind coming thence would penetrate inland and greatly temper the heat," enabling the cultivation of grains, and perhaps even the vine, two items that signified a French environment.[15]

America was a wilderness land to Europeans, a land not yet brought under Christian dominion. It was what Europe had once been. It was also a wilderness climate, unfit much of the year for civilized life. Comparing Quebec and Paris, which shared latitude, the Comte de Buffon held that centuries of change to the French landscape had moderated the Parisian climate. Even the German climate was improving, although it was not yet as salubrious nor therefore was the culture as civilized as that of France. Indeed, by the late eighteenth century it seemed to some that Paris had acquired the climate of ancient Rome and with it the natural environment to nurture the culture and politics of Rome's modern heir.[16]

By the mid-eighteenth century, the relationship between land, water, and air, and the mediating effects of trees, had caught the attention of naturalists in certain quarters of the French Empire where deforestation had noticeably altered the local climate. As Richard Grove has argued, this led to a serious effort by the French to rehabilitate through reforestation colonies suffering from drought. In North America, however, deforestation was considered to be either a nonissue, because of the abundance of forests, or a good thing if it contributed to drying the land and climate. So whereas reforestation on Mauritius or in Pondicherry in India made sense because those were places prone to summer drought, in Louisiana the problem was more with the excess of stagnant water, a problem that might be dealt with by clearing forests away.[17]

How local climates might be changed was a serious matter. Louisiana was too warm to produce the fur-bearing animals that made Canada valuable, and too cool to produce sugar on the West Indian scale. But what if the climate were altered one way or the other? Climate change, however, involved much more than economics. Alembert wrote that harsh climates produced harsh people, and he pointed to the Japanese and Germans as examples. In contrast, moderate climates produce people of mild character, such as, he offered, Indians and Spaniards. The Comte du Buffon, among others, believed climate shaped more than temperament, that it determined the physical and moral well-being of people, and perhaps even the whiteness of Europeans, as well as the redness, brownness, and blackness of non-Europeans. In the supplement to volume four of *Histoire Naturelle* (1749), Buffon famously attributed the physical and moral differences between Europeans and "all the newly discovered people" to "the influence of the climate" and its effects on the variety, quality, and abundance of food. Microclimatic variations attributable to elevation, proximity to the sea, as well as to winds, temperature, and humidity, could be crucial, Buffon explained, because of their effects on diet and health. In a second entry on climate for the *Encyclopédie*, supplementing the one written by Alembert, the physician Gabriel-François Venel wrote that in medicine, unlike in geography, climate is defined by more than mean temperature. It necessarily included everything that could affect health, including quality of air, water, soil, food, all to which, Venel explained, could be attributed the physical and moral differences between peoples.[18]

In 1733 Englishman John Arbuthnot, a royal physician, penned an influential essay published in French nine years later on the subject of health and the environment. Arbuthnot specifically discussed the effects of air on the human body, explaining that "a rich fertile Soil, abounding with Variety of active, volatile, and unctuous Particles, with a considerable Degree of Heat, must necessarily produce inflammatory Distempers in Human Bodies; such are rich Meadow Grounds, upon the Banks of Rivers, which, with the increasing Heat of the Spring, bring Fevers, especially intermitting: Such rich Grounds, in very hot climates, are extremely unhealthy, as we find by the Relations of Travellers. On the other hand," he continued, echoing Bressani, "a gravelly Soil, on the Banks of a running Stream, is generally healthy." Rivers that were prone to flooding were particularly dangerous. Arbuthnot's observations of the Nile River were applied by others to the Mississippi River near New Orleans. According to Arbuthnot, while floodwaters could temporarily cause the abatement of extreme heat as they receded, those who lived nearby were "subject to all the Diseases from putrid and stagnating Water, and Exhalations from Heat after the Inundation is over; and these are often pestilential; therefore such as can, live remote from the Channel of the River."[19]

In light of these theories of the unhealthy effects of hot, humid climates, mounting evidence that people could change microclimates presented risks, but also exciting possibilities if it meant the extremes of heat and cold could be moderated, diseases could be reduced, and agriculture made not only more profitable, but in the case of food crops, more nourishing. Most of all, the notion that human activity affected climate held out the possibility that foreign climates could be made more like that of France. If Louisiana was not quite like Languedoc, perhaps it could be. To put the matter another way, within the framework of a theory of geosymmetry that explained the heat and cold of some places as excessive, that is to say, abnormal or anomalous, tinkering with climate change at the local level amounted to normalizing and thus naturalizing climate.

Writing in the 1750s, Antoine Simon Le Page du Pratz bemoaned the disappearance of the cypress forests around New Orleans. "The cypresses were formerly very common in Louisiana," he wrote, "but they have wasted them so imprudently, that they are now somewhat rare." However, reports by du Pratz and others of the disappearance of the cypress forests were greatly exaggerated and probably referred to a selective culling of the largest and most accessible trees along the rivers. Cypress forests on the whole remained quite extensive for more than another century.[20]

Why, then, was Le Page du Pratz so quick to sound an alarm about the disappearing cypress forest? The answer in part lies in the value of cypress timber as a natural resource, relative to the costs of extracting it. But there was another, perhaps more urgent reason to fear the loss of forest cover in Louisiana. Trees were thought to be climate modifiers. The climate of New Orleans, though on the same latitude as North Africa, had, according to Le Page du Pratz, a climate more like that of the south of France. Louisiana was more temperate, and healthier, than it should have been. Why? "I ascribe [this] to two causes," Le Page wrote: "the first is, the number of woods, which though scattered up and down, cover the face of this country: the second, the great number of rivers. The former prevent the sun from warming the earth; and the latter diffuse a great degree of humidity." Clear the forests, and the result might be the Africanization and Caribbeanization of a European-like climate, and perhaps the Africanization of French colonists.[21]

Not everyone agreed. Some, Louis Vivier for example, writing at about the same time as Le Page, expressed his view that Louisiana was already too hot, too African, too West Indian, and not at all like France, precisely because of the forests and swamps. Clearing and drying the land would, in his view, cool the local climate. Dumont believed the climate had already begun to cool. "Throughout this space of ground that is not found in lakes and marshes in these immense forests are planted lands," wrote Dumont, "for some years, winter is more severe than it was at the beginning of the establishment of the colony, whether we should attribute this change to the clearing of land, or some other unknown cause." Of course, whether Louisiana was too hot or just right and whether it was warming or cooling was a matter of perspective. Le Page du Pratz was a salesman of sorts, determined to put the best face on French colonization. However, like Le Page du Pratz, those who believed Louisiana was too hot for proper French colonization associated local climate conditions with trees, water, and vapors and argued that if trees were cleared away, cooling winds and a drying sun would modify the temperature. Moreover, all associated climate with health. These were stakes far greater than those of the cypress lumber trade. The extent of forest and wetlands seemed directly related to the suitability of Louisiana for French settlement.[22]

The arduous process of clearing forests and draining wetlands, undertaken primarily by the forced labor of enslaved Africans and indentured Europeans had no noticeable effects on the colony's climate, which remained far from frenchified. That much was clear to Pierre Laussat, the last French governor, who arrived in 1803 to find a decidedly non-French environment. Writing from New Orleans, he described the weather as pleasant but variable, warm one day, quite cool the next. "Such was May in Louisiana," he wrote. "We were to see what the summer months, about which people frightened us, were like." Summer weather was upon him all too soon. "The great heat waves began about mid-June with stifling mornings, a storm in the afternoon, and in the evening a coolness that was deeply appreciated. It was said that the summer of 1803 was less unbearable than usual. During the month of August, we even had some dismal days interspersed with fresh air. The sun alone was scorching; its rays darted forth ruthlessly upon the body. The thermometer, in the shade of my study, registered as high as thirty-two degrees [90 degrees Fahrenheit]; its average was twenty-eight or twenty-nine. Some days were unbearable—like the desert heat of Africa, as I imagine it." That summer Laussat got sick, suffering he thought from a touch of yellow fever. The "excessive heat retarded and prolonged my convalescence," he wrote.[23]

At about the same time Laussat was experiencing the long, hot summers of New Orleans, others were looking to the former colony for ideas on how to improve the climate in France. In 1809, at the behest of the Institute of France, Simon-Louis Pierre de Cubières proposed to rid France of unhealthy wetlands by importing cypress trees from Louisiana. Caught up in the optimism of the early French Republic, when some thought that climate, like politics, could be perfected, Cubières argued that wetlands in Flanders, la Bresse, and Saint-leger could be reclaimed by planting them with southern bald cypress. This American tree, he believed, would dry up and purify wet, brackish, muddy, and generally unhealthy wetlands in France as it had in Louisiana.

> When I reflect on the immense quantity of water that one tree draws up in the space of twenty-four hours, to restore the large part to vital area, I am struck by the great advantage which will result from the cultivation of cypress in the cesspools of stagnant water that surround so many villages and hamlets. The presence of this tree neutralizes the noxious miasmas that the mires exhale, contributes to the healthiness of the air, and the inhabitants of those rotting countrysides, by that means to be sheltered from autumn fevers of which they are so often the victims.

Cubières perhaps associated, incorrectly, the reduction of wetlands in Louisiana with the expansive cypress forest; levees, drainage ditches, and agriculture were the true causes, and together they would take quite a toll on the forest. Nevertheless, the theories that had explained the cold of Canada and the heat of Louisiana in terms of forests and wetlands persisted into the nineteenth century, when they became even more scrutinized by men of science on both sides of the Atlantic.[24]

Laussat's primary responsibility while governor of Louisiana was to effect the transfer of the colony from France to the United States. In the succeeding years new arrivals from the United States once again tried to change the Louisiana environment, to de-frenchify and de-Africanize it. Former US Army surgeon Jabez Heustis drew attention to the dangers posed by swamps, humidity, and vapors, when he warned of New Orleans's unhealthy environment, with its "noxious effluvia" and "putrefying fish." Other newcomers from the United States expressed similar concerns, faulting not only the wetlands and its fish but also the people that caught, marketed, and consumed them. Louisiana was a degraded environment inhabited by degraded people. Drying wetlands, clearing forests, ridding the river banks and city streets of rotting fish, improving climate, health, and morals, and re-ordering society along new racial and ethnic lines that would Americanize the former French colony, were aspects of a single project that was at than moment about to commence. The new project was no more successful than the old. Nevertheless, Heustis was not exceptional. For many northerners, New Orleans and the South generally, with its long, hot summers, its humidity, its reputation dating back to the era of slavery for moral decadence, would seem un-American. This was the case until the advent of air conditioning, which made possible the phenomenon of the Sun Belt South, although for some, the southern climate and culture continue to seem exotic.[25]

Initially frustrated in his efforts to conceptualize the best way of approaching the restoration of New Orleans after Hurricane Katrina, Cuban-born architect and New Urbanism advocate Andres Duany had an epiphany: "I had been predisposed by the media to think of New Orleans as a charming but lackadaisical and fundamentally mismanaged place." Then, as he pondered a house framed by banana trees, he suddenly realized that "New Orleans was not really an American city, but rather a Caribbean one." Indeed, it was "the most organized, wealthiest, cleanest, and competently governed of Caribbean cities." According to Duany, the problem was that New Orleans was measured against Minneapolis, not Havana or Kingston. Considered in its proper context, of the Caribbean, not North America, New Orleans made sense. Of course it did not occur to Duany that the banana trees, a tropical plant, were as exotic to the New Orleans climate as Minnesota-style government was to its politics. That New Orleans and the South are measured by the standards of other cities and regions in other environments, social, cultural, and natural, is it turns out, nothing new.[26]

Notes

1. Jacques Marquette, "Voyages du Pere Jacques Marquette, 1673–75," in *The Jesuit Relations and Allied Documents: Travels and Explorations of the Jesuit Missionaries in New France 1610–1791*, vol. 59, *Lower Canada, Illinois, Ottawas, 1667–1669*," ed. Reuben Gold Thwaites (Cleveland: Burrows Brothers, 1899), http://puffin.creighton.edu/jesuit/relations/relations_59.html#_ednref43 (accessed January 6, 2013).

2. Clarence Casson, *Ninety Degrees in the Shade* (Chapel Hill: University of North Carolina Press, 1935). Ulrich B. Phillips, *Life and Labor in the Old South* (Boston: Little, Brown, 1929), 3. See Ray Arsenault's article, "The End of the Long Hot Summer: The Air Conditioner and Southern Culture," *Journal of Southern History* 50 (November 1984): 597–628, on the significance of the air conditioner in the South. On the difficult adjustment of Europeans to the southern climate, the heat and humidity in particular, see Marion Stange, *Protecting Settlers' Health in Colonial Louisiana and South Carolina, 1720–1763* (Goettingen, Germany: Vandenhoeck & Ruprecht, 2012). Recent inquiries into the relationship between climate and southern identity include Joyce E. Chaplin, "Climate and Southern Pessimism: The Natural History of an Idea" in *The South as an American Problem*, ed. Larry J. Griffin and Don H. Doyle, 57–82 (Athens: University of Georgia Press, 1995); Joyce E. Chaplin, *An Anxious Pursuit: Agricultural Innovation and Modernity in the Lower South, 1730–1815* (Chapel Hill: University of North Carolina Press, for the Institute of Early American History and Culture, 1993), 66–91; and Mart Stewart, "Let Us Begin with the Weather?: Climate, Race, and Cultural Distinctiveness in the American South," in *Nature and Society in Historical Context*, ed. Mikulas Teich, Roy Porter, and Bo Gustafsson, 240–56 (Cambridge: Cambridge University Press, 1997).

3. On history and space, see Richard White, "The Nationalization of Nature," *Journal of American History* 86 (December 1999): 976–86. On climate and the first European empires, see Richard H. Grove, *Green Imperialism: Colonial Expansion, Tropical Island Edens and the Origins of Environmentalism, 1600–1860* (Cambridge: Cambridge University Press, 1995); Richard H. Grove, *Ecology, Climate and Empire: Colonialism and Global Environmental History, 1400–1940* (Cambridge, UK: White Horse Press, 1997); and Sherry Johnson, *Climate and Catastrophe in Cuba and the Atlantic World in the Age of Revolution* (Chapel Hill: University of North Carolina Press, 2011). Histories of Louisiana and the French North American Empire say little if anything about climate, although Sophie White, "'This Gown ... Was Much Admired and Caused Much Jealousy': Fashion and the Forging of Identities in French Colonial Louisiana," in *George Washington's South*, ed. Tamara Harvey and Greg O'Brien, 86–118 (Gainesville: University Press of Florida, 2004), briefly mentions the effect of climate on dress in colonial New Orleans.

4. The Lescarbot quotation comes from Samuel Purchas, *Hakluytus posthumus, or, Purchas his Pilgrimes*, 20 vols. (Glasgow: James MacLehose and Sons, 1906), 18:239–40. W. L. Grant, ed., *Voyages of Samuel de Champlain 1604–1618* (New York: Charles Scribner's Sons, 1907), 147–48. Kenneth J. Carpenter, *The History of Scurvy and Vitamin C* (Cambridge: Cambridge University Press, 1986), 10–11. According to Richard Guthry, a Scot who in 1629 witnessed the ravages of scurvy in a new colony in Nova Scotia, scurvy was "a sickness insident to that country the maner and nature of this scurvy disease is, if any fall sicke of it in the winter usually they die of it, but if in summer, bathing with the scurvy leafe pottage, and

drinks of wilde pise [peas, although probably not a legume, but a spurge or euphorbia], but especially the wilde fitche, frech victuals and bear which fishermen doe bring heir, are great means of the recovery of there healths." N. E. S. Griffiths and John G. Reid, "New Evidence on New Scotland, 1629," *William and Mary Quarterly*, 3rd ser. 49 (July 1992): 502. Stéphanie Tésio, "Climat et médecine à Québec au milieu du 18e siècle," *Scientia Canadensis: Canadian Journal of the History of Science, Technology and Medicine / Scientia Canadensis: revue canadienne d'histoire des sciences, des techniques et de la médecine* 31 (2008): 155–65. Tésio discusses the physician Jean-François Gaultier, who lived in Quebec in the mid-eighteenth century, where he meticulously recorded temperatures and illnesses. Gaultier concluded that cold winters brought on fevers, colds, and upper respiratory illnesses, whereas warm, humid summers brought on dysentery and other illnesses of digestive tract. Gaultier apparently made no mention of scurvy.

5. Geoffrey L. Hudson, ed., *British Military and Naval Medicine, 1600–1830* (New York: Editions Rodopi B.V., 2007), 34. Thomas Trapham, *Discourse on the State of Health in the Island of Jamaica* (London: R. Bolter, 1679). Genevieve Miller, "Airs, Waters, and Places in History," *Journal of the History of Medicine and Allied Sciences* 17 (1962): 129–40. Kupperman, "Fear of Hot Climates," 224–25. Darrett B. Rutman and Anita H. Rutman, "Of Agues and Fevers: Malaria in the Early Chesapeake," William and Mary Quarterly 33 (January 1976): 44. John B. Blake, "Yellow Fever in Eighteenth Century America," *Bulletin of the New York Academy of Medicine* 44 (June 1968): 674. Elsewhere in the British colonies, people reached similar conclusions about the relationship between clearing, cultivation, and health. See Chaplin, "Climate and Southern Pessimism," 70.

6. Jacques Gravier, "Relation of Journal of the Voyage of Father Gravier, of the Society of Jesus, in 1700, from the Contry of the Illinois To the Mouth of the Mississippi River," in *The Jesuit Relations and Allied Documents: Travels and Explorations of the Jesuit Missionaries in New France 1610–1791*, vol. 65, *Lower Canada, Mississippi Valley, 1696–1702*, ed. Reuben Gold Thwaites, 109, 159, 161 (Cleveland: Burrows Brothers, 1899). Paul du Poisson, "Letter from Father du Poisson, Missionary to the Akensas, to Father Patouillet [1726]," in *The Jesuit Relations and Allied Documents: Travels and Explorations of the Jesuit Missionaries in New France 1610–1791*, vol. 67, *Lower Canada, Abenakis, Louisiana, 1616–1727*, ed. Reuben Gold Thwaites, 289 (Cleveland: Burrows Brothers, 1900).

7. Jean-François-Benjamin Dumont de Montigny, *The Memoir of Lieutenant Dumont, 1715–1747: A Sojourner in the French Atlantic*, trans. Gordon M. Sayre, ed. Gordon M. Sayre and Carla Zecher, 77, 83, 372, 373 (Chapel Hill: University of North Carolina Press for the Omohundro Institute of Early American History and Culture, 2012).

8. Emily Clark, ed. *Voices from an Early American Convent: Marie Madeleine Hachard and the New Orleans Ursulines 1727–1760* (Baton Rouge: Louisiana State University Press, 2007), 41. Antoine Simon Le Page du Pratz, *Histoire de la Louisiane*, vol. 1 (Paris, 1758), 139–140.

9. Louis Vivier, "Letter from Father Vivier, of the Society of Jesus to a Father of the Same Society, Among the Illinois, November 17, 1750," in *The Jesuit Relations and Allied Documents: Travels and Explorations of the Jesuit Missionaries in New France 1610–1791*, vol. 59, *Lower Canada, Illinois, Ottawas, 1667–1669*, ed. Reuben Gold Thwaites, 209 (Cleveland: Burrow Brothers, 1899). On the Little Ice Age, see Emmanuel Le Roy Ladurie, *Times of Feast, Times of Famine: A History of Climate since the Year 1000*, trans. Barbara Bray (Garden City, NY: Doubleday, 1971).

10. Alain Manesson Mallet, *Description de l'univers, contenant les differents systêmes du monde, les cartes generals & particulieres de la geographie ancienne & modern*, vol. 1 (Paris, 1683), 34, 66. Pierre Biard, *Relation de la Nouvelle France* (Lyon, France, 1616), 9.

11. Jean le Rond d'Alembert, "Climat," in *Encyclopédie, ou dictionnaire raisonné des sciences, des arts et des métiers par une Société de Gens de lettres*, ed. Denis Diderot and Jean le Rond d'Alembert, vol. 3, 532–34 (Paris, 1753). William C. Woodbridge, "Isothermal Chart, or View of Climates & Production, Drawn from the Accounts of Humboldt & Others," dated January 13, 1823. Engraved map, with added color, 20.3 × 28.2 cm., from Woodbridge's *School Atlas to Accompany Woodbridge's Rudiments of Geography: Atlas on a New Plan* . . . (Hartford, CT: Oliver D. Cooke, [1823]). Karen Kupperman, "The Puzzle of the American Climate in the Early Colonial Period," *American Historical Review* 87 (December 1982): 1262–89. Robert Markley, "Monsoon Cultures: Climate and Acculturation in Alexander Hamilton's *A New Account of the East Indies*," *New Literary History* 38 (Summer 2007): 527–50.

12. Father Francesco Gioseppe Bressani, "A Brief Account of Certain Missions of the Fathers of the Society of Jesus in New France," in *The Jesuit Relations and Allied Documents: Travels and Explorations of the Jesuit Missionaries in New France 1610–1791*, vol. 38, *Abenakis, Lower Canada, Hurons, 1652–1653*, ed. Reuben Gold Thwaites, 219–27 (Cleveland: Burrows Brothers, 1898), http://puffin.creighton.edu/jesuit/relations/relations_38.html.

13. Clarence J. Glacken, *Traces on the Rhodian Shore: Nature and Culture in Western Thought from Ancient Times to the End of the Eighteenth Century* (Berkeley: University of California Press, 1967), 129–30, 462, 487–88; Kenneth Thompson, "Forests and Climate Change in America: Some Early Views," *Climatic Change* 3 (March 1980): 47–64.

14. François Le Maire, "Mémoire sur la Louisiane, pour estre présenté avec la carte de ce païs au Conseil souverain de la Marine" (1717), 4–5, in *La Bibliothèque nationale de France, Gallica online* (accessed February 5, 2013), http://visualiseur.bnf.fr/CadresPage?O=NUMM-109468&T=pleinEcran.

15. Vivier, "Letter from Father Vivier," 209.

16. Glacken, *Traces on the Rhodian Shore*, 669.

17. Grove, *Green Imperialism*, 168–263.

18. Alembert, "Climat," 3:534. Alembert drew heavily on the fourteenth-century geography of Syrian scholar Abu Al-fida' Isma'il Ibn 'ali ibn Mahmud Al-malik Al-mu'ayyad 'imad Ad-din, known in Europe as Abulfeda. Georges-Louis Leclerc, Comte de Buffon, *Histoire Naturelle, Générale et Particulière, Supplément*, 4:555 (Paris: Imprimerie Royale, 1777). Gabriel-François Venel, "Climat," in *Encyclopédie, ou dictionnaire raisonné des sciences, des arts et des métiers par une Société de Gens de lettres*, ed. Denis Diderot and Jean le Rond d'Alembert, 3:534 (Paris, 1753). Chaplin, "Climate and Southern Pessimism," 75. Chaplin, *An Anxious Pursuit*, 75–80.

19. John Arbuthnot, *An Essay Concerning the Effects of Air on Human Bodies* (London: J. Tonson, 1733), 71–72, 134. Jean Arbuthnot, *Essai des Effets de l'Air sur le Corps-Humain*, trans. M. Boyer de Pebrandié, 90, 169 (Paris: Jacques Barois, 1742). James Lind, *Diseases Incidental to Europeans in Hot Climates* (London: T. Becket and P. A. De Hondt, 1768). See the relationship between climate and physical appearance in Linda Nash, *Inescapable Ecologies: A History of Environment, Disease, and Knowledge* (Berkeley: University of California Press, 2006), 27–29; Susan Scott Parrish, *American Curiosity: Cultures of Natural History in the Colonial British Atlantic World* (Chapel Hill: University of North Carolina Press for the Omohundro

Institute of Early American History and Culture, 2006), 83. Some believed hot climates dried up Englishmen's blood, causing them to become unhealthy and pale, and thus whiter rather than darker.

20. Le Page du Pratz, *Histoire*. Craig E. Colten, "Cypress in New Orleans: Revisiting the Observations of Le Page du Pratz," *Louisiana History* 64 (2003): 463–77.

21. Le Page du Pratz, *Histoire*, 140. The quotation is from an English translation of Le Page du Pratz, *The History of Louisiana* (1774; repr., New Orleans: Pelican Press, 1947), 108.

22. Jean-François-Benjamin Dumont de Montigny and Jean-Baptiste Le Mascrier, *Mémoires historiques sur la Louisiane*, vol. 1 (Paris: J. B. Bauche, 1753), 9.

23. Pierre Clément de Laussat, *Memoirs of My Life*, trans. Agnes-Josephine Pastwa, ed. Robert D. Bush, 28, 41–42 (Baton Rouge: Louisiana State University Press, 1978). On frenchification of non-French, primarily Native cultures, see Sophie White, *Wild Frenchmen and Frenchified Indians*.

24. Simon-Louis Pierre de Cubières, *Mémoire sur le Cyprès de la Louisiane* (Versailles: P. J. Jacob, 1809). On nineteenth-century theories of forests and climate change, see Kenneth Thompson, "Forests and Climate Change in America: Some Early Views," *Climatic Change* 3 (March 1980): 47–64. If the French tended to be optimistic about the possibilities of climate change, the English tended to be pessimistic. See Chaplin, "Climate and Southern Pessimism," 76–78.

25. Jabez Wiggins Heustis, *Physical Observations, and Medical Tracts and Researches, on the Topography and Diseases of Louisiana* (New York: T. & J. Swords, 1817), 43. The classic account of the South as a colony of the North is C. Vann Woodward, *Origins of the New South 1877–1913* (Baton Rouge: Louisiana State University Press, 1951), chap. eleven. Woodward and others focus on economy. On climate as an inhibitor of the modernization of the southern economy in the twentieth century, see Arsenault, "End of the Long Hot Summer, 597–628. Chaplin, *An Anxious Pursuit*, 67, 83–85.

26. Andres Duany, "Restoring the Real New Orleans," *MetropolisMag.Com* (February 2007), http://www.metropolismag.com/story/20070214/restoring-the-real-new-orleans (accessed February 5, 2013).

8

INCIDENTAL IMPERIALIST

John Bartram's Florida Travels, 1765–1766

Robert Olwell

More than ninety years ago, Charles MacLean Andrews, one of the "inventors" of colonial American history, denoted 1763 "a great turning point."[1] With the signing of the Treaty of Paris in February of that year, Britain acquired a vast amount of new territory. In North America, they gained Canada and everything east of the Mississippi River.[2] In the Caribbean, the British were ceded the islands of Dominica, Grenada, Saint Vincent, and Tobago.[3] On the eastern side of the Atlantic, "His Britannick Majesty" took possession of the French entrepôt of Fort St. Louis at the mouth of the Senegal River. In 1765 this outpost was combined with Fort St. James on the Gambia River to form the colony of Senegambia, Britain's first colonial footstep into Africa.[4] Meanwhile, in South Asia, the British East India Company, reinforced by military forces sent from Britain and allied with native rulers, had, in the course of the war, decisively defeated their French rival and laid the foundations of the British Raj.[5]

In Andrews's assessment, these gains dramatically transformed Britain's role in the world and "securely established" its new "imperial status."[6] Although the word *empire* was not as disreputable in 1924 as it would later become, Andrews hastened to absolve the British of any blame for what had occurred. They "had not been consciously or aggressively aiming at empire," he asserted, "but had obtained it through efforts directed to other ends," namely, winning the Seven Years War.[7] Andrews's portrayal of Britain's attainment of empire as a fortunate windfall paralleled J. R. Seeley's remark of forty years earlier that the British "conquered... half the world in a fit of absence of mind."[8] If such disclaimers were to be taken seriously, one might argue, paraphrasing a British imperialist of the mid-twentieth century, that never was so much taken by so few so unintentionally.

Today, most scholars of the subject would agree that the decade of the 1760s marked a watershed in Britain's relations with the world, but they would likely dismiss any pleas of innocence regarding British intentions. Instead, Britain's imperial sunrise is usually set in the context of long-term and large-scale processes of market expansion and global integration and closely linked to the emergence of the British fiscal-military state at the end of the previous century. According to this view, the British Empire as it emerged after 1763 was not the offspring of an immaculate, or at least accidental, conception but instead was the child of deeply laid economic, political, and social structures mated to immediate, cold-blooded, policy.[9]

While the genealogy of the British Empire can confidently be traced to these macrolevel causes, it is still difficult to discern any single person's role in its creation (the elder William Pitt and Robert Clive perhaps excepted). Connecting individuals, that is, the microlevel of analysis, to the larger scales of historical change is a task fraught with complexity. To paraphrase Marx, while people make their own history, they are also made *by* history, or the historical circumstances in which they live.[10] We are all simultaneously both historical agents and subjects. The subject of this particular essay offers a case in point. Viewed in isolation, his actions and words may well merit being described as both innocent and incidental as regards the larger imperial project. Moreover, to secure the patronage of the wealthy and powerful, our protagonist developed a mode of self-representation that required, to a remarkable degree, an "absence of mind." Yet as will be seen, even while our subject was, quite literally, rowing his own boat, he was also, in his own small way, helping to build the empire, and also, paradoxically, helping to destroy it.

The hero of our story is John Bartram, a Pennsylvania Quaker one year older than the century (see Figure 8.1). Like most Quakers, Bartram was a pacifist, but he was also a patriot; along with other Britons and British-Americans, he closely followed the course of the Seven Years War in the Philadelphia newspapers. In common with many other colonials, Bartram idolized Prime Minister William Pitt, who came into office in the darkest days of the conflict and led the Pan-Atlantic British nation to victory.[11] Yet, amid the chorus of hosannas that followed the war's triumphant conclusion, Bartram sounded a slightly off-key, or at least skeptical, note. "Pray say no more about our great British empire while we must not be a farthing ye better for it," he wrote.[12]

Figure 8.1. Charles Willson Peale, "Portrait of John Bartram of Darby." The name of both the artist and sitter are written in 18th-century script on the back of the 13 × 10 inch painting; no date is given, but the portrait must have been made in the interval between Peale's arrival in Philadelphia in June 1776 and Bartram's death in September of the next year; from the image as printed in Francis Harper, ed., *Transactions of the American Philosophical Society* 33 (December 1942): i.

After the war, when Bartram gazed upon maps of the new "British Empire and Its Limits" on sale in Philadelphia bookshops, he did not see imperial glory as much as the prospect of a safe passage through the American interior.[13] "I make no difference who got it," he remarked, "if I could but travail safely in it."[14] Bartram's wanderlust was stoked by a story he "read lately in our news paper of a noble & necessary scheme . . . to search all ye country of Canada & Louisiana for all natural productions, convenient scituations for manufactories & different soils minerals & vegetables." Despite his advanced years, Bartram volunteered for the job, or at least the southern half of it. "I should be exceedingly pleased," he enthused, "to make a thorough search not only at Pensacola but ye coast of florida Alabama, Georgia & ye banks of ye Misisipi."[15]

However, in Bartram's mind, before any such expedition could be launched, Britain had first to secure the peaceful acquiescence of the Natives. He knew that the sight of a Briton (or colonist) traveling through their country taking note of "convenient scituations for manufactories" and collecting samples of soils and minerals "would alarm ye Indians to the highest degree." Native Americans knew that naturalists and surveyors blazed a trail that settlers would eventually follow. Consequently, if King George's new Indian subjects were not first "subdued," Bartram feared that "ye discoverers would be exposed to the greatest Savage cruelty[:] ye gun[,] tomahawk[,] torture[,] or revengeful devouring Jaws."[16]

Bartram knew of Indians' "cruelty" firsthand. In 1711 his father was killed by a Tuscarora war party while pioneering land in North Carolina.[17] Moreover, at the same time that Bartram was expressing his desire to explore Britain's new American territories, the region was torn by violence. In May 1763, led by the Ottawa leader, Pontiac, and inspired by the Delaware prophet, Neolin, Native Americans responded to the news that by the terms of the Treaty of Paris, the British claimed sovereignty over both them and their lands by unleashing a coordinated attack upon traders and forts throughout western Pennsylvania and the region north of the Ohio River.[18] By the fall the war, which most subsequent historians have called Pontiacs' Rebellion (thus taking the Indians' new subject status for granted), had degenerated into a bitter stalemate of ambushes and raids. One example of colonists' hardened attitude toward the Indians was a letter printed in the *Pennsylvania Gazette* in September 1763 that advocated offering "a Reward for Scalps."[19]

Bartram addressed his letters to Peter Collinson, a fellow Quaker and a wealthy London merchant. Collinson was also a fellow of the Royal Society and an accomplished botanist.[20] While Collinson declined to fund such an exploratory expedition himself, as perhaps Bartram had hoped, and hinted, he might, he soothingly agreed that if "Wee had some Wealthy publick Spirited People who would encourage a search of those fine countries," there was "No One as well Accomplished for that work as thy self." Unfortunately, Collinson added, "Court politicks so engross the attention of the Great Men that they have no room to think of any thing Else."[21]

Collinson could vouch for Bartram's qualifications from personal knowledge. For three decades the two men had been engaged in a remarkable transatlantic collaboration. In 1732, while perusing a book of leaf prints sent to him by Joseph Breintnall, a Philadelphia scrivener and a member of Benjamin Franklin's Junto (an artisan-based mutual improvement society), Collinson read in a marginal note that some of the leaves had been gathered by one "Jno. Bartram."[22] Collinson, who had long been in search of an American plant collector, quickly wrote to Bartram proposing that he assume this role. Bartram agreed, and for the next thirty-two years, he painstakingly collected, prepared, and shipped plants and seeds to Collinson. Eventually, Bartram procured specimens not only from southeastern Pennsylvania but on collecting expeditions that ranged as far and wide as Lake Ontario, Virginia, and the Carolinas.[23]

When he received Collinson's invitation, Bartram was living with his wife and children in a modest farmhouse that he had built himself on the west bank of the Schuylkill River four miles from Philadelphia. Although he had only a rudimentary education, Bartram was very inquisitive, or in the language of the time, "curious," and had, as he later described it, a lifelong "inclination to plants." (Both of these traits are indicated by his hobby of keeping an eye out for interesting looking leaves that he could give to Breintnall during his trips to the city.[24]) He was also keen to broaden his horizons beyond the narrow confines of his farm and the ordinary routines of his life. Thus, Collinson's invitation offered mutual advantage. If Bartram's location in the colonies promised to provide Collinson with "exotic" botanical specimens, the latter's metropolitan connections gave Bartram an entrée into the Enlightenment project of ordering nature.

Their correspondence and collaboration began at a propitious moment in the development of natural history. In 1735 Carl Linnaeus, a Swedish naturalist, published a new taxonomy for classifying plants by easily observable characteristics.[25] The ease and utility of the Linnaean method sparked a quest among gentleman botanists to collect and categorize all of creation according to the new system. More was at stake than the advancement of knowledge. The first person to "discover," that is, identify, a plant, might be honored by having their name bestowed upon it. In 1739, for example, Linnaeus named a newly classified plant species "Collinsonia Canadensis" after Peter Collinson. Linnaeus had received the specimen from Collinson, who had, in turn, received it from Bartram. Overcome with gratitude, Collinson replied that Linnaeus had given him "a species of Eternity.... That is, a name [that will last] as long as Men and Books Endure."[26] Bartram may have been similarly gratified the following year, when Collinson presented a letter that he had written describing the dissection of a rattlesnake's head to a meeting of the Royal Society that was subsequently published in the society's *Philosophical Transactions*.[27]

Besides his collecting expeditions, Bartram also planted an eight-acre garden between his house and the Schuylkill, where he cultivated many of the seeds he gathered.[28] This made it possible for him to fulfill requests from Collinson and his circle for additional specimens without having to return to the wild to procure them. Bartram and his garden became a destination for "enlightened" visitors to America.[29] Three days after arriving in Philadelphia after a six-week ocean crossing in September 1748, Linnaeus's student, Pehr Kalm, walked to "John Bartram's seat," where he remained for most of the next two months.[30] Kalm was utterly charmed by Bartram, who, he wrote, "possessed that great quality of communicating everything he knew."[31] For his part, Bartram, perhaps tired of his guest's incessant questions, could not resist playing a prank on his more learned visitor. With a straight face, Bartram told Kalm "that when a bear catches a cow, he kills her in the following manner: he bites a hole into the hide, and blows with all his power into it, till the animal swells, and dies."[32] The credulous Swede eagerly copied down this story and eventually printed it verbatim in his book.

Word of the acquisition of Florida in 1763 aroused great interest in British botanical circles because the region promised to contain many "undiscovered," that is, unclassified plant specimens. The ink had hardly dried on the Treaty of Paris before British botanists began to scheme how they could acquire Florida seeds for their greenhouses and planting beds; very few had any interest in traveling to the colony themselves. Prominent botanists with strings to pull, pulled them. When James Grant, the colony's newly appointed royal governor, departed for St. Augustine in the summer of 1764, he carried "extensive commissions" from both Lord Bute (the king's trusted advisor and former prime minister), and the Duke of Cumberland (the king's uncle and the commanding general of the army), to send them each a "collection of seeds" as soon as possible following the establishment of his government.[33]

By the fall of 1764, as the violence on the frontier began to wane and the "subdued" Indians began to negotiate the terms of their subjection within the British Empire, Bartram became impatient. Fretting that he might "yield to the infirmities of age, or death" before Collinson or another "public-spirited" person stepped forward to fund his proposed expedition, and perhaps equally that someone else might beat him to it, he took matters into his own hands. In a precocious example of scientific entrepreneurship and also provincial presumption, Bartram packed up "a little Box of such specimens as I am sure . . . never came to England before" and sent it to Collinson with strict instructions that it was to be given directly to the king. (George III, whose palace stood on the site of the modern royal botanical garden at Kew, was known to have a green thumb.) It was Bartram's hope that this botanical calling card might at last persuade "men of curiosity" at court to provide him with enough money "either by public authority or private subscription" to enable him "to travel [for] a year or two through our King's new acquisitions, [and] to make a thorough natural and vegetable search."[34]

Although he later grumbled "thou knows nothing [of] what it is to solicit at Court any favour," Collinson carried Bartram's box of botanical treasures to the palace.[35] To Collinson's obvious surprise, the gambit paid off. In April 1765, he wrote to tell Bartram that "thy wishes" have been to "some degree accomplished." "Our gracious King," Collinson explained, has "appointed thee his botanist, with a salary of £50 a year" and has given you a commission to travel to Florida and "make observations on the soil, [and] the country ... [as well as] gather specimens of plants, fossils, ores, etc."[36]

Fifty pounds was not a princely sum, and Bartram's appointment might easily be dismissed as a quixotic gesture of royal largesse. But his appointment came in the middle of a formative decade for British "imperial science," that is, for putting the acquisition of knowledge in the service of the state.[37] Bartram's "commission" can be set alongside other contemporaneous examples of government subsidies for scientific enterprises. In 1761, for example, astronomers had been dispatched to the far corners of the world to measure the transit of Venus.[38] At the very moment of Bartram's appointment, Captain John Byron (Lord Byron's grandfather) was in command of the frigate HMS *Dolphin* as it voyaged across the Pacific on a circumnavigation of the globe that has been described as "the first recognizably scientific voyage undertaken by the navy."[39] Similarly, in August 1768, when Captain James Cook and HMS *Endeavour* departed from Plymouth bound for Tahiti, the ship's company included an astronomer, Charles Green (brought along to record the 1769 transit of Venus), as well as two botanists, Joseph Banks and Daniel Solander.[40]

As soon as he received word of his appointment, Bartram made arrangements to travel to Florida. On July 1, 1765, he boarded a ship in Philadelphia bound for Charleston, South Carolina. It was his first sea voyage, and he proved to be no sailor; in his diary he wrote that the tossing waves made him "extream sick & head very dizey."[41] Once in Charleston and back on firm ground, he called upon Alexander Garden, a physician and botanist (the gardenia flower was named for him). Garden received Bartram cordially but was incredulous and obviously green with envy when he learned of the royal commission. "Is it really so?" Garden immediately wrote to John Ellis, another botanist and the London-based agent for the colony of West Florida. "John is a worthy man," the doctor grudgingly admitted, "yet to give the title of King's Botanist to a man who can scarcely spell, much less make out the character of any one genus of plants, appears rather hyperbolical." Garden asked Ellis if Bartram was in reality merely a hired hand: "Is he not rather appointed or sent, and paid, for searching out the plants of East and West Florida and for that service only to have ... his expences?"[42]

Garden's surmise reflected the Enlightenment distinction between physical labor (or direct observation) and mental reasoning, or in this specific case, between mere plant collecting or gardening and botanical science. The painstaking task of locating, gathering, preserving, and shipping specimens was less important than the next step: applying "science," that is, knowledge and reason, to identify, classify, and, if needed, name the new plants.[43]

From the start of their long correspondence, Collinson sought to employ Bartram as a gardener and plant collector while reserving to himself the role of "natural philosopher." Although it was Bartram who found the plants in nature, it was Collinson who received the lion's share of the credit for their "discovery" when he first introduced them to European botanical circles. According to Collinson's ideal of scientific "mercantilism," Bartram's task, like that of a dutiful colony, was to export raw materials to the metropolis where Collinson could transform them into the more valuable commodity of science.[44]

Whenever Bartram sought to transcend this instrumental role, he was gently put back in his place and reminded that his job was to produce data and not deductions. For example, when he included a carefully prepared analysis of the contents of one shipment, Collinson replied that "thy remarks ... are very curious, but I think take up too much of thy time and thought."[45] Collinson found Bartram's speculations an unnecessary and unwelcome trespass into his own self-appointed role. "As to thy care of the names," he wrote dismissively, "it does not much signify; for when I see them grow or flower, [I] can soon distinguish them."[46] Similarly, when Bartram asked to be sent botanical treatises, Collinson demurred, replying that "I would not have you puzzle with ... the Ancient & Modern knowledge of Botany" and bid Bartram to "Remember Solomon's advice, in [the] Reading of Books there is no End."[47] Instead of studying botany, Collinson advised Bartram to tend to his farm and "proceed gently in these curious things, which belong to a man of leisure."[48]

Reading through their accumulated correspondence, it is clear that the two men came to have a genuine regard for one another but also that they engaged in a decades-long song and dance over the precise nature of their relationship. What Bartram wanted to see as a transatlantic partnership of equals, Collinson preferred to perceive as a more hierarchical arrangement between a metropolitan philosopher and his colonial assistant.

A comic but also revealing contretemps concerned "an ould fine velvet cap" that Collinson sent to Bartram much as one might pass on well-worn clothes to a beloved servant. Upon opening the package, Bartram immediately recognized the implication of the gift and rejected it. The hat, he wrote Collinson, must have been sent by some mistake; it "was so rotten that I never brought it home."[49] His benevolent, if also paternalistic, gesture rebuffed, it was Collinson's turn to be insulted. He tried to turn the story around by accusing Bartram of putting on airs. It "very much surprises Mee to Find thee . . . art a philosopher prouder than I am," he replied. "My Cap it's True, had a small Hole or Two, [but] Instead of giving it away I wish thee had sent it . . . back again. It would have served Mee . . . to have worn in the Country in Rainy weather."[50] Bartram ended the affair of the cap with an apology of sorts but also with a clear warning to Collinson not to send such things in the future. "I am sory" to have discarded your gift, he began, but the "cap . . . was so rotten mouldy & eat full of holes [that] I never did believe it was thine. . . . I thought some sory fellow had thrown it [away]."[51]

While Bartram may have resented both Collinson's paternal pose (the Englishman was only five years his senior) and his metropolitan condescension, he nonetheless became adept at providing the raw and unprocessed information that was most likely to meet with Collinson's approval. It was precisely the "absence of mind," or reasoning, in Bartram's nature writing that Collinson and his colleagues most highly praised, for it enabled them to imagine him almost as an objective lens through which they might observe a world that lay thousands of miles away.[52]

When Collinson circulated examples of Bartram's nature writing among other members of his circle, the Pennsylvanian was lauded as "a mightily exact observer," "a most accurate observer of nature," or "naturally a wonderful observer."[53] The great Swede himself praised Bartram as the "greatest natural botanist in the world."[54] By describing Bartram's talent or his prose as "natural," Linnaeus and the others emphasized the fact that he was unlettered and uneducated. For their purposes, this was considered one of his greatest assets. They worried that Bartram's "natural," although in fact, carefully cultivated, technique of close description would be diminished if he acquired too much learning and began to "puzzle" (that is, theorize) over what he observed. Collinson's description of Bartram to another botanist as "a down right plain country man" was both patronizing and affectionate, but it also suggested just what it was about Bartram that made him so remarkable and valuable.[55]

Departing from Charleston on horseback, John did not ride southward toward Florida, but northward. His first errand was a mission of mercy.

Years before John had often taken his son, William, along with him as a companion on his plant-collecting travels. Young Billy had gained some skill as an artist of nature and John had proudly sent a few drawings made by "my little botanist" to Collinson, who also admired them and showed them to others.[56] As William grew older however, he showed little inclination to take up a remunerative trade. "Botany and drawing are his delight, but I'm afraid won't get him his living," John wrote.[57] When William turned sixteen in 1755, John apprenticed him to a Philadelphia merchant and six years later sent him, along with a few hundred pounds worth of goods to sell, to North Carolina (near where John's brother lived) to open a store. But William's business had not prospered. By 1764 John was writing to Collinson that he worried his son "will be ruined in Carolina, Everything goes wrong with him there."[58]

Soon after he received word of his appointment, John wrote William and invited him to close his shop and join the expedition. Perhaps John hoped to turn the post of "King's Botanist" into something of a family business and reasoned that as his assistant, William would be well positioned to succeed him in the post. John may also have felt slightly responsible for William's predicament. By encouraging his son's "delight" in nature, had he rendered him unable to earn a living? ("Hard labor does not agree with him," John once wryly noted.)[59] Or John may simply have wanted to take one last wilderness camping trip with his son. Whatever John's motives, William read his father's invitation as a reprieve. He sold his stock and closed his store in anticipation of his father's arrival. After they were reunited, the pair spent a week collecting fossils and plants along the lower Cape Fear before heading back toward Charleston and eventually southward on to Florida.

At last, on October 11, 1765, the Bartrams, father and son, rode through the north gate of St. Augustine. That evening they "dined with ye Governor" at his residence on the town plaza.[60] Governor Grant was very pleased to make their acquaintance. Although he had by now been in Florida for more than a year, Grant had thus far been unable to fulfill the commissions he had carried with him from London to collect plants for Lord Bute and the Duke of Cumberland. Ironically, only the day before the Bartrams arrived, the governor had written an apologetic letter in which he claimed that his failure to satisfy their request was not due to any want of zeal or gratitude on his part but to the fact that "botanists and proper people to assist them were wanting." (Grant abjectly described himself as a "bad Botanist.")[61] But now, he reported eagerly, "with the assistance of Mr. Bartram of Philadelphia," he would soon be able to send them a "considerable assortment of seeds."[62]

However, before he could help the governor, and belying the exaggerated accounts of the colony's healthy climate that Grant had been sending to Britain since his arrival, the elder Bartram fell dangerously ill. The symptoms and the timing suggest that the culprit was mosquito-borne malaria that he had contracted during his long ride through the coastal low country.[63] In his diary, John first noted feeling "very bad of Ague & fever" a few days after arriving in St. Augustine.[64] Despite a self-administered "vomit," which, he noted, "worked both ways," his condition quickly grew worse.[65] Within a few days, he described himself as "so very weke [I] cannot stand with reeling."[66] Soon he became too ill to keep his diary, and William took up the pen. As he lay in bed shaking with chills and fever, John may have wondered if, just as he had written to Collinson the year before, he might die before he could undertake his expedition. However, after remaining bed ridden for two weeks, nursed by his anxious son, the elder Bartram slowly began to regain his strength.

Fortunately for history, Bartram's recovery came in time to allow him and his son to attend a conference Governor Grant and John Stuart, the Indian superintendant for the southern colonies, were having with thirty-one Creek "headmen" at Fort Picolata, a Spanish-era blockhouse on the east bank of the St. Johns River, fifteen miles west of St. Augustine. On November 13, Grant and Stuart departed for the conference escorted by several hundred soldiers from Fort St. Marks. Two days later, the Bartrams, riding "in company with severall Gentlemen," left St. Augustine one hour after sunrise in pursuit.[67]

The party reached the site of the conference by late afternoon just in time to witness the opening ceremonials. As Bartram depicted the scene, "Ye Indian Chiefs assembled about 150 yards distance . . . to about 50 in number." To the sound of a "rattle box," the Indians slowly "marched [forward], sometimes dancing, singing, & shouting, & every now & then halting." When they were only fifty feet away, the main party of Indians stopped and two individuals approached "with a kind of dance." The two came up to the seated governor and superintendant and "stroaked . . . [them] all over thair faces & heads" with eagle feathers. After the two feather-bearers had "gently retired" back to where the other Indians had halted, the Creek "headmen" walked up "with an easy pace," shook hands with Grant and Stuart, and then sat down upon blankets that had been spread out upon the ground. Finally, the governor, the superintendant, and the "chief Indians" took turns taking puffs from "ye pipe of peace."[68]

What Bartram described was a "calumet ceremony," a Native American ritual whose purpose was to create a space and time for negotiations between enemies or rivals to take place.[69] Although he did not think it worthy of description, doubtless the British had also performed their own ceremonial "dance" as the redcoated soldiers of the governor's military escort marched onto the field, drums and fifes playing, and presented arms.

According to Bartram, the ensuing treaty talks took place in a "Pavilion . . . 9 paces long & 4 wide" that was covered on top, back, and along half of each side with "pine branches."[70] Bartram's description of the "Pavilion" is corroborated by another remarkable source. Among the British officers in attendance at the conference was Lieutenant William Sharp. During the conference, or perhaps soon afterward, Lieutenant Sharp, or more likely, a soldier in his command, engraved a powder horn with images of the conference that provide a unique visual record of eighteenth-century British-Indian treaty making.[71]

John Bartram was not among the British officers and "curious" gentlemen depicted on the powder horn as standing behind the seated governor, superintendant, and transcribing clerk. Instead, still weak from his illness, he "ly down upon ye ground, close by . . . that I might observe what passed."[72] (What the assembled Creeks may have made of the plainly dressed elderly man lying on the ground nearby was left unrecorded.) In his introductory speech, Governor Grant told the Creeks that "the Great King, my master and your father commanded me . . . to assure you . . . that he would always consider you as his children and love you as such." Grant suggested to the assembled Indians that since Florida was so vast and so recently won from the Spanish, "giving up a little [land] to the white people will be no loss to you."[73]

However, when their turn came to speak, the Creek headmen quickly brushed aside the governor's words. Instead, they began their oration by airing a list of grievances: white people were settling upon land reserved to the Indians at an earlier congress and the price of trade goods remained high despite promises that they would be reduced. The Creeks were determined, their spokesmen declared, "not answer to give away any lands" until these earlier wrongs were put right.[74] The governor did nothing to hide his displeasure at the Creeks' demands. Grant later described himself as acting "sulky and cross as the devil."[75] The conference recessed for the day in a tense atmosphere.

That evening, John asked, "as a particular favour," if he and William might sleep inside the blockhouse rather than in the tent that had already been pitched for them. Although he had noted the morning temperature as a comfortable 65 degrees, Bartram claimed that his request was prompted by the fact that "the fort chamber was warmer."[76] However, given his own prejudices and fears of Indians and the acrimonious conclusion of the first day's negotiation, it seems more likely that John may have wanted to wrap Fort Picolata's three-foot-thick walls and four swivel guns around himself as a comforting security blanket when he shut his eyes for the night.

When the conference reconvened the next morning, the two Bartrams excused themselves and went upon a "botanical excursion." While "Rambling in a swamp" nearby, William came suddenly upon an enormous rattlesnake (he described it as six feet long and as wide as a man's leg). In keeping with the common Euro-American custom of killing all such "vermin" on sight, he immediately found a branch and dispatched the serpent.[77] Tying the dead snake to the branch, he dragged him back to the Fort, "his scaly body sounding over the ground." Upon entering "the camp with him in triumph," William was "soon surrounded by the amazed multitude, both Indians and my countrymen." Governor Grant, who claimed to be "fond of the flesh of the rattle snake," insisted upon serving William's prize that night at a dinner he was giving to several of the Indian leaders.[78]

Later, in his famous *Travels*, William Bartram described southeastern Indians' "extraordinary veneration or dread of the rattle snake."[79] If Grant, or more likely Stuart, already knew something of the creature's symbolic importance to Native Americans, they may have ordered the snake served up for dinner in order to make an impression on their Indian guests. Thus, William Bartram's "triumph" over the rattlesnake may have helped to alter the mood of the Congress, which came to a satisfactory conclusion, at least from the British perspective, a few days later. Although, it must be admitted, a more likely explanation for the Creeks' more cooperative attitude was Grant's declaration to the assembled Indians "that if they gave me no Land, they would neither get presents [manufactured goods] nor Rum."[80] Throughout the conference, these highly desired items lay in sight but out of reach aboard a ship that lay at anchor in middle of the river.

Whatever effect the rattlesnake barbecue may have had on the outcome of the Picolata Congress, William Bartram remembered the dinner as a milestone in his life. When the plate containing the snake meat reached him, he later wrote, I "tasted of it, but could not swallow." His appetite was spoiled by a profound remorse. That day, William, daydreaming as usual, had almost stepped on the snake before he was alerted by a shout from his father. Now, he reflected that the creature, although within easy striking range, had not harmed him although "he certainly had it in his power to kill me almost instantly, and I make no doubt but that he was conscious of it." As penance for his deed, William vowed that he would never harm another rattlesnake.[81] This pledge (as well as the impulse to endow an animal

Figure 8.2. Portrait of William Bartram? Detail from Lieutenant William Sharp's powder horn. Image reproduced with permission of the Royal Ontario Museum ©ROM.

with human thoughts and emotions) marked the beginning of the intuitive sense of the "benevolent and peaceable disposition of animal creation" that would so strongly mark the *Travels* and account for much of its influence on English Romanticism.[82]

The Picolata conference may also have planted the seeds of William's lifelong fascination with and sympathy for Native Americans. Throughout his *Travels* (based upon a solo return to Florida in the early 1770s), William showed far more curiosity toward, and a greater admiration and appreciation of, Indians and their culture than his father had ever done. In this light, it is perhaps interesting that one of the images carved onto Lieutenant Sharp's powder horn appears to show young William (or at least a young Euro-American figure in a Quaker-style hat) sitting contentedly amid a circle of Indians, a necklace of treaty beads draped around his neck (see Figure 8.2).

After returning to St. Augustine to recuperate for another month, John at last felt well enough to fulfill his commission to explore the colony and "make observations on the soil, [and] the country . . . [as well as] gather specimens of plants, fossils, ores, etc." Inspired perhaps by the broad sweep of the St. Johns at Picolata, where the river is three miles wide, John decided to undertake a nautical expedition to explore its course. (It may also be that he still felt too enfeebled to spend weeks or months on horseback.) Approving of the plan, Governor Grant wrote the Board of Trade in London that "I have given the Botanists a Boat, provisions, and hunters to attend them up the River St. Johns . . . they expect to make great discoveries and promised to go up the river as far as they possibly could go."[83]

The governor arranged for Robert Davis, a planter pioneering a thousand acre plot on the east side of the St. Johns River twenty-five miles north of Picolata, to provide logistical support to the expedition.[84] The exploratory party, as John described it, consisted of five people: "I, my son William, Mr. Yates [David Yeats, the clerk of the Council, representing the governor], and Mr. Davis, [who] was not only to conduct us, but also to hunt venison for us, being a good hunter, and his Negro [who] was to row and cook for us all, the Governor bearing our expences."[85] The boat, which could not have been very large since one man could handle the oars, pushed off from Davis's landing three days before Christmas 1765.

At first they, or more precisely, their unnamed slave companion, rowed the boat upriver. They kept a slow pace, stopping to explore or camp upon most pieces of high (and dry) ground they came to (Bartram called them "bluffs," although they never rose more than twenty feet above the water). As they proceeded southward past Lake George, the river grew gradually narrower, shallower, and more weed-choked. At last, on January 12, after having proceeded upstream approximately 150 miles (a pace of only seven miles per day), they reached a place where "the weeds and reeds stopped our battoe in such a manner that it was impossible to push her any farther."[86] Because the Bartrams lacked the surveying tools and skills needed to accurately measure their position, determining precisely where they were at any point in the expedition is a matter of conjecture.[87] But the most likely location for their impasse was a narrow and multichanneled stretch of the river just south of Puzzle Lake (a spot midway between modern Orlando and Cape Canaveral).[88]

Further progress upriver deemed "impossible," the party "set out homeward," that is, they reversed their course. For the next month, they followed the flow of the St. Johns northward. The pace downstream was even slower than it had been going up, only five miles per day, suggesting that they were content to simple drift along with the river's torpid current. The boat arrived back at Davis's landing in the evening of February 12, fifty-three days after the party had departed. The Bartrams, accompanied by Yeats, returned to St. Augustine two days later.

The record John kept during the river journey reads like a marriage of Lewis and Clark's journal and *Huckleberry Finn*. Each morning, when he first stuck his head out of his tent, John took note of the weather conditions ("rainy," "foggy," "hazy," or "cool") and recorded the temperature. He had to abandon the latter practice when, to his "great disappointment," he broke his thermometer by using it to extract honey from a beehive.[89] Using only their common names throughout, Bartram listed the types of trees that grew along the banks (and especially on the "bluffs" where they camped). He noted the extensive swamps that lined the river for most of its course. No animals were mentioned (save those that ended up on the menu), except for a wood rat, a rattlesnake, the howling (but unseen) wolves, and the ubiquitous alligators.

The party encountered no Indians, or at least Bartram did not mention their meeting any. However, he did carefully make note of the ancient shell middens and "pieces of broken Indian pots" that he often found near their camps on the bluffs. Likewise, although they stopped at several plantations or pioneer settlements, Bartram did not describe any of the Euro-Americans or Africans they encountered along the way. Perhaps he did not believe humans to be a part of "nature," or at least not the kind that he was being paid to observe and describe.

For the most part, the journal is a chronicle of pure description. One day's record might serve as an example of the whole:

[January] 8th. Fine clear Morning Therm[ometer]: 44. Wind W[est] by N[orth]. Rowed by much Reedy ground, which is generally very wet, being often covered a foot more or less deep, after great Rains, but the Banks are in many places raised a foot or more by the Trash floating down the River, which being drove on shore by the Wind there rotts and is converted into stiff Soil, on which the Alligators love to lye & bask in the Sun shine every 20, 50, or 100 yards we find them, we encamped on a pleasant dry Bank but middling Soil, in a grove of live Oaks, beyond which is a plain on the Westside of the River, and beyond that a great Inland Pond or lake, below where we lodged several inlets appeared to the Northward, and above the River forked & we rowed up the N[orth].E[ast]. Branch.[90]

Read through, the journal has an almost childlike quality of pure experience. At times it almost approaches to poetry. For example, one day's entry begins, "Fine warm Morning. Birds singing, Fish Jumping and Turkeys Gobling."[91] But like a child's letter sent home from camp, Bartram also recorded his minor discomforts: "The Muskettoes were troublesome last night and this Morning, the Ticks creeping all about us, and the Lizzards running about our Tent."[92] One recurring motif in the journal is Bartram's growing appetite for bear meat, brought into camp by their hunter and prepared by the enslaved cook. He "loathed the sight [of it] at first" but eventually came to prefer it to venison or turkey for its "Sweetness and good Relish."[93] By journey's end, Bartram wrote that cabbage palm stewed in bear's fat "agreed the best with me of any Vegetable I ever eat."[94]

In his effort to make himself into an instrument for collecting and transmitting raw data back to Britain, Bartram put all of his senses to work. Whenever the party came upon a spring, he used his eyes to record its color ("like milk and water mixed,") his hand to gauge its temperature ("Warm to a Coolish hand" or "not so hot as one's blood"), his mouth to determine its taste ("sweet" or "loathsome"), and even his nose ("Smelt like Bilge Water or the Washings of a Gun Barrel").[95] Likewise, to determine the quality of soil, Bartram noted its color and its smell and crumbled it between his fingers to feel its texture.[96]

When they put their deductions onto paper, eighteenth-century philosophers usually employed an "omniscient third-person voice" that was thought to embody "ultimate authority" (i.e., the "voice of reason").[97] However, because Bartram's goal was merely to provide the first ingredient in this enlightenment alchemy, namely, direct observation, he wrote his Florida journal in the first person. To modern readers, of course, this simplicity and unadorned subjectivity is what gives Bartram's journal an air of immediacy and authenticity and also much of its charm.

In the journal, Bartram did not employ any taxonomy beyond a simple chronological narrative in which one observation followed upon another as the days passed and the boat floated along the river. Likewise, the only analogies Bartram used were homely ones. For example, the volume of a spring or stream might be described as "big enough to turn a Mill" or "small enough to run thro' the Bung hole of a Barrel."[98] Only once, in a journey of almost eight weeks and a journal of forty-five handwritten pages, did Bartram hazard to explain what he saw rather than merely describe it. After noting "a close compact mass of ground sea shells" in the river bank, he wrote (in perhaps what was meant as a memo to himself), "Quere: Whether or not some sorts of Clay formed out of sea-shells ground minutely to Powder in a long series of time?"[99]

After their return to St. Augustine, the Bartrams spent another month as the guests of Governor Grant. At the governor's request, John drew a map of the river (now lost). He spent several days "riteing" his journal, perhaps making a fair copy, or expanding upon his entries, and also appending "remarks" about different aspects of the journey.[100] He and William then assisted the governor in fulfilling his long overdue promise to gather an assortment of Florida seeds and ship them to London.

Finally, on March 17, 1766, John boarded a ship anchored off St. Augustine to begin the long journey home to Pennsylvania. He arrived back at the doorstep of his farmhouse on June 30, exactly one year to the day after he had left and a few months after his sixty-seventh birthday.[101]

John returned alone, for William had decided to remain in Florida. Beguiled by the beauty of the natural landscape, and perhaps seeking a livelihood better suited to his solitary and contemplative nature, William had persuaded his father to stake him in establishing a plantation on the east bank of the St. Johns River, midway between Fort Picolata and Davis's farm. Stopping in Charleston on his way home, John purchased plantation supplies, seeds, and six slaves and then sent them back to his son in Florida. However, William proved to be as inept an indigo planter and slave master as he had been a storekeeper. A visitor to his estate wrote to John lamenting the "forlorn state of poor Billy Bartram" and noting with worry that not only did his slaves refuse to obey his commands, one had actually threatened his life.[102] Within a year, William had abandoned his Florida plantation, and perhaps his slaves, (if the latter escaped into the interior they may have joined up with the Seminoles), and returned, empty-handed, to Philadelphia.

In traveling to and exploring the colony, collecting and packaging seeds, and keeping and transmitting a journal of his observations, John Bartram had amply fulfilled the commission he had been given as His Majesty's Botanist for the Floridas. What happened to these materials once they were put on a ship for England was, in a purely contractual sense, none of his business. Nonetheless, tracing the career of Bartram's intellectual progeny can reveal something of the nature of the British Empire in its first decade (as well, perhaps, as satisfy our own curiosity). When the packaged seeds and manuscript pages that Bartram had carefully prepared in St. Augustine reached the other side of the Atlantic, they took root, sometimes in unforeseen ways or unintended places.

Beginning in the decade of the 1760s, the estate surrounding the royal palace at Richmond-Kew was being developed into an elaborate showcase of Britain's new imperial identity and ambitions.[103] The gates of the palace grounds were opened to the genteel public every Saturday. By the end of the 1780s, among the "Exotick" plants "from every Part of the Globe" that visitors could see growing in the royal greenhouses and planting beds were several that a catalogue reported as having been cultivated from seeds collected in East Florida by "Mr. John Bartram."[104]

The journal that Bartram kept during the St. John River expedition bore even stranger fruit. Before he left for home, Bartram submitted a manuscript copy of the journal to Governor Grant, who duly forwarded it to the Board of Trade. In September 1766, the board, in turn, passed the manuscript on to William Stork "for the information of several adventurers in the settlement of that province."[105]

The previous spring, "Doctor Stork" had established himself as the foremost promoter, or "Puff General," of East Florida in Britain.[106] In May 1766, Stork published *An Account of East-Florida with Remarks on Its Future Importance to Trade and Commerce*, a short book that lauded the colony's economic potential in hyperbolic terms.[107] Stork's book, coupled with the monthly meetings of the "East Florida Society of London"—a club that Stork both founded and presided over, stoked interest in the colony and produced a dramatic rise in the number of Britons who petitioned the Privy Council for large land grants there.

However, Stork soon discovered that keeping Florida's speculative "bubble" inflated, and keeping the colony (and himself) in the eye of the British public, required constant "puffing," and this necessitated a continuous flow of new information about the colony. Thus, although the Board of Trade may have merely intended for Stork to circulate Bartram's journal in manuscript at a meeting of the East Florida Society, he instead immediately appended it to a second edition of his book, revising the title to *An Account of East-Florida with a Journal, Kept by John Bartram of Philadelphia, Botany to His Majesty for the Floridas, Upon a Journey from St. Augustine up the River St. Johns*, so as to highlight (and inflate) Bartram's royal credentials.[108]

In the preface Stork wrote to accompany the text of Bartram's journal, he described Bartram as "well known and well respected in the learned world as an able Naturalist." Stork did not claim a personal acquaintance with Bartram, and it is unlikely that the two men had met. Stork had visited Florida sometime in 1765, and it is not entirely impossible for the two men to have seen each other across the governor's dinner table in St. Augustine that fall.[109] However, as Stork was in London by mid-February 1766, he likely departed Florida no later than mid-December (that is, before the Bartrams had commenced their St. Johns River expedition).[110] In any case, Bartram never mentioned Stork in any of his letters or his journal, and it seems certain that Stork published the journal of the river expedition without Bartram's knowledge or permission.

Readers of Bartram's journal as published in the second edition of Stork's *Account* did not know what to make of it. Bartram's objective descriptions and plain prose came in sharp contrast with the promotional puffery employed by Stork in his own description of the colony, which preceded Bartram's journal and which was unchanged from his first edition. But Bartram's use of the first person, and the lack of scientific classification and discourse in his journal, also deviated from the contemplative and omniscient voice that was to be expected in the natural histories of the era. One baffled reviewer described Bartram's account of his river trip as something that could "afford entertainment only to a botanist, and to a botanist not much."[111] Another critic judged it "a very loose performance, and principally defective where we might expect it most compleat, viz., in the botanical articles."[112]

Peter Collinson's response to the book was, perhaps predictably, personal. He first complained to Bartram about the high cost (he refused to buy one) and resented the fact that Bartram did not "engage [with] Stork to Send & Complement Mee with a Book." Collinson worried that this neglect suggested that Bartram had found other, more elevated, patrons. "My friend John did not think Mee worthy," he wrote, "not the least Notice is taken of Mee." In a warning about the sin of pride, Collinson noted that Stork's description of Bartram as the Kings Botanist to the World (his pique led him to exaggerate; the actual title Stork bestowed upon Bartram was only Botanist to his Majesty for the Floridas), was one "which ... thou assumes without the King's Leave or License which is making very free with Majesty." Collinson worried (or half-hoped?) that "for this undue Liberty thy annuity may be withdrawn."[113] However, the two old friends patched up their quarrel and Bartram continued to collect his fifty-pound stipend until the outbreak of the American Revolution.[114]

If one were to add up the tangible results of John Bartram's Florida journey, the list would be short. A few plants growing in European greenhouses, a few seeds or dried leaves added to European herbariums, a few new specimens added to the Linnaean system of botanical classification. Likewise, John Bartram's account of his travels through Florida in 1765–1766 is now completely overshadowed by the journey made eight years later to the same region by his son, which was eventually published in 1791 as the classic natural history now known simply as *Bartram's Travels*. Although John Bartram remains something of a "father figure" in the history of American natural history, his 1765–1766 journey to Florida is little more than a footnote in the history of early America.

Much the same might be said about British Florida itself. Acquired from Spain by the terms of the Treaty of Paris of 1763, it was returned by the terms of another treaty of the same name twenty years later. In their two decades of possession, the British failed to make anything of the colony. In some ways, British Florida seems almost to never have existed as a real place at all. Far more documentary evidence survives for the colony in promotional pamphlets like that written by William Stork or in the letters of "adventurers" who claimed large land grants in the colony but who never left Britain, than were actually written in the colony by the few people who ventured to go and settle there.

Similarly, for historians of early America, the greatest significance of British Florida's brief history and of John Bartram's Florida expedition lies in the light these entwined histories can shed upon the attitudes and ambitions that prevailed among the members of the British establishment toward America in the years that followed the Seven Years War. Bartram's appointment as Botanist to his Majesty for the Floridas is an early example of the partnership between inquisitiveness and acquisitiveness, science and empire, or knowledge and power that would so shape the modern world. However, in the decade of the 1760s, Britain's imperial reach and ambitions still exceeded its grasp. In South Asia, the British were able to eventually expand and consolidate their control over India. But in America, the new imperial imperative for greater order and centralized control was met with resistance, rebellion, and ultimately, independence.

John Bartram died four days before the British army marched into Philadelphia in September 1777, but he and William, like most Pennsylvania Quakers, were bystanders rather than participants in the American Revolution.[115] Likewise, the journey he made to Florida a decade earlier was more a reflection than a cause of historical change. In terms of his own life, Bartram was hardly passive; he was both the agent and subject of his history. He shrewdly made use of the rising "spirit of imperialism" that emerged in Britain after 1763 to secure financial support for his personal dream to explore the Southeast.[116] For similarly pragmatic reasons, Bartram was pleased to accept both the title of His Majesty's Botanist for the Floridas and the stipend that came with it.

However, John Bartram's impact on larger events was largely inadvertent. The publication of his journal in the second edition of Stork's pamphlet may have helped to sustain British interest in Florida (and in Florida land grants). Moreover, by encouraging prominent Britons in the belief that they could accurately perceive and profitably possess a world that lay three thousand miles away, Bartram's Florida seeds and Florida writings may have fueled the flames of a fatal hubris that, ten years after his return from Florida and four miles from his farmhouse, would provoke the Declaration of Independence and the downfall of Britain's American Empire.

Notes

1. Charles M. Andrews, *The Colonial Background of the American Revolution* (New Haven, CT: Yale University Press, 1924), 122. For Andrews's role in establishing the field of Colonial American History, see Richard R. Johnson, "Charles MacLean Andrews and the Invention of American Colonial History," *William and Mary Quarterly*, 3rd ser., 43, no. 4 (October 1986): 520–41.

2. Colin G. Calloway, *The Scratch of a Pen: 1763 and the Transformation of North America* (New York: Oxford University Press, 2006).

3. During the course of the war, the British had also conquered the islands of Martinique and Guadeloupe and the city of Havana, but during the peace negotiations, in the (vain) hope that restoring to France and Spain some of their losses would reconcile them to their defeat, it was decided to return these and retain Canada and accept Florida instead.

4. See Christopher Leslie Brown, "Empire without America: British Plans for Africa in the Era of the American Revolution," in *Abolitionism and Imperialism in Britain, Africa, and the Atlantic*, ed. Derek Peterson, 84–100 (Athens: Ohio University Press, 2010). The one exception was the North African city of Tangier, which was received as a dowry gift (along with the city of Bombay) from the king of Portugal upon the wedding of his daughter, Catharine of Braganza, to King Charles II in 1662; Tangier remained in English hands until 1684. See Alison Games, *The Web of Empire: English Cosmopolitans in the Age of Expansion, 1550–1660* (New York: Oxford University Press, 2008), 293–98.

5. Although Clive's victory at Plassey in 1757 is often portrayed as the decisive battle, to Lawrence Henry Gipson it was the East India Company's acquisition of the Diwani, or taxing power in Bengal, eight years later that marked "the real beginning . . . of the British Raj" (direct rule in India). Lawrence Henry Gipson, *The British Empire Before the American Revolution*, vol. 9, *The Triumphant Empire: New Responsibilities within the Enlarged Empire, 1763–1766* (New York: Knopf, 1956), 345.

6. Andrews, *Colonial Background*, 122.

7. Ibid., 122.

8. John Robert Seeley, *The Expansion of England: Two Courses of Lectures* (Cambridge: Cambridge University Press, 1883), 8. Seeley might well be considered to be one of the "inventors" of imperial history, not least for his remark that after the eighteenth century, "the history of England is not [to be found] in England but in America and Asia," 10.

9. See, for example, P. J. Cain and Anthony Hopkins, *British Imperialism, 1688–2000*, 2nd ed. (New York: Routledge, 2001), and Philippa Levine, *The British Empire: Sunrise to Sunset*, 2nd ed. (New York: Routledge, 2013).

10. The full (and famous) quote, from the *18th Brumaire of Louis Bonaparte*, is "Men make their own history, but they do not make it just as they please; they do not make it under circumstances chosen by themselves, but under circumstances directly encountered, given, and transmitted from the past."

11. For an example of another colonial American's adoration of Pitt as the leader of a Pan-Atlantic Britain, see Rhys Isaac, *Landon Carter's Uneasy Kingdom: Rebellion and Revolution on a Virginia Plantation* (Chapel Hill: University of North Carolina Press, 2004), 152–61.

12. John Bartram to Peter Collinson, March 4, 1764, in *The Correspondence of John Bartram, 1734–1777*, ed. Edmund Berkeley and Dorothy Smith Berkeley, 622 (Gainesville: University Press of Florida, 1992).

13. See, for example, "North America, and the West Indies; A New Map, Wherein The British Empire and its Limits, according to the Definitive Treaty of Peace in 1763, are Accurately described, and the Dominions Possessed by the Spaniards, the French, & other European States," Carrington Bowles, engraver (London, 1763).

14. John Bartram to Peter Collinson, March 4, 1764, in *The Correspondence of John Bartram 1734-1777*, ed. Edmund Berkeley and Dorothy Smith Berkeley, 622 (Gainesville: University Press of Florida, 1992). Bartram, whose idiosyncratic spelling is retained throughout this essay, wrote "travail," the French word for labor, but it is more likely that he simply misspelled "travel"; the meaning is virtually the same either way.

15. Ibid., 609.

16. Ibid. In the same letter, Bartram recounted an incident that had occurred twenty years before when he was walking "far beyond our Mountains" (en route from Philadelphia to Fort Oswego on Lake Ontario) and was suddenly accosted by "an Indian man . . . [who] pulled off my hat in a great pashion & chewed it all around." Bartram interpreted the Indian's gesture as meaning "to shew me that he would eat me if I came in that countrey again."

17. Twelve-year-old John had been left behind with relatives in Pennsylvania. His mother and infant brother were taken captive, but were later ransomed. Edmund Berkeley and Dorothy Smith Berkeley, *The Life and Travels of John Bartram: From Lake Ontario to the River St. John* (Tallahassee: University Presses of Florida, 1982), 7.

18. See Calloway, *Scratch of a Pen*, 66–91.

19. *Pennsylvania Gazette* (Philadelphia), September 29, 1763.

20. For Collinson, see Alan W. Armstrong's introduction to *Forget Not Mee & My Garden: Selected Letters 1725–1768 of Peter Collinson, F.R.S.* (Philadelphia: American Philosophical Society, 2002).

21. Peter Collinson to John Bartram, June 1, 1764, in *The Correspondence of John Bartram, 1734-1777*, ed.. Edmund Berkeley and Dorothy Smith Berkeley (Gainesville: University Press of Florida, 1992), 629.

22. For Breintnall, Franklin, and the "Junto," see H. W. Brands, *The First American: The Life and Times of Benjamin Franklin* (New York: Random House, 2000), 93.

23. For Bartram's life before 1763, see Berkeley and Berkeley, *The Life and Travels of John Bartram*.

24. In a letter to Collinson, Bartram wrote that "I had allways since 10 years ould A great inclination to plants & knowed all that I once observed by sight tho not their proper names having no persons or books to instruct me." John Bartram to Peter Collinson, May 1, 1764, in *The Correspondence of John Bartram, 1734-1777*, ed. Edmund Berkeley and Dorothy Smith Berkeley (Gainesville: University Press of Florida, 1992), 627.

25. This was the first edition of his *Systemae Naturae*. Linnaeus updated and enlarged the book for the remainder of his life, publishing another eleven editions before his death in 1778. For Linnaeus, see Lisbet Koerner, *Linnaeus: Nature and Nation* (Cambridge, MA: Harvard University Press, 1999).

26. Quoted in Theresa Kelley, *Clandestine Marriage: Botany and Romantic Culture* (Baltimore: Johns Hopkins University Press, 2012), 24. Bartram was later honored by having his name attached to a genus of moss.

27. "A Letter from *John Bartram*, M.D. to Peter Collinson, F.R.S. concerning a Cluster of small Teeth observed by him at the Root of each Fang or great Tooth in the Head of a *Rattle Snake*, upon dissecting it," *Philosophical Transactions* 41 (1740): 358–59. It is revealing that Bartram was misidentified here as a doctor, perhaps to provide him with the proper genteel and academic credentials.

28. Bartram's house and garden (the latter regarded as the oldest surviving botanical garden in the United States) are today owned and operated by the nonprofit John Bartram Association and are open to the public.

29. For example, in the eleventh of his famous *Letters from An American Farmer*, Hector St. Jean de Crèvecouer described a (perhaps apocryphal) "visit . . . to Mr. John Bertram, the Celebrated Pennsylvania Botanist."

30. After his return to Sweden, Kalm published an account of his journey (in Swedish) as *En Resa til Norra America*, 3 vols. (Stockholm, 1753–1761); an English translation was published in 1770–1771 with the title *Travels in North America*.

31. Peter Kalm, *Travels in North America*, trans. John Reinhold Forster, 3 vols. (London, 1770–1771), 1:114.

32. Ibid., 1:116–17.

33. James Grant to Henry Bouquet, August 15, 1765, James Grant Letterbook, James Grant Papers (microfilm 22671, reel 1), Library of Congress, Washington, DC.

34. John Bartram to Peter Collinson, September 23, 1764, in *The Correspondence of John Bartram, 1734–1777*, ed. Edmund Berkeley and Dorothy Smith Berkeley (Gainesville: University Press of Florida, 1992), 638–39.

35. Peter Collinson to John Bartram, May 1765, in *Memorials of John Bartram and Humphrey Marshall, with Notices of Their Botanical Contemporaries*, ed. William Darlington, 269 (Philadelphia, 1849).

36. Peter Collinson to John Bartram, April 9, 1765, in *The Correspondence of John Bartram, 1734–1777*, ed. Edmund Berkeley and Dorothy Smith Berkeley (Gainesville: University Press of Florida, 1992), 644–45.

37. See, for example, Richard Drayton, *Nature's Government: Science, Imperial Britain, and the Improvement of the World* (New Haven, CT: Yale University Press, 2000).

38. See Andrea Wulf, *Chasing Venus: The Race to Measure the Heavens* (New York: Vintage, 2012). The quest did have a practical purpose, as it was hoped that the information might be used to help determine longitude while at sea.

39. See Steve Ragnall, *Better Conceiv'd than Describ'd: The Life and Times of Captain James King (1750–1784) Captain Cook's Friend and Colleague* (Leicester, UK: Troubador, 2013), 32.

40. See Introduction to James Cook, *The Journals of Captain Cook*, Penguin Classic ed. (New York: Penguin, 2003).

41. Entry of July 1, 1765, in John Bartram, "Diary of a Journey Through the Carolinas, Georgia, and Florida, From July 1, 1765 to April 10, 1766," ed. and annotated by Francis Harper, *Transactions of the American Philosophical Society* 33 (December 1942): 13.

42. Alexander Garden to John Ellis, July 15, 1765, in *A Selection of the Correspondence of Linnaeus and Other Naturalists*, 2 vols., ed. James Edward Smith (London, 1821), 1:537–38. Garden's critique was not entirely motivated by jealousy, for when he first met Bartram ten years earlier, he also noted that Bartram's descriptions of plants were "rude, inaccurate,

indistinct, and confused, seldom determining well between species and varieties." Alexander Garden to John Ellis, March 25, 1755, in ibid., 1:537.

43. See Pamela Regis, *Describing Early America: Bartram, Jefferson, Crevecoeur, and the Rhetoric of Natural History* (DeKalb: University of Northern Illinois Press, 1992), 9.

44. Ultimately, Bartram was responsible for collecting and shipping to Europe 150 new plant species, one-fourth of all North American species classified between 1492 and 1775. See Thomas Slaughter, *The Natures of John and William Bartram* (New York: Knopf, 1996), 51.

45. Peter Collinson to John Bartram, January 24, 1735, cited in Thomas Slaughter, *The Natures of John and William Bartram* (New York: Knopf, 1996), 95.

46. Cited in Regis, *Describing Early America*, 9.

47. Peter Collinson to John Bartram, December 14, 1737, in *The Correspondence of John Bartram, 1734–1777*, ed. Edmund Berkeley and Dorothy Smith Berkeley (Gainesville: University Press of Florida, 1992). Bartram retorted that perhaps "if Solomon had loved women less, and books more, he would have been a wiser and happier man than he was." John Bartram to Peter Collinson, May 1738, in ibid., 89.

48. Cited in Regis, *Describing Early America*, 97. Bartram's "business" did prosper; during the three decades that he acted as Collinson's plant collector, he enlarged his farm to three hundred acres and bought three town lots in Philadelphia on which he built rental housing. At the same time, his family grew from two children to nine; Berkeley and Berkeley, *Life and Travels of John Bartram*, 14–15.

49. John Bartram to Peter Collinson, [n.d.] 1738, in *The Correspondence of John Bartram, 1734–1777*, ed. Edmund Berkeley and Dorothy Smith Berkeley (Gainesville: University Press of Florida, 1992), 96.

50. Peter Collinson to John Bartram, [n.d.] 1738, in *The Correspondence of John Bartram, 1734–1777*, ed. Edmund Berkeley and Dorothy Smith Berkeley (Gainesville: University Press of Florida, 1992), 96.

51. John Bartram to Peter Collinson, July 18, 1739, in *The Correspondence of John Bartram, 1734–1777*, ed. Edmund Berkeley and Dorothy Smith Berkeley (Gainesville: University Press of Florida, 1992), 122.

52. As David Scofield Wilson notes, Bartram "trained himself to become the type of nature reporter most valued by the system he elected to serve." David Scofield Wilson, *In the Presence of Nature* (Amherst: University of Massachusetts Press, 1978), 91.

53. Peter Kalm, cited in Edmund Berkeley and Dorothy Smith Berkeley, *The Life and Travels of John Bartram: From Lake Ontario to the River St. John* (Tallahassee: University Presses of Florida, 1982), 129; Cadwalader Colden to Peter Collinson, June 1746, and Alexander Garden to John Ellis, July 15, 1765, both cited in Thomas Slaughter, *The Natures of John and William Bartram* (New York: Knopf, 1996), 97.

54. Cited in David Scofield Wilson, *In the Presence of Nature* (Amherst: University of Massachusetts, 1978), 90.

55. Collinson to John Custis, December 24, 1737, cited in David Scofield Wilson, *In the Presence of Nature* (Amherst: University of Massachusetts, 1978), 88.

56. John Bartram to Peter Collinson, August 20, 1753, in *The Correspondence of John Bartram, 1734–1777*, Berkeley and Berkeley; Edmund Berkeley and Dorothy Smith Berkeley,

The Life and Travels of John Bartram: From Lake Ontario to the River St. John (Tallahassee: University Presses of Florida, 1982), 354.

57. John Bartram to Alexander Garden, March 14, 1756, in Edmund Berkeley and Dorothy Smith Berkeley, *The Life and Travels of John Bartram: From Lake Ontario to the River St. John* (Tallahassee: University Presses of Florida, 1982), 403.

58. John Bartram to Peter Collinson, March 4, 1764, in Edmund Berkeley and Dorothy Smith Berkeley, *The Life and Travels of John Bartram: From Lake Ontario to the River St. John* (Tallahassee: University Presses of Florida,, 1982), 622.

59. John Bartram to Peter Collinson, 27 April 1755, in Edmund Berkeley and Dorothy Smith Berkeley, *The Life and Travels of John Bartram: From Lake Ontario to the River St. John* (Tallahassee: University Presses of Florida, 1982), 384.

60. Entry of October 12, 1765, in John Bartram "Diary of a Journey Through the Carolinas, Georgia, and Florida, From July 1, 1765 to April 10, 1766," ed. and annotated by Francis Harper, *Transactions of the American Philosophical Society* 33 (December 1942): 33.

61. James Grant to Edward Mason, October 10, 1765, James Grant Letterbook, James Grant Papers (microfilm 22671, reel 1), Library of Congress, Washington, DC.

62. James Grant to Lord Bute, December 24, 1765, James Grant Letterbook, James Grant Papers (microfilm 22671, reel 1), Library of Congress, Washington, DC. When he wrote, Grant could not have known that the Duke of Cumberland had died in October.

63. For malaria in the colonial lowcountry, see H. Roy Merrens and George D. Terry, "Dying In Paradise: Malaria, Mortality, and the Perceptual Environment in Colonial South Carolina," *Journal of Southern History* 50 (November 1984): 533–50.

64. Entry of October 16, 1765, in John Bartram, "Diary of a Journey Through the Carolinas, Georgia, and Florida, From July 1, 1765 to April 10, 1766," ed. and annotated by Francis Harper, *Transactions of the American Philosophical Society* 33 (December 1942): 33.

65. Entry of October 18, 1765, in John Bartram, "Diary of a Journey Through the Carolinas, Georgia, and Florida, From July 1, 1765 to April 10, 1766," ed. and annotated by Francis Harper, *Transactions of the American Philosophical Society* 33 (December 1942): 33.

66. Entry of October 23, 1765, in John Bartram, "Diary of a Journey Through the Carolinas, Georgia, and Florida, From July 1, 1765 to April 10, 1766," ed. and annotated by Francis Harper, *Transactions of the American Philosophical Society* 33 (December 1942): 34.

67. Entry of November 15, 1765, in John Bartram, "Diary of a Journey Through the Carolinas, Georgia, and Florida, From July 1, 1765 to April 10, 1766," ed. and annotated by Francis Harper, *Transactions of the American Philosophical Society* 33 (December 1942): 35.

68. Bartram, "Remarks On Ye Congress Held in a Pavilion," in John Bartram, "Diary of a Journey Through the Carolinas, Georgia, and Florida, From July 1, 1765 to April 10, 1766," ed. and annotated by Francis Harper, *Transactions of the American Philosophical Society* 33 (December 1942): 51.

69. Bartram's account of the calumet ceremony at Picolata was the easternmost account of the ceremony ever recorded. For an examination of the proceedings at Picolata by a historian of Native America, see Kathryn Holland-Braund, "The Congress Held in a Pavilion: John Bartram and the Indian Congress at Fort Picolata, East Florida," in *America's Curious Botanist: A Tercentennial Reappraisal of John Bartram, 1699-1777*, ed. Nancy E. Hoffman and John C. Van Horne (Philadelphia: American Philosophical Society, 2004), 79–96.

70. Bartram, "Remarks On Ye Congress Held in a Pavilion," in John Bartram "Diary of a Journey Through the Carolinas, Georgia, and Florida," ed. and annotated by Francis Harper, *Transactions of the American Philosophical Society* 33 (December 1942): 51.

71. The powder horn is now in the collection of the Royal Ontario Museum in Toronto, Canada.

72. John Bartram to Peter Collinson, June [n.d.] 1766, in *The Correspondence of John Bartram, 1734–1777*, ed. Edmund Berkeley and Dorothy Smith Berkeley, (Gainesville: University Press of Florida, 1992), 669.

73. James W. Covington, *The British Meet the Seminoles: Negotiations between British Authorities in east Florida and the Indians, 1763–68* (Gainesville: University Press of Florida, 1961), 25.

74. Ibid., 27.

75. James Grant to William Knox, December 9, 1765, James Grant Letterbook, James Grant Papers (microfilm 22671, reel 1), Library of Congress, Washington, DC.

76. Entry of November 16, 1765, in John Bartram "Diary of a Journey Through the Carolinas, Georgia, and Florida," ed. Francis Harper, *Transactions of the American Philosophical Society* 33 (December 1942): 35.

77. Many colonies offered bounties for rattlesnake skins. See Vance Dunbar, *Rattles and Snappers: Reptiles, Amphibians, and Outlaws* (Bloomington, IN: Author House, 2007), 29.

78. William Bartram, *Travels Through North and South Carolina, Georgia, East and West Florida*, (1791; repr., New York: Penguin Nature Classics, 1988), 224.

79. Ibid., 218.

80. James Grant to William Knox, December 9, 1765, James Grant Letterbook, James Grant Papers (microfilm 22671, reel 1), Library of Congress, Washington, DC.

81. Bartram, *Travels Through North and South Carolina*, 225.

82. Ibid., 222. For the influence of Bartram's *Travels* on the English Romantic poets, esp. William Coleridge, see John Livingston Lowes, *The Road to Xanadu: A Study in the Ways of the Imagination* (Boston: Houghton Mifflin, 1927).

83. James Grant to William Knox, December 21, 1765, James Grant Letterbook, James Grant Papers (microfilm 22671, reel 1), Library of Congress, Washington, DC.

84. Robert Davis submitted a claim for one thousand acres in East Florida on July 20, 1765, and the survey for his plat was run on September 12, 1765. National Archives, Kew, UK: T/77/16/400.

85. Entry of December 20, 1765, in John Bartram, "Diary of a Journey Through the Carolinas, Georgia, and Florida, From July 1, 1765 to April 10, 1766," ed. and annotated by Francis Harper, *Transactions of the American Philosophical Society* 33 (December 1942): 43 Edmund Berkeley and Dorothy Smith Berkeley, *The Life and Travels of John Bartram: From Lake Ontario to the River St. John* (Tallahassee: University Presses of Florida, 1982), 36.

86. Entry of January 25, 1766, in Edmund Berkeley and Dorothy Smith Berkeley, *The Life and Travels of John Bartram: From Lake Ontario to the River St. John* (Tallahassee: University Presses of Florida, 1982), 43.

87. Except of course those instances when the expedition visited places whose location is easily determined (for example, the site of Rollestown, or the entrance to Lake George).

88. For estimates of where the expedition turned back, see Map 7 in "Travels of John Bartram in Florida, 1765–66," in John Bartram, "Diary of a Journey Through the Carolinas,

Georgia, and Florida," ed. and annotated by Francis Harper, *Transactions of the American Philosophical Society* 33 (December 1942), Plate 7. See also Bill Belleville, *River of Lakes: A Journey on Florida's St. Johns River* (Athens: University of Georgia Press, 2000), 38.

89. Entry of January 14, 1766, in John Bartram, "Diary of a Journey Through the Carolinas, Georgia, and Florida," ed. and annotated by Francis Harper, *Transactions of the American Philosophical Society* 33 (December 1942): 42.

90. Entry of January 8, 1766, in John Bartram, "Diary of a Journey Through the Carolinas, Georgia, and Florida," ed. and annotated by Francis Harper, *Transactions of the American Philosophical Society* 33 (December 1942): 41; Francis Harper suggests that this particular portion of Bartram's journal describes a section of the St. John's just upriver from what is now called Lake Monroe and that Bartram's "pleasant dry bank" is today known as Lemon Bluff, ibid. 72.

91. Entry of January 19, 1766, in John Bartram, "Diary of a Journey Through the Carolinas, Georgia, and Florida," ed. and annotated by Francis Harper, *Transactions of the American Philosophical Society* 33 (December 1942): 43.

92. Entry of January 15, 1766, in John Bartram, "Diary of a Journey Through the Carolinas, Georgia, and Florida," ed. and annotated by Francis Harper, *Transactions of the American Philosophical Society* 33 (December 1942): 42.

93. Entry of January 13, 1766, in John Bartram, "Diary of a Journey Through the Carolinas, Georgia, and Florida," ed. and annotated by Francis Harper, *Transactions of the American Philosophical Society* 33 (December 1942): 42.

94. Entry of January 17, 1766, in John Bartram, "Diary of a Journey Through the Carolinas, Georgia, and Florida," ed. and annotated by Francis Harper, *Transactions of the American Philosophical Society* 33 (December 1942): 43. Bartram's acquired taste for bear meat resembles that gained by the members of the surveying expedition that William Byrd II had satirized in his "Secret History of the Dividing Line" more than thirty years earlier. For Byrd, the surveying party's growing appetite for bear meat suggested a decline into savagery; although Byrd's satire was written around 1730, it was not published until the nineteenth century. However, it is intriguing to note that Bartram visited Byrd at his Virginia plantation in 1738 on one of his plant collecting excursions, see Berkeley and Berkeley, *Life and Travels of John Bartram*, 57–59.

95. Entries of January 7, 1766 and December 27, 1765, in John Bartram, "Diary of a Journey Through the Carolinas, Georgia, and Florida," ed. and annotated by Francis Harper, *Transactions of the American Philosophical Society* 33 (December 1942): 40–41, 38, 43.

96. Entry of December 30, 1765, in John Bartram, "Diary of a Journey Through the Carolinas, Georgia, and Florida," ed. and annotated by Francis Harper, *Transactions of the American Philosophical Society* 33 (December 1942): 38.

97. Neil Safier, *Measuring the New World: Enlightenment Science and South America* (Chicago: University of Chicago Press, 2008), 255.

98. Entries of December 27, 1765, and January 7, 1766, in John Bartram, "Diary of a Journey Through the Carolinas, Georgia, and Florida," ed. and annotated Francis Harper, *Transactions of the American Philosophical Society* 33 (December 1942): 40.

99. Entry of January 20, 1766, in John Bartram, "Diary of a Journey Through the Carolinas, Georgia, and Florida," ed. and annotated Francis Harper, *Transactions of the American Philosophical Society* 33 (December 1942): 44. The age of shells (and of the earth)

was an old interest of Bartram's and of Enlightenment geologists (like Thomas Jefferson). Twenty-five years earlier the discovery of a deposit of "sea shells set in stone" [i.e., fossils] in the Allegheny Mountains had led Bartram to speculate whether they had been deposited prior to the biblical flood, in an age "before beasts lived on dry land, or fowls flew in the air." See Slaughter, *Natures of John and William Bartram*, 57.

100. Entries of February 17 and 20–22, 1766, in John Bartram, "Diary of a Journey Through the Carolinas, Georgia, and Florida," ed. and annotated by Francis Harper, in *Transactions of the American Philosophical Society* 33 (December 1942): 48; In his diary on February 20, Bartram penned "began to write my Journal," which might seem to suggest that he was creating it from scratch, i.e., after the fact. However, given the laconic, day-to-day, quality of the text this seems very unlikely. Most probably he was copying or putting into a fair hand the daily notes that he had made during the journey, and perhaps elaborating on them and appending to them the concluding "remarks" as described above.

101. For the date of Bartram's departure from St. Augustine, see entry of March 17, 1766, in John Bartram, "Diary of a Journey Through the Carolinas, Georgia, and Florida," ed. and annotated by Francis Harper, *Transactions of the American Philosophical Society* 33 (December 1942): 49. For his arrival at his home, see John Bartram to Collinson, June 30, 1766, in *The Correspondence of John Bartram, 1734–1777*, ed. Edmund Berkeley and Dorothy Smith Berkeley, 668 (Gainesville: University Press of Florida, 1992).

102. Henry Laurens to John Bartram, August 9, 1766, in *The Papers of Henry Laurens*, 16 vols., ed. George C. Rogers, David R. Chesnutt, Peggy C. Clark (Columbia: University of South Carolina Press, 1968–1992), 5:151–55.

103. See Robert Olwell, "Seeds of Empire: Florida, Kew, and the British Imperial Meridian in the 1760s," in *The Creation of the British Atlantic World*, ed. Elizabeth Mancke and Carole Shammas (Baltimore: Johns Hopkins University Press, 2006), 263–82.

104. *A Description of the Gardens and Buildings at Kew, in Surrey* (London, 1768), 6; William Aiton, *Hortus Kewensis*, 2 vols. (London, 1789), 2:43, 47.

105. Journal of the Board of Trade, September 1, 1766, cited in Charles L. Mowatt, "The First Campaign of Publicity for Florida," *Mississippi Valley Historical Review* 30 (December 1943): 359–76.

106. Adam Gordon to James Grant, February 14, 1767, Ballindalloch Castle Muniments, Ballindalloch Castle, Scotland, 50/474. I am grateful to Mr. Oliver Russell for allowing me access to these documents.

107. William Stork, *An Account of East Florida with Remarks on Its Future Importance to Trade and Commerce* (London, 1766).

108. William Stork, *An Account of East-Florida with a Journal Kept by John Bartram of Philadelphia, Botanist to his Majesty for the Floridas, Upon a Journey from St. Augustine Up the River St. John's, with Explanatory Notes* (London, 1766).

109. Evidence that Stork was in Florida in 1765 is provided by James Grant to Archibald Grant, April 10, 1768, James Grant Papers, Library of Congress (microfilm 22671, reel 2), Washington, DC.

110. The Bartrams returned to St. Augustine from their journey up the St. Johns River on February 13, 1766. The previous day, on the opposite side of the Atlantic, Richard Oswald reported that Stork was staying at his London house, see Berkeley and Berkeley, *The Life and Travels of John Bartram*, 262; Richard Oswald to James Grant, February 12, 1766,

McPherson-Grant Papers, Ballindalloch Castle Muniments, Ballindalloch Castle, Perthshire, Scotland, CM 34/295 (consulted by the kind permission of Mr. Oliver Russell); even allowing only eight weeks to travel from St. Augustine to London (a very fast passage), Stork must have left Florida no later than mid-December.

111. *Gentleman's Magazine* (London), October 1766, 486–87.

112. Bernard Romans, *A Concise Natural History of East and West Florida* (1775; repr., ed. and intro. Kathryn E. Holland Braund (Tuscaloosa: University of Alabama Press, 1999), 260.

113. Peter Collinson to John Bartram, [no date, probably February 1767], in *The Correspondence of John Bartram, 1734–1777*, ed. *The Correspondence of John Bartram, 1734–1777*, ed. Edmund Berkeley and Dorothy Smith Berkeley (Gainesville: University Press of Florida, 1992), 679–80.

114. Bartram apparently responded in a similar spirit, leading Collinson to answer, "I can take a squib from John Bartram without the least resentment, Friends may be allowed to rally one another when it is not done in anger.... If I can be thought too quick, my dear John, thou wast too slow & so we will let the matter go." Peter Collinson to John Bartram, July 31, 1767, in *The Correspondence of John Bartram, 1734–1777*, ed. Edmund Berkeley and Dorothy Smith Berkeley (Gainesville: University Press of Florida, 1992), 684. After Collinson's death in 1768, John Fothergill became Bartram's British patron; he also privately financed William Bartram's return to Florida in 1773–1774.

115. For Quakers' response to the American Revolution, see Arthur J. Worrall, *Quakers in the Colonial Northeast* (Lebanon, NH: University Press of New England, 2002).

116. Andrews, *Colonial Background*, 143.

URBANITY AND THE ENDURANCE OF GLOBAL EMPIRE

Charleston and Calcutta before and after the American Revolution

Jonathan Eacott

On any given day in 1790, men and women in the British Empire gazed into their looking glasses to consider not only their physical appearance and that of their surroundings, but how that appearance reinforced, or failed to reinforce, their position in both their local community and in a greater imperial space. Looking glasses had become desired items in cities as geographically distant as Charleston, South Carolina, and Calcutta, Bengal.[1] Despite being on nearly opposite sides of the world, the scenes reflected by these looking glasses were connected both in theory and practice. In reflecting the local, looking glasses also reflected broadly global strands of empire. This duality was deeply embedded in the imperial system, encouraging and tapping into a sense of belonging to a greater British ideal that might helpfully be called *imperial urbanity*. Imperial urbanity describes both the importance of the network of urban ports in the trade and administration of the empire and a sense of the shared everyday fashions, habits, and practices that the middling and upper sorts who managed the empire sought to develop locally as well as in a broader imperial frame.[2]

Over two decades ago Jack Greene encouraged historians to rethink the relationship between the American North and South in the colonial period, stressing the ways in which the South flowed "in the mainstream of British-American development."[3] Looking in another direction, historians of the

Atlantic world have similarly elevated the question of linkages between the Old World and the New by tracing the development of transatlantic commerce and of an Anglo-American genteel culture. These productive and important thrusts to trace the continuities between the North and South, the Old World and the New, have nevertheless tended to perpetuate the division of the history of the British Empire into the Atlantic "First" Empire and the Asian and African "Second" Empire. In this framework, there seems to be little reason for Atlantic historians to consider the Pacific and Indian Oceans. Likewise, historians of British India have rarely considered America. Studies focusing on one region or even one whole ocean of the empire rarely reflect back upon the imperial system as a whole. There are, however, more global approaches emerging. Conferences and works on the Pacific Rim have begun to broaden our understanding of British America beyond the colonial Eastern Seaboard and beyond the West Coast.[4] Works by historians such as Peter Marshall, Linda Colley, and Maya Jasanoff, meanwhile, have expanded the global politics of the British Empire and revealed the global movement of individuals throughout the empire, amongst Europe; Africa; the Americas; and the West, and importantly, East Indies. The questions of whether or how a subject or visitor might know if they were in the British Empire, or when they were in it, however, remain unanswered. These are important questions, for their answers offer us a new perspective on whether our atomized historiography reflects the contingencies of the development of that historiography more than the contingencies of the empire that it tries to understand.[5]

Of course, one might quickly respond, Charleston was not part of the British Empire after the American Revolution. This is true in a certain formal sense. Nevertheless, the notions of formal and informal imperialism that are often used in binary to think about the exercise of imperial power obscure the processes through which the physical, legal, and ideological imprints of the British Empire on Charleston and its inhabitants were developed and through which they lasted beyond the Revolution. Historians often describe such ongoing and new imprints as Anglicization, but this tends to load too much centralizing force in Britain itself. Imperial imprints were often products of Britons out in the colonies, in America and India, forming and exercising power as part of the empire to which they belonged and as part of their own imperial ambitions, as Alejandra Dubcovsky, Travis Glasson, Robert Olwell, and Joshua Piker show in this volume for the American South. Similarly, Carl Nightingale has shown that ideas of race and segregationist policies in the American South and India influenced each other. As I argue elsewhere, Anglicization was part of a larger process of imperialization. Here, bringing Charleston and Calcutta side by side reveals clear patterns of British imperial urbanity. These patterns suggest that Britain and its northern colonies were in many ways on the fringe of an increasingly subtropical and tropical, or more simply, southern global imperial urbanity that in many respects survived the American Revolution. In their everyday lives, fashions, economic pursuits, and structure of their enslaved labor systems, Charlestonians continued to participate in this southern mainstream of the British Empire even if after 1783 most, though not all, would have readily disclaimed their membership in it, and even if their political institutions were no longer directly under British authority.[6]

• • •

Both Charleston and Calcutta were port towns in similar regional geographies, of a similar age, with comparable numbers of people of European descent who accounted for a minority of the population. The British founded both cities near large saltwater harbors that were connected to the interior through systems of navigable freshwater rivers. These specific locations allowed for the ready exchange of products, fashions, and ideas with the rural hinterlands and with other locations across the oceans. Calcutta's hinterland had a non-European population density several times higher than South Carolina, where white settlers were displacing the Native population through disease and violence. The closer demographic analogue was between Asian Indians and American blacks. British colonists, and later Americans, imported Africans to be the local majority underclass in Charleston, a role filled by Asian Indians in and around Calcutta. In 1790, Charleston County had about 47,000 residents, 34,846 blacks and 11,801 whites, although within the city itself the ratio was much closer to 1:1. Nevertheless, Charleston had a much higher proportion of blacks than other major American cities.[7] In 1756 greater Calcutta had an estimated 117,744 residents, rising to 179,917 in 1819. Of these totals, the white population typically amounted to perhaps less than one to two thousand individuals.[8]

It must be stressed that the details of Asian Indian and African American negotiations with the white minority frequently differed. Both British and Indian people in Calcutta lacked access to some types of political institutions available to whites in Charleston, such as elected assemblies, although they were far from powerless in negotiating with the East India Company. Much work remains to be done in understanding the political positions, freedoms, and unfreedoms of Indians under British rule, but chattel enslavement was a more pronounced and common life experience in South Carolina. Asian Indians belonged to various long-rooted and not easily displaceable networks that included elite merchants and bankers who interacted as business partners with people of British and other European descent.[9]

Language and print reflect the greater levels of political and economic agency available to at least some such Asian Indians and give a sense of how these differences became manifested as a varying degree of cultural exchange. Blacks in the South Carolina low country developed a local creole language combining English and African vocabularies and syntaxes.[10] This language did not become integrated into structures of control, even though it reinforced a creole identity and served as a mode of resistance. All of Charleston's newspapers ran in English. In contrast, the *Calcutta Gazette* contained numerous advertisements as well as official statements in any combination of English, Bengali, and Urdu. The adoption of local languages in structures of imperial power is one of many indicators that the political and economic strength of elite Asian Indians was greater than that of Native Americans or leading blacks in South Carolina. Still, both port cities were profoundly shaped by the rule of the British minority.[11]

These British rulers, and their American descendants in Charleston, tended to be relatively mobile, but collectively they also found it difficult to permanently relocate back to Britain—they consciously created permanent urban environments in both America and India. Again, the language used at the time is instructive in thinking about how Britons viewed these distant communities. Britons identified Calcutta and Charleston alike, along with other colonial towns in both India and America as "settlements," showing an embrace and awareness of the creation of permanent communities even if the individuals making up the communities were often locally and globally mobile.[12] Merchants and others frequently traveled to Britain, Europe, and ports within and without the British Empire and back again. Writing and talking about returning permanently to Britain appears to have been more common in colonial India. Nevertheless, mortality rates and other difficulties suggest that patterns of permanent return to Britain were not remarkably different between Calcutta and Charleston. Most died in their colonial settlements. Probate records further indicate that many of the Europeans who died in Calcutta relied on local kin to be estate administrators and left their possessions to children, spouses, or extended family members who often continued to live in, and themselves often died in, the town or elsewhere in the colony. Children sent to Britain for schooling also often returned to

Figure 9.1. Charles Fraser, "A Scene in the Theatre Charleston," Charles Fraser Sketchbook, c. 1790s, p. 17, from the Collections of the South Carolina Historical Society.

the colonies, although such return rates remain an area in need of further study. Additionally, Charleston and Calcutta shared a similar predominance of rental housing, frequent moves within the city, and migration into and out of the countryside.[13]

The built environments of Charleston and Calcutta manifested the permanence of settlement and the location of the ports within a shared British imperial culture, divided in many ways more by wealth and climate than by ocean. Britons in both towns shared local civic pride, and both towns were often proclaimed respectively as the most urbane in India and the North American South, boasting theatres, music halls, fine churches, orphanages, and public lamps.[14] As shown in Figures 9.1 and 9.2, the central townscapes of Calcutta and Charleston shared much in common. Contemporary descriptions and images reveal public buildings and homes with similar proportions, shapes, and styles, if some different details. Buildings tended to be inspired by and to conjure up the classical imperial civilizations of Greece and Rome with Doric and Ionic columns, friezes, and cornices. If the allusions were lost

Figure 9.2. Note the similar classically influenced religious and secular architecture to Charleston, as well as the carriage-style palanquin distinctive to India in the foreground. James Baillie Fraser, "View of St Andrew's Church, from Mission Row," Views of Calcutta (1824–1826), X644, Plate 13, copyright the British Library Board.

on Indians and African Americans, they were not lost on those seeking to justify their power.[15] Even detached from their references to the empires of antiquity, the construction and size of the homes of the wealthy presented common messages of permanence, wealth, and strength to the populations of Charleston and Calcutta. Additionally, the Mughal custom of walling in urban property adopted by Britons in India fit easily with British customs of fencing and hedging used in Britain and America alike.[16] Britain was, nevertheless, much cooler than Charleston and Calcutta, and the climate differentiated buildings in both cities from those in London. Balconies and verandas as retreats from the oppressive summer heat were common in Charleston and Calcutta but not in Britain, although in the early nineteenth century Rudolph Ackermann, one of London's fashion leaders, encouraged their adoption. These broader imperial designs were often combined with local stylistic elements, such as North American clapboard siding or South Asian finials.[17]

Housing advertisements for the middling and upper sorts in Calcutta were interchangeable with those in Charleston, with the exception of street names and the occasional reference to cypress or "pucka," while the homes of the poorer sorts shared a far lower standard. In Charleston, Michael Kaltisen advertised homes with "every necessary and convenience, either for a publican or a merchant in cellars, kitchens, stables, &c. &c." and a tenement "two stories high . . . with outhouses, garden, &c. . . . well suited for public or private business." In Calcutta, Mr. Hamilton let a five-room house, similarly "with Office . . . Coach House, and stabling, sufficient garden grounds." Jacob Eilbracht offered a "large and commodious House pleasantly situated on the banks of the river [with] . . . six lower and three upper rooms . . . a warehouse and six store-rooms, a cook room, and a garden."[18] Calcutta homes may have been more open than those in Charleston: living spaces flowed together, rooms often lacked doors, doors often lacked locks, and servants lacked specific hidden quarters. In any case, servants or enslaved people in both towns were often intimately close to white families despite broader patterns of segregation. According to Lord Valencia, who visited Calcutta in 1803, the lower ranks lived in roughly constructed homes of wood and mud. He drew a transoceanic and imperial comparison, finding them similar to "the cabins of the poorest class in Ireland." If he had visited North America, he would likely have found the lower-rank housing of South Carolina similar again.[19]

Britons and Americans in Charleston and Calcutta also shared a broadly imperial consumer culture. If Americans were engaged in a distinctly American form of commercialism, one should find major differences between the types of consumer goods purchased by Britons, and later Americans, in the two cities. Through comparing Charleston and Calcutta probate inventories (records of possessions owned at an individual's death) and advertisements, however, the picture that emerges is one of a common consumer culture. This common culture included a shared attraction to many products and fashions from throughout the empire as well as modes of adapting purchasing patterns to local conditions. Thus, one can imagine two overlapping circles of consumption: one a shared transimperial space, the other local and place specific. In the overlap, one finds items that combined characteristics from both the shared and the local.

The following analysis is drawn from 250 probate inventories from South Carolina for the periods 1760–1765, 1790–1795, and 1808–1809, as well as 272 inventories from the Bengal presidency for the periods 1760–1765, 1790–1800, and 1820–1829. A smaller number of inventories for additional years were studied but not included in the statistical analysis. The bulk of the analysis focuses on a subset of fifty-eight and fifty-two inventories for individuals who lived in the city of Charleston, and fifty-two and fifty-seven inventories for individuals who lived in Calcutta in the 1760s and 1790s respectively.

The Charleston inventories were further divided into three categories based on the value of the individual's non-real estate possessions to give an approximate sense of the ownership of goods at different wealth and status levels. Seventy-eight inventories were in the lower wealth group, sixty in the middling, and twenty-four in the highest. Inventories primarily cover merchants, army officers, lawyers, doctors, educators, ship's officers, planters, shopkeepers, unmarried women, and a broad range of artisans. All of these people were participants in imperial urbanity. The bulk of the inventories recorded were for men, and women are considered separately in the analysis. The inventories underrepresent the poor and working poor in Charleston and Calcutta who had few or no possessions, and they do not represent the possessions of the enslaved.[20]

In the 1760s slavery was legal in both Charleston and Calcutta, although rates of ownership and the number of enslaved people owned per estate were substantially higher in Charleston. Approximately two-thirds of Charleston estates included enslaved people, compared with approximately one-third in Calcutta. Britons in India tended to defend Indian slavery as being substantially different from the chattel slavery of the Atlantic, although such defenses must be recognized as serving their specific interests in deflecting criticism back toward the Atlantic colonies. Legal slavery was, nevertheless, on the decline amongst Calcutta's whites. Calcutta inventories for the 1790s and 1820s did not include enslaved people.[21] Nevertheless, a typical British household in Calcutta employed several Indian servants whose range of freedom remains unclear. Likewise, in the 1790s, the average urban Charlestonian owned eight or nine enslaved people. Britons throughout the empire saw enslaved people and servants as fashionable before the American Revolution. After the Revolution, the abolition movement in Britain and the northern US states forced the question of the trade in enslaved people and their ownership, legally and morally. As the antagonist, Sir Matthew Mite, in Samuel Foote's play *The Nabob*, noted, "I had some thoughts of importing three blacks from Bengal . . . but I sha'n't venture till the point is determined whether those creatures are to be considered as mere chattels, or men."[22] Nevertheless, many enslaved people and servants accompanied their masters to Britain from Charleston and Calcutta alike, flowing the southern cultural mainstream into the metropole. Even as the forms of household labor differed, Asian Indians and Africans served white Britons and Americans, and they were integral to the maintenance of imperial urbanity.[23]

This system depended on violence and the threat of violence, as manifested in high levels of weapon ownership in both cities. Gun culture was decidedly imperial and not British-Atlantic or American. In colonial Charleston more white men owned guns at their death than in Calcutta, but in early Republican Charleston the reverse was the case. In Calcutta gun ownership levels amongst white men increased slightly over time from 40 percent to 46 percent in the 1820s, a shift with little statistical significance. Meanwhile, the total number of guns averaged over all estates in Calcutta declined in each period, from nine guns per estate in the 1760s, to two guns in the 1790s, and 1.4 guns in the 1820s. Pistols, in particular, were more popular in Calcutta than in Charleston, but overall ownership levels stayed higher as well. In Charleston the number of guns per owner peaked at 1.4 averaged over all estates in the 1760s, falling to 0.6 in the 1790s and 1809. The number of men who owned at least one gun at their death in Charleston declined from 72 percent in the 1760s to 36 percent in the 1790s. This decline was particularly sharp in inventories of people with less valuable personal possessions at their death, falling from an ownership rate of 71 percent to 25 percent. This suggests a preference away from gun ownership in favor of other goods amongst people with more limited resources. Amongst middling estates, owning guns declined more modestly from 74 percent in the 1760s to 58 percent in the 1790s. These men were easily wealthy enough to own guns if they chose, and the majority continued to choose to. The pattern of ownership likely reflects that men with more valuable possessions tended to have more enslaved laborers, more wealth to lose, and greater positions of authority than those with less valuable possessions. Newspaper advertisements further suggest the importance of firearms as high fashion, offering in Calcutta, for example, "very valuable, highly finished double and single barrel fowling pieces and pistols from Joseph Manton and other eminent makers." Similarly, in Charleston the merchant Joseph Winn offered "elegant Fowling Pieces" or shot guns. Gun ownership was decidedly masculine: one out of twenty-three women in Charleston owned a gun, and one out of twenty-seven women in Calcutta owned a gun barrel.[24]

Indeed, high levels of weapon ownership correlated with long periods of war and the number of men active in the military. During the Seven Years War, the Nawab of Bengal, Siraj-ud-daula, briefly seized Calcutta in 1756, and in South Carolina the Cherokee defeated colonists at several points. British forces then launched major victorious offensives in both regions in the late 1750s and early 1760s. War returned during the American Revolution in South Carolina and eastern India, but after 1783 war was not a significant part of life in Charleston for decades and gun ownership began to decline. In India, meanwhile, major conquests continued to be aided by British forces from Calcutta during the Mysore Wars and through the early nineteenth century. In 1830 the East India Company's and royal armies were by far the largest employers of Britons in India, employing 36,409 mostly British Europeans. The correlation of weapon ownership and military action can also be seen in the ownership trends of swords, which were useful in the army but generally less preferable to guns for hunting or personal defense. Estates of white men in Calcutta more frequently included swords than estates in Charleston. By the 1790s, swords appeared in less than 10 percent of Charleston inventories.[25]

Given the boycotts of the American Revolutionary era, permanent declines in the consumption of goods associated with the British Empire in Charleston might be expected, particularly of tea which had been at the heart of colonial resistance. In Charleston inventories between the 1760s and the 1790s, the number of tea kettles decreased somewhat while the number of teapots increased somewhat. Notably, however, the rate of teapot ownership increased between each period in Calcutta, with over twice the rate of ownership in Calcutta compared to Charleston in the 1790s. The rate of coffeepot ownership in Charleston, meanwhile, stayed consistent at just under one-third. Charlestonians were not replacing tea drinking with coffee drinking. Coffeepot ownership varied somewhat more widely over time in Calcutta, but overall rates were broadly similar to Charleston. Both tea drinking from China and coffee drinking from the Middle East reflected the power of the empire in mediating the transfer of specific cultural goods and their incorporation into genteel fashion, but independence in America does appear to have coincided with limited increases in tea consumption compared to India.[26]

Other elements of diet more closely reflected local influences. Some urban Charleston inventories contained "Indian" corn (maize) as well as corn mills, and both were common in rural South Carolina inventories. Colonists had rapidly adopted maize, indigenous to the Americas, from Native American peoples throughout the Atlantic Seaboard. Maize did not become popular in Calcutta. Britons in Calcutta did, however, adopt and adapt Asian Indian curries and a range of associated goods, such as curry dishes. By the middle of the eighteenth century, curry recipes appeared in British cookbooks, with the first in Hannah Glasse's influential and frequently reprinted and revised *Art of Cookery* (1747).[27] Such recipes were available in Charleston. Frederick Grunsway, for instance, owned Glasse's *Art of Cookery*, and curry powder was advertised in Charleston after the Revolution. Still, there is no evidence that Charlestonians cooked and ate curries as frequently as Britons in India. The first American cookbooks did not include curries, suggesting that cookery authors believed such recipes should have no place in American diets.[28]

Inside urban homes, wall covering had developed into an art heavily influenced by Asia, with careful combinations of looking glasses, wallpapers, curtains, pictures, and windows working together to create illusions of openness and of the outdoors. Looking glasses themselves were standard items in Charleston. As wealth increased, so too did the number of looking glasses, and almost all decedents at the higher ownership levels owned looking glasses. Wallpaper remnants occasionally appear in Charleston inventories, but generally inventories are not a helpful guide for the incidence of wallpaper. We know from surviving images and structures, however, that wallpaper had become common in the homes of prosperous families throughout the British Atlantic. Wallpaper was less common in India due to the damage caused by insects, despite its Chinese inspiration.[29] Approximately one-third of inventories in Calcutta and Charleston included window curtains in the 1790s, with people having more valuable possessions more frequently owning curtains. Similarly, over a third of inventories in both cities contained wall art, again with people with more valuable possessions more frequently owning it.

Complicated and multivalent identities were suggested by a mixing of imperial space and of local place in Charleston wall art that included British cultural examples and celebrations of British figures and imperial victories alongside celebrations of American valor in the face of British enemies. John Lloyd, a planter living in Charleston with the most valuable estate in 1809, owned several landscape paintings that depicted British and local scenes painted by Britons or by Americans trained in the British school of landscape painting.[30] Lloyd also owned six prints of plays by Shakespeare that had become iconographic of British nationalism.[31] Lloyd owned eight prints depicting Roman gods and glories, which like classical architecture, conveyed messages of virtue and strength while justifying authority and empire. These were not images of Roman republicanism that might have reflected the American political experiment. Yet Lloyd did own two American patriotic prints, *Death of Montgomery* and *Battle of Bunker Hill*. These were likely copies of John Trumbull's works, possibly the 1808 prints done by Andrew Maverick. Both of these depictions echoed Benjamin West's use of light, grouped figures, and the martyr's death in *Death of General Woolfe*, painted in 1770 to celebrate the British capture of Quebec. West himself was born in America and moved to Britain; this was imperial exchange at work and not simply Anglicization.

The Charleston merchant Alexander McDowall owned a similar mix of art celebrating both Britain's empire and America. McDowall had lived in Charleston for some time, along with several other McDowalls.³² Strikingly, he owned a picture of George III and a range of celebrations of British naval victories over the French in the French Revolutionary and Napoleonic Wars, including a picture of British naval hero Horatio Nelson, a "Tribute to the Memory of Nelson," a copy of Thomas Whitcombe's *Admiral Duncan's Victory off Camperdown*, and two plates of a 1795 painting celebrating Lord Howe's famous June victory over the French fleet. This last was a particularly intriguing image to be in the collection. Howe had substantially weakened the French fleet, but nevertheless a major grain shipment from the United States made it through to France. In effect the moment could be seen as a victory for all three parties. McDowall also owned a view of London, four views of Scotland, and a picture of the Scottish military hero Ralph Abercromby, who had been sympathetic to the Patriots during the American Revolution but had become, in the 1790s, the commander of British forces in the West Indies, and then Ireland, before he was finally killed fighting the French in Egypt. Ambercromby had openly praised George Washington. And, similarly, McDowall owned an "Inscription to Washington" and a picture of Washington's family.³³ McDowall's art collection indicates that he maintained pride in his Scottish heritage, alongside pride in both his larger British identity and his more recent American one.

Calcutta wall art followed a similar pattern of balancing standard transimperial and locally adapted fashion, although its owners need not wrestle with competing messages of the Empire and the independent Republic. Shakespeare prints and portraits of the king and queen tell a similar story of the integration of white Calcutta into a specifically British imperial space. The popularity of landscapes of India among white settlers reflected, as in America, the application of the British landscape school to local place. Francis Swain Ward, for example, advertised a collection of engravings of his drawings in the 1784 *Calcutta Gazette*. Each depicted "Gentoo Architecture, &c"; his catalogue included no views of European settlements or buildings. The drawings of India had been sent to England for engraving, from where the engravings would then be delivered to India. Lest there be any doubt of both its broader and local fashionability, he described his work as "well known, and esteemed in Europe and India."³⁴

Books similarly maintained and replicated British imperial themes in a literary community from Charleston to Calcutta even after the American Revolution. The majority of decedents in both cities owned books at their death, with overall ownership rates between 60 and 74 percent and with rates amongst those in the two higher inventory categories higher still. In all periods, books by British authors predominated and imperial themes were common. In 1760s Charleston, for example, Daniel Hunt owned collections of the works of John Locke and Joseph Addison, which both appeared in many other probate inventories as well. Frederick Grunsway owned several books with imperial influences and themes including, *Robinson Crusoe,* the *Imperial Magazine,* and Glasse's *Art of Cookery.* In the 1790s, Charlestonian James Down owned the works of famous British literary figures Oliver Goldsmith and Alexander Pope, as well as John Bell's collection of British poetry and Lewis Theobald's collected works of Shakespeare. Much like they owned prints of Shakespeare's plays, decedents in both cities owned various editions of the plays themselves. Down also owned the works of Scottish enlightenment thinker David Hume, as well as William Blackstone's *Commentaries on the Laws of England.* In 1809 the Charleston merchant Tobias Cambridge owned books on classical history and the history of Britain, as well as Blackstone's *Commentaries* and the *Encyclopaedia Britannica.*[35] Importantly, he also owned four of the five volumes of *Asiatic Researches,* written by the members of Calcutta's Asiatic Society. The society had been formed by Britons under the leadership of the famous orientalist William Jones, who had considered moving to America.[36] Cambridge also owned Johnson's famous dictionary and forty-two issues of the British *Universal Magazine.* Cambridge owned only one issue of the *Pennsylvania Magazine.* In Calcutta many of the same works appeared, as well as many books on Asia and military affairs and some on America, such as William Robertson's *History of America.* As in other aspects of consumer culture, these book collections suggest that Charlestonians remained very much a part of a broader British imperial urbanity.

British, Asian, and American craftsmen made bookshelves, trunks, chests, chests of drawers, desks, tables, and chairs using British pattern books and materials influenced by the empire and its trade. The furniture market combined imported products crafted in Europe, products made locally from fashionable imported materials, and products made locally from local materials. Construction styles and finishes incorporated elements from India, China, Japan, the Americas, and Europe, including lacquering, japanning, and stylized Asian paintings.[37] Inventories and advertisements indicate that mahogany from the West Indies and South America had the most fashionable appeal not just in the British Atlantic but in British India as well. In Calcutta, R. Duncan, for example, advertised "elegant mahogany furniture, after the newest fashion in London."³⁸ Less expensive furniture was made from local woods, such as sissoo, pine, or cypress. An 1803 Charleston directory listed twenty-two cabinetmakers, ten chair makers, and one speciality Windsor chair maker. An 1800 Calcutta directory listed six European cabinet makers, and there were many Asian Indian carpenters and furniture makers as well.³⁹ The biggest difference was in the type of furniture used for rest. Most Charleston inventories included formal bedsteads, often with curtains or pavilions. In contrast, less than 10 percent of Calcutta inventories contained bedsteads until the 1820s. Instead, most inventories contained cots made with thin mattresses over rattan lacing that were lighter, cheaper, and cooler than bedsteads.⁴⁰ As bedsteads increased in prevalence in Calcutta in the early nineteenth century, cots also increased in prevalence in Charleston, bringing sleeping furniture patterns closer together.

Outside of the home, means of transportation also reflected a balance between imperial trends and local conditions. The existence of horses in Charleston and Calcutta should not be taken for granted as horses were indigenous to neither region. In 1815 "HIGH-BRED FRESH UNTRIED ARABS, RECENTLY IMPORTED" continued to be advertised in Calcutta papers.⁴¹ Horse ownership levels were approximately one-third in Charleston and Calcutta alike, except for the 1760s in Charleston, when about 45 percent of deceased men owned at least one horse. Horses were used for plantation work, riding, and pulling a variety of carriages. London-styled horse-drawn carriages, often using imperially sourced materials, represented fashionable transportation in both cities. Advertisements for fashionable carriages imported from London, such as "A neat crane-neck'd London built Chariot," frequently appeared.⁴² Whether made in London or locally, such carriages were expensive and their wide track and heavy weight made them unsuitable in large parts of Carolina and Bengal. Midcentury colonists in Charleston took up the colonial invention of lightweight Windsor chairs mounted on horse carts.⁴³ Britons in Calcutta adopted and applied London style to palanquins, customary Indian conveyances carried by servants on long horizontal poles rested on their shoulders. Palanquin passengers typically reclined as at rest, although some palanquins were more akin to sedan chairs. Palanquins were most suited to rural, roadless, nighttime travel. A growing number of British estates in Calcutta included at least one palanquin, rising to over 80 percent in the 1790s, before declining again in the early nineteenth century. Palanquins required substantial human labor, which was cheaper in India than in South Carolina, and they were also used in the West Indies, Africa, and South America.⁴⁴ Neither palanquins nor sedan chairs appeared in the

Charleston inventories, although sedan chairs were used in Carolina as they were throughout the empire.[45]

Local influences also shaped means of water transport. Seven percent of Charleston inventories for men listed at least one canoe, the design borrowed from Native Americans particularly for river navigation. No canoes appeared amongst city decedents in 1809 and no other vessel style appears to have replaced the canoe for inland navigation. Canoes disappeared with the improvement of regional roads and the decline of the local deerskin trade. Britons in Calcutta did not own canoes, although some of the wealthiest did own large Indian *budgerows*. Budgerows provided comfortable spaces, sometimes with several rooms. Although much larger than canoes, their shallow draft and lack of keel made them ideal for river travel.[46]

Fashionable dress and accessories were particularly strongly influenced in the colonies and Britain by imperial exchange with the southern parts of the empire. For men, banyan gowns, shirts, and coats had spread from Asia to Britain and from there to the American colonies, though by the early nineteenth century they were falling out of fashion. In Calcutta but not in Charleston or London, many British women owned *cholis*, form-fitting Indian blouses with short sleeves that typically exposed part of the midriff, "Uncurb'd by forms of prudish fools," as a poet wrote in the *Calcutta Gazette*.[47] Women across the empire, including in Charleston and Britain, took up Asian-inspired parasols or sun umbrellas in the eighteenth century, but men only adopted them in the southern parts of the empire. A man from a southern colony quoted in the *Pennsylvania Gazette* was shocked in 1771 that Philadelphians complained of the sun's heat but did not use umbrellas as protection. Umbrellas, he explained, were a useful and internationally recognized defense that had come from India. They offered protection against "Vertigoes Epilepsy Sore eyes Fevers" and general illness caused by the sun. He noted that men spent more time outside than ladies and did more important business; therefore, they had even more reason to use umbrellas for protection from the sun. If umbrellas were effeminate, he reasoned, since "the Ladies wear Shoes let the Men therefore go barefooted."[48] By the turn to the nineteenth century, men throughout the British Empire and in America alike were adopting umbrellas for the rain instead of the sun. In Charleston the number of men's inventories listing umbrellas increased steadily from 10 percent in the 1760s to 28 percent in 1809. These totals, however, likely underestimate the rate of umbrella ownership as many inventories, particularly in the later decades, do not itemize wearing apparel and accessories. Similarly, the East India Company helped to popularize brightly colored bandanna-style handkerchiefs from India in America, goods which were prohibited in Britain itself for much of the eighteenth century.[49]

Britain did continue to mediate many fashions, but even London's fashion was much more imperial than intrinsically British. The Committee of Buyers of East-India Piece Goods explained, "London is known to impose her fashions as to dress, more or less, upon the greater part of Europe." "Her" example had most recently been followed "in the adoption of muslins in general."[50] Indeed, after a ball in 1801 Ann Steele wrote from Georgetown, "Ms. Murray was there, she is just back from Europe of course very fashionable. She was dressed in black Muslin . . . a cambrick muslin handkerchief tied around her head." Steele enclosed a sample pattern of a handkerchief design.[51] The wording of advertisements in Charleston underscore this association between goods from the British Empire and genteel London fashion. In 1783 George Lockey made sure to highlight that his "fashionable assortment of printed linens, calicos, linen handkerchiefs, India chintz, silk handkerchiefs, and Romalls" had all been "IMPORTED . . . from London." Calicoes, and later muslins, and the forms of unstructured dress to which they were suited had been adopted in London from India and classical Rome and Greece—they were not essentially British, although British manufacturers increasingly produced them.[52]

Conclusion

In the years around the American Revolution, the British Empire was a tropical and semitropical empire. To borrow and adapt Jack Greene's expression, Charleston and Calcutta flowed "in the mainstream" of British imperial urbanity, even as Charleston became part of the United States. Charleston, near the western extreme of the empire, in some ways shared more in common with Calcutta, near the eastern extreme, than with the much physically closer ports of the northern United States. Their geographies and their pasts within the empire shaped not just their economies but their cultures and urban environments. Their urbanity was a British imperial one, premised on exploiting nonwhite people, violent conquest, and commercial and fashionable exchange, adoption, and adaptation. The middling and wealthy sorts demanded products drawn from throughout the empire. Many of these goods were not British, although they reflected Britain's global power and often, though not always, reflected London tastes. Simultaneously, people of European descent in Calcutta and Charleston diversified their consumption patterns and habits by adapting imperial fashion locally and adopting additional local goods ranging from canoes to cholis. From the dialectic of imperial space and place, people in Calcutta and Charleston developed a shared imperial urbanity, stabilizing and participating in the flow of the British Empire, both before and after the American Revolution.[53] In their looking glasses, Britons in Calcutta as well as Britons and, later, Americans in Charleston saw not only themselves, their local communities, and Britain, they saw Britain's global empire.

Notes

1. Looking glasses were vital tools in many countries over millennia. Sabine Melchior-Bonnet traces the role of the mirror in imagining and preparing one's image from classical antiquity, through the Renaissance, to the twenty-first century. Sabine Melchior-Bonnet, *The Mirror: A History*, trans. Katharine Jewett, 101–29, 176–82 (London: Routledge, 2001). The author thanks the participants of the European Empires in the American South Conference, University of Mississippi, Oxford, MS, 2013, and Catherine Cangany, Dena Goodman, David Hancock, Robert Kruckeburg, and Jennifer Palmer for comments on earlier versions of this essay as well as the Department of History, International Institute, and Rackham Graduate School at the University of Michigan, Ann Arbor, MI, which provided funding for research in the United Kingdom and India.

2. Imperial urbanity goes beyond fashion or style to include what Pierre Bourdieu calls habitus, the unthinking practices and associations that affirm social norms. Pierre Bourdieu, *Distinction: A Social Critique of the Judgement of Taste* (Cambridge, MA: Harvard University Press, 1984), 170, 483.

3. Jack Greene, *Pursuits of Happiness: The Social Development of Early Modern British Colonies and the Formation of American Culture* (Chapel Hill: University of North Carolina Press, 1988), 5.

4. See, for example, Paul W. Mapp, *The Elusive West and the Contest for Empire, 1713–1763* (Chapel Hill: Published for the Omohundro Institute of Early American History and Culture, Williamsburg, VA, by the University of North Carolina Press, 2011).

5. P. J. Marshall, *The Making and Unmaking of Empires: Britain, India, and America, c.1750–1783* (Oxford: Oxford University Press, 2005); Linda Colley, *The Ordeal of Elizabeth Marsh: A Woman in World History* (New York: Anchor Books, 2008); Maya Jasanoff, *Liberty's Exiles: American Loyalists in the Revolutionary World* (New York: Knopf, 2011).

6. Carl Nightingale, *Segregation: A Global History of Divided Cities* (Chicago: University of Chicago Press, 2012), 2–3, 69–70; Jonathan Eacott, *Selling Empire: India in the Making of Britain and America, 1600–1830* (Chapel Hill: University of North Carolina Press for the Omohundro Institute, 2016), 10–11. On Anglicization before the American Revolution, see Timothy Breen, *The Marketplace of Revolution* (Oxford: Oxford University Press, 2004), esp. 35–71; Timothy Breen, "'Baubles of Britain': The American and Consumer Revolutions of the Eighteenth Century," *Past & Present* 119 (May 1988): 73–104. For examples of works

on Anglicization in the United States after the American Revolution, see Elisa Tamarkin, *Anglophilia: Deference, Devotion, and Antebellum America* (Chicago: University of Chicago Press, 2008); Kariann Akemi Yokota, *Unbecoming British: How Revolutionary America Became a Postcolonial Nation* (New York: Oxford University Press, 2011); Sam Haynes, *Unfinished Revolution: The Early American Republic in a British World* (Charlottesville: University of Virginia Press, 2010). The global southern perspective is shared in this volume by Christopher Morris in his work on the French.

7. Walter J. Fraser, *Charleston! Charleston! The History of a Southern City* (Columbia: University of South Carolina Press, 1989), 178.

8. For a detailed consideration of the problems with the various population estimates, see A. K. Ray, *A Short History of Calcutta* (1902; repr., Calcutta: Raddhi, 1982), 133–43.

9. Peter Marshall, "The Whites of British India, 1780–1830: A Failed Colonial Society?," *International History Review* 12, no. 1 (February 1990): 30–35, 44.

10. Philip D. Morgan, *Slave Counterpoint: Black Culture in the Eighteenth-Century Chesapeake and Low Country* (Chapel Hill: University of North Carolina Press for the Omohundro Institute, 1998), 566–79.

11. Several historians have discussed successful East Indian businessmen. For two different perspectives, one stressing East Indian interactions with Americans and the other with Britons, see Susan Bean, *Yankee India: American Commercial and Cultural Encounters with India in the Age of Sail, 1784–1860* (Salem, MA: Peabody Essex Museum, 2001), 101–11, and Anne Bulley, *The Bombay Country Ships, 1790–1833* (London: Curzon, 2000), 101.

12. There are countless examples. See, for instance, Joseph Price, *Five Letters from a Free Merchant in Bengal, to Warren Hastings, Esq; Governor General of the Honourable East India Company's Settlements in Asia: Conveying Some Free Thoughts on the Probable Causes of the Decline of the Export Trade of That Kingdom* (London, [1777?]).

13. Julie Flavell, *When London Was Capital of America* (New Haven, CT: Yale University Press, 2010), esp. 7–26; Jeanne A. Calhoun, Elizabeth A. Paysinger, and Martha A. Zierden, *A Survey of Economic Activity in Charleston* (Charleston, SC: Charleston Museum, 1982), 58; Emma Hart, *Building Charleston: Town and Society in the Eighteenth-Century British Atlantic World* (Charlottesville: University of Virginia Press, 2010), 80–96.

14. For comments praising the cities, see L. de comte de Grandpré, *A Voyage in the Indian Ocean and to Bengal, Undertaken in the Year 1790* (Brattleborough, VT: William Fessenden, 1814), 136–37, and Thomas Twining, *Travels in India a Hundred Years Ago, with a Visit to the United States* (London: J. R. Osgood, McIlvaine & Co., 1893), 73. For civic energy in Charleston, see Fraser, *Charleston*, 107–130, 179–184; Robert Olwell, *Masters, Slaves and Subjects: The Culture of Power in the South Carolina Low Country, 1740–1790* (Ithaca, NY: Cornell University Press, 1998), 33–36; and Hart, *Building Charleston*, 132–55. On Calcutta see Thomas Spear, *The Nabobs: A Study of the Social Life of the English in Eighteenth Century India* (London: Oxford University Press, 1932), 34; Ray, *Short History of Calcutta*, 160; and Peter Marshall, "White Town of Calcutta under the Rule of the East India Company," *Modern Asian Studies* 34, no. 2 (May 2000), 324–25.

15. For more, see Rhys Isaac, *The Transformation of Virginia 1740–1790* (Chapel Hill: University of North Carolina Press for the Omohundro Institute, 1982), 33, 36–39; Richard Bushman, *The Refinement of America: Persons, Houses, Cities* (New York: Alfred A. Knopf, 1992), 115, 193–96; Marshall, "White Town of Calcutta," 314–19.

16. Patricia Seed, *Ceremonies of Possession in Europe's Conquest of the New World 1492-1640* (Cambridge: Cambridge University Press, 1995), 20-31.

17. Jan Morris, Charles Allen, Gillian Tindall, Colin Amery et al., *Architecture of the British Empire* (New York: Vendome Press, 1986), 186, 191; Rudolph Ackermann, "Design for a Verandah," *Repository of Arts* 8 (September 1812): 242-43; Rudolph Ackermann, *Engravings of Fashionable Furniture* (London: Ackermann, 1823), 49. John Plaw had earlier recommended verandas for rural homes in Britain; see John Plaw, *Sketches for Country Houses, Villas, and Rural Dwellings; Calculated for Persons of Moderate Income, and for Comfortable Retirement* (London: S. Gosnell, 1800), 11, Plate 7.

18. *South Carolina Gazette*, May 17, 1783, 1; *Calcutta Gazette*, March 11, 1784, May 5 and 6, 1784.

19. In India, British houses often reserved the first floor for storage, unlike in Charleston. On housing in Calcutta, see Swati Chattopadhyay, "Blurring of Boundaries: The Limits of 'White Town' in Colonial Calcutta," *Journal of South Asian History* 59, no. 2 (June 2000): 158-63, 166-77; Philip Davies, *Splendours of the Raj: British Architecture in India, 1660-1947* (London: J. Murray, 1985). On Charleston housing, see Hart, *Building Charleston*, 73-76; Leila Sellers, *Charleston Business on the Eve of the American Revolution* (Chapel Hill: University of North Carolina Press, 1934), 17; Lord Valencia quoted in Ranjit Sen, *The Stagnating City: Calcutta in the Eighteenth Century* (Calcutta: Institute of Historical Studies, 2000), 15.

20. Charleston County Probate Inventories, 1761-1763, 1763-1767; B, 1787-1793; C, 1793-1800; D, 1800-1810, http://www.fold3.com/page/282784161_estate_inventories_for_charleston. The 1760s Calcutta inventories are from Inventories of Deceased Estates, Bengal, IOR/P/154/62-69, British Library, London (hereafter cited as BL); Inventories from 1790-1799 and 1820-1829 are from Inventories and Accounts of Deceased Estates, Bengal (1780-1840), IOR/L/AG/34/27/13-22, 69-93, BL. For issues of coverage, consistency, and detail in colonial American inventories, see Lois Green Carr and Lorena S. Walsh, "Inventories and the Analysis of Wealth and Consumption Patterns in St. Mary's County, Maryland, 1658-1777" *Historical Methods* 13, no. 2 (Spring 1980): 81-90. Calcutta inventories are more consistent and detailed.

21. For more on Charleston slavery, see Hart, *Building Charleston*, 103. For more on slavery and India, see Andrea Major, *Slavery, Abolitionism and Empire in India: 1772-1843* (Liverpool: University of Liverpool Press, 2012), esp. 3-6, 34.

22. Samuel Foote, *The Nabob; A Comedy, in Three Acts* (London: T. Cadell/Colman, 1778), 38.

23. Flavell, *When London Was Capital of America*, 27-43; Michael Fisher, *Counterflows to Colonialism: Indian Travellers and Settlers in Britain 1600-1857* (Delhi: Permanent Black, 2004), 44-45, 57. For more on enslaved people as fashion, see Morgan, *Slave Counterpoint*, 244-46, and James Holzman, *The Nabobs in England: A Study of the Returned Anglo-Indian, 1760-1785* (New York, 1926), 91.

24. *Calcutta Gazette*, December 8, 1814, 3; *South Carolina State Gazette*, November 13, 1799, [3]; see also Swinton C. Holland's advertisement, *City Gazette and Daily Advertiser* (Charleston, SC), November 20, 1799, 3. The findings do not fit with Michael Bellisles's claim that guns rarely appeared in probate inventories. Michael Bellisles, *Arming America: The Origins of a National Gun Culture* (New York: Knopf, 2000), 229. For an example of other research that has contradicted Bellisles's reading of inventories, see James Lindgreen and

Justin Heather, "Counting Guns in Early America," *William and Mary Law Review* 43 (2002): 1777–1842.

25. Marshall, "Whites of British India," 26.

26. Breen, *Marketplace of Revolution*, 195–331. Data for 1809 is unreliable, as many inventories no longer itemized kitchen goods. For more on the importation and adaption of coffee culture in London, from where it spread to the colonies, see Brian Cowan, *The Social Life of Coffee: The Emergence of the British Coffeehouse* (London: Yale University Press, 2005).

27. Hannah Glasse, *The Art of Cookery, Made Plain and Easy*, 6th ed. (London: A. Millar and T. Trye, 1758), 101.

28. Amelia Simmons, *American Cookery; or, The Art of Dressing Viands, Fish, Poultry, and Vegetables, and the Best Modes of Making Pastes, Puffs, Pies, Tarts, Puddings, Custards and Preserves, and All Kinds of Cakes, from the Imperial Plumb to Plain Cake* (1796; repr., New York: Oxford University Press, 1958); An American Lady, *New American Cookery, or Female Companion* (New York: D. D. Smith, 1805); Lucy Emerson, *The NewEngland Cookery; or, The Art of Dressing all Kinds of Flesh, Fish, and Vegetables and the Best Modes of Making Pastes, Puffs, Pies, Tarts, Puddings, Custards, and Preserves and all Kinds of Cakes from the Imperial Plumb to Plain Cake, Particularly Adapted to this Part of the Country* (Montpelier, VT: Josiah Parks, 1808).

29. N. E. Kindersley, *Letters from the East Indies* (London: J. Nourse, 1777), 279.

30. For more on "how codes of landscape representation developed in England were deployed in an American setting," see Stephen Daniels, *Fields of Vision: Landscape Imagery and National Identity in England and the United States* (Cambridge: Polity Press, 1993), 7–8. See also John Michael Vlach, *The Planter's Prospect: Privilege and Slavery in Plantation Paintings* (Chapel Hill: University of North Carolina Press, 2002), 10–12, 60–65.

31. Thomas Cartelli, *Repositioning Shakespeare: National Formations, Postcolonial Appropriations* (London: Routledge, 1999), chaps. 2–3.

32. There was an Alexander Mcdowal in a Charleston summary process role in 1786, and another Alexander McDowell apparently arrived from Dublin as a saddler about 1795. See Alexander Mcdowall [signed Mcdowal], Indorsee of Nobby Murttis vs John Richey, Summary Process Roll, November 1786, S136011, South Carolina Department of Archives and History, Columbia, SC; *City Gazette & Daily Advertiser*, May 3, 1795, [2]. Given the value of his possessions, it appears more likely to be the former. A merchant McDowell ran several advertisements in Charleston in the late 1790s; see, for example, *City Gazette and Daily Advertiser*, December 8, 1798, [3].

33. Charleston Inventories, D, 1800–1810, 516; David Gates, "Abercromby, Sir Ralph, of Tullibody (1734–1801)," in *Oxford Dictionary of National Biography* (Oxford: Oxford University Press, 2004), online ed., October 2007, http://www.oxforddnb.com.proxy.wm.edu/viewrticle/45 (accessed June 5, 2013).

34. *Calcutta Gazette*, March 4, 1784, 5.

35. It is unclear when or where Tobias Cambridge was born, but a Tobias Cambridge was married in Charleston in 1778; *Register of St. Philip's Parish, Charles Town, or Charleston* (Charleston: University of South Carolina Press, 1927), 230.

36. Garland Cannon, *The Life and Mind of Oriental Jones: Sir William Jones, the Father of Modern Linguistics* (New York: Cambridge University Press, 1990), 171–74, 199, 203–8.

37. Beatrice Garvan, *Federal Philadelphia 1785–1825: The Athens of the Western World* (Philadelphia: Museum of Art, 1987), 66–71; Amin Jaffer, *Furniture from British India and Ceylon: Catalogue of the Collections in the Victoria and Albert Museum and the Peabody Essex Museum* (London: Victoria and Albert Museum, 2001), 76–89. For descriptions of colonial furniture and its stylistic heritage, see William Voss Elder III and Jayne E. Stokes, *American Furniture 1680–1880: From the Collection of the Baltimore Museum of Art* (Baltimore: Museum of Art, 1987); J. Michael Flanigan, *American Furniture from the Kaufman Collection* (Washington, DC: National Gallery of Art, 1986).

38. *Calcutta Gazette*, April 22, 1784, 7.

39. *Bengal Kalendar & Register for the Year 1800* (Calcutta, 1800); Eleazer Elizer, *Directory for 1803; Containing Names of All the Housekeepers & Traders in the City of Charleston* (Charleston, SC, 1803).

40. Kindersley, *Letters*, 280.

41. *Calcutta Gazette*, January 12, 1815, 3.

42. *South Carolina Gazette*, April 5, 1783, 3. For more examples of British-built carriages, see *South Carolina Gazette*, June 24, 1783, 2, which includes a list. For Calcutta see *Calcutta Morning Post*, February 12, 1813, 1; March 26, 1813, 1; May 7, 1813, 1.

43. Nancy Goyne Evans, *American Windsor Furniture: Specialized Forms* (New York: Hudson Hills in association with the Henry Francis du Pont Winterthur Museum, 1997), 227.

44. On palanquins in Africa, South America, and the West Indies, see Paola Collo and Silvia Benso, eds., *Sogno: Bamba, Pemba, Ovando e Altra Contrade dei Regni do Congo, Angola e Adjacenti* (Milan: Franco Maria Ricci, 1986), 79; Amédée Frézier, *Relation du Voyage de la Mer du Sud aux Cotes du Chili du Pérou, ét du Brézil* (Amsterdam, 1717), 2, Plate 35; William Elmes, *Adventures of Johnny Newcome* (1812), Plate 1. On the suitability of palanquins for use on India's roads see, Harry Verlest to Charles Playdell, March 22, 1761, MSS Eur. F218/79, BL; Samuel Stennett, *Memoirs of the Life of the Rev. William Ward, Late Baptist Missionary in India* (London: Simpkin and Marshal, 1825), 137. On sleeping see Neil Edmonstone to William Edmonstone, May 27, 1788, June 19, 1788, Neil Edmonstone Papers, MS Add. 7616, Department of Manuscripts and University Archives, Cambridge University Library, Cambridge. On palanquins and the heat, see Gerard Gustavus Ducarel to his Mother, January 1766, Ducarel Papers, D2091/F11, Gloucestershire Archives, Gloucester, UK; Philip Dormer Stanhope, *Genuine Memoirs of Asiaticus, in a Series of Letters to a Friend, During Five Years Residence in Different Parts of India* (London, 1784), 36, 73.

45. Sedan chairs appear in the Pennsylvania tax lists for 1785. William Henry Egle, ed., *Pennsylvania Archives*, 3rd ser., vol. 13, vols. 14–16 (Harrisburg: W. S. Ray, 1897); see, for example, William Richardson, Bucks County, 3rd ser., vol. 13. It is unclear who carried these chairs. For Carolina, see Carson I. A. Ritchie, *Frontier Parish: An Account of the Society for the Propagation of the Gospel* (Cranbury, NJ: Associated University Presses, 1976), 60. For London, see H. W. Hart, "The Sedan Chair as a Means of Public Conveyance," *Journal of Transport History* 5, no. 4 (1962): 206–9.

46. For an outline of the low country skin trade, see Sellers, *Charleston Business*, 169–77. For descriptions of large *budgerows*, see Henry Abbot, Diary, vol. 1, 47, MSS Eur. B412, BL; William Peacock to Anna Peacock, October 25, 1828, MSS Eur. C180, BL. Henry Thomas Colebrooke, *Remarks on the Present State of the Husbandry and Commerce of Bengal* ([Calcutta], 1795), 124.

47. *Calcutta Gazette*, August 12, 1784, 2.

48. *Pennsylvania Gazette*, August 8, 1771.

49. "Apparel," extracted from Watson's *Annals of Philadelphia*, reprinted in Samuel Hazard, ed., *Register of Pennsylvania* 6 (July 1830–January 1831): 90–91; Susan S. Bean, "Bandanna: On the Origins of an All American Textile," *Annual Proceedings* (*Dublin Seminar for New England Folklife*) (1997), 169.

50. *Letter to the Right Honble. Henry Dundas, One of His Majesty's Principal Secretaries of State, From the Committee of Buyers of East-India Piece Goods for Home Consumption, Respecting the Prohibition of India Muslins* (London: J. Debrett, 1793), 10.

51. Ann Steele to Margaret Steele, December 11, 1801 and Ann Steele to Mary Steele, December 25, 1801, John Steele Papers, ser. 1, Correspondence, Records of AnteBellum Southern Plantations from the Revolution through the Civil War, ser. J, Selections from the Southern Historical Collection, Manuscripts Department, Library of the University of North Carolina at Chapel Hill, Part 13: Piedmont North Carolina (microfilm).

52. *Calcutta Gazette*, September 6, 1783, 1. On muslin dresses, see Aileen Ribeiro, *The Art of Dress: Fashion in England and France, 1750 to 1820* (New Haven, CT: Yale University Press, 1995), 64–71, 109–13; Aileen Ribeiro, *Dress in Eighteenth Century Europe, 1715–1789* (New Haven, CT: Yale University Press, 2002), 222–28; Eacott, *Selling Empire*, 281.

53. For more on the space/place dialectic, see David Harvey, *Justice, Nature, and the Geography of Difference* (Cambridge, MA: Blackwell, 1996), esp. 316.

AFTERWORD

Kathleen DuVal

As long as there has been colonial American history, there have been historians studying the British southern colonies. But until recently, New England was the cornerstone of the scholarship. The mainstream historical profession generally labeled colonial historians who looked south or west as regional historians, whereas historians of New England were the real early Americanists. According to this thinking, only those who studied New England could tell us about the origins of the United States, which eventually spread across the continent.

In the 1970s, a few historians began pushing for inclusion of the South, not as quirky anecdotes, foils to the industrious settlement of North America, or a foreshadowing of the Civil War a couple of centuries later, but as an integral part of America's origin story. Gaining a wide reading audience and earning prominent positions in the profession, these historians made the South central to colonial America and made "the South" more than just Virginia.[1]

Through the 1990s, this argument's resolution was in doubt. Perhaps New England scholarship would remain dominant, or perhaps the standoff would be perpetual. But the advocates of expansion won. No book or course today could claim to represent colonial America while drawing all of its conclusions from New England. Scholars who study New England now see it as an important region that interacted with other colonies and the world beyond, just as people do who study Maryland, New Mexico, Iroquoia, and Berbice.

European Empires in the American South shows how far we have come from arguments over whether Charleston is an important part of the pre-Revolutionary American past. These nine far-flung, cutting-edge essays define the South as not only the British colonies from Maryland to Georgia but also Spanish Florida and French Louisiana; the Creeks, Yamasees, Choctaws, and other Native polities; and the porous and contested borderlands over which countless insiders and outsiders sought to make their mark on the land—or slip through without attracting attention. Reflecting trends in American history more generally, we see many Souths, a wide variety of forms and experiences of slavery, and myriad and changing empires, nations, confederacies, and towns. Most of the action takes place on the North American mainland, but the authors take us around the world, not only to Havana, Rio de Janeiro, Bermuda, La Rochelle, and the Barbary Coast, but across the Pacific to Calcutta and Pondicherry. This is empire as we should understand it: worked out on the ground in countless permutations, with economic and political connections around the world. As such, this book brings together the most influential movements in early American historiography. American Indian history and continental history emphasize local and regional power and practice, while imperial and Atlantic World history explain how systems of trade and slavery infiltrated Europeans into the world beyond Europe.

All of these forces and peoples came together in the colonial South. Three powerful empires—Spain, France, and Britain—competed here for two and half centuries, from the first Spanish slave raids at the start of the sixteenth century and the bloody clash between Spanish St. Augustine and French Fort Caroline in the 1560s through the wars for Florida in the 1810s. Powerful Indian polities—first Mississippian peoples and later Creeks, Cherokees, Choctaws, and Chickasaws—controlled the interior and parts of the coast for the same centuries, usually considering one another their most serious rivals.

At first Spain saw little use for this land with no gold and lots of war, but as France and England aimed to join Spain in reaping profits from distant lands, they looked for places in the tropics and subtropics where Spain and Portugal had not yet established themselves. India, West Africa, the West Indies, and what would become the American South, might be too hot to grow wheat for bread. But enslaved men and women could clear the land (or plant on the abandoned fields of Native women) and grow the indigo, sugar, rice, and tobacco to stoke a global empire.

Recognizing how the regions and peoples of the American South were connected to one another and far beyond reveals a complex and fascinating place, one far removed from traditional stories of the planting of Jamestown and the quick conversion of Pocahontas. The English men and women who attempted silk cultivation in the seventeenth-century Chesapeake were trying the same thing in the same place for the same reasons as Spaniards did in the 1520s. Virginia's silkworm advocates sought to copy a Chinese imperial model to build an empire as rich as Spanish Peru.

Throughout the colonial period, Europeans found themselves on Indian borderlands and recruited into Indian wars and diplomacy. Someone familiar with only the nineteenth-century story of Native resistance to American westward expansion might expect Indians to oppose an imperial fort on their lands. On the contrary, Creeks and Tuscaroras in 1721 welcomed Fort King George. They valued the trade goods and British alliance opportunities it could provide, and they sought to expand the fort's intended function into a site to host their own Creek-Tuscarora diplomacy. At St. Augustine, Yamasee Cacique Jorge (whose very name conveys the connections of the colonial South) cited Spanish slave policy, which he recognized as different from Yamasee policy, to support the freedom petition of several African slaves. If there is a central narrative of the colonial South, it is one of contested power among a variety of peoples and polities. The historians in this collection have shed assumptions of imperial power to look with clear eyes at who had the power, who was trying to get more, and how power dynamics shifted over time.

Europeans claimed to have colonized North America, but their empires were full of places like Fort Frederic: a short oystershell wall called a fort and marked on European maps as a fortress that granted dominion over a third of a continent. Perhaps it is little surprise that the French King's house in Natchitoches had no curtains, but Fort Frederic was no backcountry attempt at expansion. It was a coastal fort, designed to protect Charleston, a vital colonial port and one of the largest cities north of Mexico. European posts created swaths of possession on European maps, but they were really, as Alexandre Dubé said at the symposium where this volume began, a "scattered archipelago of buildings lightly deposited upon the Native grounds of North America." A couple of decades before Fort Frederic's founding, a Spanish party of six traveled by land from St. Augustine to Fort King George and surprised the British not only by their undetected approach but also with their self-professed mission to negotiate the border between Spanish Florida and British South Carolina. South Carolina's governor insisted that this was not how empires were supposed to work. Meanwhile in London, Spanish and British representatives, trying to negotiate the border in the proper way, could not even find the contested rivers and fort on a map. As Joshua Piker puts it, "while the empire's reach was long, its arms were weak."

Lest we overcompensate by exaggerating Native control over the South, it was not just Europeans who projected more power than they possessed. Malatchi and Mary Bosomworth both called themselves Creek emperors to enhance their status among the British, and Malatchi carried British goods and imprimatur back home to bolster his position among the Creeks. Still, when we compare 2,000 Creek warriors in the 1740s to the 200 soldiers that South Carolina Governor James Glen requested but did not actually receive, it is not much of a contest. Colonizers' claims fooled historians of the colonial Americas for a long time, but no more.

Still, imperial projection had quite real effects on the South and on the world. The desperate drive for profitability and monopoly is a nasty thing. It forced men and women far from home, millions of them into hard labor with no sharing in empire's benefits, and many of those into a life of slavery that they passed on to generations and generations. Imperial competition and Indian control over trade drew the British into the Indian slave trade in part to enslave and thereby incapacitate Spain's Indian allies. Britain's involvement in turn accelerated the Indian slave trade far beyond what anyone had imagined and enslaved and dispersed whole communities that had nothing to do with the Spanish. As fruitless as Chesapeake silk cultivation turned out to be, empires in enough times and places did figure out how to produce goods valued in the world economy and leverage a whole lot of unfree labor and un-granted lands to make it happen.

Global empires could fail or compromise in some places while directing fleets and armies to conquer chosen places, all the while claiming to rule a vast space that was by nature not governable by any one group. Indeed, part of what made the language of empire appealing (why Malachi and Mary Bosomworth called themselves "emperor" and "empress") was its combination of flexibility and sticking power. We vividly see this insidious duality in Robert Olwell's John Bartram: a man exploring the margins of empire for his own dilettante purposes but also a small advance guard for the knowledge and reach of empire.

This book and the current scholarship that it represents show us an American South in which late eighteenth-century Charleston was more like Calcutta and the Creek town of Coweta was more like Natchitoches than any of them were like the plantations and statehouses of the antebellum South. No one expected equality or independence in this pre-Revolutionary and largely pre-Enlightenment place, but neither was the dichotomy of white supremacy and black subjection the monstrosity it would become.

One might ask if this South, so different from the antebellum South, makes sense as a region before the 1830s, but its climate, labor systems, staple crops, and political organizations have distinguished it from other parts of the continent since ancient times, as recent scholarship including in the journal *Native South* has shown. Long before it was the land of cotton, it was the land of corn, where some Native southerners leveraged forced labor to build and maintain Mississippian city-states, which at times had empire-like reach in trade and in military power within the region that six centuries later would be the Confederate States of America.

When Europeans and Africans came beginning in the 1500s, it was to a hot and fertile land of some promise and more peril. New empires and changing Native polities developed new forms of organizing land and labor, both relying on slavery even more than in the region's past. By the American Revolution, Europeans had settled on the Atlantic coast and a few places on the Gulf of Mexico and in the interior. Most Native southerners had combined into a few powerful confederacies, while many smaller communities survived by allying to one or multiple European or Native powers. Here longer than in any other region, multiple powerful Native peoples interacted with multiple ambitious empires and their substantial but not dominant colonial populations. Slavery was ubiquitous yet seldom defended as a positive good. It was a place far removed from later Souths but a region that made sense as such to its peoples: a world of small regionally-focused places with ties to a global system of trade and slavery.

Notes

1. For important early scholarship on the colonial South, see, for example, Wesley Frank Craven, *The Southern Colonies in the Seventeenth Century, 1607–1689* (Baton Rouge: Louisiana State University Press, 1949). For expansion in the 1970s and 1980s, see Richard S. Dunn, *Sugar and Slaves: The Rise of the Planter Class in the English West Indies, 1624–1713* (Chapel Hill: The Institute of Early American History and Culture by the University of North Carolina Press, 1972); Peter H. Wood, *Black Majority: Negroes in Colonial South Carolina from 1670 through the Stono Rebellion* (New York: W. W. Norton, 1974); Edmund S. Morgan, *American Slavery, American Freedom: The Ordeal of Colonial Virginia* (New York: W. W. Norton, 1975); Jack P. Greene, *Pursuits of Happiness: The Social Development of Early Modern British Colonies and the Formation of American Culture* (Chapel Hill: University of North Carolina Press, 1988).

ABOUT THE CONTRIBUTORS

Allison Margaret Bigelow is an assistant professor in the Department of Spanish, Italian, and Portuguese at the University of Virginia. She has published articles in the *Anuario de Estudios Bolivianos, Ethnohistory*, and *Early American Literature*. Her book *Cultural Touchstones: Mining, Refining, and the Languages of Empire in the Early Americas* is committed to the Omohundro Institute of Early American History and Culture (University of North Carolina Press).

Denise I. Bossy is an associate professor of history at the University of North Florida. She has published articles in *Early American Studies* and the *South Carolina Historical Magazine*, and she is currently completing a monograph titled "A History of the Yamasee Indians: Ethnogenesis, Strategic Diaspora, and Resurgence."

Alejandra Dubcovsky is an assistant professor of history at the University of California-Riverside. Her publications include *Informed Power: Communication in the Early American South* as well as articles in *Native South, Early American Studies, Ethnohistory*, and the *William and Mary Quarterly*.

Alexandre Dubé is an assistant professor of history at Washington University in St. Louis. He is completing a monograph on the politicization of buying, selling, and supplying in colonial French Louisiana and the larger empire of France.

Kathleen DuVal is a professor of history at the University of North Carolina, Chapel Hill. Her publications include *The Native Ground: Indians and*

Colonists in the Heart of the Continent and *Independence Lost: Lives on the Edge of the American Revolution*.

Jonathan Eacott is an associate professor of history at the University of California-Riverside. The author of *Selling Empire: India in the Making of Britain and America, 1600-1830*, his other publications include articles in *Quaderni Storici* and the *William and Mary Quarterly*.

Travis Glasson is an associate professor of British and Atlantic history at Temple University. He is the author of *Mastering Christianity: Missionary Anglicanism and Slavery in the Atlantic World* as well as articles in the *Journal of British Studies* and the *Journal of Southern Religion*.

Christopher Morris is a professor of history at the University of Texas-Arlington. He is the author of *Becoming Southern: The Evolution of a Way of Life, Warren County and Vicksburg, Mississippi*, and *The Big Muddy: An Environmental History of the Mississippi and Its Peoples from Hernando de Soto to Hurricane Katrina*.

Robert Olwell is an associate professor of history at the University of Texas-Austin. He is the author of *Masters, Slaves, and Subjects: The Culture of Power in the South Carolina Low Country, 1740–1790* and coeditor of *Cultures and Identities in Colonial British America*.

Joshua Piker is a professor of history at the College of William & Mary. His publications include *Okfuskee: A Creek Indian Town in Colonial America* and *The Four Deaths of Acorn Whistler: Telling Stories in Colonial America*. He is also the editor of the *William and Mary Quarterly*.

Joseph P. Ward is dean of the College of Humanities and Social Sciences at Utah State University. His publications include *Culture, Faith, and Philanthropy: Londoners and Provincial Reform in Early Modern England*; (with Robert Bucholz) *London: A Social and Cultural History 1550–1750*; and (as editor) *Britain and the American South: From Colonialism to Rock and Roll*.

INDEX

Abercromby, Ralph, 229
Acapulco, 22
Ackermann, Rudolph, 223
Addison, Joseph, 230
Africa, 6, 22, 171, 174, 175, 178, 181, 182, 188, 219, 231
Alabama, 66, 100, 190
Altamaha River, 37–40, 43–47, 51, 52
American South, 3, 4, 6, 23, 42, 87, 169–83, 222, 241, 243
Amsterdam, 97, 100
Amy, Anne, 132
Amy, Thomas, 132, 133
Andrews, Charles MacLean, 188
Antilles, 171
Apalachee, 40, 42–44, 65–67
Aquinas, Thomas, 139
Arbuthnot, John, 179, 180
Aristotle, 138, 177
Arkansas, 100, 173
Asia, 171, 178, 208, 219, 228, 230, 232
Aviles, Pedro Menéndez de, 63
Ayala, Francisco Antonio de, 44
Ayala, Juan de, 47

Bahamas, 122, 125, 130–32, 135
Banks, Joseph, 194
Barbados, 125, 140
Barbary Coast, 174, 241

Barnwell, John (Tuscarora Jack), 38–42
Bartram, John, 6, 188–202, 204–8, 210, 211, 216, 217, 243
Bartram, William, 161, 197–202, 204, 205
Beaufort, 42
Bell, John, 230
Bénac, Étienne de, 102
Benavides, Antonio de, 40, 43, 47, 48, 50, 51, 52, 77
Bengal, 170, 175, 209, 218, 224, 225, 231
Bennet, Thomas, 139
Bermuda, 15, 122–33, 135, 140, 141, 241
Bernard, William, 30
Biard, Pierre, 175
Bienville, Jean-Baptiste Lemoyne de, 95, 105–8, 111
Bigelow, Allison Margaret, 4, 241, 245
Biloxi, 91, 173
Blackstone, William, 230
Blake, Joseph, 123
Blathwayt, William, 23
Blith, Walter, 12
Bonnet, Stede, 123, 131, 138
Bonoeil, John, 9, 15
Boone, Joseph, 38, 39
Bordeaux, 97
Bosomworth, Abraham, 156
Bosomworth, Mary, 5, 149–51, 153, 154, 156, 157, 159, 160–64, 243

Bosomworth, Thomas, 149, 161, 163, 167
Bossy, Denise I., 5, 54, 57, 80, 82, 85, 245
Bray, Thomas, 133, 134, 137, 141
Breintnall, Joseph, 191, 192
Bressani, Francesco Giuseppe, 176, 177, 180
Brims, 78, 155, 165
British East India Company, 188, 209, 220, 227, 232
Buffon, Comte de, 178, 179
Bullock, William, 22
Burbage, Mrs. Thomas, 30
Burghill, Francis, 129
Bute, Lord John Stuart, 193, 197
Byron, John, 194

Cabrera, Juan Marquéz, 68, 72
Calcutta, 6, 170, 218, 220–34, 236, 241, 243
California, 15, 33
Cambridge, Tobias, 230
Canada, 6, 100, 108, 170–72, 175–79, 182, 188, 190, 209
Canzo, Gonzalo Méndez de, 64, 65, 82
Cape Fear River, 197
Caribbean, 87, 94, 102, 109, 116, 139, 183, 188
Carlier, Alexis-Philippe, 104
Cartier, Jacques, 172
Cason, Clarence, 170
Chandernagore, 170
Charles I, 8
Charles II, 127, 209
Charleston, 6, 69, 72, 73, 75, 110, 123, 152, 157, 159, 166, 194, 196, 197, 205, 218–34, 237, 240–43
Charles Town (Charlestown), 38–42, 44, 45–48, 51, 52, 133, 136, 143
Chesapeake, 21, 23, 125, 242, 243
Child, Robert, 9
China, 21–26, 33, 87, 175, 178, 227, 230
Church Act, 135, 136
Church of England, 5, 122, 123, 133–36, 140–42
Cicero, 138
Clayton, Robert, 126, 127, 129, 131

Clive, Robert, 189, 209
Coke, Edward, 138
Colley, Linda, 219
Collinson, Peter, 191–98, 207, 217
Company of the Indies, 90, 91, 96–100, 104–7, 109, 111, 116
Cook, James, 194
Coote, Richard, 132
Cowell, John, 138
Coweta, 150, 155, 243
Cuba, 64, 69
Cubières, Simon-Louis Pierre de, 182
Cumberland, Duke of, 193, 197
Cumberland, Richard, 138
Cupide, Andrés del Coro Barruita y, 44–46, 48, 55
Curaçao, 87

d'Alembert, Jean le Rond, 175, 179, 186
Daudin, G., 98
Dauphine, Durand de, 173
Dauphin Island, 93
Davis, Robert, 202, 205, 214
d'Iberville, Pierre le Moyne, 172
Dickens, Charles, 133
Diderot, Denis, 175
Diggs, Edward, 30
Dominica, 188
Down, James, 230
Duany, Andres, 183
Dubcovsky, Alejandra, 4, 37, 86, 219, 245
Dubé, Alexandre, 5, 87, 117, 121, 242, 245
Dublin, 28, 237
Dupérier, Léon de Saint-Léon, 97, 99
DuVal, Kathleen, 6, 245

Eacott, Jonathan, 6, 246
East Indies, 22, 132, 219
Egypt, 14, 174, 229
Eilbracht, Jacob, 224
Eleuthera, 130
Elliot, John Huxtable, 26
Ellis, John, 194

Emerson, Ralph Waldo, 20
Escovar, Juan de Ayala y, 77
Evelyn, John, 13, 177
Every, Henry, 132

Fermiers-Généraux, 98
Ferrar, John, 8, 11, 12, 18, 19, 21–30, 36
Ferrar, Richard, 24, 36
Ferrar, Virginia, 8, 10, 12, 19, 21, 22, 25, 27–29, 36
Ferrar, William, 28, 36
Flanders, 142, 182
Florida, 6, 23, 38, 42–52, 59, 62, 63, 65, 68, 70, 71, 73, 75, 190, 193–97, 199, 201, 204–9, 241, 242
Foote, Samuel, 225
Fort Caroline, 62, 241
Fortescue, John, 141
Fort Frederic, 152, 153
Fort Johnson, 152
Fort King George, 37–52, 55, 56, 242
Fort Oswego, 210
Fort Picolata, 198, 200–202, 205, 213
Fort Rosalie, 92
Fort St. James, 188
Fort St. Louis, 188
Fort St. Marks, 198
Fort Tombecbé, 104, 108
Fort Toulouse, 87, 100
Frankland, Thomas, 137
Franklin, Benjamin, 191
French Guadeloupe, 173

Gagnier, John, 137
Gambia River, 188
Garden, Alexander, 194, 195
George II, 151, 156, 158
George III, 191, 193, 229
Georgia, 5, 15, 41, 59, 60, 64–66, 69, 70, 105, 110, 149, 150, 152, 153, 155, 159–62, 190, 241
Gervais, Widow, 102
Gibson, Edmund, 134, 140, 141
Glasse, Hannah, 227

Glasson, Travis, 5, 122, 147, 219, 246
Glen, James, 152–54, 157–60, 243
Goddard, John, 130
Godefroy, Denis, 138
Goldsmith, Oliver, 230
Gracia Real de Santa Teresa de Mose, 77
Grant, James, 197, 198–202, 204, 206
Gravier, Jacques, 173
Green, Charles, 194
Greene, Jack, 218, 233
Grenada, 188
Grove, Richard, 179
Grunsway, Frederick, 227, 230
Guale-Mocama (region), 42, 43, 60, 65, 68–70
Gulf Coast, 61, 171, 172
Gulf of Mexico, 91, 93, 172, 244

Hachard, Marie Madeleine, 174
Hakluyt, Richard, 9
Hale, Matthew, 138
Hamilton, Alexander, 151
Harper, Thomas, 16
Hartlib, Samuel, 8–12, 20, 22, 23, 26–29
Havana, 172, 183, 209, 241
Heustis, Jabez W., 183
Heydon, John, 129
Hog Island, 131
Hooghly River, 170
Hooker, Richard, 139
Howe, Lord Richard, 229
Hudson, Geoffrey, 173
Hudson Bay, 172
Humboldt, Alexander von, 176
Hume, David, 230
Hunt, Daniel, 230

India, 6, 87, 170, 178, 179, 208, 219, 220–33, 241
Ireland, 10, 21, 29, 224, 229

Jamaica, 11, 13, 109, 173
James I, 9

James II, 129
James River, 22, 23
Japan, 22, 37, 230
Jasanoff, Maya, 219
Johnson, Nathaniel, 134, 135
Johnson, Robert, 124
Johnson, Samuel, 230
Johnston, Gabriel, 138, 147
Jones, William, 230
Jorge, 77–79, 85, 242

Kalm, Pehr, 193
Kaltisen, Michael, 26, 223
Kingston, 183
Kolly, Jean-Daniel, 94
Kublai Khan, 26
Kupperman, Karen, 14

La Florida, 42, 44, 61, 63, 64, 66–69, 72, 73, 75–79
Lake George, 202
Lake Ontario, 192, 210
Languedoc, 100
La Rochelle, 87, 94, 97, 98, 102, 174, 241
La Salle, René-Robert Cavelier de, 105
Laumet, Antoine (Lamothe Cadillac), 105
Laussat, Pierre Clément de, 181–83
Le Maire, François, 177, 178
Le Page du Pratz, Antoine Simon, 174, 180, 181
Le Roy, Magdeleine, 102
Lescarbot, Marc, 172, 173
Linnaeus, Carl, 192, 193, 196, 210
Little Gidding, 29
Lloyd, John, 228
Lobs, George, 30
Locke, John, 230
Lockey, George, 233
London, 4, 15, 16, 38, 39, 43–48, 52, 122–24, 126–30, 132–36, 140, 141, 144, 147, 150, 152, 156–58, 160, 161, 163, 166, 191, 197, 201, 204, 206, 217, 223, 231–33, 242
Louisiana, 5, 6, 37, 40, 87–100, 102–4, 106–12, 158, 170–72, 174, 175, 177–83, 190, 241, 245

Louis XV, 5, 92, 97, 100, 102, 104, 110
Luis, 63
Lyonnais, 100

MacMahon, Laurent-Patrice, 93, 95
Malatchi, 5, 149, 150–60, 162, 165, 166, 243
Mallet, Alain Manesson, 175
Manila, 22
Manton, Joseph, 226
Markham, Gervas, 12, 13
Marqués, Francisco Menéndez, 47, 48, 50, 51
Marquette, Jacques, 169, 170
Marshall, Peter, 219
Marx, Karl, 189
Maryland, 23, 134, 142, 240, 241
Mascarene Islands, 91
Massey, Edward, 37, 56
Mauritius, 179
Maverick, Andrew, 228
Mazan, Balthazar Ponfrac de, 102
McDowall, Alexander, 229, 237
Memphis, 173
Menéndez, Josef Rodriguez, 47
Menéndez, Pedro de Avilés, 42, 63, 67
Merenciana, Cacica, 68
Mexia, Juan, 47
Mézy, Sébastien-François-Ange Lenormant de, 101, 108
Michel, Honoré-Gabriel, 101
Middle East, 20, 21, 24, 30, 227
Middleton, Arthur, 45, 49
Mississippi, 89, 106
Mississippi Delta, 87
Mississippi River, 91, 92, 98, 169, 170, 172, 173, 180, 188
Mississippi Valley, 5, 87, 89, 92, 99, 102, 105, 106, 110, 111, 171
Mobile, 87, 91, 93, 98, 99, 105, 107
Molière, 97
Montauban, 97
Montesquieu, 97
Montigny, Jean-François-Benjamin de Dumont, 173, 174, 181

Montpellier, 97
Montreal, 174
Moore, James, 135
Morris, Christopher, 6, 23, 246
Morris, Robert, 126

Nairne, Thomas, 74, 76
Nantes, 93
Nassau, 131, 132
Natchitoches, 100, 110, 242, 243
Native Americans: Ais, 63, 65; Alabama, 100; Altamaha, 60, 62, 63, 65, 72, 74; Apalachee, 60, 64, 72, 76; Apalachicola, 60, 66, 72 (*see also* Lower Creek);Caddo, 87, 90, 92, 100; Calusa, 63, 73; Cherokee, 63, 73, 76, 82, 153, 157, 226, 241; Chickasaw, 94, 241; Chiluque, 70; Choctaw, 76, 87, 90, 92, 105–10, 241; Coweta, 72, 158; Creek, 5, 37, 40–43, 49, 60, 70, 72–74, 76–79, 86, 90, 92, 108, 110, 149–51, 153–67, 198–200, 241–43; Guale, 64, 68, 72, 74, 83; Ichisi, 60–63, 65; Illinois, 90, 92, 100, 107; Kuscetaw, 72; Lower Creek, 37, 49, 60, 70, 72–74, 76, 78, 79, 151, 161; Menominee, 169, 170; Mocama, 68; Natchez, 90, 92, 94, 105, 106; Ocute, 60–63, 65; Ottawa, 191; Ouacha, 87; Pamunkey, 66; Petites Nations of the Delta, 92; Pontiac, 191; Quapaw, 87, 90, 92; Sapella, 72; Sapickay, 72; Saturiwa, 62, 63; Savannah, 76; Soho, 72; Surruque, 65; Tequesta, 63, 64; Thimogona, 62, 63; Timucua, 42, 60, 62, 64, 66, 69, 71, 72; Tocobaga, 63; Tuscarora, 38, 41, 42, 73, 191, 242; Uchize, 70; Upper Creek, 76, 151, 161; Westo, 60, 65, 66, 70, 72; Yamasees, 5, 37, 38, 40–43, 46, 47, 49, 51, 52, 57, 59–79, 82, 84, 85, 241, 242, 245
Nawab of Bengal (Siraj-us-daula), 226
Nelson, Horatio, 229
Neolin, 191
Netherlands, 100
Nevis, 140, 172

New Brunswick, 172
Newcastle, Duke of, 44, 48
New England, 15, 33, 142, 240
New Hampshire, 140
New Orleans, 87–91, 93–96, 98–102, 104–8, 110, 116, 119, 173, 174, 180–84
New Providence, 131, 132
New Spain, 21, 22, 26, 87, 91
Nicholson, Francis, 47–51, 140, 142
Nightingale, Carl, 219
Nile River, 180
Normandy, 100
North Africa, 175, 178, 181
North Carolina, 191, 197
Nova Scotia, 142

Oaxaca, 22
Ocmulgee-Oconee Region, 60, 65
Oglethorpe, James, 160
Ohio River, 169, 191
Olwell, Robert, 6, 14, 219, 243, 246
Orry, Philibert, 92, 94
Outina, 62

Paris, 92, 95, 97, 100, 105, 178
Pays d'En Haut, 107
Pennsylvania, 140, 189, 191, 192, 205, 208, 210, 238
Pensacola, 87, 91, 92, 190
Périer, Étienne, 105, 106
Persia, 22–25, 175, 178
Peru, 18, 242,
Phélypeaux, Jean-Frédéric (comte de Maurepas), 92, 94, 96–99, 104, 106–10
Philadelphia, 189–94, 197, 205, 208, 210, 212
Phillip, Ulrich Bonnell, 170
Philippi, 177
Piker, Joshua, 5, 219, 242, 246
Pitt, William, 189,
Platt, Hugh, 12–14
Plymouth, 194
Pocotaligo, 78
Poisson, Paul du, 173

Ponce de Léon, Nicolás II, 69
Pondicherry, 91, 179, 241
Pope, Alexander, 230
Popple, William, 140
Port Nelson, 172
Port Royal, 70–74
Portugal, 241
Potter, William, 27
Pradel, 93
Prieto, Martin, 64
Pristo, John, 130
Pufendorf, Samuel von, 138
Puzzle Lake, 202

Quebec, 100, 172–74, 178, 228
Queen Anne, 139
Quiroga, Diego de, 75

Rebolledo, Diego de, 69
Rennes, 97
Rhett, Sarah, 124
Rhett, William, 135
Rhode Island, 140
Richier, Isaac, 129, 130
Rio de Janeiro, 241
Rivera, Joseph Primo de, 43
Robertson, Robert, 129, 130
Robertson, William, 230
Robinson, John, 134, 137
Rochefort, 97, 99
Roper, L. H., 141
Rouen, 97, 109, 174
Russell, Richard, 30
Russia, 23

Saavedra, Alonzo de Avila, 47
Saint Domingue, 99
Saint-Malo, 98
Saint Vincent, 188
Salmon, Edme-Gatien, 98
Sanderson, Robert, 139
Sandoval, Juan de, 47
Santa Catalina de Anhoica, 71, 72

Santa Catalina Island, 50
Savannah, 5, 149–51, 155, 156, 159
Savannah (incident), 150–52, 155, 160, 161
Savannah River, 72, 73
Savano Town, Florida, 73, 76
Schuylkill River, 192
Scotland, 9, 138, 229
Seeley, J. R., 188
Senegal River, 170, 188
Seven Years War, 188, 189, 208, 226
Seville, 6
Sharp, John, 139
Sharp, William, 199, 201
Skene, Alexander, 140
Smith, John, 9, 15
Smith, Nathaniel, 127
Smyrna, 127
Snyder, Christina, 58
Solander, Daniel, 194
Somers Islands Company, 125–30, 141
Soto, Hernando de, 60–62
South America, 230, 231
South Carolina, 5, 37–45, 47–52, 57–59, 65,
    66, 69–71, 73–79, 122–27, 130, 131, 133,
    135–38, 140–42, 144, 152, 155, 160, 194,
    218, 220–22, 224, 226, 227, 242, 243
South Carolina General Assembly, 74, 76
Spain, 4, 18, 22, 38, 43–46, 48, 49, 52, 207,
    209, 241, 243
Stadacona, 172
St. Augustine, 45, 50, 63–65, 67–70, 72, 75–79,
    85, 193, 197, 198, 201, 204–6, 217, 241, 242
St. Croix, 172
Steele, Ann, 233
Stephenson, John, 16
Stevens, Robert, 127
St. Francis River, 169
St. Helena Island (Santa Elena), 65, 66, 70,
    74
St. Johns River, 198, 201, 202, 205, 206, 216
St. Lawrence River, 170, 172
Stono River, 130
Stork, William, 206–8, 217

Stuart, John, 198, 200
Suarez, Francisco, 138
Sweden, 100

Tahiti, 194
Talbot, Charles, 130
Tamil Nadu, 170
Tangiers, 142
Taylor, Jeremy, 139
Tenison, Thomas, 134, 137
Theobald, Lewis, 230
Theophrastus, 177
Thessaly, 177
Tillotson, John, 139
Tobago, 188
Trapham, Thomas, 173
Treaty of Paris, 6, 188, 191, 193, 207
Trott, Nicholas, 122, 124–32, 133, 140, 141, 143–45, 146
Trott, Perient, Jr., 124–31
Trott, Perient, Sr., 124, 126
Trott, Samuel, 124, 126–30, 133, 143, 144
Trumbull, John, 228

Usner, Daniel, 108

Valencia, Lord, 224
Vaudreuil, Pierre de Riguad de, 110
Venel, Gabriel-François, 179
Vera Cruz, 109
Versailles, 88, 92, 105, 107, 111
Virginia, 4, 8–10, 12, 14–16, 20–24, 26–30, 31, 65, 66, 125, 140, 142, 173, 192, 215, 240
Virginia Company, 8, 16
Viviér, Louis, 175, 178, 181

Ward, Francis Swain, 229
Ward, Joseph P., 246
Ward, Lawrence, 30
Ward, Mary Mapletoft, 29, 36
Warwick, Earl of, 126, 128
Washington, George, 229
West, Benjamin, 228

West Africa, 170, 241
West Indies, 6, 22, 170–72, 175, 178, 181, 219, 229–31, 241
Whitcombe, Thomas, 229
Williams, Edward, 16–19, 23, 24, 33
Williamsburg, Virginia, 6
Willis, Jane, 124
Winn, Joseph, 226
Wood, Thomas, 138
Woodbridge, William C., 176
Woodward, Josiah, 139
Wright, John, 73, 76
Wyatt, Francis, 15
Wyse, John, 127

Yeats, David, 202
Yfallaquisca (Mad Dog), 77–79

Zahedieh, Nuala, 125

www.ingramcontent.com/pod-product-compliance
Lightning Source LLC
Chambersburg PA
CBHW030617230426
43661CB00053B/2032